IL BEL CENTRO

A YEAR IN THE BEAUTIFUL CENTER

MICHELLE DAMIANI

RIALTO
PRESS

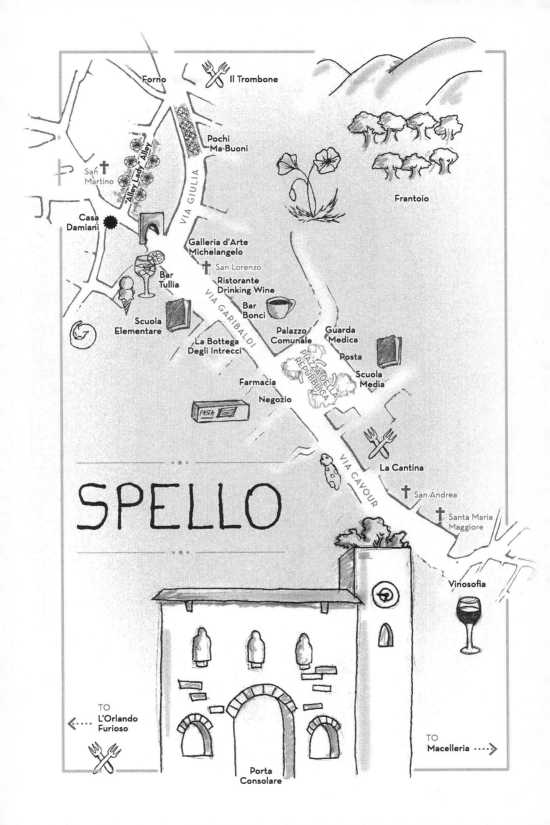

ACKNOWLEDGMENTS

For Il Bel Centro blog readers

Without you, I would not have known that our story was universal, and worthy of telling. You comforted me in the dark times and enlivened me in the bright ones with your collective wisdom and encouragement.

For my friends and family

Without you to follow our journey, to read drafts for content or grammar or Italian, to offer an artist's garret to scribble in, to listen to my ranting about the hopelessness of ever turning this into a book with a hug and an offer of a *kir royale*, I would not have been able to stir myself out of the doubt that too often colored my confidence. Plus, without your discerning eye, this book would be sagging with sentence fragments and incorrect pronouns.

For Emily

Without you, this book would be a cluttered mess, and four times too long.

For those Spellani that graced our lives

Without your spirits to Light the pages, this book would be a boring series of colorless meals.

For Nicolas, Siena, and Gabriel

Without you, my book would be a short story. You are my teachers, my joy, my heart, my home.

For Keith

Without you, this story would never exist. You are my rock and my wings, and I'm still not exactly sure how I got so lucky as to walk through this wild and astonishing thing called life with you at my side.

PRE-LAUNCH

25 July, 2012

I hand Keith a serving of casserole, smashed into a coffee mug; these days, he won't eat unless his food has a handle. The trail of abandoned plates corresponds with his belt cinching tighter, so I'm determined that he eat. He takes the cup distractedly, too sidelined by the needs of our 100-year-old house to focus on the needs of his evaporating body. It was easy a few years ago to assume the house would be renovated in time for the arrival of our renters, even with Keith doing the lion's share of the work himself. But as the calendar pages turned inexorably to the date stamped on our plane tickets, the amount of work seems to have hardly diminished. Keith, usually unflappable, looks downright panicked.

I get it. I do. All five of us are tense, coiled. Tomorrow, a scant few hours after the renters enter our ostensibly finished house, we leave for a year-long sojourn in Italy. And there appears to be three months' worth of work left to complete. Friends who drop by—to lend a hand, or to collect our children—grow still when they see the paint cans scattered throughout the house and the piles of lists and tools heaped on the counters. I see the fear in their eyes, a reflection of my own. We'll never be done.

Two days ago, when I walked into the kitchen and realized that Keith had once again worked through the night, I burst into tears. "You're going to die!" I wailed. He patted my paint-spattered head against his sawdust-covered shirt and consoled me. Gracious, if you think about it, to comfort me when there were so many bare wires erupting from the walls of our house, and I had yet to find time to shower. I called my friends, "Keith's going to die!" And they soothed me, telling me I could fatten him up when we reached Italy. Remember, they add, you are about to embark on your dream.

Empty words. Yes, in an academic way, I remember those nights Keith and I wove together a dream of moving abroad. I can vaguely recall the decision to make Umbria our home for a year, the scouting trip when we discovered Spello and began the process of enrolling our three English-speaking children into the public school. I have an image like a photograph of the moment we signed the lease on an apartment. But it all feels like somebody else's memories. Some star-addled innocent who had no idea what picking up and moving half a world away would entail—the bureaucratic tangles made more complicated when our original visa was denied, the timeline looming with our house (and ourselves) ill prepared, the search for a family that would agree to rent our house at a price that would cover our mortgage and lease on an Italian apartment, the selling our car, the squabbling with the FDA that for some reason has jurisdiction over our cats' travel, the horror at the grove of grey hairs that suddenly sprouted from my hairline. Maybe I am just too old to begin again. Too old, too perennially anxious, too settled into my roots laid into Virginia soil.

I have misplaced the dream, along with my children who are around some-where, and my cats probably hiding under the bed. And yet tomorrow we leave. Italy is waiting. Hopefully Italy won't mind that I still haven't found a chance to shower.

JULY, AUGUST

A PEACH
OUT OF WATER

26 July

Iawake, gasping for air. My heart trips with a sudden surety that moving my family to another country cannot possibly end well. I try to remind myself that the worst must be behind us. The turbulent last two months of preparing the house is over, and our renters who arrived late last night from Israel didn't flinch at the still unpainted doorways. Yet I can't quite quell the rising certainty that moving to a foreign country is beyond stupid. I struggle to remember why I ever thought this was a good idea. What is adventure compared to this sense of impending doom? I order myself to just focus on the car ride to the airport. As Nicolas, Siena, and Gabe pile into the rented van, Keith adjusts the mirrors and announces, "Okay! This is going to be a long journey. Someone is going to throw up and someone is going to cry and someone is going to yell. Our job is to roll with it." Everyone laughs, the first time we've all laughed together in weeks, and all of a sudden it feels, just our being gathered in one place, like a mini-vacation. My breathing slows, but I still flirt with the image of our plane drifting into the airless reaches of the galaxy.

Ten minutes north of Charlottesville, the cat vomits. That she beat Siena to it is a surprise. But not as surprising as our other cat's gift—in her caterwauling hysteria, she expresses a foul musky liquid, which drips out of her carrier and nauseates us to the point of incoherence. Gabe waits until the cats are safely delivered onto the plane before he reports that he feels sick. His fever crests over the Atlantic, and I hold him while he shivers and mutters. I can't sleep. Instead, my mind casts back to five years ago, when Keith and I decided to move abroad for a year. It was our anniversary, and in our reminiscing about our shared history,

I remembered our old dream of living outside the States. We love traveling, the unknown inherent in every day, and wanted a long-term sense of discovery. I suppose the dream of having a family supplanted the dream of a grand adventure. As the cabin lights blink on and off, and Gabe finds a more comfortable position on my lap, I remember the moment when I asked Keith, "We couldn't move abroad with kids, right?" And Keith swirled the wine in his glass and considered before replying, "Why not?"

Immediately the air between us became charged with possibility. How? When? Where? More quickly than I would have imagined, we sketched out a plan. In five years, we could complete the renovations and save enough money to take a year off. My flashback is broken by Gabe thrashing and throwing his arm over my shoulder, and Nicolas peering over the seat in front of us to make sure his brother is okay. This sickness feels inauspicious, though it makes me grateful that we chose to go to Europe, a known destination. Over that anniversary dinner, I had wondered if we should consider a year someplace completely novel to us like Malaysia, and Keith had laughed and said that living abroad would be enough of a challenge. He'd advocate for a country where the language and culture were not so dissimilar that we'd spend the entire year just trying to find our feet. I agreed, and so we settled on Europe. We toyed with Spain, France, or Italy. All three seemed magical and surreal. Gabe was just a baby; it was hard enough to envision him five years old, let alone five years old living in another country. I nuzzle Gabe and his eyes briefly flutter open before he falls into a more solid sleep.

We didn't decide where we'd go in that conversation. In fact, we agreed that the "where" hardly mattered. The place we landed would be mere backdrop to the act of leaping. It occurred to me that diving into an entirely new life would likely force me to confront aspects of myself I'd never considered. I could, we all could, be utterly transformed. I was struck by a sudden thought, and impulsively confessed, "But what if the me I discover by doing this isn't someone I even like?" Keith guffawed and took my hand. "You mean you'll realize you hate cheese and love Civil War reenactments? Doubtful."

"Okay," I countered. "What if I become someone *you* don't like?"

"Even more doubtful."

I smile at the memory and look backward at Keith. Siena's head is lolling on his shoulder, her mouth with its sweet little overbite slightly ajar, but Keith's eyes are alert. He reaches to touch my disheveled hair. There are no words. Just this shared knowledge that the dream we spun over the last of a bottle of wine is now commencing.

Gabe's fever breaks as we enter German airspace. He wakes up feeling so fantastic that he waxes lyrical about the celery that is curiously placed next to his morning danish. The dimple in his right cheek, identical to Nicolas', flickers as he smiles and says that he loves having salty celery for breakfast. I hug him close.

As we fly past snow-covered peaks and glittering blue water, the man across the aisle asks how long we'll be in Italy. His eyes widen when I answer, "A year." Frankly, I don't think he's any more surprised than I am. It's one thing to plan an adventure. It's a thing apart to begin. He asks if work is bringing us to Europe, and I struggle to articulate that Keith and I yearned to break free from our assumptions about the constructs and colors of our lives. Not just for us, but for our children: Nicolas, who at 13 is beginning to cross the boundary between goofy boy and goofy man; Siena, ten, with a tendency toward quiet observation and gentle compassion; and Gabe, five, who could worry before he could talk.

Not knowing how to explain to the balding man from Detroit that we want to shake up our lives and see what hides in the corners, I offer, "We want a change."

Touchdown.

27 July

Sleep deprivation and speechless wonder twist into a jittery knot in my stomach as the cab driver steers us north from Rome's airport, into Umbria, the green heart of Italy. The landscape resembles a shifting series of Renaissance paintings. Sunflower fields beckon. Cypress and umbrella pines march across sloping landscapes. Glowing villages crown hilltops with skirts of silvery olive orchards. And then we glimpse our new home—Spello, rosy in the early afternoon light.

The rubber tires speed incongruously up ancient streets, past arches constructed by men in togas, to park outside a small café. We step out of the van and turn slowly in circles, luggage and cats forgotten. Though Keith and I have been here before, we are as wide eyed as the children. I wordlessly point out the yellow-hued walls of the elementary school, and notice that the adjacent patio for the café, Bar Tullia, is filled with people casually living their Italian lives. Across the street from the school the buildings are all stone. A jackhammer sounds from within a church under reconstruction. Stretching down the hill is a line of serene shops, edged in hand painted signs and flower boxes. Our silence is broken by the sight of Patrizia, our landlady, appearing from under the arch just up the hill from the bar. She's tiny, with short black hair swept across her right eyebrow, and fashionably dressed in an outfit that might fit my forearm. Her impossible freshness stands in startling contrast to our rumpled selves stained with travel and cat effluvia. She greets us is in a voice low-pitched and warm, and leans to kiss our cheeks. My eyes are too full and I botch the greeting. She laughs easily, and helps us drag our suitcases the 50 meters up the narrow street to our apartment.

My head swivels from side to side as we walk. I want to let my fingers graze the rough, oddly pink-tinged stone of the walls, but I'm weighed down by suitcases that seemed sensible back in Virginia, but now feel garishly colored and uncomfortably shiny. Patrizia chatters in mellifluous Italian but I can't make out a word, despite the fact that my workbook progress suggests that I should be able to use the present and past tense of at least 20 verbs. The five of us gather behind Patrizia as she unlocks a heavily waxed wooden door. She pauses and points out our name, Damiani, under the doorbell to our apartment. My brain goes into overdrive and I suspect I'm on the verge of short-circuiting. None of this feels real.

We haul our bags up the polished steps that are the same rosy color as the outside walls and enter our apartment. The eat-in kitchen to our right is filled with light from the glass door that leads to a *terrazza*. Windows with deep ledges line the left side of the long room we stand in. A heavy dining room table fills the first part of the room, and black leather chairs and a loveseat surround a coffee table at the far side. Just beyond the living room area is another *terrazza* door. The children scatter, Nicolas into what he knows must be his bedroom to the right off of the living room, and the younger two up the glossy steps beyond the kitchen doorway. The staircase ends at a landing with their room, marked by a bunkbed, on the right, a bathroom straight ahead, and our large and lofty bedroom to the left. Our room is notably spectacular because of the steps leading up to the *loggia*, an arcaded gallery. The children race outside and lean over the wall to gaze over the roof tiles of Spello. Patrizia points out the armoires filled with sheets and towels, and then leads us back downstairs, to open the doors of the hutch filled with dishes and table linens.

This apartment is outfitted with more precision than our house in Charlottesville.

As we release the cats, hoping Patrizia won't notice the odor, I realize that our landlady is asking a question. We stand looking at her, puzzled. She uses her hands to aid her dramatically slowed speech. Keith and I turn to each other in unison and say, "She's offering to take one of us grocery shopping." My heart quickens as a blooper reel of outtakes plays suddenly across my mind. Before I can linger too long at a scene of tragic comedy that involves me holding a bag of figs, *fichi*, while shouting about vaginas, *fiche*, to incredulous stares, I volunteer. I am determined to get past the apprehension that restrains me. Besides, food is universal. I may not be able to use the imperfect tense, but I do know at least 15 words for pasta. I follow my Italian landlady out of my Italian apartment to go Italian grocery shopping.

On the way, I admire *"il bel panorama"*— the tiny streets framing views of intensely green countryside. Admiring in another language is easy, all lush sighs and pointing. At the bottom of the hill lies the modern part of Spello, called the *borgo*. I grow giddy as we pass a fresh pasta shop, and Patrizia smiles at my eagerness before pointing out the fish market. I ask if the fish market sells *gambe*. Her eyebrows shoot up and she darts a curious look at me. As we pull into the parking lot, I realize that I had asked if the fish store sold legs. I had meant *gamberi*, shrimp. Now my landlady thinks I'll be storing body parts in her pristine fridge.

My well-rehearsed list of items evaporates into the chilled air of Superconti, and I'm left with a pervasive uncertainty of what to do with my hands. I force myself to start with the first step. Produce. I struggle to remember the Italian word for lettuce, and suggest *lattuga*. Patrizia takes a breath and tells me that we will not be getting vegetables. My cheeks flush. My mind spins. Have I offended her and asked for too much? Are we just getting staples? Should I apologize? Patrizia leans toward me and whispers that the Superconti is good for fruit, but not vegetables, we'll go to her *fruttivendolo* later. I sigh. Yes, please, just fruit.

Fruit, and also the cookies that Patrizia thinks I'll need for breakfast (do Italians feed their children cookies for breakfast? The picture on the back of the bag suggests that cookies and a box of juice are a wholesome start to the day), a selection of pasta, cat supplies, and coffee. Patrizia fills out an application for a frequent shopper card for me, while I stand at attention at the checkout. As I hand over the large bills, I'm lost in thought about how Italian checkers sit, rather than stand as they do in America, and which would be better for one's back? I'm pulled into the present by the checker barking at me. Patrizia rushes over and gives the checker a few euro pennies so that my change is all in bills, rather than coins. I'm befuddled by what just happened, but nonetheless, I'm proud of the bags of groceries now lining the back of Patrizia's car.

After a brief stop at her *fruttivendolo* to pick up vegetables, Patrizia drives me home. When I enter the house, Keith and the children greet me with excited descriptions of their trip to Bar Tullia for gelato. We quickly unpack the groceries, the children squealing at the apricot-flavored yogurt, and then head out to explore Spello together. My heart suddenly thuds in my chest. This is not the same as wandering towns we stay in when we travel—the people we pass will be our neighbors through fall and winter and spring and summer, what if we inadvertently do something wrong? The concern fades into excitement as we close the wooden door behind us, and stroll down the cobblestone street, past the elementary school and Bar Tullia, toward the *piazza*. Old men gathered on benches look at us curiously, but then return to their speeches punctuated by snappy hand gestures. Nicolas wanders to the left of the *piazza* to look at the middle school while his siblings follow the skinny cats that trot between the rose bushes encircling the fountain. I notice the *negozio*, a little grocery store, which will be handy for all the things I'm sure I forgot today. Keith just stands and beams.

The lanes branching off of the *piazza* invite us forward and we wander tiny alleys. The heaviness of the stone walls is lightened by the trilling grace of flowers, everywhere. The children race ahead, laughing at cats sleeping in the foliage, and Keith languidly follows behind, as if in a dream. I stop. There is my family, glowing with the setting sun reflecting off ancient walls. I can't believe we're here. I close my eyes and breathe in the scent of coffee. Above my head, I hear the clattering of dishes as someone prepares dinner. The resonant, warm air sinks into my skin. My nerve endings tingle, not in their well-carved anxious way, but in a novel way. Some sort of fog is lightening in my brain.

Keith turns to face me, still beaming. I move toward him and into his arms. The quiet embrace lasts just a few moments before Gabe realizes a hug is happening without him, and launches at our waists to wrap his skinny arms around us. We laugh and decide to walk to dinner. Patrizia recommended Il Trombone, and so we turn back up the hill. We duck into the restaurant and are shown to the outdoor patio, situated above pasture land hemmed by terraced olive orchards drifting into green hills. I realize that Spello lies along the crest of one of these hills. Our house is on one side of the hill, looking out toward Assisi and farmland scattered with industry. This side faces a diminutive valley, tucked away from main roads. Once we are seated I find that I have developed some sort of Spello-induced ADHD. My eyes bop between the swoop of fields into mountains, the menu, my children jiggling in their seat, a lanky cat climbing an olive tree beside us, and the waitress threading her way around the patio carrying plates heaped with heavenly smelling meats and pasta.

I order my brain to cooperate and decipher the menu for the children. The boys order *tagliatelle* with wild boar sauce, Keith and I order *gnocchi* with gorgonzola and radicchio, and Siena requests *gnocchi* with cheese and truffles. Keith's posture assumes the relaxed ease he adopts in Italy as he orders a *mezzolitro vino rosso*, a half liter of house wine. The wine arrives with a basket of bread. The children excitedly reach for bread, and Keith and I laugh aloud as we watch their faces turn from thrilled expectation to confused revolt. We tell them that Umbrian bread isn't salted, and they place their uneaten pieces on the edges of their plates. Keith is still laughing as he pours us both glasses of wine. At home we rarely drink wine, in deference to our tight budget, but here the wine is about as inexpensive as the bottled water, and I feel like a queen sipping the currant-red wine as I contemplate the distant hills.

Our dinner arrives to cheers, such is the excitement around our first meal in Spello. The *gnocchi* are a small variety I've never had, the sauce is creamy and unctuous, with a tang from the gorgonzola. For our *secondi* we share a platter of grilled meats, and I breathe in the peppery scent of olive oil drizzled over the caramelized chops and sausages. Keith cuts sausage for Gabe, and Siena and I surreptitiously gnaw on the bones, as I consider how few family meals we've shared lately. The realization makes me appreciate this sudden sense of completion. Before the leave-taking chaos, we ate around the dinner table almost every night. Weekdays that dinner was often easy quesadillas or something I threw in the crockpot—what was on the plate was less important than being together. Weekends were for more labor-intensive meals to linger over. Because of cost constraints, we almost never dined out as a family. So now—given how long it's been since we've been able to enjoy any family meal with all of us eating off plates, and how satisfying the meal is, and how glittering the adventure before us lies—it's no wonder we tune into every miraculous aspect of the restaurant, the meal, and the vista. We observe how the landscape shifts with the waning light, and how much cooler the breezes become as the darkness gathers. The children sigh that they already love the cats and alleys and flowers of Spello. We agree that our brains are continually grappling with the idea that this is our home.

We walk back to the apartment, and Keith and I tuck the children into their new beds. Keith brings a bottle of wine and two glasses to the *loggia*, and gestures for me to follow him. As he uncorks the wine he asks, "Happy?" I think about it. This feeling is something unknown. Happy approaches it, but it's also like mild stage fright. What we planned on paper is now happening, and that just feels strange. I nod, and ask him if he's happy, but I know the answer already. Keith's happiness is unalloyed. I remember when we finally settled on Italy as a destination for our year abroad. It was partly because I realized that I felt more expansive in Italy than in any other country, and because the food, language, and history were compelling to both of us. But it was also because Keith just seems to unfold in Italy. Perhaps because it's where his ancestors are from, though his living links to his Italian heritage have never actually set foot on Italian soil. Maybe it's the effusiveness of the culture. Then again, Keith himself is not particularly effusive. His hand gestures are barely perceptible. But his heart is warm and though he characterizes himself as a misanthrope, he's appreciative and generous with anyone he feels remotely attached to. So maybe he has that Italian sense of community that drew us here, though, as he's worked on the house, he's refused to ask for help, even from people who have offered. That fierce independence seems more American to me. He looks a little Italian, with his expressive brown eyes, but I can see more of the Northern European parts of him—he's tall and his skin is more pink than olive. Plus, he's balding and don't Italians all have full heads of lustrous hair? He is effortlessly thin and loves coffee, but I don't think that explains how he rounds and mellows when we are in Italy. So, no, I can't place what it is, but I know that when we took a family vacation to Italy years ago, when flights were $250 round trip, I looked out at the Roman suburbs flashing as we drove from the airport and I was awash with this feeling of "I finally got Keith home."

And he does seem at home now, already. Sipping his wine and smiling out over the Umbrian plain. It's not the tight smile of "I'll be okay" that I've grown used to over the last months, but rather the broad grin that makes his eyes crinkle in the corners. The grin I fell in love with. We speak of our relief to have made it, to be here. I inhale the fragrance of warm stones and wood smoke, and wonder aloud what the next few days will bring. The fact that we've arrived seems odd enough, the fact that there is a year's worth of life to live here, that's a twist I can't get my brain to reach past. We sink into the darkness, mellowed by wine and the breeze that softens the edges of night. We're quiet together and the last month of panic-drenched chaos feels like it happened to other people, far away.

28 July

I've been asleep for less than an hour before Gabe starts crying out in his sleep, "What did *I* do?" I snuggle his thin body against mine, his dark blond cowlick tickling my nose. I'm unable to fall asleep for hours as I worry over his labored breathing. Only the merry church bells announcing noon alert me to the fact that I'd finally fallen into a deep sleep. A sleep that unfortunately does nothing to ease Gabe's breathing, and the catch of a wheeze sends me recklessly flinging clothes out of suitcases until I locate the inhaler I'd thankfully remembered to pack, despite the fact that he'd seemed to outgrow his babyhood habit of developing a wheeze when struggling with a virus. Gabe grows suddenly still. And then he vomits. Trying not to panic, I tell him this is probably just his strategy to be the first to use the shower. Third children have to pull out all the stops. The water perks him up, and he raves about his new shampoo's advertised cotton-flower fragrance.

He shuffles downstairs damp and red-cheeked to greet our landlords as they arrive. Patrizia is more impossibly fresh and fashionable than the day before, and Loris stands easily beside her, gazing around at what was his home until he and Patrizia married. His handsomely coiffed head thrown back, he carries himself with such authority, it's difficult to gauge his height. Loris instructs us on how to turn on the gas, operate the videophone doorbell, and open the bathroom skylights. He starts talking about hooking up a phone line, but it becomes clear that this conversation involves a level of nuance beyond our basic Italian. Wouldn't he rather discuss pasta shapes? Keith begins to apologize for our lack of Italian, but they interject, "No, no!" and Loris assures us that we'll be speaking perfect Italian in a month. It's such a gracious lie, I want to weep. Gabe's labored breathing makes the whole process ahead seem labored. How we'll ever be able to form seamless sentences is beyond me.

Gabe's breathing improves, however, releasing the tension in my shoulders. I spend the afternoon unpacking, while Gabe follows behind me chattering in the tender way he has when he's recovering from being sick. I listen to Nicolas and Siena as they plan movies to make with Nicolas' computer. Movies that will star the cats, Juno and Freja, who are cleaning themselves in advance of their Italian film debut. As I move from room to room, Gabe on my heels, I wonder about my two eldest. Born four years apart and separated by gender and personality, they have always shared a bond without being particularly close. Will the smaller house in a foreign country serve to divide them by forcing their edges to grate, or connect them via a need for companionship?

I look up from my musing at the sound of the doorbell. Keith buzzes in our landlords, who have returned to take Keith to Foligno, the nearest town of consequence, to get a mobile phone. Apparently, we've agreed to this. One must relinquish a significant amount of control when one has no idea what's happening.

The kids draw pictures and watch the Olympics, while I peek into cupboards and investigate the sauté pans. Nicolas yells that judo is on, and I join them, curious. We watch together, confused at how to discern who is winning. As the gold-medal winning Korean rips off his top, Siena tucks a long strand of dark hair behind her ear and wishes aloud that the Italian silver medalist would rip off his top, too. Perhaps Italy will mature her in ways I hadn't anticipated. I turn off the TV.

Keith returns home, brimming with stories of his trip to Foligno. While he describes the foam on his *espresso*, the doorbell sounds. I can't seem to remember where the buzzer is, so I dart in the wrong direction, while Keith decides to walk downstairs to open the door. He finds a woman with Gabe. Gabe, who I was sure was drawing on the *terrazza*. My son tells us that his pencil had dropped from the ledge, so he'd walked outside to get it, but the door had closed behind him. He'd stood on the steps and pushed his pencil through the mail slot—here he throws out his chest at this piece of cleverness—but couldn't fathom how to get past the door. A passing woman witnessed his quandary and rang the doorbell.

The incident would have been more alarming if the street were wider than an ox-cart, but it does prompt us to talk about house rules, until the tolling bell alerts us that the dinner hour is upon us. We walk down to the *borgo* for pizza at Il Vecchio Opificio, where we revel in the very Italian-ness of our surroundings: Gabe copying a gladiator from a brochure for an ancient Roman festival while Siena draws a bottle of wine, Nicolas ordering pizza with his broad smile, and the sounds of ancient Umbrian music from a nearby *piazza*. While we chase strings of cheese from our pizza, I notice that the family seated in front of us is becoming friends with a family at a nearby table. I watch the parents lean toward each other, their children holding hands. I try to imagine ever having this sort of instant camaraderie with a family here, and fail. I had reconciled myself to this being a lonely year, but it hadn't occurred to me that it will be a year lacking in the easy banter of people just meeting. Without a shared language, a bubble separates our family from the rest of society. I suddenly not only feel self-conscious but also distanced. I admonish myself for getting too ahead of where I am, and instead take my children's hands as we walk back up the hill in the moonlight.

Despite the late hour of our return, I am determined to do a load of laundry. Which is more complicated than I anticipated, as there are about 15 settings that vary in pre-wash, temperature, and amount of spinning. I select a program that promises to work on clothes that are *molto sporchi* (I defy anyone to come up with a better word for "dirty" than "*sporco*"). These clothes are definitely *sporchi*. I feel fairly confident that I figured it out. But still wonder if we'll wake up to a sudsy kitchen floor. I fall asleep with the house quiet—no wheezing—just Umbrian music drifting up the hill from the *piazza*, echoing along the patient stones.

29 July

After a third gelato at Bar Tullia in as many days, I realize I'm going to need more drawstring pants. Unfortunately, it's swimsuits, not drawstrings, that are the order of the day, as we've been invited to Loris and Patrizia's pool. On a whim, I suggest we go through the tiny alley just a few meters down from our front door to see if it connects to the road to our landlord's. Once we're walking, none of us cares if it's a shortcut or if we'll have to double back. It feels like we've stepped back in time. The alley is narrow, with just enough room for us to walk single file and allow Gabe to zoom and twirl around us. Green chairs are settled against the stone walls that rise like cliff sides. Arches span the distance between the walls, some heavy and sturdy, some light and airy. A white-haired lady in a flowered apron steps out of a door and settles herself onto a chair with a bowl of greens to sort. Keith greets her, *"Buonasera,"* good afternoon, while I nod and smile as we continue walking. The cobblestones lead us past the high wall of a garden with tree foliage leaning out over the path. A black and white cat sits in a doorway and stares at us imperiously. The alley ends with steps down to the main road, and I'm thrilled to have discovered what feels like a secret passage. The children clap and point when they spot a tiny bakery at the junction of the alley and the road. They gather around the display window decorated with a scene of mushrooms and snails made from bread, while I peep past the strings of beads that mark the entrance to the bakery. The scent of almonds wafts out over the street. This little bakery with no sign, I wonder if it will be part of my life in the coming months? It's odd to have no real idea about what my days will look like—what my go-to dinners will be, what I'll wake up thinking about, who I'll see enough to become familiar.

Turning left out the alley, we pass Il Trombone and notice that the restaurant is firing up its wood-burning oven. We continue walking past homes interspersed with art shops and alleys that open onto that view of the pastoral valley. At the top of the hill we arrive at our landlord's house. Loris welcomes us heartily and leads us to the pool with a view of red tile rooftops, deeply green cypress trees, and golden hills. The children fling off their clothes, Nicolas carefully resting his glasses in arms reach of the edge of the pool. Siena is the first to jump in, and she immediately floats with her hair fanned around her, the inky fringe of her lashes grazing her pale cheekbones, as her belly, pale and still slightly baby rounded, greets the sun. Nicolas tucks his lanky body into a ball and hurls himself into the water, while I help Gabe wade in slowly. Soon they are splashing with an elation that comes from feeling the release from heat and stone. Suddenly though, Gabe winces and shouts that he has a splinter. I take him by the hand, lead him to Loris, and say, *"Gabri ha una pezza di legna in la sua detto."* Turns out, many of those words don't actually exist. But show and tell works in any language, and after investigating the proffered finger, Loris leaps up, chuckling under his breath. He returns, brandishing tweezers with a flourish and insists on removing the offending sliver of wood.

I thank our host, then return to the pool with the children, while Keith sits on the lounge chair beside Loris and makes conversation. I can't tell what they are talking about, but it involves gestures and laughing. Not for the first time, I wish I had Keith's comfort with speaking a foreign language. Our language progression has been fairly well matched—I pick up Italian more quickly than he because of my Spanish background, but Keith doesn't second guess himself, which means he doesn't stumble as much as I do. That difference is particularly evident now that we've landed. My accent may be closer to an Italian accent, but there is Keith, eager to try speaking, while I'm happy to be the one in the pool with the children.

I was hoping to see Patrizia, but she arrives just as we announce to Loris that it's time for us to go. He looks surprised. Don't we want to stay to eat and drink? Keith and I look at each other, unsure of how to move forward. Is Loris just being polite? Or is it rude to refuse a meal? In America, we'd protest in a vague way, our host would either accept the protest and we'd leave, or push past our protest and we'd stay. But we don't know how to protest vaguely. Keith tells Loris that I've already made dinner. This, Loris can respect. I breathe a sigh of relief at Keith's cleverness. This was a conversational impasse I couldn't see my way through.

Keith was honest, I had prepared a tomato sauce during *pausa*, the afternoon rest time, while a storm blew past our open *terrazza* door. Once home from swimming, I set the sauce to simmer and pasta water to boil, while I place salami, *mortadella*, and fennel on a plate. Packaged pasta with a simple sauce is perfect for these early days when I'm trying to get the hang of the heat generated by the gas stove and the contents of my tiny refrigerator, but I look forward to long afternoons cooking as I've been wanting to cook. I select a marbled piece of salami to chew while I step into the living room and watch a bit of Olympic swimming. I tell Keith that I find swimming impressive because I can't even swim in a straight line. He wraps his arm around my waist and pulls me close, laughing that maybe I'd be the first swimmer in history to get a yellow card for banging into a competitor. I smile and return to the kitchen, grateful that there are no yellow cards for bumbling a conversation so thoroughly that I smack and bruise those around me.

30 July

Sometimes I fixate on irrelevant details. This morning it is dishwashing detergent. I forgot to buy a box at the Superconti, and our dishes are only growing more fetid in the hot dishwasher. On an ordinary morning, in the States, I can count on my ability to saunter to the store and purchase a box of dishwashing detergent. With a sponge for good measure. Here, details paralyze me. So when I wake up, exhausted from a night of sleep continually interrupted by Siena, who is having bad dreams, and Gabe, who keeps falling out of bed, I have dishwashing detergent on my mind. I think about dishwashing detergent when Keith hands me the cup of coffee that barely brightens my thinking. I think about dishwashing detergent when Loris appears on our doorstep, handsome and vital and clearly not worrying about dishwashing detergent.

Instead, he's arrived to accompany us to the *comune*, the civil office, to begin the work of acquiring the *permesso* that will allow us to stay in Italy. The visa authorizes our stay, but the *permesso* is the culmination of that process. It will prove to officials on the street, at the bank, and on the border, that we are here legally. But we are not exactly sure how one turns the visa into a *permesso*. We don't even know what a *permesso* looks like—if it is affixed into our passport like the visa, or if it's a piece of paper we carry. All we know is that process of acquiring the *permesso* must be started within ten days of arriving into Italy.

Loris believes we begin at the *comune*, and so we follow him like baby geese, past Bar Tullia, past the elementary school, past a café called Bar Bonci, through the doorway into the civil administration building. Within the yellow walls of the *comune*, confusion reigns. The front desk employee insists that we need a signed lease for each member of the family. Loris is incredulous, shouting and laughing that this is ridiculous. He asks, in Italian, "Even the children need a registered lease?" Even so, answers the man. We're sent upstairs where everyone bustles, stamping papers and gesticulating wildly, oblivious of the frescos that have witnessed civil business for centuries. Here, the woman is emphatic. We need a registered lease to get the *permesso*. And also, we need the *permesso* to register the lease. Loris announces that he is taking Keith to the *questura*, police station, in Foligno, to resolve how to proceed. Then he storms out, five Americans in his wake.

Keith kisses me goodbye, then lopes off beside Loris, a goofy smile plastered on his face. What feels like a rat's maze to me is part of the adventure for him. I watch the two of them turn the corner, and then, like any self-respecting Italian, I use the sudden opening in my day to go to the bar. Which, to American sensibilities, probably sounds more desperate than it is. In Italy, bars are family affairs—a spot to pick up a pastry or sandwich, a shot of caffeine, often gelato, as well as alcohol. I just need coffee. And space to breathe. I order a *cappuccino* and three assorted *cornetti*, Italian croissants. The *barista* cheerfully directs us to the garden where I watch the gleaming, chestnut-colored eyes of my children drink in the stunning prospect—farms burrowed into the valley's curves and groves of olive trees stretching into the hills. The children carefully select a table with maximum shade and optimal view, and we dive into our treats. The *cornetti* filled with Nutella are especially praised. Revitalized, I gather my strength and my children, and walk to the *negozio*, the little supermarket on the *piazza*, to buy dishwashing detergent. It wasn't actually all that complicated.

Keith returns soon after we do and tells me that the police officer at the *questura* was amused at the idea of our children needing registered leases. He directed Keith to go to a post office to complete and mail in our *permesso* application. The application will take three months to complete, but in the meantime the receipt and our visas are all we need to prove we're here legally.

Bureaucracy done for the day, we head to the *borgo* to explore the playground. It stretches across a city block, and is separated into play spaces and resting spaces by flowers, cypress trees, and bay bushes filled with butterflies. Spying rosemary bushes, I wish aloud for a sprig. Obligingly, Nicolas breaks a twig and hands it to me saying, "It's more forgivable for a child to pick the plants." I nod gratefully and shove the fragrant sprig in my purse, already dreaming of olive oil and rosemary-cloaked potatoes. The children gravitate toward the play equipment created without concerns about American lawsuits, like the eight-foot plastic donut, tilted so that people standing on its higher edge rotate down, and children who gather on it can spin it fast enough to whirl at least one toddler entirely off and into the mulch. There aren't many children here, though. I wonder if they are all on vacation.

Our outing continues as we walk in search of the *macelleria* Patrizia recommended in the *borgo*. It is here that I discover that Italian butcher shops are even more entertaining than Italian playgrounds. I summon my courage and order pork chops by offering the word *maiale*, pig, while miming slicing. The woman helpfully suggests, "*Bistecca?*" "*Si, si! Bistecca!*" She removes a ribcage from the case, and her husband rhythmically carves the chops with a satisfying thwack! It's a music I bob to as I drift toward the case of *salumi*, cured meats. The butcher wraps our chops in paper, and asks if we'd like a taste of salami. We exclaim, "*Si!*" and he laughs, a merry bellow. Still smiling, he hands us thin slices of salami. Delicious. Then a larger one, with more fat. Even more delicious. Then two kinds of *prosciutto*. Silky and delicious. He asks how to say "*salami*" in English. We reply, "Salami!" and he and his wife look at each other and burst into fresh laughter. He wraps our purchases and I hand him €20 for five pork chops, a whole salami, *mortadella*, and acacia honey. It feels like I pulled a fast one on this nice man.

In the evening, I nibble our new salami while rubbing a fragrant clove of garlic over the thin pork chops and the creamy white ribbon of fat that I was advised to score to keep the chop from curling. I massage peppery local olive oil into the meat, and then sprinkle it liberally with salt and pepper. The chops and seasonings grow familiar while I roast the small, waxy potatoes with the illicit rosemary needles. When the potatoes are almost cooked through, I fire up a pan until a drop of water dances on the surface. I quickly sear the chops and let them rest on a platter with a zesty hit of lemon juice. I dress a salad simply with salt, a good quantity of olive oil, and a splash of balsamic. The crisp and slightly bitter leaves are a bright consort to the feathery potatoes and the juicy pork. Meat in the States can often taste like the absorbent pad it's packaged on. This pork, packaged with conversation and laughter, is more tender and flavorful than any I have ever had.

31 July

Although we maneuver the shutters according to Patrizia's directions—open at night, but closed first thing in the morning, the heat hangs heavy. We're used to Virginia summers, notable for humidity that feels like a warm wash cloth pressed against one's face. So we don't find it terrible, as long as we stick to the shade. And yet we stubbornly perseverate in our quest to find children at the playground. It is empty. Again. Are there no children in Spello? Undeterred, our three chase each other in a zombie game that would likely repel other children had there been any, until they grow red and blotchy and more than a little moist. Just as I call them, Nicolas takes a spectacular dive across the concrete skinning his knee. The scrape is mild, but his face grows ashen. He moans that he might vomit, and I spare a moment to pray that this passes, and that it proves to be the worst medical drama we'll encounter in a year without our doctor. I lead my stumbling boy to the cistern and wash his neck with water, clean and cool. His eyes close as the tension leaves him, and the planes of his face fall into the simple innocence I remember from his babyhood. After a few deep breaths, he announces he's feeling better and ready to celebrate our successful crisis aversion with gelato. He runs his hands through his short brown hair, so much like Gabe's only without the cowlick, and walks purposely toward the *gelateria*.

As we delight in the fruity, icy goodness, I can't stop touching Nicolas' face. By the time we walk to the *macelleria*, he's swatting my hands away. He must be feeling better. As we enter the *macelleria*, the butcher greets us with a shout of "cheese!" He must remember that yesterday I had said I'd be back for *formaggio*. I wonder if he's actually looked up the English word. I nod, laughing with him, and walk to the cheese counter to select a wedge of pecorino. Then I ask for a whole chicken. The woman cocks her head and furrows her brow. As she goes to the back room to get a chicken, my mind begins its now familiar spinning—is summer an idiotic season for roasting a chicken? I file this under: Things I don't consider when in the land of endless cool convenience. I console myself with a packet of twirling pasta, *umbricelli*.

The hill seems steeper in the searing afternoon heat. Keith stops into the *negozio*, and when he joins us in the *piazza*, he holds up bottles of gin and tonic water. "Now we can pretend to be British expats!" Siena and Gabe start speaking in a British accent, and Nicolas mutters, "We can never take them to England."

Back home, Keith mocks our tiny ice cube tray, which not only hampers the proper chilling of our current cocktails but will certainly put a damper on his martini habit. I sip a warm gin and tonic while cooking the chicken. I opt for cutting the chicken to pan fry, rather than heating the house by roasting it whole. I season the pieces with the *porcini* pepper I found in the cupboard, and then cook them in a very hot pan of olive oil, skin side down first. While it pops and sends out the scent of crackling fat, I boil the curly *umbricelli*, which I dot with butter and flourish with grated parmesan and cracked pepper. We settle around the dining room table to eat. Oh, that chicken must have had a happy life. She must have clucked with moxie and scratched with purpose and gazed out to the throbbing blue sky with joy. *Grazie*, sweet chicken.

While Keith is glaring at the chicken—as he does when he's dumbfounded that something can be so tasty—his cell phone rings. We sit confused at the unfamiliar sound. Keith fumbles picking it up, and then fumbles trying to get a signal, until he realizes that the thick stone walls that keep the house cooler than one would expect also block a cell signal. He jogs out to the *terrazza*. I hear him laughing and talking in Italian, and I'm bewildered. I have a tendency to freeze when asked what I want at the *negozio*, the thought of communicating without pointing, grunting, and gestures leaves me weak. Keith, however, approaches the call like a game, a challenge. I can see this, and yet it doesn't attenuate my own desire to speak only when I'm fairly certain I'll make sense. Keith comes back to the table with a wide grin. We're invited to go to Loris and Patrizia's after dinner. Not after our dinner, which is just finishing, but after *their* dinner. At 9:30.

Long past our children's bedtimes, we walk through the streets to our landlord's house. Once there, we make small talk. Very small talk. They admire Gabe's sketchbook, and laugh at his tendency to answer all questions with *"grazie."* I'm glad they find it endearing, but I can't help but think that soon he'll be in school where *grazie* might not get him far. Gabe warms to Loris and Patrizia, and soon he's chattering at them as if they're only pretending not to understand.

Over ice cream bars and Chino, a soda that tastes like cola with bay leaves, we begin discussing the internet. Their son, Filippo, who rides up on his motorcycle and rushes to press his handsomely stubbled cheek against ours, facilitates this conversation with his excellent English. When I admire his fluency he laughs, saying he watches a lot of American TV. Though I have to speak deliberately, it's a relief to smile and share pleasantries with relative ease. He assists Loris in explaining that there are three internet options. Each one must be emphatically discussed while I sit back and observe. The internet is a foreign language unto itself, all I can do is nod like I understand. Finally, it turns out everyone agreed all along.

Patrizia rises to get ice cream, to the wide eyes of our children. They are going to have TWO desserts? Gabe hurries back to his seat, and in his haste scoots the bowl off the table. It shatters in an explosion that leaves us all quiet. Gabe freezes, and then sags his head into his arms and begins wailing. Loris and Filippo rush to kiss his head while giggling into their hands. Gabe eventually sniffs and rallies, and dives into his new plastic bowl of gelato.

Filippo brings out watermelon, and the children gloat at their third dessert. We then announce our departure before our hosts can offer more dessert, drinks, or yet another household item that Patrizia is sure I can't live without (I'm already walking home with kitchen towels, a board for making pasta and pastries, and several canisters). Gabe screams that he never wants to leave, and our hosts embrace him and laugh at his charm. I find it less than charming and wrangle him out, attempting some semblance of grace. Though something tells me that my grace is a delusion—as shattered as Gabe's gelato bowl. All that's left is the grace of others.

1 August

I love outdoor markets. I seek them out in every town I visit as a place to get cheap, local food. In fact, my travels are connected—like a string of beads—by memories of markets. From the line of stalls in Paris that filled the air with the smell of brown and juicy chickens turning on a rotisserie, to the Barcelona covered market that boasted crispy crusted rolls so excellent with local cheese, to the bridge in Prague filled with people selling from tablecloths spread over the ground. I love the chatter of customers and vendors, I love the groundedness of food recently tugged from the earth, I love the olives and berries and artichokes all spilling out of crates. The Spello market is not that market. Instead, it is mostly cheap clothes. Even while I'm chiding myself for acting spoiled, I worry the corner of my lip between my teeth in disappointment. I buy five peaches from the one produce truck while Keith stops into the Vodafone store to make copies of our *permesso* application in advance of our trip to the *posta*.

He returns a half hour later, chuckling. I'm barely able to concentrate on his narration of the odd workings of the Vodafone store because I'm trying to control the peach juice running down my arm. But I catch enough to tell him he should apply for a job. He answers, "That'd be great, and the first thing I'd do is teach them that when you print, you can select 'three' copies, rather than hitting print three times."

After washing off at the cistern, we present ourselves to the post office. Our optimism fades in the face of a line that moves like aged balsamic in the Dolomiti. Finally, it is our turn and we step to the window, our smiles barely containing our nerves to begin the process that will make us residents. The worker scowls and berates us in what sounds like Klingon. A woman at the next window calls out in slow Italian that the post office will be closing in a half hour, and since the *permesso* process is lengthy, we'll need to come back tomorrow.

We trudge, defeated, up the hill. As we reach the corner, a man hails us. His neatly trimmed mustache bristles against his tanned and aging face, and he wears his seersucker shirt casually untucked. He tells us, in Italian, that he is married to a French woman, and has smart children. I nod in admiration, and Keith reciprocates by telling him, "*Viviamo a Spello.*" We live in Spello. The man nods, unfazed, and answers with a smile, "*Io lo so.*" I know.

2 August

Another day at the *posta*, another endless line. Finally the woman who dismissed us yesterday beckons us to her window, but dismisses us once again because we haven't noted the fee for the *permesso* on the application. Why it isn't listed on the application, or at the *posta* where one completes the process, I have no idea. We use the *piazza*'s free wifi to find the fee for each of the 20 different kinds of *permessi*. Ours cost €80, plus a processing fee, a mailing fee, and a fee for the *marca da bollo* stamp, required on almost all official documentation. They get you coming and going.

We join the line. Finally, the Klingon man calls us to his window. He speaks slowly, and I'm relieved to recognize Italian. He begins methodically going through our paperwork, and then stops and hands us back our application. I'm certain we're being rejected again, but he asks us to write the cost of the *permesso* in words, rather than numbers. Keith corrects the error, and I am flooded with satisfaction as the man bangs on our application with an ancient wooden stamp.

We celebrate that evening with a trip to Patrizia's favorite *pizzeria*, L'Orlando Furioso. It's a quiet celebration, as all of our energy is focused on our pizza—cracker crisp, with a bright tomato sauce and perfectly stretchy cheese. The pizzas are heavenly, the restaurant is bustling, and the price is incredible—about €5 per individually sized pizza. With a multi-page menu, we'd struggle to try a quarter of them in the course of our stay. Once sated, we stagger homeward, certain that this *pizzeria* will become a fixture of our year here.

Yawning, we approach the playground, but stop short when we hear an unfamiliar sound. People. It's 10:00 and the park is full of families eating gelato, preteen boys showing off soccer tricks, and little children toddling around. Now I understand why the playground is always empty. Only crazy Americans would venture out of their stone houses during the heat of the day.

Keith and I settle onto one of the few empty benches, and watch our children join the throngs of youngsters racing around in the darkened cool. I tell him that I have noticed a rhythm to the day here that moves with the rising, then falling, temperature. Shops open early, and close around 12:30, when the heat is settling in. Everyone goes home to rest in the cool and then heads back out when the sun begins to sink and the breezes shift and gentle down the harsh glare of the day. I am used to a culture that adapts the existing structure to suit the convenience of people. This is a culture where people adjust to structure imposed by weather and history and architectural landmarks. Keith says that earlier Gabe asked him why Italian cars are so tiny. Keith pointed out the tight, medieval roads. Gabe counters that people should knock down the city to build wider roads. I can see, coming from a disposable culture, he would think that razing what is inconvenient would make sense. Mom-and-Pop stores cost more and don't have everything you need? Bulldoze them in favor of a Walmart! With air conditioning!

As we watch Spellani children pedaling their bikes erratically in the dark, I think about how we'll have to adapt to this new rhythm. Aspects of my life that I never think about, like my trust that I can put in a load of laundry and have it clean and dry in an hour, I'm going to have to reconsider. Keith, who has grown quiet, mulls, "It's strange to not have things be easy and convenient, but also kind of satisfying." I answer, "I know. We have to really focus on what we are doing." It is a change, and I think a good one. At least until we are late to the post office without clean underwear, I suppose.

3 August

With excitement, we step onto the *navetta*, the free shuttle. But it's really more like Mr. Toad's Wild Ride. We tear through the streets of Spello, inches from stone walls and tourist toes, barrel around hairpin turns, and kick up dust all over the Umbrian countryside. We stumble off at the Superconti, a bit green around the gills, though the children perk up when we enter the store. They love the novelty of using plastic gloves to select garlic, weigh it, print a sticker, and put the sticker on the bag. They're floored at the entire Nutella section that includes Nutella that comes packaged with bread sticks and tea, called, fittingly, Nutella-and-GO! The *biscotti* aisle, the blood orange juice, the Haribo and other candies, the row of pasta four times as long as the cereal section, the carrot and celery packaged with a mini bottle of olive oil as "*pinzimonio*," olive oil dipping sauce.

The *navetta* ride home is blessedly shorter, and leaves us in the *piazza*. Impulsively I decide to stop into the *negozio*, because I remember they have a bin of marinated eggplant I've been wanting to try. The thin, white-haired proprietor with the gaunt face and wide eyes is less flustered than usual. I order *melanzane sott'olio*. While he's scooping the oil-soaked eggplant into a container, I see an intriguing container of marinated silvery fish. Though I'm embarrassed at my limited language skills, I'm emboldened because the store is empty, so I ask what kind of fish they are, "*Che tipo di pesche sono?*" The owner looks confused. "*Qui?*" He asks, pointing to the oil-cured tomatoes next to the fish. "*No, le pesche. Qui.*" I point. He hesitates and offers, "*Alici,*" which I know to be anchovies. Hooray! Successful transaction.

Maybe he looks alarmed because he can't believe a tourist speaks so well. That's probably it. I'm probably some sort of language prodigy with an effortless accent. And then, it dawns on me—*pesche* doesn't mean *fish*. It means *peaches*. *Pesce*, no hard 'c' sound, is *fish*. To my embarrassment, I realized I had just pointed at fish and asked the poor man for peaches.

4 August

Feeling the urge to explore the region, we decide to head to Perugia, Umbria's capital. On our walk to the train station, we pass the man who is married to the French woman, enjoying his morning *espresso* at Bar Tullia. He hails us with a hearty "*buongiorno!*"

We hop off the train after a half-hour ride, and follow signs for the *centro*, assuming that walking is a reasonable way to reach the city center. After six steep kilometers of leg-quivering, shirt-drenching, soul-crushing walking, we realize we were wrong. Really, really wrong. Poor little Gabe's mosquito-bitten legs tremble, and Nicolas cajoles his brother with games, "Let's think of all the gelato flavors that start with 'p'!" He should probably consider a career as a camp counselor.

When Jack climbed his magic beanstalk, he reached a world of giant proportions with hens that laid golden eggs. In Perugia, we leave behind the memory of the crushing walk for the new reality where everything is larger, loftier, more ethereal. Our necks crane back to see the stone work on Etruscan arches, Roman arches, and medieval arches. I'm dazed at porticos several stories high tracing azure skies and golden mountains. A fountain springs water merrily above our heads. A wide avenue framed by impossibly grand buildings feels like it's on top of the world. Perugia is celestial.

Lunch is notable for my *pasta alla Norcia*, a cream-based pasta with sausage and mushrooms, and Keith's thin, fresh pasta with wild fennel fronds and *guanciale,* pig jowl. I wish I could find wild fennel fronds and *guanciale* at home—the dish has a subtle complexity that surprises me when I consider the kind of heavy, tomato-laden Italian food found in Charlottesville.

Once we exit the patio cooled by misters, the heat hits us and we decide to move indoors, to the Galleria Nazionale dell'Umbria—the museum that houses art of the region. It's a small museum, with the art arranged chronologically, which allows us to observe how artistic style has transformed over time. Nicolas and Siena notice how the feeling of the pieces change as artists discovered methods of capturing movement and expression. And they are excited to discover patterns, like one saint who always wears a red hat. Gabe, however, is not the ideal museum patron. Though he's initially entertained by the task of hunting for images of St.

Francis by looking for the stigmata, he quickly tires out. And then he's storming through rooms announcing, "Yes, yes, that's pretty, so's that, let's move on."

He does perk up at the exhibit of ornate communion wafer irons. I explain how Catholics and Protestants differ in their belief in the meaning of the communion wafers, and that those differences spurred more than one beheading. Beheadings always catch the imagination of tired youth. "Jesus is a cookie?" becomes their refrain, as the communion wafer irons resemble the *pizzelle* cookies we make at home.

All this delving into religion requires gelato at Gelateria Veneta. Though these days, it seems breathing necessitates gelato. Afterwards, we stroll to a courtyard where a quartet plays the overture from *Barber of Seville*. The jolly music is mere soundtrack to Gabe's scratching. He is so covered with mosquito bites that I wonder if he actually has chicken pox until I discern that the welts are only present where his clothes don't cover his skin. With Gabe moaning as his hands fly over his increasingly red legs, we creep out of the concert in search of a *farmacia*. We douse Gabe with an anti-itch cream, which relieves him enough to enjoy his pizza.

Earlier, Keith and I had remembered we'd heard of a "Minimetro" that runs between the station and the *centro*. So at dinner, we find a metro stop on our map. We arrive to find nothing but a locked elevator. Our train back to Spello is scheduled to depart in 20 minutes. Where's the station? In desperation, I ask a passing woman. She shyly says that we're in the right place, but this station is closed. She hesitates, and adds a run of quiet words that include *vado*, I go, and *seguite*, follow. I deduce that she's headed for another Minimetro station and we can follow her. And we do. She barrels forward, neither looking back nor adjusting her pace, until she finally ducks through an archway into a park with a ticket machine for the Minimetro. She continues down the escalator.

We purchase tickets and jog to the platform. Nicolas, Gabe, and I insert our tickets into the reader, and the turnstile releases. Seeing the metro waiting with open doors, we run, yelling for Keith and Siena to "hurry, hurry!" The doors begin to close. Nicolas and I hold them open as Keith and Siena race to join us. Riders are shouting. Probably, "Stop blocking the door! You'll stain our lovely Italian shoes with your squished American entrails!" Our guide studiously looks out the window at the blank tunnel wall. The five of us collapse into the metro and I feel a surge of embarrassment for creating all this drama. Particularly when I pretend that everything's normal by casually reading the signage on the car and realize that metros arrive every 45 seconds.

At the train station, I race with the children under the tracks to line two, while Keith wrangles with the ticket validation machine. Once at the track, I spy another validation machine, so I shout, "Keith! Try this one!" over the bell announcing the incoming train. He hightails it through the tunnel to our platform, and in the silence that follows my yelling, I'm once again mortified, standing self-consciously across the tracks from a line of effortlessly elegant Perugians. Keith joins us right as the train arrives, quickly validates the tickets, and we leap on the train. The whole experience drives home the reality that we'll have to grow comfortable being a spectacle.

5 August

Spello is just waking up. Shutters are opening, men are hanging sheets on lines that run from window to window, and an *ape*, the three-wheeled truck favored by corpulent farmers, is clattering down the street. I walk through the narrow, stone alley lined with green plastic chairs where the ladies gather to wash greens and gossip. Pots along the walls spill over with a riot of flowers, and sticks to keep the town's cats from using the pots as open air litter boxes. The large orange and white cat that lives next door to us peeks his head out from the foliage. He doesn't seem to mind the sticks. At the end of the alley is my destination, the bakery, but it is Sunday, and the shop is closed. I turn left on Via Giulia and discover one tucked-away *piazza* after another brimming with more flowers and chairs, these occupied with elderly people talking over each other as they gesture with their canes and shout words of greeting to passersby.

Full of good feeling, I step into Bar Bonci, and Letizia, the owner, turns toward me, smiling as if my presence were the exact thing she has been waiting for all morning. Her eyes glint, brightening her already glowing complexion as she asks if I'd like a *cappuccino,* my usual order. I nod, surprised. After Letizia hands me my cup with an amiable, "*Eccola,*" here it is, she tucks an errant strand of short blond hair behind her ear and turns to wash dishes. She sings along with the radio, mostly quietly, but sometimes full-throated. It's impossible not to rock my hips as I stand to sip my *cappuccino*. I try to discretely listen to the other bar patrons, but they are speaking far too quickly. No one on Rosetta Stone talks this fast.

On my way home, I'm delighted to see that Doreen is back in Spello and having coffee at Bar Tullia. We greet each other like old friends and I'm startled by the rush of affection I have for a woman I've met only once before. Loris had arranged to have Doreen translate when he showed Keith and me the apartment during our scouting trip, and she offered to accompany us to the schools. It was Doreen who made sure we wrote down contact information for the English teachers who would help us enroll the children. The warmth of her spirit illuminated our impression of Spello and probably influenced our belief that this town would be a friendly place to settle for a year. We've kept in contact since then, and her messages have been spots of sunshine in my inbox. I can't stop smiling as I hug her. Her beaming face framed by blond shoulder length layers of hair is animated as she tells me that she's having coffee with her Italian teacher, Arturo, and wants to introduce me to him. She turns, and Arturo rises from the table with a gallant smile and a small lift of his white fedora. With his gray ponytail and colorful silk shirt, he has the air of a Mexican artist emerging from a cabana. I stumble trying to tell him that I have been hoping to find a *maestro*, teacher, and he offers me a lesson tomorrow. We agree on a time, and that Nicolas, who also wants lessons, can meet with him afterwards. Arturo speaks no English, but he smiles at the challenge of combining slow speech, charades, and repetition to aid my understanding. I walk away with a shiver of anticipation.

When I arrive home, I find the children sitting around the dining room table, drawing. Gabe runs to show me his ram with "theological breasts and an udder that shoots pineapple juice." I fear the mosquitoes may be giving him malaria. The bites are lessening with our new arsenal of products, but he is still covered. In the afternoon, Patrizia yelps at the sight of him before running to fetch plug-in bulbs with citronella. I thank her before climbing into the pool with the children, me imagining the cool water soothing Gabe's angry welts. Patrizia laughs at the children splashing, while I practice saying the Italian word for mosquitos—*zanzare*. It sounds just like those whizzing little bastards.

After we return home, I start dinner while Nicolas and Siena read in their rooms and Keith and Gabe copy Umbrian town seals and flags with their own silly flair (Keith's oddly proportioned falcon is dubbed a pigeon, and thus Montefalco will now be referred to as Montepiccione). As the kitchen fills with the smell of browning onions, I serve a bowl of the peaches-as-anchovies I bought at the *negozio*. Gabe reaches for an anchovy and plops the entire fish into his mouth. And then another. He declares the fish's feet delicious. I watch my splotchy baby devour silvery fish tails as if life could furnish no greater pleasure.

7 August

Doreen accompanies me to Arturo's house, a scarce ten second jaunt up the hill from my door, then right after the tiny chapel dedicated to San Martino. As we approach, Doreen whispers a warning that Arturo is a bit of a character, and his apartment can be—surprising. Thus prepared, Doreen knocks. From within I hear, "*Arrivo!*" and the door is thrown open. Even with the advance warning, I startle. Colorful gauzy tapestries are draped in the entryway and across transition spaces. Hundreds of pieces of jewelry are nailed across the mantle. Mismatched gilt pillows are scattered on chairs beside a wooden replica of the statue of Venus de Milo. Arturo has turned pack-rat syndrome into an art form. There's so much action in that room, my eyes can mostly just take in a searing amount of shiny noise. It's like a Fellini movie exploded.

My friend takes her leave, and I seat myself across the large wooden desk from my new *maestro*. Arturo begins with Italian letters and their pronunciation. He is detail oriented, and we spend ten minutes on the difference between "*capello*," hair, and "*cappello*," hat. The lesson moves swiftly. I duck out at 10:30 to meet Nicolas at the chapel that marks the turn to Arturo's alley. I walk him in, giving him the same warning Doreen offered, and yet when the door opens, he stiffens and his mouth falls open. I hesitate leaving Nicolas looking shellshocked. And why wouldn't he be? Alone in the crazy apartment of an aging gentleman who speaks no English and who, as evidenced by his deeply open collar, shaves his chest. I'm sure Nicolas wonders if he'll get out alive. His voice is forced cheerfulness as he bids me goodbye.

The time passes slowly, as I imagine Nicolas tense and desperate for escape. Noon finds me watching out the window, and then I catch sight of him strolling down the street, face lifted toward the sunshine. I shout to the rest of the family, "He's home!" Nicolas hurries in. He admits that he'd been nervous, but Arturo put him immediately at ease. He loves the old world style of learning with repetition and handwritten worksheets, learning possessives by using candy, and the cat named Monet who plopped in the middle of the desk. He insists he needs four lessons a week.

I'm in awe of him. I have to push past my fears of being imperfect. Of making a fool of myself. This is my work, and a place where I can learn from my child, because he has no such fears. He'll throw himself into an experience without fear of being wrong or different. Unless that experience is making his bed.

In the afternoon, Keith off-handedly tells me that he spied cherry yogurt gelato at Bar Tullia and I'm struck with the surety that we must celebrate our Italian lessons with gelato. On Tullia's patio we find Arturo, so Nicolas introduces Keith, and Arturo patiently corrects my son's grammar. It's reassuring to have another adult in town looking out for Nicolas, even if it's just for his subject-verb agreement. We each order our gelato and I laugh in incredulity at the overflowing cups—they seem fuller each visit. My tastebuds tingle in anticipation of Tullia gelato, creamier and less sweet than the gelato found at home. Once settled on the patio, Gabe approaches Arturo to say hello and admire his silk shirt covered with flags. Arturo swoops him up in a hug and then introduces us to his friends, who welcome us to Spello. All of a sudden, without ceremony or fanfare, we've arrived.

8 August

Craving sweets, the children and I decide to visit the *panificio* across from the playground while Keith goes to Foligno with Patrizia to acquire our *codice fiscale*, the Italian equivalent of a social security number. We admire the rows of captivating little cookies before we realize that bakers are avoiding us. Finally, a customer indicates that we're next, and a baker sighs in resignation before approaching us. I might be awkward, but I can't see that I merit this much scorn. I ask what the chocolate cookie is called, and her eyes hostile, she sarcastically answers, "*Biscotti*," as if I'm an idiot. I may be an idiot, but I'm an idiot who knows that each of the 40 cookies on display are *biscotti*. We leave with a small bag of unspecified *biscotti* and a decision to not return.

We impulsively decide to pick up modeling clay at the Superconti, and while the cashier is ringing up my purchases, I ask Nicolas to help Gabe put away his little cart. Gabe is incensed. As I'm trying to count out the exact change so important to Italian cashiers, Gabe is shrieking, "MOMMY! MOMMY! I CAN DO IT MYSELF!" Which makes me seethe because even this simple transaction feels complicated, and I need to focus.

As we exit, Gabe apologizes and slips his hand into mine. I catch sight of his skinny, masticated legs and my blood pressure dips back into the normal zone. We walk hand in hand, Siena and Nicolas running ahead. Siena calls us, pointing up into a tree. Following her finger, we catch sight of curious fruit, which Siena has recognized as pomegranates. The children laugh and wonder at seeing pomegranates in trees.

It's curious that our lives can suddenly be so different—the vegetation, the food, the amount of thought required for an interaction. And yet so much is the same—everyday annoyances, surly shop workers, parenting with a short fuse, and aggravation at a youngest child who simply resents being the youngest, even when he's in the mystical land where pomegranates grow.

9 August

I wake up sweating from a dream that Keith has injured his foot and opted to self-amputate rather than spend time seeking medical attention. I suppose I'm still processing the weeks before our leave-taking. The dream lingers, and it's a relief to see Keith walking ably into the room, bearing a cup of coffee for me.

He sits beside me, and I giggle as he tells me about his newfound love of the *bomba,* a cream-filled donut. Apparently, when he goes in Bar Bonci, Letizia says, "*Buongiorno, Keet!*" (No Italian can pronounce his name). "*Un espresso?*" Yesterday, she asked how he was, and he told her, "*Bene, ma dopo una bomba… benissimo!*" Good, but after a *bomba*—wonderful! And she laughed in pleasure.

10 August

As we're preparing ourselves to walk down to the school for our appointment with Alessia, the teacher who shepherded us through the school enrollment process, the doorbell chimes. It's the technician here to install our internet. Strange that it's been weeks since we've had an in-home internet connection. Luckily, Spello has free wifi in the *piazza,* which we've made use of almost daily to coordinate the last of the transitions for our tenants and assure our families that we're still alive. But for the most part, we've been unplugged and the quiet is oddly comforting. I imagine radio waves all around me, connecting people in buzzing lines, and myself separate and still.

Patrizia arrives, and soon she and the technician are shouting and waving their hands. Keith asks if there is a problem, and they look at him confused. No, no problem. Keith stays behind to oversee this mystifying process, while I take the children to the *scuola elementare.* I suffer a moment of nervousness when I realize I'll have to face the school without my Keith-buffer, but I ease upon remembering that Alessia speaks English.

The secretary leads us to through the school, and I smile to see the children gape in awe. The school entrance opens into a courtyard with yellow walls that highlight the blue of the sky. From there the school is built like a labyrinth, with a catwalk over a former chapel that is now a library, terraces that overlook ancient rooftops, and views onto the Umbrian plain.

Alessia greets us with hugs and kisses. She introduces us to other teachers who smile and tousle Gabe's hair. His head seems to bewitch Italians, for which I credit the cotton-flower shampoo. Alessia tells us that there will be an orientation for *prima,* first grade, a chance for Gabe to familiarize himself with the school before classes begin on September 12. We're also told that we can walk the children in the first day, which relieves my worry that they'll wind up in the wrong classroom. She adds that the school is still unsure if the elementary school will run five or six days a week (as the middle school does). Everyone is friendly, yet I leave feeling disconcerted. I've never been good at flying by the seat of my pants and rolling with the punches. Instead, I favor lists and flowcharts. Now, not only do I lack a clear idea of even how many days a week my children will be in school,

I feel self-conscious in our American-ness. Our very gestures mark us as "different." Plus, I realize belatedly that I should have asked if the orientation is just for Gabe, or if we should all be there.

Nicolas and Siena are quiet after the meeting. Perhaps they are realizing that this is not vacation. They've been coasting, approaching each day as a new adventure. For the most part cheerful and obliging, but entering school, talking to teachers—suddenly, the hurdle ahead of them must seem gargantuan. Or maybe they, too, are suddenly feeling how alien we are. Gabe, on the other hand, is tickled with excitement. I wonder what he is picturing. Clearly it is not the isolation and confusion that I'm picturing.

11 August

On our way to the *macelleria* this morning we pass an elderly lady watering her flowers. She chatters to us, and Keith and I chuckle knowingly in response. Heh, heh, heh…Yes, we know just how that goes. We wave goodbye and continue down the hill. After a suitable distance, Nicolas asks what the woman said, and we admit that we haven't a clue. The children laugh and Keith muses, "You know, she might have been telling us that she was going to soak her drunken sot of a husband."

At the *macelleria* the butcher hails us with a shout of "Good morning!" to our *"Buongiorno!"* Pleasantries past, I realize that the shop is uncharacteristically empty, which allows me to play meat charades. I point at every unfamiliar item in the case and ask, *"Che cos'è?"* and the butchers mime the animal and cut. I select a roll of pork filled with sausage, *mortadella*, chicken, and herbs. The Italian version of turducken is wrapped for me, and I then request five slices of pounded beef covered in soft breadcrumbs. When I ask how to prepare it, the butcher takes down a bottle of sunflower oil to demonstrate and I tell him I have this oil at home. Actually, what I say is, *"Io ho! Io ho!"* I have! I have! The butcher and his wife look at each other fondly, I'm sure amused by a woman speaking like a proud two year old.

Over a dinner of crispy beef slices sprinkled with a bracing squeeze of lemon juice, we discuss this oddness of not having our language. Language has been my life—in therapy, in writing—words have served to connect me. Now words serve to define my place outside the mainstream, and it's monkeying with my sense of self. It's not necessarily an aversive feeling, more like a burr in my sock—a constant reminder of my guest status. Keith agrees, but he finds the whole language barrier a lark, rather than an obstacle. Nicolas nods along; he likes the humming his brain does when he's searching for an Italian word. Siena and Gabe have been relatively quiet, both at dinner and when we are about town. I can tell that Gabe, though, is eager to begin trying to reach out. Though he has historically been an anxious child—known for sidling up to me when one of his siblings is in trouble to whisper, "But I'm okay, right?"—his desire to be faultless seems to be weakening in the face of wanting to engage with his new life.

After dinner, we walk down the hill for our nightly gelato trip to Bar Tullia, where I see Arturo. I tell him that I'll have to miss my next lesson because we have to make an appearance at the *questura* for our dreaded *permesso* application. Arturo nods, and then pauses. He starts telling me something that seems important, judging by his slow and deliberate speech. I look at him confused, and he summons his friend Antonio with a wave. Arturo tries again, and Antonio translates in halting English that if we ever run into trouble—any at all—we can call Arturo, and he will help. "*Volontieri,*" happily. Antonio chimes in that he too would be happy to assist us. Arturo describe what sorts of situations might require assistance, but I'm too busy blinking back tears of gratitude to pay strict attention. I suppose the blessing of feeling alien is bearing witness to the beauty of people who reach across the divide.

12 August

Keith has realized that he should probably assure his clients back home that he hasn't entered some sort of wine-and-pasta-induced fugue state. We now have internet, it's time to return to work. We had planned to abandon our businesses during this year, but ballooning renovations costs forced us to dip into our sabbatical savings. Now, we need some income to stay afloat and travel a bit. As a clinical psychologist, I can't work here, but Keith can continue to do graphic design from Italy.

I feel restless, and the unanticipated cooler temperature is an invitation to explore the countryside. The children and I walk to the top of Spello, where we spot a sign directing walkers to a Roman aqueduct. Not the high arches spanning a valley I expected, this is a humble version of water transport. It resembles a simple stone wall, and only the periodic gaps revealing the inner structure hint at a storied purpose. Olive groves spread out below us and stretch above the aqueduct, and the path is bordered by wild fennel and mint. The children periodically break an herb to chew, and the scents drift as we walk.

The air is warm, but the breeze graces us with its sigh. Abruptly, we stop, in unison, listening. We strain to make sense of a thumping noise, like a heartbeat. The noise gets closer, until we realize it's an animal running. An animal loud enough to run audibly. Below us, we see a flash of grey hindquarters before the footfalls begin to recede. We exhale. Gabe says the animal was a fox. I say it was a *cinghiale*, a wild boar. Nicolas says he wants to turn back. To which Gabe cries that he wants to walk all the way to Jalapeño, his interpretation of Collepino, the town six kilometers from Spello. I tell him that journey is too far for today.

On our walk back, Siena collects a handful of porcupine quills. Gabe cries that he wants quills, too, and Siena hands him half her haul. Gabe is mollified, and we're quiet again until Nicolas observes that none of us have gotten bitten by mosquitos on the walk. Are the mosquitos town dwellers? Perhaps, but one thing I know is that they are ninja mosquitos. I'll blink and Gabe will have four new bites on his earlobe. I've read signs cautioning Spellani to not leave standing water because of the mosquitos, as well as an admonishment to place red fish in pots. Or maybe it's red peaches. Neither makes sense.

We burst through the door, eager to tell Keith about our adventure. We're so elated that we don't notice Freja slip past our feet until Keith heads out for an *espresso* and I hear him in the stairwell calling out, "Well isn't this a nice place to relax!" He picks Freja up from her curled position by the front door and carries her back upstairs. She acts weird for the rest of the day. Weird, that is, for a cat. She undulates with a strange power, like, "I explored strange lands and found them habitable." Which is ironic since she's living half a world away from her homeland, and that hardly raises her cat brow. But she opened a tiny crevice into unexplored territory, found a bit of novelty, even if that novelty was only the umbrella stand, and her world has expanded.

13 August

When I hear the word "Assisi" I think of Saint Francis' birthplace. I never considered this spiritual destination as home to a FIAT dealership. And yet, it was at the Assisi FIAT dealer that Keith was granted a car, with no contract, no forms, no problem. I didn't know that St. Francis was the patron saint of car leasing. It's a relief to have wheels in the family, even if they are Keith's wheels. I elected against getting an International Driver's License, since we'll only need one driver, and unlike Keith who thrills to driving in Italy, I tend to panic and brake when people ride my bumper too closely. It occurs to me that our family dynamic will inevitably shift, since Keith will now be responsible for shuttling children, as well as doing any large grocery shopping trips. I wonder if he realizes that he is now responsible for every non-Spello-bound errand. Judging by his smile as he spins the keys on his finger, he either hasn't realized, or has realized and finds the prospect amusing. Either is possible.

We celebrate our newfound ability to sally forth by venturing to Bevagna. The town is on flat terrain, which is unusual in Umbria. There is a canal running alongside the walls, as well as gardens everywhere. Bevagna seems to belong in the English countryside, but it's deeply Italian—there are the remains of a Roman bath and a Roman theater. On every street, people on stools confer emphatically, surrounded by breezes that smell of garlicky tomato sauce. We wander, and then stop for dinner at Osteria Scottadito, a restaurant whose tantalizing smell of grilled meats had earlier prompted us to make a reservation during our walking tour.

We find our table, marked with a scrap of paper that reads, "Damiani." Laughing in sheer pleasure at not having to spell our name, we take our seats. A constant sizzling sound emanates from the kitchen as the restaurant fills with diners, chattering in Italian. The children draw on their paper placemats, Keith pours the local wine into my glass, and we muse aloud that we are *really in Italy*. Home seems like another universe—the past has all the reality of a dream and the future, even with school on the horizon, feels the same. *Now* is the entire focus of our conversation.

The meal is an affront to vegetarians but a *tour de force* for meat lovers. As we are perusing the menu, the waitress brings us *bruschette* topped with pâté, creamy and garlicky. I'm not sure why I thought *bruschette* were only topped with tomatoes.

We order an *antipasti* of *salumi*. The selection includes *lombo*, a cured pork tenderloin I've never had before, and a soft salami on warm Umbrian flatbread. Siena comments that she's surprised by the salami's pillowy texture. I've never heard of a soft salami either. *Antipasti* devoured, I wait with curiosity for the *agnello scottadito*, grilled lamb chops, I ordered even though I'm skeptical about whether I like lamb. Turns out I *adore* lamb. Keith tucks into his *bistecca alla fiorentina*, and Siena and Gabe dine on slices of grilled steak. And Nicolas has a grilled pork chop. When I ask him if it's hard to resist the urge to nibble the crispy parts on the bone, he said he wouldn't know, since he doesn't bother resisting the urge. That's my boy.

14 August

Siena joins me at Arturo's today, as she's considering taking lessons. She spends the lesson in a fit of giggles—laughing at Arturo's description of an *urlo*, a yell, as he pantomimes me yelling at my kids to be quiet. How does he know? And she stares rapt as he demonstrates the gesture for "clever like a fox," thumb on the cheek, fingers up, then fingers rotate down.

Afterwards, I pop in the Italian-dubbed movie *Spirited Away*, and enjoy the quiet of Italian screen time babysitting. At home we don't have cable, and our DVDs are limited, so movies are an occasional treat, usually while we eat take-out Chinese food. Here, I'm happy to have them watch the same movie repeatedly in the service of more language exposure, but really so I can write. I catch a bit of the movie as I putter about making lunch. It looks strange to me, and makes me wonder what they are actually learning. Probably just to avoid people with enormous heads. Nicolas saw it in English and said it was bizarre to the point of creepy. I'm going to go ahead and assume that the chilling elements will be downgraded to eerie when watched in a foreign language.

This is exactly the sort of rationalization that makes me wonder if my parenting skills have been lost in translation, along with my attitude toward nutrition. Once I monitored sugar intake, but my new cavalier attitude is, You're hungry? Have a *biscotto*! Still hungry? Hmmm… I'm kind of tired of making things, let's go out for gelato. Part of me wonders if my children will become screen-and-sugar-addicted automatons with an irrational fear of big heads. The other part thinks that avoiding creatures with gargantuan appendages is probably for the best.

15 August

It's *ferragosto!* It's *ferragosto!* Wait, what in the world is *ferragosto?* Outside our window, people are calling, *"Buon ferragosto!"* which makes it seem like something exciting is happening. But nothing seems different, aside from hordes of people walking the streets.

I decide to ask Arturo and knock on his door. He beckons me to sit at my student seat across his desk. Pushing his overlarge glasses, broken and carefully mended with black tape, higher onto his nose, he gazes at me seriously. I tell him that Siena enjoyed her lesson and would like to continue. He smiles that he is *contento*. We begin to map out a schedule, his on a monthly calendar, mine on a scrap of paper. He stares at my scrawl and pauses.

"Non va bene così." It's not so good. With a fresh sheet of paper, he neatly rewrites the schedule in careful grid form. I wonder if he has a fixation for tidy charts. Or if perhaps my handwriting is just that bad.

As we stand to walk to the door, I ask him, *"Che è Ferragosto?"* He laughs and says *"Ferragosto è niente."* *Ferragosto* is nothing. He explains that *ferragosto* is the middle of August, therefore the middle of summer, the hottest day of the year. A good day for farmers and factory workers to take a day off. Now, it is a day when people escape to the mountains or the sea. They travel and eat, and enjoy a change. He adds that there is an expression, *"Ferragosto moglie mia no ti conosco."* At *ferragosto*, I don't know my wife. Arturo claps his hands and slides one forcefully away to indicate flight, *"Perché va!"* Because he goes! Or maybe she goes? I'm not sure I understand, but maybe the flight encouraged by the heat is more than just a flight to cooler climes; maybe it is a flight from the shackles of morality itself? He then goes on to tell me that if I went to Rome today, I would look around (here he cranes his head around in confusion and stumbles around as if stunned) and wonder, who killed everyone? Because there would be nobody there! *Capito?* This doesn't surprise me, I think everyone is in Spello.

Ferragosto or no, I put my children to work, as there are shrimp to prepare.

Siena has been brittle lately, mad when Nicolas won't play with her, cross at our enforced *pausa*. She grows easier as she peels each shrimp, and I wonder if working helps bridge the space between vacation and home. When she's done, she asks to make a vegetable platter, and places it on the table with pride.

The fresh *tagliatelle* that I purchased yesterday at Casa delle Tagliatelle soak the simple sauce I make from shrimp and olive oil, becoming suffused with flavor. Keith takes thirds of the succulent pasta, and requests that we always have this pasta for *ferragosto*. Nicolas wonders if we should make it with legs next time, his sidelong jab at my mistaking legs and shrimp on my first shopping trip with Patrizia. While we sop up the last of the sauce, I share what Arturo told me about *ferragosto* being an excuse to get away. Gabe wants to know, "Are we going on a trip?" Honey, right now your whole life is a trip.

16 August

Siena is ready five minutes before her first lesson with Arturo. No amount of my telling her it's a 20-second walk appeases her eagerness to get out the door. Though I have some reservations about being the wall she hides behind, I agree to stay with her during her lesson. As it turns out, Siena is so engaged with Arturo, I'm left to indulge my inner snoop and try to make sense of his house. While Arturo teaches Siena commands that she'll learn at school like "listen," "repeat," and "write," I marvel at the mobiles and pendants hanging haphazardly across his sloping stone ceiling. I try not to look too closely at the huge painting of the naked man enjoying what looks like "private fun time" in a ripe field of wheat, incongruously hung beside a small cross-stitch of kittens sharing a bowl of milk.

I do pay enough attention to note that Siena's pronunciation improves throughout the lesson. But even better than her progress in pronunciation is her progress in voice. Arturo asks Siena to recite the alphabet, and as she begins, he stops her and tells her to use *una voce alta*. *Capito?* No, Siena does not understand. Arturo runs to his kitchen and loudly tells her that now he's far away and she'll have to speak more loudly. She giggles, and begins. He shouts that he wanted *tutti*, everyone, to hear her! She laughs again and recites the rest of the letters like she really means them. He settles back in his chair and gently tells Siena that in school, she'll need to speak like people are far away, so that the teacher will call her *"brava,"* and not to do an *urlo.* He pantomimes yelling to Siena's helpless giggles. Arturo turns to me and beams, *"Capisce subito,"* she understands right away.

Now Siena has her own information to contribute to family conversations about Arturo's oddities. Lunch is typically the time we share our observations, and for the first time, she has stories of her own. Siena tells about the card Arturo gave her to keep under her hand while she wrote to soak up grease that would otherwise clog his pen. Nicolas shares that Arturo asked him to trace his hand on paper in order to write down the names of the fingers. But when Nicolas placed his hand on the paper, Arturo grew silent, and glared at Nicolas' outstretched hand muttering, *"Non va bene così."* He opened his desk drawer to retrieve special scissors, and began clipping the errant pieces of skin below Nicolas' fingernails. While Nicolas simply waited. What's funny is that as rigid as Arturo seems to be in ways of personal grooming, his own nails are of various lengths. He's an enigma.

An enigma who warmly greets us at Bar Tullia when we arrive for our afternoon gelato. He seats Gabe next to him, hands him a candy, and asks him in Italian what it is. Gabe nods sagely and replies, *"Sì, sì."* Arturo tells him it's a caramella. Gabe nods again and with great seriousness answers, *"Sì, sì."* Arturo guffaws before stopping to note the peal of bells. He tells us that there are bells to announce the hour, and also bells for celebration and bells to announce a death. We listen to the merry chiming and decide together that these bells must mark a celebration. Arturo wonders if perhaps a baby has been baptized. As Gabe gets up to select his gelato, Arturo sees those bitten legs. He tells us that the voracious insects attacking us aren't ordinary mosquitos. They aren't mosquitos at all but *papatacci*, a tiny dun-colored sand fly, silent, and virtually impossible to see. I *knew* they were ninja mosquitos! They can walk as well as fly, so when they find a nice feasting ground (like under my knee), they can eat, mosey, eat some more, mosey. And their bites are pernicious, they irritate more than ordinary mosquito bites and the itch burns for days rather than hours.

It is a time of discoveries.

17 August

We're lost. Well, maybe not lost exactly, but desperately tangled. I hate being late, and being late for *permesso* meeting scheduled for 10:21 makes my stomach clench in way that I haven't felt since the day we left for Italy. On the bright side, at least the stress of being late for an appointment that is scheduled to the minute is insulating me from the stress of the meeting itself. Keith is clearly rattled as he consults maps while whipping his head around to spot street signs, but I know he's excited about the meeting. He finds every logistical tangle a game where he gets to practice speaking in what seems like code. He's looking to Level Up on this video game called Italian Bureaucracy.

As we rush down yet another useless alley we reassure each other. They can't deny us a *permesso* for being five minutes late, right? Maybe they're even running behind. It turns out, a truer sentence was never written. We aren't seated in front of the *permesso* officer until 12:30. Two hours of sitting in a crowded, smoky hallway, trying to understand why no names are being called, and how we are supposed to sort out our order in the midst of all the shouting and elbows.

While the children create games out of coins and paper, Keith swims through the horde to puzzle out the business. By the time it's our turn, I'm jittery and tense. Thank goodness Keith is calm. He's already learned the secret to massaging bureaucracy in Italy—blame another agency. This officer informs us that we should have indicated on our application that the children need a *permesso*. Rather than answer that there was no place to indicate this on the application, Keith tells the officer that the *posta* told us to add the children to our *permesso* at the *questura*. The officer guffaws at this idiocy and asks why the children don't have a visa in their passport. Keith matter-of-factly blames our consulate. Which sends the officer on a harangue in which Keith catches the word for birth certificates. He asks if the officer needs the birth certificates, and the officer pauses before hedging, "*Sì*." Keith whips out three birth certificates, certified by the State of Virginia. We watch the officer's eyes widen at their shiny golden seals. Seals must indicate power and authority because the officer grunts and begins the paperwork granting a *permesso* to each child. This strikes me as a miracle.

We coast into Spello on a tide of bureaucratic success, and saunter into Bar

Tullia for celebratory gelato. I consider trying out an expression Arturo has suggested: *"Il normale,"* the usual, to indicate our five cups. Before I can, Assunta, one of Tullia's owners, starts placing cups on the counter while asking, *"Cinque coppette?"* Gabe orders first, loud and clear. She laughs and says, *"Bravo, Gabri!"* Three weeks in and the owner of the gelato shop calls my son by his name. The *permesso* may legalize our place here, but gelato cements it.

18 August

When I arrive for my Italian lesson, Arturo tells me that yesterday, Nicolas accidentally referred to Keith as the pope, *papa*, rather than as his father, *papà*. When Arturo asked Nicolas about his religious background, Nicolas answered that he is a Quaker. Arturo admitted to me that he'd never heard of Quakers. I wish I could tell him that he's not alone. Even my father often refers to me as Amish. I wasn't raised Quaker but was attracted to the faith because of the core principle that the Light of God is in everyone. This means that there is no minister. Instead, worship is held quietly, with members rising to stand and deliver messages that fill them during the course of the meeting. Because of the fundamental tenet of Light in all, the history of Quakers is marked by advocacy for abolition, suffrage, and now, gay rights.

What my children like about being Quakers is that decisions are made not by majority rules but by unanimity. As a family, we can't do this for all decisions, but when we had to decide whether or not we'd bring the cats to Italy, we had a Quaker-style meeting. Keith reminded us that the cats are part of the family, and we couldn't leave them behind simply because it was inconvenient. Siena mused that so much would be strange, she wanted to have something familiar. Gabe added, "Plus, I love them." Nicolas and I shared our concerns, which mostly revolved around the hassle of bringing cats and finding cat sitters if we traveled. But Nicolas and I saw how important it was to the rest of the family, so we decided to stand aside for the vote. No one felt railroaded, and no one "won." As it happens, I'm now shocked that we considered leaving the cats behind. So is Nicolas. Freja is as permanent a fixture on his bed as Juno is on mine, and I can't imagine being across an ocean from our beloved cats.

I have wondered how our faith will be perceived in a country where there is a cross in every public building and a Madonna and Child in every school. Will we be proselytized to, as we so often are by roving groups of people knocking on our door and insisting that we see God in the same form they do? I'm tense, waiting for Arturo to speak his next words. He looks at me searchingly, and says, "*Complimenti.*" He praises the Quaker belief that everyone carries the Light of God. His eyes widen at the faith's emphasis on equality and pacifism. Then he rushes to get his book of world religions so he can show me the passages he's underlined. What a surprise to have someone acknowledge who I am.

I carry this interaction with me the rest of the day, and notice subtler moments of feeling seen. Letizia won't listen to our drink order, instead reciting it with an expectant grin, before insisting that we wait in the garden. The owner of the *negozio* refuses to let Keith pay for a bunch of basil. And later, Gianni, who owns Bar Tullia with his sister, Assunta, accepts Keith's €10 for our gelato, and asks him to pay the other €1 tomorrow, rather than paying with a €20. Being seen is an unexpected comfort. It makes me wonder both how we feel seen at home and how we give the gift of seeing the Light in others.

20 August

We follow Arturo's yellow Fiat Punto through the Umbrian countryside to Lago Trasimeno, the largest lake in the region. Arturo has invited us out for a day on the lake. We arrive and park, then hop on the ferry to Isola Maggiore, one of the three islands in Lago Trasimeno. The island is small, inhabited by fewer than 40 people. Once we dock, Arturo leads us up the hill behind the houses to the ancient olive grove, and shows us the chapel that Francis lived in during his residence on the island, pre-stigmata. Nicolas, whose stomach often defines his reality, asks, *"San Francesco mangia...che mangia?"* Arturo explains that the monk's *amici,* friends, would leave him with provisions. As we continue walking, Arturo starts telling us the history of the island, but he stops to address us all in his slow and intentional Italian. As we stand on the dusty path, Arturo tells us that Tuoro, the town we see across the water, was attacked by Hannibal in 217 BC, taking advantage of the early morning mists. Fifteen thousand Romans died in a humiliating defeat, so many that the river ran red. Farmers still find bones of the slain Roman soldiers.

Another chilling episode: In World War II, the people of nearby Passignano hid on Isola Maggiore. When the Nazis goose-stepped into town, they found it deserted. Not easily thwarted, they rowed to the island and killed all the people too aged or slow to avoid capture. We struggle to fit the knowledge of this sense-less bloodshed with the day's mellow serenity.

As we pass a bakery, I tell Arturo about my failed attempt at *panzanella*, bread salad. He stops dead in the street and orders me to recount my procedure. He shakes his head and clucks when I confess that I did not used wood-fired bread. This was, it seems, my downfall. Despite his troubled expression, discussing food with Arturo is cheerier than talking about man's inhumanity to man. As he tells me about his childhood spent helping his mother, I imagine a five-year-old Arturo, just like our current Arturo, complete with huge glasses and grey ponytail, standing beside his mother in the kitchen, obediently poking his fingers into each *gnocco*.

We set up our picnic, and Keith treats the children to Fantas, which are fresh and tart here. The soda seems to be the siren song for *vespe*, wasps, as they descend immediately once we pop the tops. Gabe runs laps around our table, shrieking in fear, and Arturo kills a wasp, flinging a *panino* to the ground in the process. For the rest of the day, we call him Arturo, *gladiatore* of *vespe* and *panini*, and he smiles modestly as if we've crowned him emperor of Umbria.

—

22 August

Spello is proud of her Roman heritage, and celebrates with an annual festi-val called Hispellum, the ancient word for "Spello." We pore over the program to search for events, and discover there will be a parade tonight. As the evening pro-gresses, and candles are lit all over town, we notice an increasing number of people in Roman garb. Strolling through the *piazza*, we linger at vendors selling wooden swords and local olive oil and incense, and shiver whenever we hear the bellow of the long horn. We watch the falconers and stand together, breathless, as a falcon screeches into the inky sky. While we wait to see if it returns, an American voice behind us wonders if the falcon will come back with a pigeon. We turn and meet Max, a Franciscan monk who's making a pilgrimage to Assisi, Francis' birthplace and Spello's neighbor to the north. I tell him about seeing Francis' dwelling at Isola Maggiore, and he excitedly says he was there last week. He tells me that, according to legend, Francis arrived on the island with two loaves of bread, and at the end he had one and a half left. Max speaks animatedly about how sharing what we have feeds our own soul, and I felt the pull of a saint born just a few kilometers away.

Even with the wonder of the filling streets, I am unprepared for the parade. The children point excitedly at gladiators on horseback, Vestal virgins in flowing robes, the falconer now carrying a sedate owl, scampering toga-clad children holding hands, patricians with golden laurel crowns, senators striding with gravity, and slaves hinged together with rope. It's thrilling, but I can't help feel outside the celebration. This history is not mine. But as flame throwers career past us, it's easy to ignore the sense of being a witness rather than a participant.

As I stand in amazement, I feel a tug at my elbow and turn to greet Doreen. She impulsively hugs me, and then introduces us to Paola, who owns a clothing shop across the street from Bar Bonci. Paola smiles broadly at the introduction, laughing at our awe at the parade. She agrees that it's spectacular, and I'm appreciative of her excellent English. She tells me she lived in London for a time, but has made Spello her home for the last 20 years. With a hand on my arm, she tells me that if I need anything, I can ask her. Looking into her warm eyes, I sense her sincerity and smile in return.

The parade continues to thread past us, and Paola tells us that 400 people participate in the festival. Spello provides the costumes, and participants commit to being part of the festivities for all four days. We fall silent as a gladiator with golden arm bands and a giant dog strides past us. I'm beginning to comprehend the reverence that country people must have experienced in watching ancient Romans march into their lands with axes and armor and arrows. And also how proud those who considered themselves Romans must have been to watch their armies return, triumphant.

23 August

My day of crankiness begins with a trip to the playground. The kids play Hug Zombie until Siena storms off because "the boys aren't being fair." Without the clannishness of the three of them together, the boys become open to the overtures of a curious child. Nicolas brokers a conversation between Gabe and the boy, which he notes is grammatically flawed, but he's proud of his effort. I notice a little girl clutching a stuffed puppy watching Siena, but Siena is too intent on perfecting her pout to notice. She answers my suggestions to engage the girl with complaining and grumbling. It is frankly annoying. Complaining is so rarely helpful, and she's missing an opportunity to form a connection. Plus, I can't stand having my suggestions summarily dismissed.

We continue to the *macelleria*, where my worsening mood slips irrevocably as Gabe insists on repeatedly barreling into me while shouting that I am an "evil deed" and Siena grows more petulant. The Superconti fails to improve their mood, despite Nicolas taking Gabe aside to cajole him into good behavior, and putting his arm around Siena to soothe her. Unable to make headway with his siblings, he jokes with me that I may single handedly re-energize the Euro with my shopping. I smile at his effort, but my mood is sinking under the weight of being responsible for four of us when three of us are heavy, and getting heavier.

As a final blow, we wait 45 sweltering minutes for our *navetta* ride to the *piazza*. I feel like a moron for not understanding the schedule, and this annoys me. Then I blame the crazily unclear schedule, which also annoys me. Gabe running around with no self-control annoys me, Siena's gloom annoys me. I resent the walk up the hill from the *piazza*, I resent Siena finding the energy she'd claimed had disappeared because she was tired, and sprinting to ring the bell for Keith to buzz her inside while we're 40 feet behind her. I am thoroughly, unequivocally cranky.

I eat lunch by myself because I don't want to deal with anyone's needs or expectations. Afterwards, I apologize to Keith for being crabby, and he tells me I'm allowed to be crabby. Even in paradise. Unexpectedly, my shoulders lighten. I realize I've been feeling guilty for not being able to look past the trivial annoyance of the day to the bigger whole—I'm living my dream, and I've been too fractious to care. I wonder if the guilt of not being grateful was weighing on me as much as the cumulative annoying moments. I also wonder why I can't give myself permission to feel what I feel. I'm distracted from my thoughts as Gabe and Siena snuggle against me. They take turns massaging my back and kissing my arms. They are sweet kids, and they are allowed to be difficult sometimes, too. I guess I'll keep them.

24 August

Gladiator school. I had no idea there was such a thing. But Keith used Google Translate to decipher the Hispellum program, and unless "*scuola gladiatori per bambini*" means something different from the literal translation, then there is a Gladiator School in Spello this evening. Gabe is beside himself.

When we arrive at the *piazza*, we find five boys with wooden swords clustered around a man in a blue loincloth demonstrating gladiator moves. Gabe clutches my hand, his body tense with yearning to join the circle. I encourage him to practice the moves, but though he starts bending his knees, he quickly stops and says, "I feel embarrassed because I don't have a sword." He doesn't know how to join the group, and his parents are useless, as we only understand one word for every 20, and most of these are body parts. Gabe keeps looking up at me. His shoulders are so small, and his ache to belong is tangible. Keith leaves to make reservations as the two of us are dining out alone, and Nicolas joins him, unable to stomach watching Gabe any longer.

To my consummate relief, eventually enough new children appear that more wooden swords are distributed, and I make sure Gabe gets one. He now joins the line—smaller than the other children, and in our eyes, infinitely more vulnerable. After enough repetition, Siena and I finally understand the instructions and translate for Gabe: First, attack the head, then the neck, then the other side of the neck, the legs, and finally the stomach. Gabe practices alongside the rambunctious gladiators-in-training—always a step behind. His little body quivers with determination as he matches his steps to the teacher and shouts, a beat behind everyone else, words he doesn't understand.

When it's time for the students to spar with the teacher, Gabe announces that he's going to keep participating. My stomach drops—this provokes all my fears of language impasses and awkwardness. Only this time with swords and an audience thrown in for good measure. When the teacher calls for volunteers, we have to shout for Gabe to raise his hand, and he keeps it stretched high long after the chosen child has begun to circle with the teacher, and everyone else is waiting for the next call for volunteers.

Finally, Gabe is called to fight, and all his power evaporates. He is downright delicate. After a few gentle parries, the teacher dramatically drops to the ground with a groan, then leaps back up with a smile to congratulate Gabe with a hearty "*bravo!*" Gabe switches teachers and now he's found his footing, leaping away with a mischievous grin and lunging forward to parry. When he's successfully knocked down his second teacher, he runs toward us, arms flung wide. Keith presents him with his own wooden sword, purchased in the *piazza* on the way back from making reservations. Gabe's face is wreathed in pride and disbelief. He hugs his sword and walks home with an unfamiliar swagger in his steps. He doesn't want to relinquish his sword, but we don't want him battling. He asks, "Can I draw a picture of my sword?" Yes, that's safe enough. We show Nicolas our phone numbers as we head out the door, and he assures us that all will be well. He can run down to La Cantina, and Arturo is around the corner.

As Keith and I walk through the lively street, we chuckle at the sight of centurions with plastic water bottles in their sword sheaths and gladiators texting. At the sounds of his laughter, it occurs to me that this is our first time out alone together in longer than I can remember. When we sit down at La Cantina and look at each other, we laugh, out of the initial strangeness. As we pick up our menus, Keith tells me about a conversation he had with Letizia this morning, which launches him into how much he loves ducking out of the house multiple times a day for a pick-me-up. He tells me of the relative merits of the *espresso* at Bar Tullia, Bar Bonci, and Bar Cavour. They all taste the same to me.

Keith leans back and says, "It's nice to think about coffee instead of work." He is working just a few hours a day, which is quite a shift from his frequent 18-hour work days back home. He tells me that he often catches himself feeling that he should be doing something, and the sudden awareness that there is nothing he must do is freeing. As for me, I've replaced my therapy practice with daily writing during an extended afternoon *pausa*. So I'm still working, but it doesn't feel like working at all. It's hard to explain to Keith, but I finally liken it to angioplasty. My husband laughs aloud, almost dropping his fork, but then quickly leans forward to understand what I mean. I've always honored the work of diving into the hearts of my clients. But, there were days of talking to people all day when, by dinner, I just wanted someone to ask me how *I* was. Writing does that for me. It encourages me to sit and contemplate the state of my own being, to look for metaphors in my life, to make connections and realizations. I'm asking myself how I am, and it's opening channels of understanding. I'm diving into my own heart.

We stop talking when our food arrives. We had planned to share, but I am so smitten with my *agnello scottadito* that I can't bear to part with more than just a bite or two. Luckily, Keith is equally enamored with his beef cheeks in local Sagrantino wine, so he doesn't mind not swapping plates. When we stop remarking on our meals, our conversation turns to language. I shake my head in wonder at Keith's language acquisition. He tells me that I know as much as he does, but he suspects my brain freezes because I insist on saying things correctly. This is true, and when my brain freezes, I find myself hiding behind him. Which is easy because he exudes competence, even when he has no idea what he's doing. I wonder aloud if it's a Y-chromosome thing, and Keith counters that it's more likely to be a speech-and-debate thing. That's what he did in high school when I was busy writing poetry steeped in desolation.

Over a shared plate of tiramisù, and an *espresso* for Keith, we brainstorm places we'd like to visit this year. It's odd, like dreaming within a dream, but this month has whizzed by so quickly, I know that if we don't make plans, we may never move. Inertia is a powerful thing. We agree that we'd like to see the southern parts of Italy, perhaps an island, like Sicily or Sardinia. Food is always a driving force behind our travels, and the culinary culture of Lyon appeals to me, though we'll be limited to locations where we can get inexpensive flights. We decide that we'll plan our first trip next month, and choose a location based entirely on ticket cost.

As we walk out of La Cantina, I feel a little fuller and a little lighter. My nerves are less jangly, and a sense of peace has quieted my thoughts that can sometimes move too quickly. I bump against Keith's hip, and he takes my hand. The quiet of the town surrounds us in a warm hush, and we walk under stars brighter and more fluid than I remember.

The bliss is short lived. When we walk in the door, Nicolas tells me that though the little ones behaved beautifully, the evening was not without drama. He had barely tucked the kids in, when Siena yelled that Gabe was bleeding. He ran upstairs to find Gabe clutching his nose, which was pouring blood. Nicolas goes on to say that Siena didn't have the lightheaded response to blood that he did, and she applied pressure to Gabe's nose, cleaned him up, and washed his bedding. They both tucked him back in. Nobody had seemed to miss our presence during the bloodshed, and it's reassuring to know that they can handle this kind of situation together. Our own little gladiator team.

26 August

Sometimes this notion of moving to a place where we don't speak the language or know anyone seems wholly insane. Why would we abandon a town, friends, and school that we love just for a new experience? Maybe because underneath that craving for the growth that a "fish out of water" venture embodies is a desire to create a home out of the unknown. The urge toward creation is a powerful one.

Looking back at this past month, I can see the ways that we've deepened our connection to Spello. Making meals, doing laundry, writing, studying. On vacation, we're always looking for the next fun activity. Working toward a sense of competence and industry in a new place translates into feeling like this is life, not vacation. It also connects who we are as people with the place we are living. Even the bureaucracy is useful for gaining a sense of place. Keith has gone to the bank four times trying to set up an account and keeps getting the runaround—someone is on vacation, someone is gone for the day. But these acts of business, loony as they sometimes are, give us an understanding of the underpinnings of our community. Or at least the propensity of employees to be on vacation. Taking care of business is dull and often aggravating, but it's a consistent reminder that this is our daily existence.

As I watch tourists stream back and forth past my house, while the side streets remain empty, it occurs to me that residents feel comfortable attempting alternative avenues. I believe a recent craving for Asian food speaks to my readiness to shake up our gastronomy. Or maybe I'm just in MSG withdrawal. Branching out also means trying different shops, like the new *fruttivendolo* I visited yesterday. The owners were friendly, and when I left, the woman ran after me to ask if I wanted a bundle of *prezzemolo*, parsley. And then the man handed me the vibrant bundle with a grin. I felt like our presence was appreciated, not just tolerated. I live here now, I make choices, and those choices create a pattern. And the patterns stretch and grow, creating a fabric of community.

This also means experimenting with language, asking people how they are doing or where they are going instead of just "*buongiorno.*" Last night, Nicolas went to Bar Bonci to get a treat. Letizia asked if he was alone. Nicolas said, "*Sì, sono molto coraggioso.*" Yes, I'm very brave. He stretched himself by going out on a limb, and in doing so made a connection though language and humor. That's what's going to make this feel like home.

It's strange now, to remember the day that we told the children that we were moving to Italy. Saying the words aloud was like letting go of the ropes that had held us in place for so long. Gabe, once he understood that the plane ride wasn't imminent, went back to tinkering with magnets, but Siena curled against me while Nicolas stirred out of his open mouthed shock.

"Wow, just wow…but we don't know any Italian."

"That's true, but we're going to start Italian lessons next week."

"Will I go to school there?"

"Yes."

"Even if I haven't learned Italian?"

"Yes. You'll learn more quickly once we arrive. And if you don't understand the lessons, that's okay."

"But then I'll get bad grades."

"You are allowed to fail every class but English. Actually, maybe math, too. That should be universal."

"Where will we live?"

"We're not sure yet, somewhere in central Italy. Probably Umbria."

"Why there?"

"Because it's close to both Florence and Rome, both great cities, and we've been to the area and liked it, so it's not completely unknown. Do you remember Umbria? We went there for a week after our trip to Rome when you were five?"

"Was that the place with the houses on hilltops and the town with people who gave me chocolate for no reason?"

"That's it."

"Yes, I remember…Have you picked a house?"

"No, we have over a year."

"What will happen to our house?"

"We'll rent it out."

"But it doesn't have real walls in some of the rooms."

"We know, but again, we have over a year, it'll be done."

"Will someone live in my room?"

"Almost certainly. Is that okay?"

"Of course! I'll be in Italy! Wow! I can't believe it! This is *so cool!*"

And on and on, with Siena watching the conversation like a tennis match. I whispered to her, "What do you think, Bellini?"

She paused, and said, "I think it sounds exciting. I want to see a world outside of Charlottesville. But I'm afraid I'll miss my friends and my school." I assured her that was reasonable, even though Nicolas looked ready to pack his bags. I reminded her that it would only be for a year. She nodded and smiled into my eyes. I could tell she was divided, but she's a child who is tuned into her emotions, so it didn't trouble me that she was accessing a place of trepidation. I was more surprised that Nicolas wasn't. Then again, not much rattles my eldest, except when someone in the family is unhappy. That slays him.

I bring my thoughts back to the present. It's bizarre to consider that back then, we could not have imagined our lives here, now. No, Spello is not home, but it's more than we imagined a year ago. What more will it take to feel like home? Maybe a predictable rhythm. School will give structure to our days. But other aspects of predictability, too—like understanding the *navetta* schedule, appreciating the views in different seasons, communicating through instinct rather than deliberation, and anticipating the smells and sounds and sights. I can't imagine I'll feel that I belong by the end of the year, but I can understand my world enough to play with the constants, experiment with the herbs, anticipate the church bells. In short, perhaps it will feel like home.

27 August

Siena forgot to study the names of shapes, and is adamant that she shouldn't go to her lesson. I tell her, fine, we won't go, Arturo can just wonder where we are. She smiles and says, "Okay!" Damn. She's learned to call my bluff. My annoyance is tempered by empathy, I know she's been struggling a bit lately—confessing that she likes to imagine the Blue Ridge Mountains are just over the valley, growing quiet where she is usually merry. Despite all the wonder she expresses at the flowers and the cats and the gelato, the knowledge of what's around the corner must be hard to bear. I simply take her by the hand and start walking. I feel a pinch in my stomach when my mind whispers, "How will she manage school?" but I shake it off in the face of Arturo's expansive welcome. Siena easily finds her smile once more.

Later in the afternoon, Nicolas and I walk through the alley to the other side of Spello, to pick up supplies for dinner at the little shop across from the bakery. We pass one of the old ladies sitting in her green chair, and Nicolas greets her with a measured, *"Buongiorno,"* to which she replies, *"Buongiorno."* As the hour is 5:00, and therefore it is no longer morning, I instead greet her, *"Buonasera."* The woman responds in kind, tittering into her hand. We walk on, Nicolas seething at his error. On our way back through the alley, we see her still sitting in her green plastic chair. When she sees us approaching, she pauses over her lacework and looks up expectantly. Nicolas deliberately greets her, *"Buonasera."* To which she retorts, *"Buongiorno!"* And then cackles with such force, I fear she'll fall out of her chair. Her chortles follow us out of the alley. Nicolas comments, "Now I have an inside joke with one of the alley ladies." He smiles in pleasure.

The evening is cool and fine, and we stroll to the playground, merrily calling, *"Buonasera!"* to anyone who looks familiar. Nicolas is careful in his diction. Soon after we arrive at the playground, Siena bounds to me and Keith and asks in a rush, "How do you say 'hug' and 'zombie'? There's a girl who is trying to play with us and we don't know how to tell her what we're playing." We guess, *abbraccia di zombie*, maybe? But then Keith notes, "You know, they might as well call it 'chocolate pants' for all the good the name will do." The little girl, Margherita, races alongside our children for the next 20 minutes. She chatters relentlessly at my daughter until Siena tells her, *"Non parlo italiano."* At this, Margherita's brow creases, and with dramatically slowed speech, she points at the playground structure and says, *"Scala!"* Siena obediently climbs the ladder. When she climbs down, Margherita says, *"Mano!"* Siena holds out her open hand. Margherita deliberately stretches her hand over Siena's and drops a pebble into my daughter's waiting palm.

30 August

My mind continually starts when I realize that the first day of school is around the corner. I've grown protective of this unfamiliar amount of family time, and I'm loath to introduce elements of distress. Plus, I've been so busy pushing away the image of my children in a classroom without their parents and without the armor of cultural comfort, I've neglected to consider that my baby is not just starting Italian school, he's starting elementary school. It's harder to plunge my head in the sand now that today is Gabe's orientation.

I wake up anxious about clean laundry, but I know this is a veneer for the real panic—What if we can't understand? How can we stand tall when we're outsiders? What if Gabe breaks down crying because he's so confused? What if I break down crying because *I'm* so confused?

I try to think of it as an adventure, and fail. I try to remember that Quaker adage, "Way will open." Breathe—and it is time. I take Gabe by the hand, and we walk out of our door toward the *scuola elementare*. Ahead, children are walking, hand in hand with their parents. I remember that the whole *prima* class is as unfamiliar with sitting at a desk and listening to a teacher as Gabe is, since kindergarten in Italy is preschool, in a different building. The realization is a comfort, until we enter the school courtyard and it seems like we are crashing a huge family reunion. A reunion of a family that takes pride in their appearance—everyone is dressed with care, everyone's hair is meticulously arranged without a shimmer of gray, and the women's beautiful features are accentuated by makeup. Come to think of it, it feels less like a reunion and more like an informal wedding. I'm suddenly aware of my ill-fitting clothes and my hair in its usual indifferent lump at the top of my head (what my family lovingly calls "Mommy's doorknob"). The five of us stand awkwardly to the side and smile woodenly at nothing.

Finally, Alessia calls for attention. She is oldest of the three *prima* teachers, and even though she's tiny, she has a commanding air with her sharp nose and her pulled-back black hair. Her eyes radiate welcome as she addresses the crowd, a gap between her two front teeth winking with her smile. I have no idea what she's saying, though I do recognize when she starts listing children's names. I offer a prayer of thanks that our last name doesn't begin with an "A," as we'd have stood there like idiots. When Gabe is called, we step behind Alessia with the other families. When all the names are read, Alessia announces that this is the *classe prima A* and leads us upstairs to a classroom with desks too large for such little people. The students sit at the desks, and the parents line up against the edges of the classroom. I try to look like I know perfectly well what to do with my arms that suddenly seem too long.

The hour is a jumble. Alessia tells a story about a rainbow, and Gabe lolls his head about, eyes pleading as he whispers, "I don't under*stand*." I finally realize he probably thinks he's *expected* to understand. I assure him, "You're not supposed to understand, there's no way you could. Your only job is to pay attention, watch the other children to follow." His agitation decreases, but his face is still pinched with worry.

Alessia hands out paper for the children to go home and draw a picture for the classroom. Gabe clasps that piece of paper to his chest like a lifeline. Then Alessia raises her voice for attention and asks who is new to Spello schools. I'm shocked that we understand the question in time to prompt Gabe to raise his hand, as he looks at us and asks, "Why am I raising my hand?" There is one other child who didn't go to kindergarten with the rest, but he's from Foligno. Alessia asks Gabe in English where he went to school and he answers, loud and clear, "America" to a collective sigh of "*awwww!*" from the parents. Maybe it's his American accent, but Gabe is seen as adorable. I'll take it. With coupons. Any edge this child can get, I'll grab and be grateful for it.

At the end of the orientation, Alessia speeds through information on school supplies, the schedule, and the goals of *prima*, but I catch almost none of it, and suddenly we're all following her back downstairs. Keith ducks into the secretary's office to turn in Nicolas and Siena's transcripts, while I continue to follow Alessia out of the school to get those details I missed. As I approach her in front of Bar Tullia's patio, she greets me with hugs and kisses. She is breezy about school supplies, I think Gabe needs five large notebooks with squares, and two small notebooks for communicating with the teacher, as well as a pencil case. Yes, he should bring a snack, the school has no pizza until the man comes in October. I'm briefly sidelined by the curious image of an autumnal pizza man, but then refocus on more pressing matters. Alessia is telling me the kids will each need a diary. To my confused expression, she adds, "For writing down homework." Oh!

I guess that's a planner. Business complete, Alessia asks if I like the school, and assures me that everything will be fine. Just be calm! I guess I'm not hiding the terror very well. Besides, as the only woman not wearing bronzer, perhaps I appear particularly wan.

Keith rejoins me outside, and we walk to the playground to let the children play while we talk. He tells me about the forms he completed, including the spot where he'd had to note that the children are not Catholic. Keith muses, "I wonder if it's for their annual 'shaming of the heathens' ceremony." He registered Nicolas to take piano after school, which is an optional perk of the *scuola media*. My head is full, everything feels too hard, too complicated. And I'm struggling with a strange sense of releasing the reins. It's always me that handles the school—now I not only feel outside the language and culture, I unexpectedly feel outside my normal role as a parent. This realization is made more painful when I remember that if it had been me in the secretary's office I would have been frozen and useless. Incompetent and scared and feeble, that's how I feel. I confess this to Keith who tells me I need to be easier on myself—his taking over some of the school duties is part of what we wanted, to rethink our roles and habits. But being easy on myself is a skill I've never had, and it doesn't make sense to start now. Instead, I berate myself for not talking more to people, for not studying harder, for not approaching the language barrier with lightness and trust. All this self-flagellation on top of the morning's anxiety puts me in ill humor.

I buy peaches at the market, and that helps me feel better. Hunger isn't a good salve for self-reproach. Sunshiney peaches soften the hard edges. As the five of us sit side by side on the bench, the little boy from Foligno enters the playground. Gabe and the boy watch each other with unabashed curiosity. An utterly Italian child—golden complexion, wide eyes, hair spiky in the front, sweater-vest over a collared shirt, gorgeous. We exchange a friendly "*ciao*" with the father. It's not much, but it's a start. I guess. I wonder how many foreigners I've given a small smile to on the playground back home, when they could have really used an attempt at conversation to make them feel included into a society that suddenly seems too remote. This feeling of being alien and outside is just the pits.

As we walk home past Bar Tullia, Assunta stops us to ask, "*Andate scuola qui?*" Are you going to school here?

Yes. Yes, I guess we are.

Ferragosto Tagliatelle con Gamberi
(not legs)

1 pound of fresh tagliatelle

1 pound of shrimp, peeled, tails left on

6 tablespoons of butter

4 tablespoons of olive oil

4 cloves of garlic

8 basil leaves, chiffonade

salt

lemon to taste (ours are like balls of juice here, so we just needed
a quarter of a lemon, back home I'd say almost a whole one)

———————— · ❃ · ————————

1. Boil salted water for pasta, cook according to package directions. While pasta cooks, begin shrimp sauce.

2. Heat pan to quite hot and add roughly a third of the butter and a third of the olive oil, and sauté two of the garlic cloves, without browning them.

3. Add half of the shrimp to the pan, sprinkle with coarse salt, and cook without stirring until the shrimps are caramelized, then stir to complete cooking. Add half the basil, toss, and then remove the shrimp to a bowl. Repeat with the other half of the shrimp. The batches are important so the shrimp aren't crowded. Crowded shrimp steam, rather than sear to a decadent crisp.

4. Off the heat, add the leftover butter and olive oil to the empty pan, and squeeze in the lemon juice. Swirl the liquid and scrape up any bits, to deglaze the pan. When the pasta is done and drained, put it back in its pot, and toss in the shrimp, the sauce, and any stray bits of basil remaining on the cutting board. Toss, and serve immediately. *Buon appetito!*

SEPTEMBER

TUMMY BUNCH TO THE RESCUE

1 September

At Bar Bonci I screw up my courage and ask about a beverage that I see a patron drinking. Letizia's niece, Donata, tells me it is a *marocchino*—layers of *espresso*, chocolate, and frothed milk in a glass. I nod, wondering if this is the predecessor of the American mocha. Donata hands us our drinks and then asks if the children are starting school. When I say yes, she asks what grades they'll each be in. To my surprise, she then switches to English. When I compliment her, she switches back to Italian and tells me that she was going to school to be a translator, but then there were family problems, and she was forced to come home. I want to ask questions, to sympathize, to find out if she has plans to go back to school. But all I can do is make a sympathetic noise. One barrier is language, but the other is, I don't even know her. This is always the occupational hazard of being a therapist— it's easy to assume I have the right to more information than I actually do. As she turns her back to wash a cup, Keith asks me why I sounded sad when I was talking to Donata. Which makes me nervous that what she actually said was that she left school to have a baby, and I inadvertently expressed sorrow.

Donata advises Nicolas to read books in Italian, like *Frankenstein*, to help his language development. Frankenstein is probably beyond him, but it occurs to me that *Harry Potter* might be helpful. She leans forward on the bar and asks how long we are staying in Spello. We tell her a year. She responds with a smile and a shrug. Well, you never know what will happen, maybe you will stay. Maybe you will stay *per sempre*. Forever. Yesterday it seemed we were behind a wall. Today it feels like there is someone at the gate, holding it open.

3 September

The weather is turning. Storms are rolling in with regularity, pushing massive grey clouds across the Umbrian plain. When they pass, small shreds of mist lodge in crevices of the hills across the valley. Winds blow with a tactile nudge, rain beats the roof with a comforting drumbeat, rivers race down the cobblestone streets. A storm is an occasion, and we gather around the windows in awe as we watch rainwater falling off the rooftops in slices. I've put extra comforters on the beds; was it just last week that I was trying not to move in the afternoon so as not to raise my core body temperature? Umbria does nothing by halves.

We've decided to cancel tentative plans to visit Cinque Terre in favor of planting deeper roots here. I look at the basil I potted with the soil and boxes Keith surprised me with, and I notice that it is thriving despite the tempest winds trying to unseat it from its tender place. I need us to be the same—to feel fixed and safe to weather the storms ahead. The challenges that school will bring. I ask Gabe if he is more or less excited about school starting since his orientation. He pauses, then, "I'm scared. Is that an option?"

The tourists are dwindling, and thus our continued residence in Spello is now acknowledged as more than temporary. One of the alley ladies stops me in the *piazza* to ask me hopefully, "*Siete qui per sempre, adesso?*" Are you here for always now? Letizia has just realized our children are going to school in Spello, and she's become more conversational, correcting our pronunciation and asking us questions about ourselves. The butchers ask me if I am living in Spello, and when I said, "*Sí, per un anno,*" they help me find a *navetta* stop closer to the *macelleria*. Moments of bright warmth in days that are growing so progressively autumn-like that I'm planning dinners like rosemary-infused beef stew. No longer illicit rosemary, but my own, purchased from the plant vendor at the outdoor market. I can step out to the *terrazza* with bare feet, gather the piney herbs, and lift my face to the waning sun.

4 September

Juno is missing. Our cat, not the goddess. We walk through the neighborhood, calling her. Quietly at first, apologetically raising our American voices in these roads lined with ancient Umbrian stones, but by turns we are louder and more insistent. We brainstorm: How could she have escaped? Did she leap from the edge of the *loggia* to the rooftops? This would put her anywhere on rooftops of Spello. We study Google Maps to get a sense of how the rooftops connect. In short: Every way. We walk around and around trying to see what a logical path would be. In the process, I discover that putting oneself in the mindset of cat and looking for logic is daunting, to say the least.

Keith makes a poster, but pictures of Juno are scarce. I have one of her sneakily eating my yogurt, and another of our travel day to Italy when she was insisting on thrusting her noxious head out of the carrier. In both, she looks deranged. We finally settle on using a photo of her sister, Freja. Close enough. Keith leaves to hang the posters while I sit on the windowsill of Siena and Gabe's room, as it abuts the roof line. I figure if she's on the rooftops, maybe she'll sense me. This cat—this is my cat. She nestles against me when I'm anxious, she lies on my chest, head thrown back, and gazes into my eyes. I thank the universe for her daily, so the thought of her out there, alone, injured...or worse...

I'm wrested from my perch by unfamiliar voices calling for Juno. I step outside, and find neighbors combing the street, calling our cat. Apparently, one of our neighbors, Anna, who heard Keith calling Juno, approached him asking if we'd lost our cat. My eyes prick with tears at the investment of strangers in finding our pet. For hours, the sound of "Juno!" rings through the street.

Siena suggests soliciting Arturo's help, so I knock on his door to ask if he can keep an eye out for our cat. He grows serious, quickly dons a hat and vest, scoops cat food into an empty can, and orders Siena and me to follow him. First stop, our street. He says the people on our street love cats. I tell him they are already engaged. Next, the old ladies in the alley, who also *"amano i gatti."* I agree that they do love cats, and one of them already knows. He easily assumes this means they all know, because he then directs us uphill. As we walk, he teaches us how to call cats by making a whispery noise. Monet, his calico cat that has taken to lounging across my papers during lessons, races down the hill to trot at his heels.

Arturo questions the elderly couple at the top of the hill who care for stray cats, but they have no leads. We turn back down the hill, our shoulders sagging. But as we approach the house, we see Keith waving at us, and shouting, "She's found! She's found! She's safe at home!" We rush toward him and he tells us more, half in Italian in deference to Arturo. He says that a woman on Via Giulia found her, saw the poster, and called. He raced down the hill with the neighbors, trying not to hope—so many cats look like Juno. He walked into the courtyard, looked up to the window, and the neighbors were asking, *"È lei? È lei?"* Is it her? *È lei.* It was her. Puffed and tense, but definitely Juno. As we walk toward the house, Keith goes on that he'd followed the woman up the steps to the window, and scooped up our little runaway. She offered no resistance, but did start squirming when everyone started shouting in celebration. It was too much for her delicate sensibilities. She is still, despite her Italian adventure, a thoroughly American cat.

5 September

I stand in Bar Bonci, making my *cappuccino* last as long as possible. Though I try to focus on the two men shouting about something in the paper, my mind keeps returning to the email—the email from Alessia saying there are more forms to complete. I debate heading back to the house to ask Keith to go the secretary's office. After all, he began the forms, he should finish them. At least that's the excuse I tell myself to avoid admitting that I'm scared of feeling foolish and stupid. I consider just doing it myself. But that seems impossible—walking into a room full of Italian speakers and trying to even say who I am, let alone making sense of forms probably written in a tense I don't understand. It's embarrassing to admit how easily I get overwhelmed.

Letizia stands in front of me and says, "Michelle." I love the lilt in my name when it's said by an Italian. *"I bambini iniziano la scuola presto, sì?"* The children start school soon? I bite my lip and answer, *"Sì, e ho un po' di paura."* Yes, and I am a little afraid. Letizia raises her hands in a gesture of wide acceptance, and insists that the children will be fine, and adds, *"Piano, piano, e tutto bene!"* Slow, slow, and everything is well. I smile at her words of comfort and ponder her advice. Instead of focusing on the million possible awkward scenarios, I take it slow, and focus just on the one step ahead. I decide to go to the school alone. Scriptless, but undaunted. I imagine the wind of Letizia's confidence warming my back, emboldening my steps. I try to adopt Keith's attitude that this is a game, and I don't have to be perfect, I just have to dodge and weave until things make sense. Which also means, I have to trust that they will make sense. I pretend that I have that trust and ring the school's bell.

I stumble through the receptionist, and do better once in the office. There are, as I feared, times of utter impasse, but when I look at the secretary with confusion, she slowly repeats her sentence until I understand. Or, when I say a sentence that sounds perfectly reasonable, but she looks bewildered to the point of alarm, she pauses, digests, and eventually makes sense of my word salad. And so I complete the forms. Where Keith wrote in pencil, I write in pen. Where there are blanks, I fill them in. And then I leave, utterly high. I had no idea that completing a transaction in a foreign language would leave me feeling invincible. Like I burned away the underbrush, and now there is more ventilation, more space for sunlight, among the trees.

7 September

Shopping for school supplies is part of our September ritual. And here we are, September, in a mall, shopping for school supplies. It is an Italian mall, to be sure, built on the site where St. Francis was taken hostage by the Perugian army. Nonetheless, there is a McDonald's in the food court, so our shopping for supplies is tinged with the smell of stale fries.

First on my list are the pencil cases that Alessia mentioned. I'm expecting to find cases to fill, but when I see a rack of what looks like mini-lunchboxes, I realize I misunderstood. The pencil cases are box shaped with three zippered compartments for markers, colored pencils, and basic supplies—a pencil, a pencil sharpener, an eraser, scissors, a ruler, and two pens. I realize that all children must have these cases, when I remember how at Siena's last lesson Arturo taught her to both ask for and lend a pencil sharpener and a red pen. He also taught Siena how to address teachers and how to ask to go the bathroom. As I help my children choose a pencil case, I remember how Arturo heartened me by declaring that school is for all the children, not just Italian ones.

Our shopping bags full with school supplies, we pause for a hit of mall gelato, before continuing to Euro Spar, an upscale grocery store. The variety of prepared foods is thrilling, and there are more cheeses than I've seen in Umbria. I leave the boys in charge of choosing dinner while Siena and I admire the bloomy cheeses and use fetching plastic gloves to select produce. When I place our soft ripened cheese in the cart, I spy smoked pancetta, burger patties, provolone cheese, and Kaiser rolls. I look up at Keith curiously and he tells me—with a mixture of pride and sheepishness—that they've settled on bacon cheeseburgers for dinner. I've been struggling with Asian food cravings, so I laugh that Keith's first non-Italian cuisine hankering is for a food that never tempts me. But I nod, burgers sort of fit the day we're having. I remember the little flag toothpicks that Keith picked up for Gabe, who was so besotted with the flags that come on *panini* at Bar Bonci that Letizia spangled his sandwich with them. I think I'll put Italian and American flags on our burgers.

The mall, back-to-school shopping, cheeseburgers—all of a sudden, our foreign days take on a familiar hue. But our Italian lives rise to meet us when Keith drops us off at the house so we can unload before he parks outside the town walls. I place a bag on the step before returning to the trunk for more groceries and the bag slumps, releasing peaches and tortellini that roll away, gaining speed on the steep hill. While I haul the *frizzante* water to the stoop, Siena and Nicolas chase our groceries down the cobblestone street.

8 September

The morning dawns fresh and cool, ideal for a walk to Jalapeño, that is, Collepino. We pack water, heart-shaped *biscotti*, and a container of plums, and set off anticipating a beautiful walk, a long lunch, and a comfortable afternoon stroll home.

As the path enters the pastoral valley, the Umbrian sprawl fades into a view of rustling trees and sporadic farms. We read the philosophical quotes along the aqueduct, and Keith remarks that they break up the walk. Gabe asks, "What does that mean?" A question that if I were at home—stirring sauce, cajoling children to do homework, and answering the phone—would have exasperated me. But here, where the moment is everything, there is time to explain that sometimes pausing in a walk makes the journey more pleasant. The points of punctuation allow us to gather our resources and appreciate where we are.

We cross bridges, pass fruit orchards, pick wild figs, chew fennel stems, and admire the olive trees—young trees with light trunks and supple limbs, and geriatric silver trees with dark trunks split with age, glowing in the changing light. Sometimes I think we've lost the aqueduct, but then we see the chiseled stones and realize that the path has moved so that the aqueduct lies under our feet.

The final stretch to Collepino is punishing—a sheer uphill on loose rocks. As we climb, my calves convulsing in protest, I begin to regret the whole journey. But there is Gabe, leaping up the mountain like a goat, chattering about how steep the path is. We all cheer in victory when the ground levels into Collepino, a quiet little jewel of a village. We stroll past the town's communal ovens, a winsome *piazza* with views over the surrounding hills and a bar where friends strum guitars together.

We rest in the *piazza* and wait for the Taverna San Silvestro to open. A little girl capers toward us and introduces herself as Eva. She informs us that she is the town *ladro*, thief, and she steals everything. Including this *cappello!* She dashes off with Keith's hat, and then runs to return it, doubled over with laughter. Soon Eva is called home, and we continue to wait for lunchtime. Siena notices how much calmer Collepino is than Spello, and Keith wonders how many people live here. We sit gazing out to the hills, and Nicolas mutters, "I'm not sure a year here will be enough." I look at him in surprise. He continues that he loves the increasing bits of predictability in our otherwise scattered existence: The neighbor married to a French woman will invariably tell us that he is married to a French woman and that his children are smart. The old ladies seated in the alley will inevitably reach for Gabe's head and shout about his cuteness when Gabe calls, "*Buonasera!*" We will always run into Arturo wherever we are. Letizia will greet us with familiarity. The old men will always be found playing cards on the side of Tullia. And one of them will always insist on holding Gabe's hand. Sometimes it's strange to remember that this life we are living has an expiration date. I remind him that school will make things less predictable. Is he ready for that? He nods, and says that he feels ready for the challenge. Gabe starts dancing at the thought of school. Siena grows silent. As the most timid of my children, I wonder how the school transition will be for her.

The wafting scent, more than the time, alert us to the restaurant's opening. Through a narrow stone stairway, we enter what seems like a whitewashed cave and settle in for a deservedly huge meal. Everything is marvelous except my *strongozzi* with milk cap mushrooms, which is actually unpleasant with undercooked pasta and mushrooms that taste dead. But I enjoy the bite of Siena's ravioli in artichoke sauce I'm able to pinch before she practically licks her plate clean and I polish off Gabe's *pappardelle con cinghiale*, a wide noodle with a lemony wild boar sauce. We have been captivated by *cinghiale*—it's nuttier, wilder, and slightly muskier than its domesticated cousin. *Secondi* arrive, lamb, a kebab of different meats, a *scamorza* cheese covered with grated truffles. I hear "grilled cheese" and I think of the rainy day standard next to tomato soup. I love the idea of grilling a slab of cheese. And the grated truffles bring out the smokiness of the grill. We polish it all off and look around for more.

With frozen desserts from the shop on Collepino's *piazza*, we begin the walk back to Spello. It is less charming, given the rising heat, the culminated exhaustion, and the lessened novelty of the journey. Though this may just be me, everyone else is in excellent spirits, and they shout with glee when we hear the bells of Spello echoing toward us. I spend the rest of the afternoon with a wet washcloth on my head—glad of the journey but glad to be back.

9 September

Gabe has a definite case of the moans. Or the whines. Depending on the octave he can reach given his body posture. It used to be that when we told him, "No," he'd want to understand why and then either ask clarifying questions or nod in agreement. Now, he's likely to ignore us if we tell him to stop doing something ("Stop picking other people's flowers, stop climbing that structure that is too big for you, stop touching that thing that could be poop!"), or cry if we tell him he can't do something ("No, we can't eat outside at the restaurant because there is no outdoor seating"). I'm not sure if it's the trauma of the transition, the toll that school apprehension may be taking, tiredness from a surfeit of late nights, or, please God no, just his innate character.

The most frequent thing he cries when he is upset nowadays is "That's *BORING!*" As in:

Gabe: Can I go into the torture museum?
Me: I'm afraid not, kiddo, it's pretty intense.
Gabe: That's BORING!

   (or)

Gabe: Can I have gelato for breakfast?
Me: We'll have some after lunch.
Gabe: That's BORING!

I'm not sure if he doesn't understand the word boring, or if he is willfully misusing it. It's aggravating nonetheless. And puzzling. Here is a child who can smilingly walk over 12 kilometers in a day. Then he's told he can't use the stapler because there are no staples and he loses his marbles. Nicolas uses this predilection of Gabe's to much humorous effect.

Nicolas: Will we be home for pausa today?
Me: No, we'll be out.
Nicolas (with a giant stamp and huff): That's BORING!

Cracks me up, every time. Though I have to muffle my laughter, else Gabe will come running in, "What is it? What's so funny?" And he is overly reactive to anything that smacks of mocking him. Hell hath no fury like a Gabe mocked.

Today he's been fairly pleasant. He's chipper at the Sicilian bakery we discover in Foligno, and seems to remember how to use his words when he's disappointed that he can't ride the merry-go-round at the park. My guard drops as we pull into the Onion Festival in Cannara, when he remarks with wonder that the field that serves as our parking lot smells like onion rings.

As far as I can tell, given how packed the town is with visitors and stands selling everything from licorice to braided onions, Cannara is a charming village. The townspeople sit on plastic chairs lining the street, observing the hubbub. There's even a donkey on display that's described as a therapy animal. Plus, there are *taverne*—pop-up restaurants that are omnipresent at Italian festivals. Hungry, we get in line, and play many, many rounds of Infinity Questions (our more enabling form of 20 questions) before we are seated in the mayhem. We quickly order fried onions and truffled scrambled eggs and a round of four *primi*—two orders of onion soup with crostini, one order of *penne* with onion and *guanciale di cinghiale*, wild boar jowl, and *gnocchi* with goose and *regaglie*. We don't know *regaglie* are, but order it anyway.

When the *primi* arrive, Gabe immediately fixates on the parmesan sprinkled on his penne. Gabe on a good day would easily cope with parmesan on his pasta, even though he loathes cheese that's not melted. He'd eat around it. This is not Gabe on a good day. This is Gabe on a very, very, very bad day. He begins shrieking that he isn't going to get any dinner because *everything* has cheese. And we are *BORING* for not giving him dinner. Huge tears fall onto his shirt, and I think the only reason we don't attract attention is that the tent is so overflowing with humanity I can barely hear Nicolas beside me, frantically begging me to quiet Gabe. Gabe shrieks and sobs. We try to reason with him, no dice. We try to ignore him, too difficult. Part of me is really annoyed. And part of me feels genuinely bad for the guy. Here he is, five years old, living in a foreign country where nothing is familiar and his routine bears no resemblance to what he's used to. He's tired, he's about to start school in a language not his own, he's just spent an hour in a slow-moving press of people such that he couldn't see or hardly breathe. And now it's 9:00 at night, and he's being served the Gabe equivalent of a steaming plate of entrails. The boy needs a therapy donkey.

Maybe it is my compassion that finally dispels his anger. I tell him that we ordered two *antipasti*, which he enjoyed, and four *primi,* and there were two *secondi* still to come. All to share. We would like him to eat, but it is his choice. He looks mollified. Taking my life in my hands, because when I suggested this minutes before I got a big yell that I was *BORING*, I offer him a bit of my soup. He lets me spoon it into his mouth, and smiles. Without even questioning the suspicious cheese-like chunks on top. Nicolas offers him a bite of his gnocchi, he loves that, too, and I decide to not tell him that I've realized that *regaglie* are giblets. Keith once again offers Gabe a bite of *penne* from the edge of his plate, where no parmesan has contaminated the pasta, Gabe pronounces it de-*li*-cious. And then he is Gabe again. He loves the *secondi* of pork and beef in a rich brown sauce served with a spoonful of delicious caramelized red onions. He skips out, holding our hands.

We buy *bombe* at a stand, with onion cream. I am skeptical, but it's actually quite delicious. There is a delicately sweet note to onions that works beautifully in custard. Though I'm not exactly planning an onion tiramisù. As I nibble the donut, the children scuttle sideways like crabs down the street and then pretend to joust with their bottoms. I ask Keith if it has ever occurred him to that our children are kooky. Nicolas overhears and in an aggrieved huff tells me I am *BORING!* I giggle as we enter a *piazza* and dance together to accordion music, before walking back to the car, all five of us trailing the sweet smell of onions.

And none of us are boring.

10 September

I am having a good strong dose of reality in the school supplies aisle of the Superconti. We've tried to pick up the children's books from the local *cartoleria* (the stationary shop with textbooks), but only half are ready. Siena and I practice saying, "The books weren't ready," so she can explain to her teacher. Alessia had suggested I ask the owner of the *cartoleria* what notebooks we'd need, and though I thought I understood, now that I'm looking at the notebooks, I have no idea. Does Gabe need notebooks with 7 mm grid? Keith thinks it was 1 cm. The big kids may be five mm. I see notebooks specifically for science or history. Do they need these, too?

The fears hit me in waves—Siena, overwhelmed and alien, staring at her teacher uncomprehendingly; Gabe, gravely nodding, "*Grazie*" to his teacher's commands, while he's confused and feels like his world is slipping out from under him and he's trying to remember if he gets to go home or if he's stuck here forever; Nicolas, shoulders back in a desperate bid to appear brave, but really hating us for putting him in a position where he is so clueless. I look blankly at the folders, turning them over and over as if the answer is written in small print somewhere, but really I'm wondering how much it would cost to get us home. Now.

What is wrong with me? The size of a grid pattern shouldn't instill hysteria. I wonder if my notebook panic is mere foreshadowing for Wednesday. The point at which I am unable to shield my children, and they must fend for themselves.

As I stand frozen in front of the notebooks, Keith proposes a plan. We'll arm each child with two different notebooks and a planner. And when we walk Gabe in, we'll ask what more they'll need and purchase whatever we're missing. I agree, dully.

I thaw a bit when we are home, poring over our few textbooks. Gabe examines every page in his books and begs to work a little. I copy out some activities for him. The books begin with letter recognition, so scholastically he's ahead of the game, which makes me feel better since linguistically he'll be years behind. Looking at how his book teaches sequence by following a vintner making wine, I realize that much of his instruction is going to be visual and experiential, which will hopefully make the language impasse less burdensome.

Siena's only available book is for her Italian class, which seems to be a blend of language, geography, and history. The book outlines the regions of Italy, with plenty of photographs. I wish it included restaurant recommendations. Lucky Nicolas has half of his ten books. The English textbook is more advanced than I would've expected, and amusing since it teaches British English. Now my son can learn how to ride on the Tube, and how to ask what guacamole is.

11 September

I wake up with my stomach in knots. But as I walk to the bakery for tomorrow's pastries and *focaccia*, a truth occurs to me—it will be hard, and that is okay. It seems too simple, but all of a sudden, the jangly energy coursing around my brain ebbs away. And what's left in its place is a trust that my children will make it through this transition intact. It makes sense. After all, our strongest fears lie deep within our hearts. So deep, we often look at the defenses around the fear rather than the fear itself. So, underneath my freezing at the Superconti yesterday? I now realize—*it will be hard*. Of course it will, how could it not? But they'll get through it. Instead of trying to convince myself that it won't be challenging, I embrace the clearer, cleaner fact. It will be hard. And they will get through it.

Now I can honestly approach the issue of school with the children without being too cheerleadery or too panicked. We agree that it will be hard. And we agree that they will get through it.

The Tummy Bunch is also part of the dialogue. The children have created a league of inept superheroes, each with particular "powers." Nicolas' favorite is "Sour Man!" He's sour. That's it. He cajoles villains to bite him and then they walk away spitting into their hands, "Man, that guy is *sour*!" Siena loves "Fruit Bat Girl!" She has the power of echolocation, but only for mangoes. Gabe is a fan of "Chatter Girl and Cheddar Girl!" Twins who can either talk you to death or instantly turn milk into cheddar. Which creates all kinds of hilarious mix-ups when the populace calls for Chatter Girl and end up getting too much cheese.

My favorite is "Eyelash Girl!" She has super-long eyelashes, so if there is a dust storm, she just bats her eyelashes and murmurs, "I don't mind." This sets me giggling until my ribs hurt. Maybe it's the lackadaisical and self-involved tone, so different from the usual Marvel fare.

Over dinner, when the children are creating new members of the Tummy Bunch, I suggest that tomorrow, they be "Eyelash Girl!" Situations will be confusing and unsettling, they need to bat their eyelashes and mutter, "I don't mind." Because, really, it is all okay. Any problem can be resolved, any sticking place will get easier with time. It's hard because it's supposed to be hard.

They nod, and Nicolas says, "You know what other power the Tummy Bunch has? Each other. 'Chilblain!' makes a block of ice around the villain, but also around himself. He needs 'Matchstick!' to create fire. But 'Matchstick!' is not fire retardant, so he gets burned. But—hooray! The Tummy Bunch also has 'Aloe Vera Man!' to soothe the burns. They work together, and that's their secret power."

After I tuck the children in, I overhear Siena reminding Gabe that even if they don't see each other while at school, they can know that they are in the same building, having similar experiences. And Nicolas is just down the road. We're all on the same page. It's scary, but nothing will happen that they won't be able to manage. Because they are the Tummy Bunch. Not perfect, not all powerful. But brave and strong. And united in facing a school of unfamiliar, incomprehensible strangers, they can take what is dished out and murmur to themselves in unison, "I don't mind."

12 September

It's midnight and Gabe has turned up at my bedside yet again to ask if some-one is clipping his toenails. Finally, I get him to fall asleep, but a few hours later I hear him wandering and find him sleepwalking, about to pee in the trash. I redirect him toward a more appropriate receptacle, then bring him to my bed. Wrapping my arms around his fragile frame, I breathe in his scent of tree bark and sun-warmed puppy. He repeatedly startles, but quiets when he feels my arms tighten around him.

When the alarm goes off, all three children spring out of bed. I head down-stairs to make them breakfast, while they dress. Unable to give them a cookie for breakfast like Italian mammas on TV, I load them with yogurt, bread and Nute-lla, *prosciutto* and melon, *insalata caprese* (tomatoes and mozzarella, really just for Siena, since my boys abhor cheese), and blood orange juice. They eat over their plates so as to avoid getting food on their carefully chosen clothes. Siena compli-ments her brother, "Oh, Gabe, you look so *classy*."

Their heavy backpacks strapped on, we follow the sound of rising chatter to school, where families are gathered around the door. I imagine the crowd in front of the *scuola media*. Nicolas has offered to go alone, so that each of his siblings can have a parent with them, but now, when we're surrounded by a sea of unfamiliar sounds and inquisitive faces, I can't imagine he still feels confident. But he insists he's ready. I watch his back recede down the hill, through the crowd, dragging what must be the only Spellani backpack on wheels—he looks so small and so adult at the same time.

I turn to the little ones and try to make light conversation interspersed with supportive messages. Gabe announces he's going to be "Cheddar Girl!" turning words he doesn't understand into words he does understand, and changing bad into good. Siena just stands there, trying to smile but the expression doesn't reach her eyes.

The doors of the primary school are thrown open, and we enter. I focus on breathing, and find that I'm actually more confused than alarmed—Do we need to check in and who do we give materials to and should we stay to settle our kids in? But that lack of anxiety must be an illusion, because my legs start to give out on the stairs, and when I walk into the classroom Alessia calls, "Michelle! Why you look worried?" She takes my face in her hands, gives me a kiss and orders, "Don't be worried! Is okay!" I wonder inanely if therapy donkeys do long-term rentals.

Gabe, meanwhile, is pale but resolved. He sits with his hands folded, quiet in the midst of boisterous merrymaking. Alessia announces that parents need to say goodbye. I kiss Gabe, running my fingers over his cheek. I walk downstairs to the courtyard, fighting tears as I hear an audible tearing sound inside my heart. Catching sight of Keith waiting for me, I reach for his hand. We step into Bar Tullia, order our coffee, and sag onto the patio. From my vantage point, I see a familiar face exit the school—it's the elegantly dressed mom with the beautifully curled hair whose son attended school in Foligno last year. She tentatively waves, then moves toward us. Apologizing, she asks, in Italian, if we prefer English or Italian. Then she motions her husband to join us, and they introduce themselves as Anna Maria and Stefano, Lorenzo's parents. Their English is excellent, and they offer to help us in any way. Their eyes full of care, they ask how many children we have in school and what levels they are. When I confess concern at my children's lack of Italian, Anna Maria's face radiates a beautiful smile and she reassures me, *"Piano, piano."* Slowly, slowly, one step at a time, and all will be well. She holds my gaze and grins once more before they say goodbye. She calls over her shoulder to contact them if we need *anything*.

Over coffee, Keith tells me that he and Siena had trouble finding her classroom, but Siena seemed collected, just increasingly nervous that she was going to be late. They asked for help from a teacher who looked like a hip musician, with his shoulder length curly hair, who shouted, "This must be the American!" He cheerfully led them to Siena's classroom, *quinta B,* class B of fifth grade, where she met her teacher. Keith reports that Siena's teacher is a thin, brittle-looking woman, but she welcomed Siena, who shrank a little when she was introduced to the class. But she sat down, and looked at least like she was trying to be strong.

The rest of the day is a blur of errands I pretend I'm interested in, when really I'm only marking time until 1:00. Or really 12:45, as we can't stand the suspense. Keith walks around to the back of the school, where we think *prima* will release, while I wait for Siena with the teeming throng of chattering parents. As I wait, fearsome images flood my vision—kids picking on the non-Italian speakers in their midst, teachers ignoring the plaintive expression of my children who don't understand what's happening, the children hating Italian school and insisting on going home or they'll hate us forever. After ten minutes of useless staring the front door, willing it to open, I feel Gabe throw his arms around my legs, and when I bend to pull him into my arms he whispers in my ear, "I had a great day." The relief nearly topples me.

Then my heart catches again as I see that students are filing out of school. And there is Siena! There she is! Holding hands with a thin girl with long hair and glasses! When Siena sees us, she cheerily waves goodbye to the girl and runs into my arms. She nestles against me and breathes, "I'm happy."

Winning the lottery pales in comparison to having your children cheerfully walk out their first day of Italian school. Only one more to go. We wait, and finally spot Nicolas straggling up the street. There's Nicolas! We can't embarrass him by shouting questions or running toward him, but in answer to our searching looks, he reports his day was great. I can't stop smiling.

This deserves gelato. This deserves gelato *before lunch*. Few events in our family narrative have been as deserving of gelato *before lunch*. We order and hurry to the patio. Gabe is spilling over with words even before we sit down. My heart twists when he begins by saying that he cried when I left, but he goes on to say that Alessia helped him locate his math book and then he felt better. He reports that he made friends, enjoyed the day, and he saw Siena on his way to recess. He wriggles with excitement about going back tomorrow.

Siena reports that she was also teary. She started the day feeling alienated by the flurry of curious conversation around her. But then a girl across the aisle shook her hand and that understandable interaction stabilized her. She was surprised to find that she understood more than she'd anticipated. Except in math—decimal places in Italian made her head spin. To her delight, it turns out that the welcoming male teacher is the English and Italian teacher for all *quinta* classes. He periodically turned to Siena to ask for help with English words, in a way that helped her feel included. At recess, she drifted, lonely, but then a girl ran up and asked her name. Soon, all the girls were jostling each other to talk to her. They kept repeating the same phrase, and when she didn't understand, they ran to the English teacher who laughed and told Siena they wanted to be best friends. Siena relayed the story with eyes wide.

Arturo had foretold this exact scenario. He had predicted that Siena's newness would attract the girls, and they'd vie for her friendship. I had responded, "*Spero.*" I hope. He'd paused and looked at me, considering. Then told me not to worry. I told him that was hard, he said, no, it's not hard. I just needed to remind myself, "Arturo knows." The man is an oracle.

Nicolas didn't begin the day crying, but he admitted to feeling overwhelmed and a little panicky when he saw the mob of people waiting at the school. All of a sudden, his plan of asking for directions felt ridiculous—who was he going to ask? He noticed that once he started to worry, his worries snowballed until he was worried he'd be lost the whole day, which he knew was silly. Once the bell rang and people started moving in, he was able to take some action, and that made him feel stronger. He leapfrogged asking one person and then another until he found his classroom. He sat down, and the students introduced themselves to him. For the rest of the day, the students noticed when he was going the wrong way, helped him translate teacher instructions, and even gave him a tour as they walked from one classroom to another. The teachers, too, were more patient and welcoming than he expected. And he surprised himself by his ability to communicate, even using the present, past, and future tense. Beyond the figuring out how to manage in Italian school, he also realized that when he slouched, he felt defeated. When he straightened into an attitude of confidence, he felt more solid.

I prepare baked *ziti*, a family favorite, and it makes the house smell kindly all afternoon as the meat sauce burbles, the béchamel thickens and gives off a festive tinge of nutmeg, and the cheese melts, oozes, and finally browns. Since school finishes so early, the children have time to unwind. They read during *pausa* and then play a clay game Nicolas invented. My ragtag gaggle of quasi-superheroes, gathering their strength for the challenges of tomorrow.

13 September

I have become a covert operator. In my quest to understand what Italian school is like for my American children, I grill my network (read: brood of three) on what they discover as they pose as mild-mannered Italian youth. I devour the crumbs of knowledge my children unwittingly drop, I would dip into our wine fund for the chance to slip a nanny cam on any of them. They are out in the world unsheltered and unchaperoned, and I have to wait till 1:00 just to know the state of their hearts. It's a rough slog. After dropping them off at school today, I climb back into my jammies, order Keith to judge-me-not, and return to bed. Tomorrow I'll use this time for writing, but right now I can hardly focus, and instead I read under the covers. It is pretty cozy, with the rain pelting at the window. I need time to adjust to the fact that I can hear my own breathing, that the sight of brightly colored Legos scattered across the living room floor creates a catch in my throat, and that I spend much of the day watching the clock ticks toward 1:00.

On day two, Gabe is not a good source of information. In his notebook, though, I see that he is learning to write *"Io amo il mondo,"* I love the world. The only tidbit I get about his day is from Siena who reports that the *prima* class marched into her classroom, around the perimeter, and then left. Gabe explains, "We were having a little explore of our school."

When Siena exits school today, she's holding hands with the same little girl. This time, the girl, Valentina, greets us with a big smile, and then runs off to the bus. She seems determined to be friends with Siena, so I want to pin a medal on her and bake her a pie. Over lunch, Siena reports that today wasn't as good as yesterday, mostly because of math. Long division is done differently here and it is hard to follow. Particularly since she can barely count to 100 in Italian. Siena seems to be managing by watching her peers. In this way, she learned that they don't have homework yet because she heard the teacher say a run of words that included *compiti,* homework, and then the class cheered.

Nicolas says that his math teacher is letting him do division the American way, which is a relief since he was as stumped as his sister. Math and science are fun for him, since many science and math words are cognates—here is where I am nodding along, secretly planning to look up "cognate." What he doesn't understand, he enjoys ferreting out. In science the teacher wrote the word *"azoto"* on the board with the letter N under it. Nicolas wrote in his notebook to check to see if *azoto* means nitrogen. Using the mini-dictionary that we bought each of the children on a whim at Superconti, he looked up *azoto* and it wasn't in his dictionary. But then he looked up "nitrogen" and found *azoto.* He's thrilled to have figured it out. I'm surprised by his tenacity. The challenge of the process is clearly resonating with him; he's even raising his hand to answer questions—the child is my hero—much to the delight of his teachers. Also, he's realized that the boys that have been the friendliest also take piano, so he'll see them at the group lesson once a week, after school. I can't believe he'll receive an hour-long private lesson in addition to the group lesson for free.

The three of them decompress through the afternoon with reading, Legos, and building an elaborate treehouse game in the bunk bed. After dinner, we walk to Bar Bonci for hot chocolate. It is decadent—thick like pudding. We cluster around the cups, and let the scent of warming chocolate fill our souls. Letizia asks about school, as the children scrape the last of the chocolate from the cups. The light in Bar Bonci radiates out to the dark cobblestones, glistening with rain, and we sit back, full and gathered and more than a bit triumphant.

14 September

There are signs that Gabe and Siena's veneer of contentment is just that—a veneer. There's a lot of snapping, which culminates in Gabe's shriek that Siena is *BORING*. And then there is the sleep. Which is marked by midnight startles and disorientation and nightmares that find me stumbling to their room before I'm fully awake.

So, this morning I force through the chill of exhaustion to make French toast. Gabe sits at the table with his head cocked on his hand and asks why the French don't make regular toast. The laughter and humble smell of melting butter thaw me. Coffee helps, too. Forms signed, snacks packed, books sorted, shoes on, out the door. After waving goodbye to Nicolas, we walk the little ones to their class-rooms. And then continue to Bar Bonci. Letizia has decided that I need a sprinkle of cocoa on my *cappuccino* nowadays. It feels like a benediction, that dusting of chocolate powder. Eyeing the pastries, I ask how to say "raisins." Letizia clearly annunciates, *"uvette,"* then, with an encouraging smile adds that the pastry with raisins was called a *"Veneziana." Perfetto.*

We pause outside Bar Bonci to organize our morning. I have my Italian les-son and then I'm going home to write. I toy with trying out the black chair in the living room for writing, but I suspect I'll wind up, as I always do, on our bed with the plush yellow blanket over my knees. Keith, as the man of wheels, will be experimenting with his role as family grocery shopper. He's decided to try out

Foligno's grocery store, the Coop. When he arrives home, I unpack the groceries, clapping at each novel item. Roast chicken, lasagna, and a peach cake. And then he tells me about his biggest find.

Raw milk. From a vending machine.

A euro in the slot produces a glass bottle. Another euro, and raw milk is dispensed right into the bottle. The stand displays information about the local cows, the health benefits of raw milk, and the environmental advantages of using the stand—reusable glass bottles, and minimal gas for transportation. The milk is delivered every morning before 7:00, and at the end of the day, the unsold milk is removed and used to make cheese. The milk is creamy, with almost floral vanilla notes.

We eat our grocery store chicken, which is delicious, and drink our raw milk, the children full of stories. Except Gabe. He only offers that he and Foligno boy, Lorenzo, "talked a lot," which seems to mean an exchange of *"bene"* and *"sì."* Nicolas shares his realization that while his classmates are already used to his presence, kids in the other classes have just discovered there is an oddity in their midst. Kids keep coming up to him and asking who he is and if he watches World Wrestling Federation, and then reporting back to their group. Other students feverishly whisper to each other, and when Nicolas glances over, they quickly stop talking and innocently look away. Nicolas is okay with that; his worry is that his classmates may resent that the teachers ask his classmates to translate classwork into English for him. They seem eager to help, but Nicolas worries anyway.

Siena described how her classmates appreciated her illustration for a story they were reading, even calling the teacher to come and see, *"Guarda! Guarda, Maestro!"* At recess, she and Valentina laughed and drew together. And then. Siena says that a boy asked her a question, and she responded, *"Non ho capito."* I don't understand. The boy laughed. Valentina stormed over to him and kicked him in the shin, and said in English, so Siena could understand, "Shut...up!" Normally I've got the whole Quaker-pacifist thing going, but I can't help but cheer.

A long, cozy afternoon of making a coliseum out of paper, and then for dinner I prepare *Chianina* steaks. *Chianina* are a type of cattle that have been raised in this area for over 2,000 years, making them one of the oldest breeds in existence. I brown the thin slices, remove them to a plate and sauté onions and garlic in the juices, deglaze, add tomatoes and herbs, cook it down, and add the beef back at the end. Often beef can have a flat, iron flavor. But *Chianina* is nuanced—sweetly herbaceous with an almost truffle-y depth. Umbria seems more a land of pork than beef, and so this steak feels like a treat. Keith takes thirds. Steak and a martini is pretty much his perfect dinner, though he jokes that sautéed *Chianina* slices and cheap local wine might eclipse his former favorite meal.

In the evening, Patrizia stops by to bring the children fuzzy blankets with jungle animal prints. She laughs when Gabe and Siena instantly wrap themselves in their blankets like superhero capes, and then plop on the floor, bundled, to draw. Patrizia had asked earlier if we needed blankets, and as I'm terrible at anticipating how I'll feel in different weather, I'd told her we were fine. It's disconcerting to realize how little I really know. However, existing without the defenses of answers and knowledge means being able to feel the grace of a shake of cocoa on my cappuccino, the tingle of learning new words for pastries I didn't know I needed, the surprise of raw milk from a vending machine, the gratitude for a loyal new friend, and the welcoming warmth of jungle-print blankets.

15 September

We've learned that the *scuola elementare* has decided on a schedule of five days of school one week, six days of school the next. The days will end at 1:00 regardless, and the *scuola media*, which is six days every week, releases at 1:05. As today is Saturday, it means Nicolas has school. I expect him to come home grumbling about the inanity of a world with school on Saturdays.

We hear him before he rings the bell—his rolling backpack clattering over the cobblestones. Then he's sprinting up the stairs, and explodes through the door, tripping over his words. He describes how in Italian class, he did the grammar exercises to applause from the teacher's assistant. And art class was even better since the time spent drawing left plenty of time for talking to his peers. Nicolas said that one boy exhausted every complimentary English word he knew remarking on Nicolas' art, including "congratulations!" The boys peppered him with questions, mostly in English. Nicolas responded mostly in Italian, and they found that they like the same music groups and video games. Nicolas can't stop bouncing, hugging us, remembering small moments. This is far beyond the fevered imaginings of a hopeful *mamma*.

The one sticking point is that Nicolas has homework he can't do. So he's relieved to run into Arturo talking to Antonio in the street. Nicolas asks if he can drop by for help with his *compiti*, and Arturo readily agrees. Then Arturo notices our shopping bags, spilling over with paper-wrapped parcels from the *macelleria*, and the talk turns to marketing. Back in the States, I just went shopping. In a grocery store. But here, only the British sounding word "marketing" fits our drifting from the meat market, to fish market, to pasta market, and then the produce market. That marketing is worthy of conversation. We discuss the relative merits of the new *fruttivendolo* next to the *macelleria*, run by Moroccan brothers. We laugh when Antonio describes how many fruits and vegetables he eats, and therefore how much he's been saving by shopping at the lower-cost store. It seems so ordinary, talking about where to buy onions, as the afternoon sunlight slants over the street, and yet it strikes me as a moment when our lives slide into that of Spello. It almost feels like we fit. Gabe admires Arturo's new hat. Arturo tells him it's his *"mezzastagione,"* midseason, hat. As we call, *"Ciao! Ciao!"* we imagine what Arturo's winter hat will be.

16 September

My boy is 14.

I am pretty sure it was just yesterday he was throwing his food on the floor in a fit of giggles, but I turn around and see him: Taller than me, comfortable in his skin, with beliefs that have little to do with mine. I was told this would happen, but when each day is like the one before, I get lulled into a sense that nothing will change, and my baby will always seek solace in playing with tractors and the comfort of my arms. It's whiplash to confront the passage of time.

We begin our celebration after Nicolas' beloved *pausa*. He has taken to this Italian custom like an old man to his Barcalounger. I suspect it is because it's the time of day that he gets to do nothing—not clean the litter, not play with his siblings if he doesn't feel like it, not interact at all. It's quiet and predictable. In honor of his birthday, we make *pausa* extra long, and then we walk to Bar Tullia. To Assunta's curious expression at Nicolas' ordering a *medio*, rather than a *piccolo*, gelato we tell her that it's his birthday. She wishes him, *"Buon compleanno,"* to a wide grin from Nicolas. It's part of Italian bar culture to pay after eating and drinking, so it is when we are leaving that we realize that Assunta didn't charge us for Nicolas' tureen of gelato. Nicolas turns back to thank her, and she winks at him.

Nicolas has a hard time walking upright after all that gelato. Assunta has been overfilling our cups as it is, the *medio* may be his undoing. Even so, he is committed to a trip to the playground. After the children exhaust all zombie and gargoyle games, we drive to Montefalco. Two weeks ago we'd dined at L'Alchemista, and Nicolas had pronounced the *tagliatelle del ragù* so stunning he wanted to return for his birthday. We drive past groves of shimmering olive orchards and up into hills trimmed with blue grapes hanging heavy on the vines, to park outside the walls of Montefalco. The light itself seems to hang heavy, and the air is clear and golden as we walk to the restaurant. We're ushered downstairs, to what looks like a wine cellar, with nubby walls painted gold, and a mishmash of tables.

Nicolas' *ragù* isn't as fabulous as last time, but he still declares it delicious. As for me, I'm initially disappointed with the first bites of my wheat polenta with gorgonzola and sausage. I continue nibbling, and grow increasingly enchanted with the toasty flavors snuggling up against the sharp cheese and smoky sausage. A few bites later, I find it overwhelming, and I'm ready to move on to our *secondi*—a stew of pork in Sagrantino wine and a dish of pork medallions wrapped in pancetta with grapes. I'm inevitably pleased by a sweet and salty combination.

Though we're stuffed, a birthday dinner requires dessert. We share a *tiramisù* and an *amaretti* dessert with chocolate and peaches. Both are decadent, but the intense flavor of the cooked peaches combined with the nutty *amaretti* cookies sends me reeling. As we step into Montefalco's *piazza*, sated, Gabe flings himself into Nicolas' arms, and Siena follows suit. They hold hands and spin, heads thrown back with laughter. Then we are all surrounding Nicolas, our child of Light and wind and bone, hugging him and laughing under a canopy of stars.

17 September

As a rule, I strive to meet expectations. Perhaps because I've always been skeptical about my adequacy, I am often overeager to meet any perceived requirement. In any case, Italy is forcing me to confront this aspect of my personality, because I'm only aware of a fraction of the expectations, and I can only hit those a fraction of the time. In short, I'm failing. A lot.

An example: Nicolas tells me that he needs his sport shirt for PE. I tear the house apart to help him look, only to find it in the washer. He puts on the wet shirt, and then tells me he can't find socks. Those were washed yesterday, and are hanging on the drying rack, but with the cooler weather, they are nowhere near dry. And so my child goes to school in a wet shirt that I belatedly notice is too small, damp socks, and shoes that I also realize are too small.

My children are no strangers to damp clothes. Even with the blessing of a dryer, I've been known to hand them a pair of moist socks and tell them to use their coping skills. But here, when the rules are different and I don't understand my children's school lives, the sense of needing to get it right consumes me. I fear that Nicolas will be found wanting by the PE teacher or his peers or anyone who pats his sodden shoulder. I'm furious at myself for not anticipating the morning's demands. Yes, I know if this were happening to someone else, I'd tell them to relax, humans make mistakes, damp and ill fitting clothing is hardly a catastrophe. I can hear that, but I also keep hearing this message, "You failed your kid. You've given him one more way to feel like an outsider." Maybe that voice is always there, but it's balanced by feeling secure in my day-to-day existence. Here, without that surety, and with the amorphous and shifting expectations, that voice is booming. So where at home, I feel fairly confident most of the time, here I'm constantly struggling with even feeling satisfactory. My balance is all off.

I could learn something from Italians—for them it seems like meeting expectations is beside the point. They drop their kids off late for school. The students wander around school asking where their class is with no compunction about not knowing. Parents trust the community to care for the children, without being worried about being judged for not adequately shepherding their offspring. Italian travelers ask questions that reveal their ignorance—What's up the hill, is it worth seeing? At home, it often feels like I'm surrounded by people who project an image of shiny implacability. But here, no one is expected to be flawless and fully prepared. I feel like I could manage not being fully prepared if only we had dry socks, but I suspect this belief is part of my problem.

19 September

This morning it's Gabe who can't find socks. *What?* But the laundry is dry now, there must be socks! I know it! Don't bother telling me that Gabe going to school in his sandals will be okay. Don't try to remind me that earlier this week I had an epiphany that I don't always have to be prepared—I just need to do what I can and let the details go? Please. In the moment, socks don't feel like details. They feel like foreground rushing toward me. There is no reasoning with me, I'll go on throwing laundry on the floor in my quest to find socks that. Must! Be! Here!

Dirty socks for Gabe.

Keith and I go to the *borgo* to buy copious quantities of socks. We take a different route, and I'm shocked to discover how little of Spello I've seen—a quiet *piazza* framed by a striking wooden *loggia* from the 1700's, bits of Roman arches embedded into the stone walls, a quiet street with grass growing between the stones. It's a small town, guidebooks suggest tourists can complete a circuit in an afternoon. How can I have been here almost two months and still be discovering? It feels like I've missed more than I've seen.

On our walk back home, I ask Keith if maybe we should have more of a routine. Our mornings are taking on a predictable rhythm—we walk the kids to school and then have coffee together while we talk about the day or his work or my writing. Then he works at the desk in our room, while I sit on the bed beside him and write, cuddled under the yellow blanket. Sometimes he'll run errands or I'll go to Italian, or we'll take a walk or go together to the *macelleria,* but for the most part, a chunk of our mornings is spent quietly working. Then we walk together to pick up the children and eat lunch and have *pausa*. The rest of our lives, though, is all over the place. Sometimes it will occur to me to do laundry, sometimes we'll walk to the playground, sometimes we'll play games with the children, sometimes I'll mock Keith for reading his new Italian murder mystery because I'm secretly jealous that he's so committed, sometimes I'll do my Italian homework, sometimes we'll all go out to get dinner supplies, sometimes Keith and I will duck out to have dinner without the children, sometimes we'll all go out for pizza. Even bedtime is a moving target, for all of us. Keith says he doesn't feel like he needs a schedule, but would be amenable if that's what I want. Part of me wants to move as I am moved, rather than moving because the schedule says I must in order to be prepared. But part of me wants socks. Mornings are easier with socks. I'm stuck between my old ways of creating a routine so that everything fits, and the way I'd like to be—effortless, aware of my leadings, rather than bogged down by *shoulds* and *musts*.

I would actually like a regular date night, regular laundry days, regular shopping days, a regular time for the kids to do homework, a regular night that we go out for pizza. For me, there is a comfort in the familiar and expected. But I wonder if it's a cold comfort. I'm not sure what the answer is. Which I'm beginning to think might be the answer. I'm just going to have to feel my way out of the depths of my own ignorance. That ignorance makes me uncomfortable, but I'm also beginning to understand that it's a divine reminder—there is more to learn, more to discover, and new areas to dig into. I suspect that every time I get frustrated with myself, it's growing pains. That's easier to remember at the end of the day, when I'm swirling a glass of wine as the sun sets over the distant hills, and hard to remember when I'm desperately searching for socks.

20 September

The children have been in school for a week. Long enough, according to the administration, to no longer need parents to walk their children to their classrooms. This is fine with Gabe, but hard for Siena, who needs connection as long as possible. Now Siena is walking Gabe to class, ostensibly so she can help him hang his backpack. I credit Alessia's warmth for Gabe's ease at school. Once, I put a note in lunch telling him I love him and when I took the note out at the end of the day, I saw that she'd added, "*Anch'io.*" Me too. My children have never been told they were loved by a teacher.

Nicolas is as fond of his piano teacher as Gabe is of Alessia, which surprises me, as he's had to do some serious ego repair work after his first lessons with her. The glory days of him being lauded for his musicianship are a distant memory. Now, his teacher sighs over his lack of technique, reprimands him for his hand curling, rejects his sheet music as trash, and in short makes him work harder than he has ever worked for the relief of a begrudging, "*Non è troppo male.*" It's not *too* bad. Watching Nicolas, I see that he copes by focusing on the satisfaction of learning. He's decided that acquiring theory and focusing on technique will make him a better player. Now he just wants to practice, so he is thrilled that Keith is going to Perugia tomorrow to collect a keyboard he bought on eBay.

I'm grateful that Nicolas is my eldest child because he models not taking himself seriously. Yesterday, he told us that the teacher asked him to recite the names for articles of clothing in Italian. The class erupted in laughter when he mistakenly said he wore scarves on his feet, and bellowed when he couldn't think of the word for boots and so said, *"scarpe lunghe,"* long shoes. When he finally recited the clothing correctly, the class rewarded him with spontaneous applause. Nicolas was doubled over telling the story. Laughing at oneself may be an ordinary superpower, but goodness, it's a powerful one.

21 September

Gabe: Are you scared to go to school?
Siena: I was the first week, but not anymore.
Gabe: I was scared today.
Siena: I know.
Gabe: Sometimes you can be scared, even if you know it's going to be okay.

22 September

Every time I ask to take home my pizza leftovers, I'm met with strange expressions. So at today's lesson, before Arturo can dive into intransitive verbs, I ask him how to properly ask for a box. This propels him to opine in Italian, "At a restaurant, you must pay for all the food! Not just what you eat! So you should bring it home. Pizza is very good heated the next day. You can drizzle it with warm tomato sauce, or some freshly grated parmesan for *nuova vita.*" New life. Here he gazes off into the middle distance. And then tells me how to ask for a box.

After discussing how cultural beliefs about leftovers vary by the wealth of nations, the conversation turns to how culture changes over time. Arturo slowly explains that 40 years ago, a Spellani boy couldn't marry a girl from outside the city walls. And if the boy told his mamma, *"Ma lei è bella,"* but she's beautiful, his mother would counter, *"Bellezza va, ma una contadina è una contadina per sempre."* Beauty goes, but a country girl is a country girl forever. I ask why the girl's parents wouldn't move to town, and he explains that they would have to stay close to the land to work it. But this changed with the introduction of factories. Factory worker salaries created a middle class, which bridged the divide between the rich and poor.

Arturo bemoans class prejudice, and then explains how the school system reinforced this divide. Back when he was in school, you could only go to school in Spello if you lived within the historic center. The school had one class per grade for girls, and one for boys. So if you were in fifth grade you would have dedicated fifth grade instruction all day, as opposed to country schools, which were the Italian equivalent of one-room school houses. Trying not to get distracted by images of Laura and Mary with *focaccia* in their lunch tins gaily calling, *"buongiorno!"* I focus on Arturo as he tells me the problem with a one room schoolhouse—namely, a fifth grader might only get an hour of dedicated instruction. And thus remained less educated than city children. When the system changed, and all Spellani children were educated within the city center, the influx of students necessitated a move to a larger building. And what had been a boarding school for novice priests became the current *scuola elementare.* Which explains the catwalk over a library that I thought resembled a chapel.

We never did talk about movement verbs.

24 September

Travel is draining, so when we pick up our children at school today after an impromptu Sunday trip to Rome, I gird myself for foul moods. And I'm not disappointed. But I bite my tongue and serve zucchini frittata, a bowl of tuna salad, and a plate of tomatoes drizzled with olive oil, imagining the vitamins and omega-3 fatty acids bludgeoning their way through our impoverished bloodstreams. I know my brain feels a bit zippier. We drift to our quiet corners for *pausa.*

Later, Gabe and Siena watch *Shrek* in Italian while Nicolas jogs to his music lesson. I begin puttering in the kitchen, remembering all the hours I've spent taking Nicolas to lessons. My former life seems a blur of chauffeuring children, often with a basket of dinner to eat on the road between activities. I stretch my arms wide in the quiet kitchen, before returning to browning *pancetta*.

The *ragù* is simmering by the time I hear Nicolas bounding up the steps. He drops onto a kitchen chair and takes an olive from the bowl I've set out for Keith, who was telling me about his conversation with Doreen at Bar Tullia. My son nods and beams, chattering about his lesson. Actually, it's less about the lesson, and more about the boys. They've invited him to the park on Saturday. He met them last weekend as well, and came home flush with stories of sharing pizza from the *rosticceria* and discussing video games and music. Teenage boys seem to be the same the world over. Nicolas practically cuts a caper in the kitchen in anticipation of whiling away another Saturday with his classmates. I smile in anticipation for him, and here again, I feel a flutter of freedom. At home, if Nicolas wanted to see a friend, I drove him. Here, he'll walk down to the *borgo*, and return when he's ready. He might well return home with a ruined appetite from pizza, but that's a small price to pay for days unblemished by shuttling.

Despite our peaceful afternoon, Siena becomes surly and cantankerous immediately after dinner. Gabe picks up on her surliness and they grow churlish to each other. Bedtime!

25 September

Our trip to Rome was marred by some Sant'Eustachio bitterness. Nicolas and I were the first of our party in the storied, and therefore mobbed, coffee landmark, and sipped our average *cappuccini*, befuddled. Only later did Keith tell me that I was supposed to order the "*Gran Espresso*" or "*Gran Cappuccino*." Sant'Eustachio's claim to fame is a creamy, sweet foam that rests upon the Gran coffee. There are long threads on coffee forums of people positing what exactly is in that foam. Egg white? Cream? Some special whipping process? Nobody knows, since the baristas hide behind a metal partition when they make it.

But when Keith was out yesterday, he accidentally found the bar that he and Loris went to our first week in Spello. The name of the bar is "Winner," which doesn't actually prepare a person for a transcendent coffee experience. But sipping his Winner *espresso* so soon after Sant'Eustachio made him realize that the cream topping is the same.

I decide to accompany Keith to the grocery store, so I can sample the goods. Winner appears to be part of a lackluster hotel, with a line out the door. We order our *espresso* and watch the magic. The barista pulls the shot of coffee, then dips a small spoon into a large glass bowl of a tan colored viscous liquid, like a sticky *zabaglione*, then hands us our tiny cups. As we stir, cream rises in a foamy layer over the top. I sip and startle in amazement. The addition adds no extra flavor to the *espresso*, but instead mellows it to sweet perfection. Sweet perfection for €0,80, rather than €2,50 at Sant'Eustachio and no fussiness around the process. The bowl is just sitting on the counter for all to see, covered with a sheet of plastic wrap.

Sant'Eustachio, with their keeping their sweetness a secret, can bite me. I have a new cure for bitterness. And it's local.

26 September

Festivals are an everyday occurrence in Umbria. It seems like every time we visit the nearby small city of Foligno a festival is coming, going, or in process. This week it is the festival of the *primi*—the first course of an Italian meal, served after *antipasti* (typically *bruschette* or *salumi* in Umbria), and followed by *secondi* (meat or fish or, if you are me, *agnello scottadito*), then *contorni* (vegetable, such as salad or potatoes), perhaps finishing with *dolci* (often *tiramisù* or *panna cotta*), *espresso*, and possibly *grappa*. Nowadays, there is much flexibility—we sometimes order *secondi* instead of *primi*, only occasionally order *antipasti*, and almost never *dolci*. In any case, *primi* are the dishes that are quintessentially considered Italian, so a festival of *primi* propels us to Foligno.

We locate the infopoint to collect a map, and then saunter to a *taverna* serving the *primi* of Le Marche. The *taverna* is beautifully situated under a lofted arcade, beside what I like to call a canal and Keith likes to call a culvert. Before we sit down, Keith pays for our meals and two mini-bottles of wine. I am enchanted with my mini-bottle. It pleases the two year old within me that would rather not share. I might start carrying a mini-bottle in my purse next to the sprigs of bay leaves I snag at the park. Once seated, the waiter brings out two bowls for each of us: One, a soup with multiple kinds of beans, pasta, and seafood, drizzled with peppery olive oil. The other bowl holds gnocchi with tomato sauce and shellfish. They are better than I expected, given how institutionalized the preparation must have been.

After eating, we wander through Foligno, passing a gluten-free *taverna*, a polenta *taverna*, and a Piedmont *taverna* boasting a variety of rice. The children run into a courtyard lined with vendors hawking many different regional products. At least, it looks like many, as I never leave the balsamic vinegar at the Acetaia San Matteo booth. The smiling owners use their English to ask questions, ply Keith and me with samples, and laugh as our faces grow in wonder with each taste. They first give us a seven-year-old vinegar that's sweet and sour, and finish with a 90-year-old vinegar that I feel sure must be caramel. I have never known vinegar could be like this—sweet and deep, with a velvety tang. Gabe intently licks it off his spoon with exuberant relish, and the man and I laugh, "*È come una lecca-lecca!*" It's like a lollipop.

It's hard to wrench myself away from these warm people, who continue to chat long after I've purchased a jar of cherry jam and ten year old vinegar, excellent for finishing grilled steak. But Gabe makes it easier by pouring olive oil from a stand all over his hands. He runs to me grinning while spreading out his slicked fingers. Time to go! I locate a sink, and then we continue to the city center, where we marvel at large replicas of famous artwork gussied up with pasta—Mona Lisa holding sheets of lasagna, Raffael's cupids reclining on curly pasta, Boticelli's Venus being born on a ravioli. Standing beside this outdoor art are two women in dresses made of pasta. Gabe is fixated on the garments, and I can see his wheels turning ("Pasta is for wearing?"), before we whisk him into the dessert tent, filled with stands with *dolci* from all over the Boot. I start to say that we'll get a treat we all agree on, but my husband is looking around like Charlie in the chocolate factory. His sweet tooth is much more developed than my own. I switch gears and suggest that we each get something, and share it all. Everyone cheers—treats! Then comes the agony of indecision. By the time we leave the tent we've acquired chocolate with *farro* (like a fancy Nestlé crunch) from Perugia, *cannoli* from Sicily, hazelnut nougat from Lombardy, and anise cookies from Genoa. Plus a crepe with Nutella from Assisi. We're making up for skipping *dolci* all those meals out.

27 September

I drag my feet to Arturo's. Sometimes my brain can produce and understand Italian without too much effort, and sometimes it's as if the words are in Mandarin. My last lesson fell into the latter category, my head too fogged and clunky to make sense of the most scintillating conversation, and besides, Arturo insisted on talking about the *posta*. If he'd wanted to talk about the *history* of the *posta*, I might have rallied, but no, he taught me how to ask, "How do I package this to send it to America?" I didn't have the heart to tell him that since it costs €1,60 to send a postcard to America, I have no intention of queuing up to send a package. That whole lesson, I kept telling myself I didn't have to think, just repeat and write. But then Arturo took my *quaderno* and asked me to tell him all the sentences I could remember about the post office, so we could have "little conversations." Blast! Not one *"brava"* on Wednesday.

So it is with some reluctance that I take my seat. But as it so often happens, whatever trials Arturo has planned—perhaps the Italian DMV?—I derail him with food and we are off and running. We chat about local farm ways, and he tells me about his friend who presses his own oil and raises pigs and rabbits. Both tasty, but when it comes to making pasta sauce, Arturo opines that duck is the king of meats. He teaches me the adage *"Una bistecca senza l'osso è come una casa senza il tetto."* A steak without a bone is like a house without a roof. We laugh over our shared love of bone gnawing. As I'm still chuckling, Arturo darts into his kitchen and emerges with a bottle that he's filled with his friend's oil, perfect, he added, for drizzling on toasted bread to make *bruschette*. Only one *must* use the fingers to spread the oil. In this way, the feelings in the heart are transferred to the food.

Looking at the clock, Arturo startles and sits erect to instruct me to start writing down sentences using the vocabulary from our discussion. Only he becomes distracted, and asks where we ate dinner at the festival. I describe the *taverna* and he sits back, looking satisfied. And then he tells me a story.

Long ago, leather workers settled at the site of the present day *taverna*. The location was ideal, as it was beside the Topino river, and water is required for the cleaning of leather. Because making leather also requires air, but not sun, the workers built an arcade beside the river. They would wash the skins in the moving water, and then stretch them in the covered area to dry. The river was important to all of Foligno, as it was the only source of water when the four city doors were closed, at night and when the city was under siege. In the middle ages, the Perugini attacked Foligno, but the doors closed, and the townspeople existed quite easily. The Perugini considered this problem, and determined to reroute the Topino *around* the town, effectively depriving the people of water. So the natural course (or *letto*, bed) of the river is the trickle that runs beside the *taverna*. The larger river going around the walls of Foligno is the artificial course created by the Perugini.

While I sit dumbfounded, trying to make sense of this history that I hadn't even imagined while sipping from my mini-bottle of wine, Arturo raises his eyebrows and suggests that next time I eat at that *taverna* I'll have my mouth pleased at the meal, and my soul pleased at the story.

Arturo continues that during this attack of Foligno, the Perugini used Spello as a base camp. After their victory, the Baglioni of Perugia rewarded Spello with a painting by Pinturicchio, which is still on display at the church of Santa Maria Maggiore. One of the Baglioni brothers actually moved to Spello, building a *palazzo*, which is the current middle school. This explains why school's music room is graced with frescos. I remember that it was the Baglioni family that refused to use the salt vendors dictated by the Vatican and so deigned that all Umbrian bread would be unsalted, and therefore dry and tasteless. And so Nicolas' school was a home for the family that single-handedly ruined Umbria's chances of taking part in the bread renaissance.

I return home with my brain humming, high on language and history. Keith is waiting to go to the *macelleria* together, but he can't get a word in edgewise, I'm too full of stories. I'm still chattering as we encounter Arturo in the *piazza*, and he laughingly asks if we're going to buy duck to make *ragù*. He turns to Keith and tells him that at our lesson, he taught me that duck makes the *"ottimo" ragù*. And furthermore, according to Spellani tradition, all pasta sauce has meat in it, or it's considered *"sugo finto,"* mock sauce. Arturo calls to an elderly lady walking by with her purse just so under her elbow, *"È vero che tutto sugo per la pasta ha carne?"* Isn't it true that all sauce has meat? She regards him as if he'd sprung tortellini from his ears. Of course! Or else it would be fake! Just some tomatoes and water! They proceed to shout at each other about the inevitability of meat in a true Spellani *ragú*.

28 September

Pecorino is good. And I mean that. It can be lovely, and it sure is versatile, what with its different stages of ripeness. But I'm a person who loves nutty gruyere in a grilled cheese sandwich and oozy raclette stretching strands of goodness and thin-skinned Èpoisses offering just a touch of resistance before it opens into rivulets of creamy stink. These are hard to find in Umbria. As is goat cheese of any persuasion, neither fresh and lively nor aged and nuanced. So our drive to Fattoria Il Secondo Altopiano, a goat cheese farm outside of Orvieto, finds me bouncing in my seat with excitement.

We follow the directions up into the hills and park at the goat barn, where Alessandra, one half of the husband-and-wife team that owns the farm, is waiting. My Italian gives out quickly, so I feel grateful that her English is excellent. Our children run to help her husband and son herd the goats, while she walks us around the farm, telling us about the history and philosophy of their venture. Her husband is a vet, and they use organic feed and primarily homeopathic medicines. Alessandra says that when they decided to start a farm, they considered raising sheep, but everyone in Umbria already makes pecorino. And anyway, "We wanted to work with an animal that was not as dumb as its cheese."

She's preaching to the goat choir. Goats are a regular item on my Christmas wish list ("But honey! Think of the cheese! And it could eat all our poison ivy!"). It's joyous to watch the herd of affectionate, amusing, and intelligent animals climb and jump and prance and nuzzle. Once the goats are safely in the milking barn, listening to classical music, Alessandra escorts us to the tasting room. Gabe and Nicolas wait in the barn with the goats—even the smell of cheese turns their stomachs. Meanwhile, the rest of us are grinning like fools in anticipation of tangy, ripened cheese. It's been so long.

We begin with wineglasses of yogurt, while I attempt conversation with Alessandra's six-year-old son. In my previous existence, I routinely bantered with children. I consider it a relative gift of mine. As it happens, my gift doesn't translate. First I try to ask him, "Who makes the cheese?" but accidentally ask him "*Where* makes the cheese?" Drat. Then I try to ask him which jam he prefers, but end up asking him which jam *I* prefer. Double drat. This sweet little boy with silky hair falling in his eyes is going to think that Americans are blooming idiots.

Unlike our conversation, the yogurt is lush and zingy. Then Alessandra produces a truffle-sized fresh goat cheese with a hazelnut on top. It is creamy and sweet, with the just the right amount of tang. Next she brings us a cheese board, laden with a beguiling array of tastes. They range from serene, *semi-stagionato* cheeses with soft paste interiors to rough, fully aged cheeses that are pungent and crumbling and seem to be covered with bark. Those mature cheeses are too powerful for my palate that has been coddled on a diet of tame pecorino and fresh mozzarella. But I swoon at the *Andantino*, a *semi-stagionato* aged on wood with a brie-like texture and caramel notes. We select two fresh cheeses and two *semi-stagionato* varieties. Alessandra carefully packages them in a box with a ribbon. And she hands us these four organic and hand-made delicacies in exchange for €17.

Goodbyes said, and our treasured cheeses nestled in my lap, we continue to Orvieto for dinner. The city rises like a mystical island, high on its rocky outcropping. We park below the city, and take the funicular into Orvieto. The streets are dark and the town is quiet as we make our way to Trattoria del Moro Aronne. Once seated, we begin with an *antipasti* of thin strips of marinated goose, draped over a light mound of creamy fennel. Goose is new to me, and I enjoy its savory taste, with a hint of orange, which marries well with the fennel. Next our *primi*— wide noodles of *pappardelle* with *cinghiale*, *tagliatelle* with *ragù*, *lasagna*, a hand-shaped thick spaghetti called *ombrichelli* with truffle, and *rigatoni* with sausage and *porcini*. Every bite feels more revolutionary than the bite before, a heady blend of flavors and textures. The wine is a perfect accompaniment—we order our usual *mezzo litro di vino rosso,* half liter of house red wine, which traditionally is served in a half carafe, but our waitress brings us the bottle, expecting us to drink half. The wine is a potent blend of caramel and raisins, with enough tannin to create depth. One of those wines where you feel like a better person just by sipping it.

Satiated, we amble to the *duomo* and admire its ornate splendor. The wind blows cool, and I am euphoric looking up at the warmly lit façade cleaving a rich indigo sky, mottled with clouds. Though that could have been the wine. Or the cheese.

30 September

For reasons he can't articulate, Gabe is nervous about entering school. I suspect it's because he had a substitute yesterday. I stand with him outside the doors, struggling with the image of him walking away from me with a quivering chin. In desperation, I tell him I'm going to hug him so tightly he'll have Mommy ziggles to last all day. Mommy ziggles? He smiles. What are Mommy ziggles? I swoop him up in a bear hug and order him to notice all the Mommy ziggles he's getting, until he's full of zinging Mommy ziggles. Things turn silly. Siena wants to give me Siena ziggles, Keith chases Nicolas down the hill offering him Daddy ziggles, Siena and Gabe gave each other fierce ziggles. And those ziggles light their faces, and they walk into school holding hands, as they wave goodbye.

In the afternoon, I refill my ziggle well—after all, how can I spoon out ziggles if I am fresh empty? After *pausa*, I suggest a walk in the pastoral valley that lies below Spello. The five of us stroll alongside fields, under trees heavy with birdsong. The pristine blue sky dappled with billowy clouds is cartoonish in its perfection, and Spello glows in the shifting light. The open space is freeing, plenty of room to run and skip and dash. Well, the children dash, while I soak in the restorative stillness of the farmland and the green all around. There are flowers to pick, a sweet chapel in the fields to admire, and grass to relieve my stone-weary feet. We do also pilfer just one juicy grape each.

While we do have some routine to our evenings now, I like to shake it up sometimes. Today I shake it up by agreeing to gelato at 5:30. Only I don't want gelato. I want to try something new. I practice in my head, and when everyone else has their gelato I tell Assunta, *"Per me una cosa diversa, per favore. Un Aperol spritz?"* For me something different, an Aperol Spritz. *"Ah!"* Assunta answers, *"Tu sei brava!"* I'm not sure if I'm *brava* because I ordered something different or because I said it well, or because an Aperol spritz will put hair on my chest. It doesn't matter. I'm ready to meet this novelty head on. After all, I'm not sure if you've heard, but I'm *brava*.

I've been curious about the Aperol spritz since my research suggested that it might be the refreshing-looking cocktail that I've seen Italians contentedly sipping. Aperol, like Campari, is a bitters made from herbs and fruit. But Aperol is supposedly sweet, whereas Campari is woody with a deeper bitter component. Campari is a bit too *amaro* for me. In small amounts I can almost enjoy its bitterness, but mostly it's a taste I only wish I liked.

I discover—as I sip my drink on Tullia's patio while gazing out over Spello— that an Aperol spritz has a fresh and sweet orange lightness, with a bitter tinge that prevents the aperitif from sinking into cloying. And the flame color is gorgeous. As an added bonus, an Aperol spritz comes with snacks. I like snacks. I feel a oneness with the world as I sip my delicately sweet aperitif with its mature bitter roundness, and nibble on savory fennel rings as we linger in the pink glow that marks the coming evening. I can't believe I spent a hot summer watching people relax with their Aperol spritz and didn't work up the courage to order one. Well, next summer is going to see a different me. A zigglier me. A spritzier me.

Once home I quickly brown a pork loin, place it on a bed of potatoes, onions, and carrots that I've moistened with white wine and olive oil, and put it in the oven. The house soon fills with the wafting scent of dinner, while I engage in Aperol wafting. Drifting here, drifting there. Bestowing beatific smiles on everyone. Everyone who, it should be said, looks at me a little alarmed. What the heck is wrong with Mommy? Why does she keep smiling at me? It's okay, she's just had a few too many ziggles.

Luckily, Doreen calls to invite me out for a glass of wine. I meet her in the *piazza* and ask about her day in Gubbio. It's hard to imagine she's spent the day traveling, as her blond hair is effortlessly rounded on her shoulders and her small frame is fresh and crisp. I tell her about my Aperol discovery and she laughs an easy laugh, her eager eyes dancing while she loops her arm through mine. I think the only thing better than an Aperol spritz on the patio of Bar Tullia (*brava!*) is an Aperol spritz on the patio of Tullia followed by wine at Vinosofia, a wine bar owned by Doreen's friend Brenda. Brenda is an expat from California, with arresting blue eyes set in a heart-shaped face. Her brilliant smile is welcoming, as she introduces me to her husband, Graziano, a tall man with thick-rimmed glasses. One of those Italian men who belongs in a scarf. Together they own Vinosofia, though it is Brenda's passion, and her creative spirit is evident in every detail. High brick ceilings give a feeling of space and lightness, and the decorations make it intimate and inviting. We sip our perfectly chilled white wine and snack on *bruschette* and *mortadella* and olives from Trevi. I catch up with Doreen who I haven't seen in a few days because her traveling has put a crimp in our coffee dates, and I get to know Brenda, who is free with extra pours from the wine bottle. On the shelves around me are beautiful cookbooks, bottles of aged vinegar, and a stunning array of wine. I sample a caper packed in salt and a *digestivo* that tastes like fig. I notice a small table for children to draw while parents enjoy a glass of wine. Excellent.

I return home full—just *full*—of ziggles.

Victorious Baked Ziti for the Tummy Bunch

1 pound ziti

2 cups of béchamel sauce:

Melt 4 Tablespoons of butter in a saucepan, add 1 ounce of flour and a good dusting of grated nutmeg. Stir constantly over low heat for several minutes, then remove from heat and add 2 cups of milk, whisking constantly. Continue to heat until thickened like pudding, and season with salt and pepper. Rest until ready to use.

2 cups of meat sauce:

Heat olive oil in a pot, and add a diced carrot, celery, onion, garlic, and a bay leaf. Add in your favorite herbs, and sautee until vegetables are soft. Add 1 pound of ground beef, and cook until no longer pink. Deglaze pan with a cup of red wine, then add a can of tomatoes, crushing as you add. Add a dash of tomato paste, and season with salt and pepper. Let simmer merrily until flavors meld, about an hour.

1 cup grated parmesan cheese

1 cup (or more) grated mozzarella

———————— • ❋ • ————————

1. Cook pasta for 5-6 minutes in plenty of boiling, salted water.

2. Drain, and then combine with béchamel, meat sauce, and parmesan. Pour into oiled baking dish and sprinkle with mozzarella. Slip under the broiler until cheese is bubbling. Savor the comforting flavors that permeate a house full of heroes, exhausted from their labors. Let rest and serve.

OCTOBER

"PIANO, PIANO..."

1 October

Siena found an acorn. It's gleaming and smooth, an invitation to be held. "I'm going to use it for a worry stone," she announces. "Only I don't worry enough to use it for that." I ask, "You don't worry?" She thinks about it and queries, "What would I have to worry about?" Which is exactly what a mother would give her eyeteeth (whatever those are) to hear from her child. However, my nascent pride in a parenting job well done is quickly tempered, as hubris generally is, by her next sentence. She adds that at night, her homesickness is "unbearable." This is *not* the thing a mother wants to hear after dragging her child away from the only home she's ever known.

Nicolas pipes up that he hasn't been homesick once. Sometimes he'll get a flash of a taste memory and miss a food, but that's it. I offer to indulge him and make him what he misses, but it turns out he misses Sour Patch Kids.

Siena misses her room—how her room felt at sunset, how cozy her bed was when it snowed. While that makes sense to me, I'm also a little bewildered by this creeping homesickness. She is a perennially sunny child that soaks in beauty and exudes gratitude. She is so characterologically grateful that she never asks for anything, because she's so damn happy with whatever is in front of her. I wonder if what she misses is something deeper that she can't explicate, like familiarity— movie nights with Chinese food and hot chocolate on rainy afternoons. During the day, she is so stimulated by the novelty, she forgets to miss the familiar, but at night it must sneak in.

Gabe contributes not a word to the conversation. I think his present has eclipsed his past, which is slightly alarming given that we've only been here two months. He can't remember the name of the gelato shop in Charlottesville, he instinctively uses the word *l'arancia* instead of orange, and he trips over the names of our former neighbors. When we went to Bar Bonci, Letizia asked him, *"Non hai scuola stamattina, Gabriel?"* You don't have school today, Gabriel? And he responded, "No," before I was finished mentally translating.

More than homesickness, I'm experiencing something curious. I get waves of the homesickness that I know I'll have for Spello a year from now. It comes at odd moments. Arturo will drop by, and as he's talking to us in the doorway, Monet runs up our stairwell and we'll all laugh, and I'll have a flash, more feeling than thought, of "I can't believe I only have a year with this lovely man and his cat." Or Letizia will call out, *"Buongiorno,"* with her back to the door, and then when she turns and sees it's me, she'll smile and laugh and give me an even heartier *"buongiorno!"* that feels like a spoken hug. Or the ladies in the alley will pull Gabe in for a kiss, and a run of mellifluous Italian endearments. Or I'll be having coffee with Keith or Doreen on the patio of Tullia with the day open ahead of me, and I'll feel this life… this life I have here is time limited. And that gives me a flash of what feels like mourning, but I can recognize that it is a deep appreciation for what I have. There's a line in *A Tree Grows in Brooklyn*: "To look at everything always as though you were seeing it either for the first or last time: Thus is your time on earth filled with glory." Precisely.

3 October

Brussels won the "what city can we fly to most cheaply" award, and so we leave tomorrow. Every time I consider that we're flying to a whole other country for the price of going out for pizza, I'm shocked anew. To avoid the flight costing the-price-of-a-pizza-dinner-*plus*-gelato, I squeeze our clothes into the tiny suitcases required to fly without paying additional fees. This means extricating the cats from the luggage they keep trying to sneak into. I assure them that they will be fine. Arturo has offered to cat sit. I suggested that he come by once during our four day sojourn, but he insisted that he'll come every day. Maybe twice a day. He claimed it's better for the cats' digestion. Of course it is.

8 October

Brussels is a hit—the food, the Magritte museum, the food, drinking beer in Mort Subite, dancing to exquisite music at the Museum of Musical Instruments. And the food. We eat our weight in *frites* and waffles and chocolate, and discover regional specialties like rabbit cooked in Belgian beer. Much of our visit is spent walking in a state of euphoria, drawn on by shifts in architecture, intoxicating smells, and friendly people. Over a dinner of mussels and fries, Keith dreams aloud of owning his own waffle van. The children put down their new Tintin comic books to brainstorm ideas for how to turn the battered and peeling 1982 Ford Club Wagon he uses to haul lumber into a snazzy waffle delivery vehicle. It's odd to notice that we're surrounded by the sounds of French mixed with Flemish, rather than the Italian which usually serves to backlight our dinnertime flights of conversational fancy. But we add Italian to those northern European tones, since we are completely incapable of saying *"merci"* and instead, no matter how much we rehearse, the word *"grazie"* flies from our mouths.

11 October

These are the gifts the universe sends: A crisp autumn morning that is an invitation for a cup of thick hot chocolate, and an unexpected and inexplicable day off of school for the one child in a family who is suddenly overwhelmed by homesickness and the demands of school. Last night Siena cried bitterly. Today, she looks calmer for having released the feelings that had clearly been building, I accept this offer of a day off of school to spend with my daughter, presented silver platter-like.

We walk to Tullia, hand in hand. The hot chocolate is warm and staying, a lovely accompaniment to our cherry tartlet. While sipping and nibbling, she says that what she misses is a feeling that her life is so routine that she can notice small changes as they occur. Like a patch of morning glory that's taken root in the corner of our yard. Spello streets, she adds, are beautiful, but the twisty lanes are maze-like. Things are still so new, it's a cacophony of change and the details are muted. She adds that she misses going outside when she's bored, or when people in our house are crabby. Which never actually happens, so I'm not exactly sure what she is referring to.

I reassure her that homesickness is normal. No, none of the rest of us struggle with it, but that doesn't mean she's wrong. In fact, it's quite common to the expat experience. And it will fade. Like grief, it doesn't blow away like dandelion fluff never to return, but rather it ebbs and flows and becomes fainter overall. I can't help moralizing by adding that in ten months this will all be a memory, and her old life of morning glory and shin guards will be her only reality. She gets one chance to enjoy this time. If what she wants is familiarity, she'll need to reach out more. The more the language is understandable, the neighborhood is navigable, and the people are known to her, the more she'll feel a sense of comfort in the expected. The alley that runs beside our house is closed to traffic. She is welcome to explore it. When its nooks and crannies are familiar to her, she'll be more likely to notice those small shifts she so delights in. Also, there are benches in the alley where she might sketch, it's a lane well frequented by cats, and having that time on her own—to feel her body in space and define her own being apart from us—will help her feel like this life here is hers.

12 October

The *scuola media* is on strike.

We have been warned of a strike that's never happened on three separate occasions, so I suppose we've grown complacent. I forgot that when there is a possible strike, a parent must accompany Nicolas to school in case he's sent home. At 9 AM, we receive a call from Nicolas to come pick him up. Poor boy had been in utter confusion. No idea what was going on, why everyone was milling around, and what he was supposed to do. Finally his friend explained it to him. All the kids were lined up to call home, so Nicolas joined the group. He called, Keith went to fetch him, and Nicolas had a nice day burrowed under the covers reading with only a quick venture out of the house for candy.

At my lesson, I ask Arturo why strikes are possible but not certain. He tells me that until the day of the strike, the school doesn't know how many teachers will forgo their pay in favor of sending a message that their wages should increase.

If there are too few teachers, the children must be sent home. I wonder why only the middle school had a strike, but we've moved on to conjugating *"venire,"* to come—Nicolas keeps getting stuck and wanted me to ask Arturo about this irregular verb. I wish I had just told Nicolas to look it up; I'm fine with the three commonly used conjugations, but then Arturo goes on to demonstrate 63 million other conjugations that make zero sense to me. Remote past, near future, pasta future— I'm pretty sure that's what he said, something about the pasta being overcooked. It's a very slow hour and a half. I perk up at the end, when Arturo suggests taking a tour of the *frantoio*, oil mill. Which prompts him to chronicle the many uses of olive oil, including rubbing it into the scalp to strengthen hair follicles. We both pause delicately, and he adds that he clearly hasn't done that.

This reminds me to ask Arturo why I don't see local olives in the stores. He tells me that if I want olives, I must go into the orchards with a plastic grocery bag and harvest my own. Then wash the olives, dry them, and pack them in salt. Wait a few days and taste them. If they are still bitter—here he makes a "pee-yew!" face of epic goofiness—let them sit longer. Once the bitterness is leeched, wash them and add olive oil, orange peel, celery, pepper, a little vinegar. I wonder if there aren't local olives for sale because everyone is poaching them.

Later in the afternoon, Nicolas is chatting on Facebook with one of his friends from school, and he asks if she's enjoyed her day off. She responds not particularly, since she'd been at school. What? *School?* Turns out, the kids were supposed to go back at 10:00. The friend soothes Nicolas' rising panic by telling him that there were only four students in class.

The nice thing—or worrisome thing, depending on how you look at it—is that I'm getting rather acclimated to missing the mark. It didn't bother me that we didn't return Nicolas to school, and I keep forgetting to resolve the problem of Siena's missing schoolbooks. Only Siena's anxiety prompts me to put it on the to-do list. A list that is probably shorter than it should be. But I'm beginning to feel much clearer on what I want, separate from the *should* statements that I now see have been pressing on me for years. The shackles of these damnable *shoulds* are shifting and turning, just a bit. Instead of crowding my day, as they do at home, I'm pausing and wondering how I feel led. Unfortunately, I'm noticing that I usually feel led to wear jammy pants while lingering with wine and Belgian chocolate on the *loggia* as the sun hesitates before quickly dropping behind the hills. Hmmm...

maybe I should connect a little more with those weakening *should* statements. But it sure is nice to develop a capacity for tolerating striking out.

14 October

I've been fielding questions about how we managed to take a year off to live in Italy. Particularly from people who know us, and know that we are not trust-fund babies, nor did we strike it rich in the dot-com boom. The answer is layered, but comes down to luck and tenacity. We are lucky to be healthy, to have jobs we can temporarily walk away from or carry. These are the obvious lucky circumstances, but there are some less obvious. It's not until landing here that we realize how lucky we are to be born American citizens. Italians we've met clearly think being born American is better than winning the lottery. Our citizenship means we've had opportunities for economic advancement that the Italians we've met clearly crave. Here, a sabbatical is a foreign concept. Plus, we were born knowing English, a world-wide marketable skill I'd never considered until now when I am surrounded by people who can't communicate outside their country. Realizing the luck involved with being born American has given me, perhaps oddly, a sense of communion with the rest of the world. After all, I'm this fortunate not because I'm worthier, smarter, kinder, or more deserving. It's sheer, insane luck that we weren't born into a destitute country or a destitute pocket of our own country. Our very lives are defined by moments of luck and grace. So, yes, we are lucky.

But there is the kind of luck that plopped us into a wealthy country and that prompted us to make good choices when we were young and stupid. And there is the kind of luck we make, and that comes from determination and openness. Otherwise known as optimism. There were roadblocks—debt to resolve, a century-old house to renovate, a visa denied, savings to build. Our optimism was sometimes shaken, sometimes wavered, but always persevered. When we were denied our visa, Nicolas shrugged and said, "You'll make it happen." The truth is, there was luck involved in that final approval. But without that luck, we would have switched gears and done a trip around the world instead. And I firmly believe I'd be writing now, saying, "Thank goodness we were denied that visa, or we would have missed this fabulous experience." It's not about "everything works out for the best." It's about allowing the way to open up ahead of us. And embracing that with enough flexibility to make it serve us.

For those who want to take this time abroad, and feel like it's unattainable—is it possible in the future? When you retire, or when your children are out of the house, or after a certain number of years saving a bit a month? Or for less time (three months or less, and you don't have to worry about the visa)? If even that is not possible—if your familial obligations, or your income, or your health status make it inconceivable—are there other ways to have a grand adventure? Travel isn't the only way to have a transformative experience. The only ingredient required is challenge. I'm realizing that as Americans, we tend to make things too easy—for ourselves, for our children. Forgetting that challenge is the first step toward strength. Can you find another way to reach and grow and thrive? Can you experiment with a change you can make in your own life, to fully integrate with your intentions and breathe your power?

What I hope for you, all of you, is that you truly live that life you were granted. That you dig deep to discover your leading, the voice of the divine within you that calls you to action. To admit to yourself what you need to feel full and complete. Perhaps the entirety of the dream isn't possible, but I bet you have the capacity and imagination to find another route toward actualizing your vision. I wish for you this—a belief that you can.

One step at a time. *Piano, piano.*

16 October

Arturo has scheduled a tour at the local *frantoio*, olive oil mill, and so we join him for a walk into the farmland below Spello. Gabe takes Doreen's hand, Nicolas and Siena run ahead, and Keith talks to Doreen, as I tell my *maestro* about the festival we visited yesterday. Our friends Colleen and Tom, whom Keith and I had met during our earlier scouting trip to the other side of the Umbrian valley, had invited us to join them for Piegaro's annual celebration of the chestnut. The children warmed quickly to Colleen and Tom, who dubbed themselves our family's Umbrian grandparents—lending us kitchen supplies and engaging each child in earnest conversation as we toured their jewel-box of a village. Arturo asks what chestnut treats we enjoyed and then tells me about his favorite Spellani festival—*L'Oro di Spello,* also known as the *Sagra della Bruschetta.* With carts hauling olive trees festooned with strings of hams. I'm sure I must have heard that wrong, why would hams hang on moving olive trees? But by now Arturo is on a tear, telling me that during the festival, Spello is divided into neighborhoods as it was in medieval times. Back then, these neighborhood distinctions weren't casual. Chains were strung across the street each night, armed by guards that would shoot anyone trying to get from one *terziere* (one of the three districts) to another. Those chains still hang on the walls along Spello's main road; one is across the street from Bar Bonci. I make a mental note to find those chains.

I ask him a question that has long been niggling at me, *"Qual è la differenza tra* sagra *e* festa*?"* What is the difference between *sagra* and *festa*? I see signs for both constantly, and haven't been able to discern a pattern. Arturo laughs, and describes a *festa* as a party, and a *sagra* as more contemplative. So *L'Oro di Spello* is an olive oil *festa* since everyone can celebrate olive oil. The *sagra* is about *bruschetta* because it is part of Spello's history. Arturo asks, did you eat *bruschetta* growing up? I hang my head. No, no I didn't. That's right. It's regional. After school when children were hungry and money was short, mammas would toast bread and streak them with olive oil. It would fill howling bellies. Arturo adds that everyone had bread in the house, and it was *più igienico.* This sounds like "hygienic," but I think it actually means healthy. The gluten-free revolution has passed Arturo by.

Arturo continues that many celebrations are both a *sagra* and a *festa.* I ask, like our Thanksgiving? Arturo suddenly stops, and leans toward me to ask, *"Perché gli americani sempre mangiano il tacchino a* Thanksgiving*?"* Why do Americans always eat turkey at Thanksgiving? His hopeful expression suggests he believes I'm about to impart a state secret. I feel silly answering it's because turkey is a typical early American food. Oh. He looks disappointed. I wish I'd told him that partisan messages were encoded in the turkey bones, turkeys being larger and therefore more appropriate for long-winded American-style memos. Doreen has mentioned celebrating Thanksgiving together, I wonder if we should invite Arturo.

At the *frantoio,* the tour guide tells us that there are 130,000 olive trees in the town's hills. The olives are harvested by the owners of the trees, and then hauled to the collective where the mill presses the olives and gives each farmer a quantity of oil proportional to their contribution. Farmers generally keep enough oil to sustain them until the next harvest, and the excess is sold to the collective.

Since olive season is just beginning the facility is quiet, but the tour guide shows us the machines that remove clinging leaves, crush the olives and their pits into a paste, separate the oil from the "salsa" that remains, and bottle the oil. I sample face lotion sold under the label "*Oro di Spello*," Gold of Spello, and Arturo remarks that tomorrow morning I'll look ten years younger, and everyone will ask, "*Dov'è Michelle?*" Where is Michelle. What a revelation to get the joke in real time.

On our walk back to Spello, Arturo tells me how to prepare polenta. This is so important that he must stop walking, slowing his speech to its most precise. First, make the polenta, and pour it over the table. Right on the table? Yes, yes, *sulla tavola*. Then cover it with a good meaty sauce. And place sausages in the middle. Everyone eats polenta from the edges. Only those that eat enough to get to the middle are rewarded with sausages. I think Italians must keep a tidier table. Mine is currently dusted with cat fur and glass rings.

Nicolas catches up and tells Arturo a story about one of his friends, a girl. Arturo asks if the girl is "*brutta*" or "*bella*." As he says each word, he gestures dramatically, a thumb going down the cheek while his eyebrows wiggle knowingly for *bella* and a thumb across the cheek in a harsh gesture and furrowed brows for *brutta*. Nicolas and I are whooping, and Nicolas sputters to ask why the hand gestures? Walking again, Arturo placidly answers that when a girl walks by, guys can make their comments without saying a word. I think about this, and tell Arturo that I love Italian, and he says sure, because Italians speak half with their mouths and half with their hands.

In the evening I start feeling like this cold I'd been fending off is creeping up on me. Rather than a pre-dinner cocktail or glass of wine, I enjoy a glass of hot broth. How sexy is that? *Che brutta!*

17 October

Describing the weather seems to be the first chapter of every language book. So it's odd that it's taken Arturo and me months to discuss meteorological events. I guess that's what happens when you continue to thwart your Italian teacher with questions about olives. This morning we go through all the standard fare, it's raining, it's snowing, the old man *sta russando*. Much of the lesson is spent on adages.

"*Rosso di sera, bel tempo si spera.*" Red in the evening, good weather hopefully.

"*Quando il Subasio mette il cappello, prendi sempre l'ombrello.*" When Mount Subasio (the mountain that abuts Spello) wears a hat (of clouds), always bring an umbrella.

"*Quando gli uccelli volano basso, fra poco pioverà.*" When the birds fly low, it will rain soon.

In the evening, I stand on the *terrazza* and watch streaks of pink darken in the sky, and the sliver of moon brighten on the horizon. As I sit in observance, the golden sickle of moon slips behind the mountains. I've never seen the moon set, and I sigh in wonder before putting my laundry outside to allow it to dry more quickly. After all, the sky is pink. Keith guffaws, "You are officially an old wife."

18 October

A flutter of colored paper caught in the cobblestones hooks my attention. It's a Chinese menu. I'm surprised to learn there is a Chinese food restaurant in Umbria, as I haven't seen any. This one also sells pizza, but still, it's written in Chinese script, which means it's authentic. And I'm reading this menu with a smile on my face. Not a sheepish smile, a grin of pleasure. I want to go there. And I'm okay with that.

Time was, seeking out Asian food in Umbria would make me feel a little embarrassed. Kind of like asking for ketchup on your fries in France. But I've made an important discovery. I'm not Italian. I had assumed that living in Italy meant I needed to fall in line with what I knew about Italians. Never leave the house with wet hair. A small and sweet breakfast is ideal. *Cappuccino* after 10:30 AM is unseemly. And the only proper cuisine is Italian cuisine. I understand why I'd want to fit in and be respectful of my host country. But it's a little ridiculous. I do want to embrace the customs of Spello—I'll put meat in my *ragù* so it's not *sugo finto*, fake sauce, and I will soften my "sc" sound from how I learned it when I was in the States. But I'll still be American. And I might as well embrace that, too.

Because I've found that when I do, I feel more at home. Like visiting the obviously non-Umbrian cheese farm. Goat cheese, particularly goat cheese in the French tradition, is too strong for Umbrian palates. And it was just that non-Umbrian quality that made me feel like I was settling into a niche of my own making, rather than skittering along the top of perceived expectations. Same with my insistence on using the raw milk stand. In my pre-Italian days, I sought out food that was local, organic, and as unprocessed as possible because that fit my belief structure. Doing that here makes me feel like *me* in Italy. Rather than a stranger to myself.

I remember that in the U.S., I was firm about protein-laden meals, particularly breakfast which featured eggs or sausage. But when we first arrived, I was happy to succumb to the allure of the Italian idea of a shot of sweet in the morning. So even while I was mocking the cookie packaging's insistence that six cookies, fruit salad, and a *cappuccino* constituted a healthy breakfast, I was eating a handful of *biscotti* in the morning. Which is totally antithetical to my American way of eating and feeding my family. Now, I feel less comfortable with tossing aside my ideas of proper nutrition. Probably because of my intense need to make sure my children are adequately fueled for the rigors of school where they don't speak the language. So sure, I'll delight in toasting some *pane al mosto*, a local bread with raisins and wine must that tastes like a cross between raisin bread and *panettone*.

But eggs are back on the menu.

19 October

Gabe has been counting down the moments until today. Not only because it is the opening of Perugia's Eurochocolate. But because we've been invited to attend with his friend Lorenzo. Lorenzo's parents, Anna Maria and Stefano, have hailed us with warmth and familiarity since we met them on Tullia's patio on the first day of school, and last week they stopped to ask us if we'd like to go together to Umbria's claim to chocolate fame. This was not a hard question. Gabe thinks that chocolate is the large bottom section of the food pyramid and Lorenzo is Gabe's closest friend. I can see why Gabe likes him so much—Lorenzo's entire face lights when he smiles, and he smiles constantly. Plus, every time we see him he trots out every English phrase he knows.

As we set off, Gabe is hyper with excitement. Siena and Nicolas are also high on the prospect of chocolate. Lots and lots of chocolate. I'm not sure what they are picturing, but the image is so beguiling that Nicolas turned down an offer to go to the movies with his friends. "The offer of the movies will come around again, when else can I go to Eurochocolate?"

We meet Lorenzo and his family at the Minimetro station, where my face promptly flushes. Luckily, Gabe and Lorenzo provide a welcome distraction from the memory of my humiliation on the Minimetro platform with their overwhelming cuteness. Heads together, they whisper conspiratorially, pointing out dips and turns in the track, and sending each other into peals of laughter. I can see they are connecting, communicating even, but I can't figure out how. Is Gabe speaking more Italian than I realize? Or is his smattering enough when coupled with the tickles and pokes that pepper young boy communication? Or could it be that the two of them are speaking beyond language, and their different nouns and verbs are immaterial when there is hand holding to do? Because these two are holding hands pretty much constantly. Boys holding hands is one of those sweet Italian sights that make me wonder about why Americans don't have such an easy comfort with physical connection.

Eurochocolate is frankly less entertaining than watching Gabe and Lorenzo hold hands. "Holy Moly, that's a lot of chocolate," is our first impression, as we pass vendor after vendor hawking chocolate in all shapes and sizes, but it quickly begins to all look the same. Though I do enjoy wandering and talking and getting to know Lorenzo's parents with an olfactory soundtrack of wafting scents of chocolate. As we drift from stand to stand, we talk with Anna Maria and Stefano about the places they've lived, and places they think we should visit before we leave. That list is getting far too long for a year stint. Anna Maria wants to know about Halloween and asks, "Is there a particular cake Americans make for Halloween?" I tell her that we make caramel apples, and her questions grow even more animated at this unfamiliar food. She is clearly my people.

As we linger at a stand selling slices off of a loaf of chocolate, Anna Maria explains that it is *gianduja*, hazelnut-flavored chocolate, excellent sliced and placed on bread. Nicolas pipes up that he's recently read that Nutella was invented because Italian parents would pack their children a *gianduja* sandwich for school, but realized that the children would eat the chocolate and ignore the bread. As I nibble a chocolate-covered nut, I imagine a playground full of schoolchildren merrily tugging their slice of chocolate from their sandwich and tossing their dry Umbrian bread to the birds.

We stop at another stand for candy-covered balls of chocolate with mandarin liquor inside, and Lorenzo asks Anna Maria if we can all have dinner together. She explains that dinner together isn't possible today, and his lip begins quivering. "Another time" does nothing to assuage his tears, or Gabe's once he understands his friend's sadness. Luckily, they both forget their disappointment in the fun of capering around the *piazza*, holding hands and giggling. We wander the festival a bit longer, breaking up the delights of chocolate-covered bananas and corn-dog-shaped waffles dipped in chocolate with Ascolana olives—large green olives, filled with ground meat and seasonings, rolled in flour and breadcrumbs and fried to a savory crisp. As we say goodbye to Lorenzo and his family, Stefano suggests that we gather for dinner sometime soon, and I surprise myself with the forcefulness of my acceptance. The chocolate has been fun, but not as decadent as the promise of burgeoning friendship.

20 October

Gabe bursts out of school, chattering about pizza. Since several times a week I have to ward off his questions about getting the school *colazione fresca,* which translates to fresh breakfast but seems to mean pizza, I try to ignore him. The children have reported that at snack time there is a table in the hallway where students swap a slip of paper for a square of pizza. Nicolas and Siena think the pizza doesn't look as good as what I pack from the *forno,* the bakery at the end of the alley, and since it seems awfully complicated to figure out, I've been distracting Gabe every time he mentions it. Only once we're home do his words register—he had gotten pizza! And it turns out, you don't need to pay for it! You just follow the line of children, stand at the table, hold out your hand, plop! Goes the pizza! Silly parents. Paper for pizza... Ha!

It takes a few moments for his excited babble to register, but when it does, Keith and I stop and look at each other, suddenly aware of what must have happened. As mildly as I can, I tell Gabe that the pizza wasn't free. That he had joined the queue, which must've been chaotic enough that the pizza man wasn't aware that Gabe hadn't paid, so he got his pizza, but he was undoubtedly supposed to pay. I see the wheels in Gabe's head turning and then he bursts into agonized tears.

"I stole the pizza!" He cries until tears are dripping onto his shirt. I ask, "Are you upset that you did something wrong, or are you upset that you are going to be in trouble?" His face distorted by fear, he wails, "I'm upset because I'm going to *jail!*" Oh, dear heart. No matter how many times we explain, he insists on being concerned that he, or one of us, will inadvertently brush against inappropriate behavior, and be sentenced to 30 to life.

I tell him, "No, no… you are most certainly not going to jail."

"Yes, yes I am, I stole pizza! That's a terrible thing to *do!*"

I explain that he would not go to jail, even if they told him he couldn't have pizza and he stole a piece when no one was looking. A glimmer of a smile. Emboldened, I tell him that he wouldn't go to jail even if he grabbed all the pizza. A definite smile. I add that he wouldn't go to jail even if he yanked the pizza out of everyone's hands and tossed the pieces out of the window. A chuckle. And a nuzzle. "Are you sure, Mommy? That I won't go to jail? How can you be so sure?"

I don't know why two of my children are so terrified of making mistakes. I'm sure it has nothing to do with me. Luckily, Nicolas learned from Keith—neither of them gives a crap. They take mistakes in stride. When Nicolas' piano teacher criticizes his playing, he acknowledges that he didn't play his best and needs to work harder. If a kid in his class doesn't like him, well, the kid is annoying and there is no use cozying up to annoying people. He botches a test. Ah, well, he'll know how to study next time.

Unlike Siena, who last week realized she'd left her math *quaderno* at school and promptly launched into wild sobs, head buried between her knees. I sometimes get frustrated at her disorganization, but I was two glasses of wine into the evening, and I think this helped me respond from my center, rather than from my anxiety. She moaned about how her teacher would be furious, and I told her that while long division is important, and learning to be organized is important, the most important lesson is keeping other people's stuff separate from your own stuff. So if her teacher gets mad at her for not doing her homework, Siena can internalize the message "I need to improve my organization," while distancing herself from her teacher's anger. That anger is irrelevant. Anyway, it sounds like the teacher is irritable, and that's her job to manage, not Siena's.

I think she's beginning to understand, because this morning she had to work on her homework at Bar Bonci, since Eurochocolate made it impossible to finish last night. Even with that morning push, she went to school with it incomplete. I geared myself up for the mounting anxiety that's been rearing its panicky head more often lately, but instead she just shrugged it off. Later, Letizia asked me if Siena had gotten her homework done, and I said no. And she said, oh well. It'll get done… *piano, piano*. È tutto bene.

21 October

Black celery. It sounds ominous—like zombie celery with ghastly fronds. It's actually just celery. More accurately, *sedano nero* is a variety of dark celery that undergoes a burying process that bleaches it to a celery-like color. Last year during our scouting mission, Keith and I happened upon Trevi at the time of the *sagra* to celebrate the celery harvest. Town menus were full of celery-laden dishes, and Keith, curious about the local specialty, ordered *sedano nero pinzimonio*. The waiter held it high through the dining room and presented it with great flourish. We stared hard at the dish. It resembled nothing so much as celery from Safeway, extricated from its purple rubber band, and plopped on a plate. Sure, it lacked the strings of regular celery, and it was a bit bigger, and certainly was tasty—crisp and fresh like an apple. But it was celery.

The *sagra*, which we've learned also celebrates sausage, since fall is the traditional time of sausage making, is underway again. Our Fiat Punto cruises the *autostrada*, bound for Trevi, bound for celery. The day is clear and shining, an invitation to dig deeper. We arrive in Trevi, park outside the town, alongside the olive groves, and walk past vendors into the *piazza*. Where we sigh with pleasure. The air is a harmonious melding of smells both green and smoky, and the gentle sunshine warms the *piazza* as townspeople mill about filled with delight for celery and sausages—two foods I rarely spare a thought for.

Crates overflowing with celery run along the side of the piazza. Each head costs €2,50, and includes a festive *sedano nero* canvas bag. The celery is larger than usual varieties, so the fronds stand above people's shoulders as they mingle and rejoice. Trevi is the only place one can find *sedano nero* and there is a reverence around those tall fronds, waving like pennants.

A stand offers free samples of sticks of celery with newly harvested oil. We crunch the celery, trying to find a hidden flavor, but it still tastes of celery. The olive oil is delicious, we drink the rest of it like juice. On to buy *bruschette* and sausage *panini*. The *bruschette* are topped with finely minced and macerated celery; I enjoy the verdant color more than the taste. The sausages' excellent flavor has been foreshadowed by their crispy-seasoned scent wafting over the rooftops of Trevi as they are grilled over wood flames. We devour our lunch, and lick the remains of sausage from our fingers before considering buying a package of stuffed celery, ready to cook. But then I realize, I should just make it. It will be a way to connect with the foodways of the hills we're calling home this year. Besides, what else are we going to do with all the celery we've purchased?

23 October

I'm a little in love with my butcher.

Yes, he's burly from swinging a cleaver, but I also love his wife, and she's not at all burly. What they lack in collective brawn, they make up for in their ravishing display case. I've never seen such an intoxicating array of freshly prepared meats. Chicken wrapped in pancetta, slivers of deeply red and tender beef with vibrant arugula prepped for a quick sauté, flavorful and juicy chicken sausages, rolls of pork or chicken that hide *mortadella* and sausage. And large hunks of meat cut to order. Pork chops ready for slicing to preferred thickness, thin slices of beef to roll around a filling and simmer in tomato sauce, beef and veal and sausage to grind together in whatever proportion one desires to make a hearty *ragù*. And things I'd never buy, but I'm nonetheless thrilled to know that they are resting in their bin, waiting for a person to decide that, say, Wednesday is the perfect day for brains.

What I never expected when I was envisioning this year abroad, was how integral to my life a simple *macelleria* would become. It's better than a cookbook. When the weather started cooling, and I began to crave polenta, I went in to pick up meat for sauce. I asked if I should get one large piece of meat, or use meat *in pezzi*, in pieces. At first, the butcher's wife told me she prefers *pezzi*, but then she considered for a moment before adding that for polenta, she makes the sauce with different kinds of meat mixed together. The butcher called from the other end of the store that her sauce is "*buonissimo*." Load me up! She packed me off with the beef cubes, pieces of pancetta, pork cubes, pork ribs, and sausage. A festival of meats, ready for the pot. That was one decadent sauce.

I love my butcher.

Last week I asked him for *osso buco*. He told me he would get the veal shanks on Thursday. I went on Saturday and asked again. Out again, no surprise since it was past Thursday. The butcher told me that he's getting more on Tuesday and would put some aside for me. I smiled at his thoughtfulness, unable to express it beyond a simple "*grazie*." Tuesday, I was hardly through the door when the butcher called a quick greeting before absconding to the back room. I heard the heavy sound of a cleaver. Slicing my *osso buco*. Then today when I step in the shop, the butcher asks how the *osso buco* turned out. And laughs as I ecstatically tell of its deliciousness.

24 October

Back in September when we registered for school, we had to indicate if our children were Catholic. Yes or no. It was a blessedly easy box to check, in a ream of paperwork that made little sense, but there are unexpected consequences. Nicolas tells us that his English teacher wants to meet with Keith. Not "a parent," but "the father," specifically. I rankle and shoulder my way into the meeting.

For reasons passing understanding, first we talk with the Italian teacher who speaks Italian at a speed any Formula One driver would envy. After she leaves, the English teacher enters and reiterates the identical information in English, and with carefully arranged eye contact away from me. Even Keith, not particularly socially gifted, is disquieted by her studiously ignoring me. After all, I have nothing on my face, and I'm not wearing my "Americans are better than U" t-shirt. Maybe it's my face bare of make-up and my hair thrown back into its customary knob. I know I startle myself when I catch my pale and inelegant appearance in a window, surrounded by a sea of perfectly coiffed and groomed Italian hotties.

What we discover while I quietly seethe is that Nicolas can only take religion if we allow it. And we can only allow it by declaring him Catholic. If we don't, then he will be removed from class during religion and sent to another class. With a start, we remember Nicolas' confusion yesterday when he was inexplicably sent to science. Which was boring, since his class had already had that lesson.

117

Upon questioning, both Siena and Gabe tell us that they've periodically been removed from their classroom and sent to another classroom. Oh, dear. It must be because of that blasted box. Once they think about it, they realize that there are often kids from other classes who sit in on a lesson in their class. Our brood must not be the only non-Catholics. There's no comment or judgment toward the kids who find seats in a class not their own, but my children are adamant that they would rather stay with their class than be pulled out during religion. And anyway, where better to learn about Catholicism than in the shadow of the Vatican? Keith and I are supportive—no, we're not Catholic, but there's wisdom everywhere.

So we return to school to change our paperwork, this time checking the box denoting that our children are Catholic. I want to make a new box labeled "Quaker" and check that, but this is not my battle to fight, nor is it a conversation I can navigate in Italian. In any case, we use our trip to the secretary's office to find out how to get school pizza through legal channels. Turns out, Gabe's illicit pizza was actually a gift from the pizza man. Definitely *not* stolen. And we can buy tickets at the bakery in the *borgo* (€6 for a book of 10 tickets), which the kids redeem for a square of pizza. Gabe is thrilled. Now he gets to be absolved of his guilt, and color pictures of the Virgin Mary in class, and have pizza for lunch. Just like every other Italian boy.

25 October

In the afternoon we walk along the *Strada de San Francesco* to enjoy the glorious weather. And also to steal olives. Which is probably a serious breach of morals on a path named after a saint, but it's just a handful. So I tell myself. What I tell Gabe is that other people will be jealous if they know we're going to cure our own olives, so we need to keep it a secret to avoid hurt feelings. What you learn in Parenting 101: How to lie to your children. No one seems the worse for our possible sin—the children caper through the olive trees, completely alight in the fresh air lilting with caressing breezes, silvery leaves throwing light and shadow, and the adventure of the harvest. Siena spies Assisi in the distance and wonders aloud how amazing it is that we live here.

Once home, we wash the olives, pick off the stems, and pack them in salt to begin curing. Siena does her math homework with one hand curled around the salt and olive filled jar. She looks up at me and sighs, lamenting that her math teacher grows angry every time Siena lapses into American ways of doing math. Or when she accidentally glues the wrong paper into her *quaderno*. This seems unreasonable to me, shouldn't the teacher be a little more patient? Siena has only been in Italian school for a month. If I were home, I'd send an irate email to the teacher to lay off my precious child. But here, that doesn't seem possible. Not only because the school doesn't use email, but also because Siena needs to learn that she can't please everyone, and some people are going to be unpleasant no matter what she does. It's hard work, I'm very clear on that, but *piano, piano*. Siena stands to hug me and I hold her close while she thanks me for talking her through it. I try to exude assurance that all will be well, but frankly I'm not convinced.

26 October

Siena is going to a party. She's so excited to attend this first *festa* she even risked embarrassment by asking Valentina to confirm who Caterina was, so she could RSVP to the right person. Keith drives her to the party while I stay home with the boys who are deep into making paper ninja accessories. I'm glad they are occupied, as I'm trying to decipher recipes for *sedano ripieno*, stuffed celery, and it's taking all my concentration. What does a "hot oven" mean, exactly?

By the time Keith returns from dropping Siena off and picking up tomorrow's pork chops at the *macelleria*, the celery is burbling in the oven, sending out an intoxicating aroma somewhere between the allure of won tons and the comfort of lasagna. Keith tells me that Caterina's parents were befuddled about why he didn't bring Gabe. Their younger daughter is apparently in Gabe's class. Caterina's father then gestured for Keith to follow him, and took him on a tour of his garage, so he could show him his American jeep. Keith made the proper noises of admiration and asked when he should collect Siena. Oh, whenever, they respond. 7:00, 8:00, it's all good. This is a change from kids' parties we're used to with fixed pickup times, themes, and guest lists.

Perhaps it's this freedom that prompts Siena to pronounce the party fabulous. Completely casual, no decorations other than a piñata the father made, no structured activities. Just a yard full of balloons and balls to toss, two tables so filled with snacks she couldn't even see the tablecloth, and the constant energy of playful children. When we arrive to collect Siena, the parents encourage us to stay, have pizza and cake. But Siena looks like a kid who needs to speak her native language for awhile, and there is celery cooling on our countertop. She calls goodbye with confidence, and I squeeze her waist against mine as we depart through the gate.

28 October

It's hard to be a 14-year-old boy at a new school. Even harder when the language isn't yours, and your classmates have been together since before they could twirl pasta. At first it was easier than Nicolas expected, but as his novelty has waned, so has his classmates' interest. To engage them, Nicolas has decided to invite a handful of boys over to our house for some "hanging out" and a movie in Foligno. This simple plan takes massive amounts of organizing. Partly because at home, Nicolas would invite boys to join him, and whoever came, came. Here, we are tenuous. So the plan shifts and changes to accommodate everyone's perceived convenience. The simplicity of the final plan belies the constant internet movie research, rearranging and reconfiguring, Facebook chatting, and even a phone call, the most dreaded of expat interactions.

Nicolas is cheerful as he trots down to the *negozio* to select snacks to win the hearts of these boys. They arrive fairly promptly, duck their heads, and walk directly into Nicolas' room. According to Nicolas, Italian kids stand when a teacher enters the classroom (which stunned him the first time it happened—his head whipped around trying to figure out why everyone was rising out of their seat), so I expected them to at least introduce themselves when they entered our home, rather than escape directly into the teen cave. But I don't spend too much time pondering this lapse in propriety because I'm stopped cold by hearing Nicolas speak. I stand breathless in the living room, and listen more closely to my son's voice coming from his room. I've never known my eldest to struggle for language. He speaks with puns, metaphors, and SAT words. It doesn't surprise me that his Italian is rough, but I hadn't expected it would be this painful to listen to. As I linger outside his room, and hear him grappling to find words, with false starts, pauses, and stumbles—I realize. This is Nicolas without his language armor. This is Nicolas vulnerable. Keith and I stand mute. Not even listening to what he's saying, just listening to him earnestly trying.

The boys may have been awkward around me, but they seem comfortable with Nicolas. Bless them. They are patient and engaged. The scene changes once at the theater. With more boys, it becomes easier to overlook him, and he becomes the odd boy out. Literally, standing outside the circle. It's awful to witness, but Nicolas is sanguine. He says he doesn't take it personally, he understands that they like him fine, but he's a conversational liability. Nicolas told me that his goal is to have one successful communication transaction a day. As long as he's doing that, the rest is immaterial.

Nicolas did that and more tonight, so he's pleased. The more so when one of the boys calls to ask if he can come home with Nicolas tomorrow and stay for lunch before they go to their group piano lesson at 4:00. At least, that might be what he said. Massimo speaks in dialect, and is hard to follow. Sometimes I'm struck by how much is novel, just having our bodies be someplace different. Our ability to comprehend the simplest encounters, our admiration for the tenacity and understanding of our child, our capacity for feeling our own vulnerability.

29 October

After several botched attempts getting an appointment to collect our *permessi,* Keith and I decide to pop into the *questura.* The officer offers us an appointment for *mercoledì pomeriggio,* Wednesday afternoon. I tell him that is not possible. He huffs a little and agrees to give us our *permessi* now. Wait, that's all it takes? We just have to raise some resistance, and then they cave? This is excellent intel.

The *permesso* officer settles himself across the desk from us. I smile at his resemblance to a shorter, less-amused Jon Stewart with a predilection for pasta. He retrieves a stack of envelopes from a box, places them on his desk, and then walks out of the door. Keith and I stare at the envelopes. We are sitting across the table from our tickets to legal Italian residency. Keith jokes that we should snatch the envelopes and run. I titter, and then hush when the officer returns. He settles into his seat, takes up the envelopes, and rips them in half in one dramatic gesture.

I suck in my breath. And then realize that the *permessi* are plastic cards, nestled into the left hand side of the envelope. The ripping opens all the envelopes uniformly to allow the *permessi* to be extracted simultaneously. Probably also to appear macho and intense. But the intensity of the moment is already instilled by the room—smelling of smoke and adorned with a gun calendar, a least six different images of the Madonna and Child, and a particularly menacing clock shaped like a shell with plastic fish hot glued to the numbers.

The officer directs us to scan our thumbprints and then he starts typing on his ancient computer. I look at Keith and gesture with my head toward the officer. Keith shrugs, and then asks, "*A posto?*" Italian Jon Stewart nods, "*Sì, a posto,*" All's in place. We make vague cheering gestures in his direction, but the officer stares at us blankly, so perhaps the celebration is not mutual. We leave, and once outside the gates we cheer for real. In utter disbelief that we really did it. We have a *permesso* for each of us, and I'm still not sure how. Without a manual, without a guidebook, just by feeling our way forward, one step at a time, and not being deterred when we were told "no." Not when our initial visa application was denied, not when our final approval rested on our getting a form that shouldn't be possible until after our move. Not when we were told we should've asked for the kids' at the initiation of the process.

Since the children are in school, there is no Gabe winnowing between us as we hug standing on a street constructed when Dante was just that upstart bean-eater from Tuscany. I pull out of the embrace to look at Keith, and the history of the process is etched in his eyes. So much doubt, so much effort, so many times we had to carry each other over the river of gloom and melancholy that this next roadblock was insurmountable. But now, we've been here for three months, and we have the paperwork to prove that the state sanctions our presence. I grin up at Keith, who brushes a wisp of my hair off of my cheek before pulling me close again. He tells me that he still wants to pursue Italian citizenship, a process that he began when our initial visa application was denied. In our frenzy to scour routes toward living in Italy, Keith realized that since his great-grandfather didn't become an American citizen until after Keith's grandfather was born, Keith himself is technically considered Italian, under a principle called *jure sanguinis*, national by blood. If it works, we'll never have to apply for a visa to live in Italy (or much of Europe) again. This sounds like a good plan. Even though citizenship would also mean fewer stimulating conversations with voluble *questura* officers. How I'd miss that fish clock.

Celebration is required. Luckily, the lights in Farruggia, the Sicilian bakery, beckon warmly from across the street. A whimsical reward for a struggle that seemed endless and impossible. Until we arrive here at the end of the road, look back and muse, *"Tutto bene."* It's all good.

30 October

Unlike his siblings, Gabe has experienced no hiccups in his adjustment to Italian school. Well, that's not strictly true—last week he asked me to look up "Do you want to play together?" on Google Translate, and for the rest of the morning, I listened to him mutter *"Vuoi giocare insieme?"* to himself. Playing used to be as effortless as breathing, and now it requires the mature process of intentional translation. It's a realization that twisted my heart. After I sent my baby into school, still repeating the words under his breath to cement them in his memory, I fervently hoped that this was as rough as things would get for Gabe. I was hoping for too much.

As I walk him to school this morning, he skips beside me and prattles animatedly about his class Halloween party. Alessia is going to distribute costumes, and he wonders which he'll get and if there will be candy—he loves tasting new Italian sweets. I kiss him goodbye and try one more time to pat down the rowdy cowlick that sends hair up all sprightly from a whorl at his crown. At 1:00 I'm waiting for him, eager to hear about the *festa*. I expect him to fly out of the doors, but when I spot him, his head is down and he's dragging his feet. When he reaches me, he looks up with alarmed eyes and a trembling chin. What could have happened? In a shuddering voice, he says that his class did a show for the school. When he walked into the room, he saw that the *prima* parents were there to watch, and he excitedly scanned the room looking for us. He ran to the front of the school to peer out of the glass door. Eventually he had to do the show without parents. Because we never showed up. As he is relaying this tale of woe, Anna Maria rushes up to me and asks if everything is okay. She puts a hand on Gabe's head and tells me that Gabriele was so upset that we weren't there. I tell her I didn't know there was a performance, and she gasps, a hand to her heart. She assures me that next time, she will make sure I know. I nod, hollowly, and continue up the street.

Once home, Keith flips through Gabe's *quaderno* and finds the information we'd missed last night because Gabe didn't have any homework, so we hadn't looked in his notebook. It was the first time we hadn't checked, in detail, every page in his *quaderno*. It was also the first time I've left a child of mine to wonder where his mother was. Or if I have, I immediately obliterated the memory with vast quantities of cocktails and thus, it never happened. So I'm grieved each time he retells the story of his tearfully running to the glass door in vain. He retells it many times, with different details. I look with beseeching eyes at Keith, but he appears remarkably unruffled. "It's too bad, but it's not the end of the world. He'll get over it, and so will we." These words make no sense to me. Gabe is clearly traumatized. Look, he's crying again.

Three hours later, Gabe is riding the mall kiddie train, cheerfully pretending that he's going to Russia. It takes all my willpower not to stick my head into the giggling compartment and ask if this makes up for missing his show. He loves the train ride, he loves his new sweatpants, he loves the pumpkin we pick up on the way home, and he loves his homework, carefully supervised by me. The good mother. As he works, he tells me about the Italian lessons the school is giving him. "I'm having *private* Italian lessons, Mommy. Private. That means no one can interrupt. And my teacher is so nice. I love her! I love my *private* Italian lessons!" After dinner there's pumpkin carving. Usually each child gets a pumpkin and Keith helps them carve while I busy myself making caramel apples because I just don't like pumpkin carving—but this year there is just one gourd for the whole family, as a pumpkin's cost rivals that of a third-hand Fiat. The children collaborate on the design, and once finished, we munch *biscotti* and sing "Five Little Pumpkins" before putting the jack o' lantern on the stoop. Gabe has stopped mentioning his tears and withering melancholy. But I'm going to have another glass of wine, just in case.

31 October

As we stand in front of the school on Halloween morning, I'm beginning to feel like we've been duped. Despite what we've been told about children wearing costumes to school, we spy only one girl wearing a novelty headband. We keep the witch's hat and pirate headscarf securely in their discrete paper bag, and our children walk into school with no sign that they'd been scanning the crowd for permission to put on their garb.

After school, Massimo and his sister, Amalia, arrive for a visit. Massimo had invited himself over for today during their piano lesson, and called later to ask if he could bring his sister, who is apparently in another *quinta* class. They are so clearly brother and sister, both with small faces, stocky bodies, and short brown hair of the same *cappuccino* color just a shade darker than their skin. They lug bags of food up the stairs, panting heavily. A box of chocolates, a package of snack cakes, a bag of sugar-covered marshmallows, and a jar of quince jam. I'm touched, but don't know what to do with the food. Is it a hostess gift? Is it to hand out to trick-or-treaters? Are we supposed to serve it? That seems the most likely, but both visitors politely decline each offer of food or drink. I'm finding social niceties in a foreign country rather laborious.

Nicolas and Massimo escape into the den of gaming, while Siena and Amalia sit. Just quietly. Amalia has a ready smile, but is short on words. She and Siena draw for a bit, then trade World Wildlife Federation cards that come with groceries at the Coop. But mostly the room pulsates with the quiet of two children studiously avoiding each other's gaze. Amalia seems to be expecting something, but what? Cheeseburgers? SpongeBob? A star spangled parade?

As the afternoon drags on, we begin to realize that having our visitors is going to complicate the evening's plans. Siena and Gabe have their heart set on trying to trick-or-treat, followed by a trip to Vinosofia, as we know that Brenda is handing out candy. But Massimo and Amalia aren't being picked up until 7:30. And Vinosofia closes at 8:00. Should we go out and take Massimo and Amalia? Should we wait until after they go home? When would we have dinner? We suggest taking our guests trick-or-treating, and they seem amenable, but when Amalia declines a costume citing that her family doesn't wear them, we abandon that idea. Having more kids not costumed than costumed would dampen the mood. Stumped, Keith and I decide to head out after our guests are picked up and just figure out details then. In the meantime, the silence in Siena's room has grown positively painful, so we put in a movie. I didn't realize how tight my shoulders were until Amalia laughs at the screen and I release the tension of this awkward afternoon. Finally, their mother arrives, full of promises to invite our children to her house, but I see Siena wince at the prospect. This was more of a work-date than a play-date.

Now it's just us, and Gabe hurriedly dresses in his self-made pirate costume and Siena throws on her witch's hat and ties on the black material she's using as a cape. We head out into the hushed streets of Spello. Where are the trick or treaters that Arturo scared last year with his antics? Is the rain keeping everyone indoors? It's just a drizzle, but the streets of Spello empty faster than a Halloween bowl of candy with a note attached reading "take one" when there is the slightest threat of rain. In that stillness, we lack the courage to knock on doors and ask for candy. It seems rude to beg. And also to assume that Spello celebrates the American way. The only surety is that trying to decipher the societal expectations around a holiday that involves going door to door and begging for candy is about as complicated as trying to get a *permesso*.

Instead, we stop in to visit Paola in her shop. She cheers in excitement when the mini-pirate and moderately sized witch walk in her door. She moans that she doesn't have anything to offer, but truly, her noisy appreciation for the costumes is enough. The children cheerfully agree to have their picture taken, and pose with flair.

As we continue to walk to Vinosofia, the children chatter about how cozy the rain sounds on their umbrellas. They don't seem the least concerned about not trick-or-treating. Though they do light up when we walk into Brenda's shop and they finally get to crow, *"Dolcetto, scherzetto!"* Doreen rushes to hug them and praise their homemade costumes, and Brenda presents them with a beautiful box of candy to choose from. She then sets them at the little table with more treats and glasses of juice made from Sagrantino grapes. I practically fall into her arms with relief. After an afternoon of trying to figure out how to manage a holiday I would have been happy to skip save for the need of my children to preserve pieces of the tradition, it's a balm to be with Americans who require no explanation. Besides, Vinosofia is warm and glowing, with a jack o'lantern whimsically carved from a winter squash, and music playing while Brenda pours glasses of velvety red wine to sip as we enjoy a plate of local salami. Suddenly, it no longer feels like we're missing something in the urge to figure it out. Rather, we realize we have everything we need, and more we never thought to ask for. Brenda keeps the shop open late, and when we leave she sends us home with all the leftover Haribo and Kinder. My little monsters go to bed with smiles on their faces, Gabe with his pirate rope still snug around his waist.

Sedano Ripieno

2 heads of celery, washed well and cut below the fronds
(about 8-10 inches, so they fit well in a baking dish)

300 grams of pork sausage

4 eggs

dash of salt and pepper (the sausage is probably salty)

2 cups of parmesan

2 cups of breadcrumbs

flour for dredging

sunflower oil

2 cups of prepared marinara sauce

butter

--------------------------- • ▪ • ---------------------------

1. Boil the celery heads in salted water for about 10 minutes, until they are almost soft. Drain.

2. Combine the sausage, 2 eggs, salt and pepper, a handful of parmesan, and a half a handful of breadcrumbs.

3. When the celery is cool, stuff the sausage mixture between the stalks, compressing the head together so the sausage binds it all together.

4. Dredge each head in flour, then roll in the last two eggs that have been whisked, then roll in breadcrumbs.

5. Heat oil until the tip of a wooden spoon bubbles when dipped in the oil, then carefully place the stuffed celery in hot oil. Rotate the sides so the breadcrumbs brown evenly.

6. Remove to a baking dish (large celery heads can be cut in half from pole to pole if desired). Cover the top of the celery with most of the marinara sauce, then sprinkle about a cup of parmesan over it and bake at 350 F for about 45 minutes.

7. When you take it out, drizzle with the last of the marinara sauce, sprinkle with some more parmesan, and dot with butter.

NOVEMBER

WELCOME,
SWEET SHIVA

2 November

We're home from a trip to the Amalfi coast. Perhaps a little more travel wise. Arturo had counseled that the area was best explored slowly, and given our limited budget for travel and the limited number of days off of school, we didn't follow that advice. Which over-compressed the trip. But I loved the Amalfi coast. The houses and streets had a wash-worn, lived-in feel. There aren't the pristine, romantic buildings of Paris, or immaculate streets of Geneva. Rather, there is peeling paint and pockmarked streets. But they are real—the heartbeat thrums loudly and clearly. The whole area is intense and evocative. There's a feeling of living history. I can see why some people wouldn't care for it, and on another day I might be disinclined to enjoy it myself. But when the weather is rainy and cool in Umbria, I know I'll be dreaming of sipping *limoncello* looking out over the vast blue Mediterranean waters.

3 November

I believe my daughter is having a breakdown. I'm considered somewhat of an expert in these things, or so that piece of paper hanging on my office wall would suggest, but I'm not unequivocal. She may be having a breakdown.

It begins innocently enough. We're finishing our pizza at L'Orlando Furioso, and the conversation veers toward Umbrian Christmas customs. All of a sudden Siena is crying that we aren't going to have a traditional Christmas. As she starts listing the facets of our holiday that she fears losing, I realize how entrenched I've made all of our celebrations. Maybe because I was the only child of a single mom without extended family (and therefore holidays were quiet affairs), I've worked to create special traditions. Christmas sure, with the opening gifts the night before by candlelight and leaving cookies for Santa and carrots for reindeer. But also having four desserts on the Fourth of July and making dumplings on Chinese New Year and having green milk with our corned beef on Saint Patrick's Day. For the record, I'm not all that patriotic, and I'm neither Chinese nor Irish. What I am is a person who uses any occasion to create traditions we can coalesce around as a family.

I have little time to ruminate on this, as my daughter is determined to spiral down the hill into grief. We can't do a thing for her. Any attempt seems to feed the fire of her weeping. I tell her that if trees and stockings are available, we'll get them. Keith tells her that if we do have to take a break from our traditions, it's just for one year. I encourage her to think about it tomorrow instead—nighttime is notoriously bad for perspective taking. Keith tells her that perhaps we'll discover something even more wonderful by following the tide of *here*, rather than forcing a a celebration of *there*. I tell her that for all we know, it's customary in Spello to have five Christmas trees, and perhaps it would be wise to hold off on the worrying until we know more. The weeping turns jagged, as she ceases bothering to blink back tears, and instead makes a keening sound over her plate. Gabe asks in my ear if he can make Siena a stocking out of paper, and when I nod, he runs to her side and announces, "Mommy says I can make you a tree and stocking and presents out of paper!" A hint of smile. I exhale as she starts to plan a stocking for her doll. But then the storm truly breaks, right over her forlorn pizza crusts, "But what if I make stockings and Santa doesn't come and I come downstairs all excited in the morning and...and...and...the stockings...are...*empty!*"

I guess now isn't the time to reveal the truth about Santa Claus.

She's beginning to draw attention, so we leave the restaurant, and make our way up the hill. She's quiet for a few moments, and then she wails into the darkness, "Doesn't anyone else care that we are losing the traditions that have made up Christmas for us? Doesn't ANYONE ELSE CARE?" Well, no. And that's sort of the problem. Because now she's not only frantic about "losing" Christmas, but she is completely alone in her grief. In fact, I can't even sympathize, because I'm so clear that in nine months Italy will be but a distant dream that it actually annoys me that she'd waste the little time we have looking backward.

Reasoning is clearly not going to work, so instead I try to distract her by asking if she'd introduced Guaffle, the stuffed hedgehog she bought in Brussels, to her other stuffed animals. She answers, "What will happen when I take Guaffle home? Will he get along with all my other stuffed animals?" My mind darts in confusion, is her psyche actually cracking here? As I'm wondering if she really believes her stuffed animals will divide along party lines, she shatters enough that the truth breaks free, *"And I'll never have any friends in Italy!"*

Ah. I see. Underneath this petulant desire for a Christmas tree, at her center, lies a dreary sense of being adrift, without the social circle that moored her. Here she is a fascinating specimen that everyone wants to get close to, but nobody really knows. Although she delights when the kids offer her friendship bracelets, none of it compares to the deep communion that comes from companionably building fairy houses for hours with her best friend, Linnea.

What does she need? I don't know. I like to think she's at the period of twisted compaction that comes right before a leap and an untangle. I don't think there is much I can do, besides give her space to figure out what lies at the center, and hold that space with compassion so she can find her way through and into the Light. It's easy to tell myself that, but harder to feel it.

4 November

There are few things more heartbreaking that waking up your child and noticing that her eyes are puffy from crying. This is a sight designed to steal the gold from your soul, and make a hole into the abyss so the darkness can creep and gather and whisper, *"What have you done to your daughter?"* Even dashing to the bakery for breakfast can't erase the image of her angelic face turned worn and gray. She might not notice the forced lilt in her mother's voice, planning cozy afternoon activities, but you will feel hollow.

This is not a hypothetical scenario. This is my morning.

Part of me wants to keep her home, but part of me worries that will send a message that I don't trust her to cope, and just prolong her pain. As she slowly puts on her shoes, she moans that at recess, Valentina always wants her to play tag, and she *hates* it. Her lip quivers as she adds that she can't say no, and anyway then the boys *tease* her and she doesn't *like* it. This is the first I've heard of this. I wonder if she's seeing through melancholy glasses that distort the warm cajoling of yesterday to the antagonizing of today? Valentina seems like a nice girl, and while their friendship hasn't progressed beyond friendliness and hand holding at dismissal, I can't imagine she'd goad Sienà into playing tag.

I offer advice—why doesn't she ask Valentina to draw with her?—which is roundly rejected. I wonder when I'll learn to stop giving advice. Stumped, I tell her that after school we'll talk about the recess problem. She nods, resigned, and finishes tying her shoes. As we head to school, Siena asks how to say "trip." And then she proceeds to plan aloud that she'll tell everyone that she's tired from traveling. I'm grateful that she's switched to problem-solving mode, rather than digging herself deeper into pessimism. She throws back her shoulders, takes Gabe's hand, and they walk into school. Keith and I watch. And sigh. And stand a little longer.

Then Keith turns to me and says, "I need a *caffè corretto*," *espresso* with a shot of *grappa*. Parenting requires serious fortification. We opt against oblivion, and instead Keith works while I clean my computer keyboard and read a book without turning pages and stare at the windows as the rain begins to beat a steady rhythm on the rooftops. I scurry to school at dismissal, and squeeze against umbrellas to nudge closer to the door. Between the colorful nylon panels, I glimpse Siena holding hands with a lanky girl whose light brown hair wafts behind her as she and Siena practically skip out of school. My daughter's face is lit with a smile so radiant and eyes so clear I have to take a step backward. She and the friend pause before breaking hands, and bid goodbye with warm affection. Siena darts through the umbrellas to hug me until I can feel her voice in my bones, "I had a *great* day!" I hug her back, with equal ferocity.

We wait for Gabe, and when he exits, I ask them if they'd like to embrace the fall weather with popcorn and hot chocolate. They cheer, and we head down to the *negozio* in the rain that is now a steadily lightening drizzle. Siena skips beside me and says that there was no problem with recess since the rain kept the class indoors. During that time, she noticed that the girl who sits beside her, Chiara, was growing upset. Siena describes a class dispute which culminated in Chiara facing the rest of the students while trembling. Siena easily took up her place next to the child who felt alone. Later, in a stroke of misbehavior that I can't summon the urge to condemn, Siena passed a note to Chiara, asking if she was okay. They passed notes the rest of the day. Siena asked Chiara if they could be friends, to an exuberant, *"Certo!"* Chiara then asked Siena if they could walk out together.

As Siena is telling me the end of the story, and looking at my face to make sure I'm not cross about the note passing, we see Chiara on the school bus, chattering with friends. Siena runs to the window and raps to get Chiara's attention, and Chiara's thin face grows animated as she enthusiastically waves back. Siena turns to me with a grin, and squeezes my arm. We duck into the *negozio,* and pause to take in the mayhem. Immediately after school, the shop fills with children racing to buy handfuls (once I saw a child with a literal armful) of candy. The pack quickly thins as the children rush back out the door to board the bus. Once the shop is quiet, I select a packet of chocolate leaves that melt dreamily into hot milk, and a bag of popcorn kernels. On our way up the hill, Paola greets us outside her shop, and pulls us in to say hello and offer macramé bracelets to both children. As we continue up the street, Siena murmurs, "She's so *nice*! Everyone's so *nice*!" I look down at my daughter's face, beaming, full of anticipation of a cozy afternoon, and a strengthening connection with another girl, based on more than just curiosity around Siena's American-ness.

5 November

Election day finds me missing land and country. The upside is the election connects me to my Spellani neighbors who are surprisingly invested in my country's politics. They all want to ask us about the election—the grocer who sells us our tart green clementines, customers in Bar Bonci, Arturo. The radio is talking about a *"photo-finish"* for Romney and Obama. Like the rest of town, I have been glued to U.S. news all day, even though I know that results won't be published until the wee hours of the Italian morning. Being this far removed, even Facebook status updates feel like a glimmer of news.

As my computer overheats, we get a voicemail from school that Gabe is sick. I scoot to the *scuola*, but I'm promptly stymied at the locked door by the lack of response to my pressing the call button. Finally, someone exits, and I'm able to enter the school along with a woman who arrived after me and pressed the button more boldly than I did, but just as ineffectually. She walks a shade faster than I and enters the office, demanding the attention of both the office workers. Meanwhile

I grow jittery. Is Gabe okay?

Finally, as an office worker approaches my orbit, I stop her with an apology and tell her that my child is sick. She's immediately loud. Italian bossy-effusive. Telling me that I should've told her, gesturing to the lady who she'd been helping as if to indicate that this woman's problems are ridiculous and well worth interrupting. She grabs my arm and propels me to the front desk attendant, who is back at her usual seat by the front door. The office worker throws me one last reassuring glance before she returns to the office.

The front desk lady yelps when she sees me, which does nothing to assuage my panic that Gabe has vomited all over the floor or has a kind of pox. But maybe she's also being Italian bossy-effusive. As she leads me to Gabe's classroom, she asks if I understood her voicemail, and when I say yes, she says she's glad, so glad! So glad that she stops in the stairwell and turns around and kisses my cheek and waves her arms while speaking loud, rapid-fire Italian about how glad she is. It sounds like she's also praising the beauty of the English language, but that can't be right. I collect a fairly well-looking Gabe from Alessia, who reassures me that his illness is mild. She orders him to give her a kiss goodbye and the class erupts in shouts of "*Gabriele! Gabriele! Ciao! Ciao!*"

As sicknesses go, it's not bad. After a lunch of rice cooked in chicken broth and a long nap, he seems okay. Well enough to create a huge American-flag display, eat a giant pork chop for dinner, and play "Go Fish" with me—accidentally ordering me to "*vai pesce.*" I kiss his forehead goodnight, and then return to my thoroughly useless search for predictions, breaking news, and connection to my country.

6 November

When one is waiting for polls to close, the time difference between Italy and the U.S. is crap. I wake up in the night to check election results that aren't in, and I'm relieved that by the time we wake up at 6:00, there's a decision. We scan headlines, and Nicolas comes running into our room at 7:00 to ask what the verdict is. Doreen calls while we're eating breakfast to cheer and ask to meet for coffee after school drop off.

After my coffee with Doreen, I head to Arturo's for my lesson. I've heard so many opinions about the election—that Romney is a flip-flopper but loves his family, that his religion is unusual but its nice that he's a man of faith, that Obama has a nice face—it's made me curious about how Italians form opinions of American candidates. Perfect fodder for our lesson, but though he greets me full of the news, he's quickly distracted by explaining the difference between coffee and *orzo*—a toasted barley drink that he claims is good for digestion.

Over lunch, Siena shares that one of her classmates entered the schoolroom shouting about Obama's victory, and the room erupted in noise and celebration. She had to field questions about whether we'd voted for this candidate, who is clearly the favorite here. Nicolas reports that every single classmate entered the room cheering for Obama, and that they'd spent much of the day discussing electoral versus popular vote. Which is pretty shaming when I consider that I'm not even sure what political party is in power in Italy.

It's odd to feel disconnected from my country while my fellow citizens process the results from elections and ballot measures. I wallow a bit by making comfort food. As I grate cheese for macaroni and sauté apples for pie, I reflect on how the distance makes the distinction between parties blurry. We are all Americans, wanting the best for our country, while being blissfully unaware of what is happening in others. I'm going to go try to read the rest of the newspaper now. Where's my dictionary?

7 November

I have no self-control. Acquaintances will balk at this, citing my ability to turn down brownies. But give me a bag of cheese curls and I will eat until I make myself sick. The reason I don't have cable? Not because I don't like TV, but because I know if I had cable, I'd become a complete sloth. I have no self-control.

But what I do have is an awareness that I can easily get sucked into behaviors that aren't good for me, and when I do, I just don't feel good. A day of munching chips and watching movies actually makes me feel gross. Physically bad, but also emotionally flat and spacey. So I use external structure to hold my limits. I don't keep crinkly bags of salty snacks in the house. That way I opt for a carrot in balsamic instead. I don't have Netflix. That way I opt for reading. We only have one car. So I am forced to walk to work, even when the weather is dreary. And then I feel pretty good.

But this has all gone out the window these past few weeks. My laptop makes it far too easy to compulsively "just check." Facebook, email, news sites, websites I regularly troll. I end up getting what feels like an almost OCD compulsion to go through my ritual of checking. Initially, I told myself it was fine, I'm keeping track of politics in my country, that's practically noble. And I might as well check this other stuff since I'm online. But now that the election is over, I realize how little that has served me. I've completely neglected to live my life in the service of reading about others' lives. And in doing so, I feel disconnected from here, from the present.

One of the reasons I was looking forward to this year is I wanted to connect to my inner landscape. Before Italy, I was so beset by obligations and habits and activities that I could hardly catch a breath to figure out where I was going or what I was doing. Only when I cooked could I make my pace slow down, and so those Saturday dinners became critical to my happiness. Over a glass of wine and runny cheese, I'd be able to catch up with Keith while I put the finishing touches on dinner. As we would sit down to a family dinner of crispy skinned roast chicken fragrant with herbs, quick-sautéed spinach with garlic and a hit of peppery olive oil, and mashed potatoes creamy with butter and earthy with gruyere, I'd sigh—this was how I wanted my life. Full of flavor and enough time to enjoy it. Now I realize that while I am appreciating the ability to make more labor-intensive meals, I am still fragmented, just with different distractions. Instead of listening for my leading, I get an itch of seeking stimulation the easy way. So yesterday I put a "NO" sign on my computer, and attempted to walk away from it.

It's hard. Harder than I'd care to admit. With no emails to read, no link rabbits to chase, I stand idly. At first all possible activities ring hollow. I feel like Gabe. "That's *BORING!*" My fingers itch to open my freshly closed computer. I quiet the impulse. And in the silence, I notice that I want to practice piano. So I sit and play from my "learn to play piano" book. And then I want to go upstairs and open my computer, but the impulse is gentler, easier to resist. And I discover a longing to read the paper. So I do, with bumps and starts.

It's definitely difficult. I cave before dinner, but I course correct. I need to remind myself that every time I choose what is easy—checking a website instead of reading, eating leftover Halloween candy instead of reheating soup, putting a movie on for the kids instead of pursuing a common interest, sending Keith to the store so I don't have to deal with it—I am denying myself an opportunity to stretch, to feel, to deepen. But at the same time, I'm not going to beat myself up for my weakness. I'll forgive myself, make my heart easy and light, so I can hear the divine within me. And now I'm going to close my computer. Luckily I can't even find my phone.

8 November

A buoyant call of *"ciao, cara!"* greets me when I walk into the *macelleria*. Hello, dear. I laugh in response, then talk meat with the butcher, and notice that the words trip from my tongue with some ease. We're talking about salami, not peace in the Middle East, but still, it feels like progress. I leave with a cheery wave and step into the *fruttivendolo*, where the vendor asks me if Gabe feels better. I say that he's better, but now my older son is sick. He nods and says, *"Uno dopo l'altro."* One right after the other. *Esatto.*

As I'm choosing artichokes, he comments with a grin that Obama won the election. I'm perennially surprised when anyone broaches a conversation with me, since they must know how bumbling I am. That moment of startle impedes comprehension, and I have to ask him, *"Come?"* so he repeats himself before I can agree with him that those were indeed the election results, and in answer to his next question, I say that yes, I voted for Obama. He nods and after telling me about his cousins that emigrated to Florida rather than his branch of the family that moved to Italy, he comments that Obama has a good face. Now that I've been trying to figure out the dizzying Italian system, I wonder if people here use their gut to guide their way through the process. That guy looks honest, let's vote for him.

As I wait for the *navetta* back up the hill, I see Calimero, the one-eyed dog. I call him over and pet him, gingerly. The dog is so filthy it's hard to work up the courage to touch him. This time I see orange peels on his shoulder. But his armpits are clean, and he's so desperate for love, I can't help but scratch him, with a plan to wash my hands in the hottest water possible as soon as I get home. Calimero looks up at me with limpid eyes, then leans against my knee. He hesitates, then flops across my shoes, stomach toward the sky. It's kind of awkward, having the grimy town dog draped across my feet, but at the same time, gently comforting.

9 November

My crush on San Martino begins with an odd sound that impels us all to look up, startled. Are those bells? They sound older, heavier, and smaller than our neighborhood church bells. With a start, we realize they're the bells of the tiny 13th century chapel that is on the corner where our road meets Arturo's alley. *La Capella di San Martino.* We momentarily puzzle at the sound, then go back to our lives. A few minutes later, we hear the bells again. Curious now, we peer over our *loggia* to investigate. Candles line our street into the church's courtyard. Siena points out a candle on our stoop. It calls to us, an invitation. Out of our house, into the gloaming, and up the street.

Where Arturo is waiting. He tells us that this is the celebration to honor San Martino. I asked if the *festa* is for congregants of the church, and he laughs. "*No, è per tutti.*" It is for everyone. Seeing the men setting the olive branches in the grills alight, and the women laying out tables with cups of wine, I ask if there's a fee to attend. He says no, but shows me a jar where I can donate a few euros for the poor. I deposit the euros in my pocket, and turn to Arturo who is explaining the story of San Martino to my family clustered around him.

Long ago, Martino, a Roman soldier raised in Hungary, was riding his horse through the countryside, when he came upon a poor man, shivering in the autumn cold. Martino climbed off his horse, ripped his cape down the middle, and handed a half to the man. That night, he dreamed that Jesus appeared to him, wearing half the cape. The vision prompted Martino to abandon the army and be baptized. And now, San Martino is celebrated with autumnal foods—roasted chestnuts, *bruschette* with new olive oil, new wine *(vino novello)*, and sausage.

The simple story finished, I realize that the old men from the neighborhood are huddled around us, their eyes full of expectation. I smile to show I understand the story, and the men lead us to the grills, sending the scents of wood-smoke, sizzling sausages, and roasting chestnuts into the night air. And underneath these earthy aromas there's a hint of incense drifting from the thrown back doors of the chapel. Golden light spills from the tiny church onto the cobblestones, polished by hundreds of years of Spellani footfalls.

Arturo and his friends hand us bags of warm chestnuts, and order us to taste the garlicky *bruschette* with good, green olive oil. I tell the men that Umbrian bread is *perfetto* for *bruschette*. The men widen their eyes in appreciation. And it's true, the bread's denseness stands up to grilling, and it soaks up olive oil "like a boss," as Nicolas says.

To drink there is *vin brûlé*—warm wine with sugar, orange peel, and cinnamon—and cups of robust new Sagrantino wine. The men lead us back to the grill and hand us plates with sausage, sizzled and crisp, leaking juice that is caught by the bread. I laugh as I polish off my sandwich, licking my fingers clean. The men laugh too, and then hand us cups full of *mele cotte*, baked apples. I begin to dip my spoon into the apples, but one of the men snatches back my bowl and asks the woman pouring *vin brûlé* to drizzle a spoonful over the apples. Obediently, the rest of the family hands their bowls to garnish, and then luxuriate in the warm and rich apples, enlivened with tart raisins. My belly warm, I pronounce everything excellent, and the men smile and pat my shoulder. One informs me that there is no bad Italian food. To which another quips, "*Solo italiani cattivi.*" Only bad Italians. We all laugh.

The bells chime, and Keith and I debate the Italian word for bell, while the old men smile and pretend to follow our English. In a startling clap of clarity, it occurs to me to ask the men. They talk over each other in their eagerness to not only answer, but also offer the words for where the bell is hung and the person who rings the bell. Is it possible that revealing my own need connects me to others who want to give?

Keith takes Siena and Gabe home for bed, while Nicolas and I stay with Arturo. Our teacher tells Nicolas, who is rooting through the empty chestnut bags, that more chestnuts are being roasted. He leads us back to the grill to show us, and to also point out ribs, and something that looks like half-inch thick slices of bacon. He tells me it is called "*magro e grasso*," thin and fat. Arturo confides that the combination of lean meat and the fat make it very flavorful, did we want to try it? What a question. I feel like it's my San Martino Day duty to accept what is proffered, even a half cape offered by a generous man on horseback.

Arturo holds out slices of bread for the grill guys to slip in ribs, and then more slices of bread for them to slip in *magro e grasso*. I thank Arturo and bid him goodnight, so I can bring the plates to Keith. I carry the warm plates up the stairs, and Keith is delighted at the unexpected treat. We spend the next few minutes in utter grill euphoria. The ribs are remarkable, tender with delicious caramelized bits. But the *magro e grasso*. Oh, that is something else. Smoky, meaty, with creamy fat, crisped on the edges. While we are staring down at our now empty plates with a mixture of joy at our unlooked-for luck and sorrow that we've eaten it all, our doorbell buzzes. We open the door to find Arturo holding out a bag of blistering-hot chestnuts. We chatter in the doorway, laughing at Arturo's self-nomination as the festival's hospitality, praising the foods, reveling in the pleasure of the evening. After Arturo says a final goodnight, Keith, Nicolas, and I huddle around the warm paper bag. Over the cracking of shells and savoring of each yammy nut, we agree that the language came more easily tonight. For me, I think it was not having time to psyche myself into the kind of fear that usually freezes me. And people seemed to understand me. Our downstairs neighbor regarded me with surprise and said, "You speak Italian!" No, not really, but it was nice of her to say so.

After the chestnut shells are cleared away, I research San Martino, or Saint Martin, and find that after his dream of Jesus, he became a monk in Gaul. He led a simple life, teaching others and, by some accounts, spreading viticulture throughout what is now France. As Saint Martin's Day coincides with the annual butchering of farm animals, there is a Spanish expression, "*A cada cerdo le llega su San Martín.*" Every pig has his Saint Martin's Day—all wrongdoers get their just desserts. I also learn that many countries call the unseasonably warm days of November St. Martin's summer, as a nod to the story of God easing the cold to further warm the half-caped beggar. I'm surprised to learn that in parts of Western Europe children go from house to house with lanterns and sing Saint Martin songs or tell jokes in exchange for sweets. In this way, it's like our Halloween. And also Thanksgiving, as it often celebrates the abundance of autumn's bounty. In some countries, Saint Martin's Day is even like Christmas, as children receive presents from Saint Martin in November, rather than Saint Nicolas in December.

Though it bears resemblance to all of these, the holiday also feels uniquely its own. Keith and I plan to celebrate the feast day of San Martino annually. We'll have traditional autumnal foods. We'll toast our friends with the classic Saint Martin's chorus, "*If you raise your glass at Martinmas, wine will be yours throughout the year.*" We'll celebrate the twists that life takes to deliver glory. The bounty the earth volunteers. The divine grace that lives within us all. The gratitude for gifts we didn't know to ask for. We'll toast San Martino—our patron saint of accidental joy.

10 November

Our spontaneous trip to visit Assisi is thwarted by a terrific storm. With rain and wind so heavy, Keith turns our car back toward Spello just as we approach Assisi's city gates. We leave our car at the lot at the top of the hill, and scamper down the slick cobblestones, alternately whooping about how ridiculous we are to be out in this weather, and shrieking when a sudden blast of icy drops pelts our backs. And then admiring the way the haze of rain falls across a beam of light in the darkened alley. Gabe remarks, "I'm confused. I can't tell if you like the rain or hate it."

Once in, I bolt to the *terrazza* to bring in the laundry, and wipe my eyes free of the cascading rain to locate my pants. Flummoxed, I squint toward the ground. There they are, in the street. I dash out, just in time to see a car run over them. I guess I'll be washing those again.

Dry and safe, we curl under animal print blankets to read *Pimpa*—an Italian comic book we bought at the bookstore in Foligno. Pimpa is a polka-dotted dog who lives with a man named Armando. We've been reading the comic strips aloud, though we can rarely make it through a whole page without breaking into peals of laughter. In one strip, Armando tells Pimpa he wants potatoes for lunch, so she goes out to the field where potatoes are playing rugby and invites them over to dine. The potatoes are honored, but worried about how dirty they are, so Pimpa offers them the use of the bathtub. The potatoes (insert gasping breath of laughter here) unzip their "suits" to dive into the bath water. Yes, we sometimes have to use the Italian-English dictionary to catch the humor, but that's probably good for all of our vocabulary building.

Over dinner, we discuss what we miss from America. My college friend Kathy and her boyfriend Dave are visiting us for Thanksgiving, and have offered to bring us a shoebox of supplies. Nicolas tries to convince us that the box should be filled with Sour Patch Watermelons. For the greater good. Siena begins practically, wishing for Sculpey clay, but then grows misty eyed as she longs for a pocket-Linnea. She misses her friend something fierce. I would stuff the box full of ethnic food supplies, and Keith dreams of a cocktail shaker. His DIY shaker of a glass and a knife isn't cutting it. Gabe struggles to contribute, but can't think of a thing he'd want from home.

11 November

For the most part, the children are adapting to their new lives. Nicolas brags that he is getting shoved by the other boys, Gabe tells me that he likes how Italy is less busy than America, and Siena feels at peace with our decision to balance our Spellani Christmas with home traditions. But the little ones tell me with anxious eyes that they are having trouble sleeping. I reassure them that their bodies and minds are still adjusting to the enormous transition—language, routine, familiarity. Siena hugs her stuffed bunny to its comforting place under her nose, and confesses that she still feels fragile sometimes. And then whispers, "When I have bad dreams, I tell my stuffed animals." Their support comforts her, even though she knows that their words of courage come from a place within her. I pat her and give her a smile of understanding. Sounds like everything is as it should be.

After another night of broken sleep, Siena's face, which usually flashes with expression, is strangely stiff. When Keith calls, "Shoe-time!" she tells me she's not going to school. It's too overwhelming—her math teacher is too mean and the children are too insistent that she play their way and it's too much. She's just not going. She may be ten, but I pull her onto my lap so we can talk. Or rather, I talk, and she grows only more removed. Trying to reason with her only gives her something to resist, while her internal voice of panic and fear gain ground. The only point that she actually swallows is my reminder that she's not a good predictor of how her day will be. In fact, she's been this nervous, and gone on to have a wonderful day—remember, with Chiara? She solemnly nods, and gets her shoes on. I bite my lip as she trudges into school, shoulders sagging, eyes on her feet.

While she's gone, Keith walks me to the *macelleria* and tries to convince me that Siena will have revived by dismissal. But instead, she only looks more hollow, and the area under her eyes seems thin. I pull her into a silent hug. And then probably watch her too closely as she picks at her lunch. Her afternoon of drawing eases the tension in her face, and by dinner she seems herself, but she shrinks with every step she takes toward bedtime. When I lean to kiss her goodnight, she whispers that she's scared to go to sleep because then she's one step closer to having to go to school. As she snuggles deeper under her covers, she tells me that she's having stomachaches. In desperation, I suggest to her that she talk to her stuffed animals about it in her mind. I'm out of tricks. I don't know how to help her and I don't know how to get someone to airmail me Xanax, and I don't even know if the Xanax would be for her or for me. I am not prepared for this.

12 November

My sleep is a tumble of guilt and anxiety, my dreams laden with an ominous beast slinking toward me. I wake up panicked that Siena's hopeless attitude toward school will prompt her to retreat into a cave of her own making, and in that retreat, she'll cut herself off from the possibility of finding joy. And then how will she outrun her fears? I lie in bed, waiting for the morning light to move toward the windowsill, and I think about how Siena did not rally during yesterday's school hours. This worries me. That is a gross understatement. It consumes me.

I'm hesitant to trust my eyes when Siena comes downstairs for breakfast looking like… well, like Siena, rather than like a faded reflection of herself. Before the boys join us, I ask her what words of wisdom Guaffle had for her. She smiles, with a hint of serenity. Leaning forward, and resting her head on her hand, she tells me that she realized that American school wasn't always easy either. The girl dynamics in her class were often painful. No place is perfect, and, she adds, "Even in Antarctica something would be hard." I stop myself from adding, "And the food wouldn't be as good." Siena goes on to say that since she can't avoid what's hard, she might as well enjoy the parts she likes. And thus my child reinvents the counter-phobic principle, which says when something scares you, move toward it. That Guaffle sure knows his stuff.

When I see her walk into school with ease and grace, I turn away, and let tears of gratitude well in my eyes. Keith looks at me searchingly, his expression a mirrored reflection of my relief. I hope I can remember this the next time I doubt my child's ability to cope. Sure, I want things to be perfect for them always. I want to protect them from any hardship. I want them always smiling. But a young tree that is always tethered to a pole to keep it straight never learns to bend. We have to try our strength to feel our strength. And Siena is my tree, bending in the wind, while I hold my breath and watch her grow.

13 November

I'm breathing easier as Siena regains her footing. It's soothing to watch her munch on a square of pizza from the *rosticceria*, then race around the playground with her brothers. Keith and I sit on the park bench, and allow the contentment to rise back in our bodies. As the sun hangs tenuously, ready to dip into twilight, we walk to the fish market, where I impulsively buy squid. I am not typically a person who spontaneously buys cephalopods. But I'm intrigued, and tickled by a burgeoning sense of confidence.

Squid in hand, we stop at the *negozio* for an oddly pink plastic bottle of frying oil while the children play with the cats in the *piazza*. As we make our way home, we stop to talk to an alley lady who is taking out her trash. She chastises Siena for wearing a tank top, and demonstrates proper layering by showing us that she is wearing a turtleneck, a sweater, and a jacket. Arturo approaches us, Monet trotting at his heels, and joins in the debate about whether or not it's cold. I declare to Arturo and the alley lady that it's *"L'estate di San Martino,"* San Martino's summer, and they beam at me appreciatively.

I hang on to the simplicity of that streetside moment, as I spend the rest of the evening watching YouTube videos on cleaning squid, since they were packaged for us whole, beaks and all. These critters are thrillingly nasty. We fry them with my impulse purchase of an *etto*, a tenth of a kilo, of tiny, silvery fish. Gathering around the platters of fried seafood, we devour every briny, crispy bit. Dinner closes with Siena tossing rings of calamari into Nicolas' mouth, while he barks like a seal. All on a Tuesday.

14 November

My baker can't seem to find his pants. He casually rings up my customary *filetta* and yogurt bread while wearing nothing but his pristine white boxers and undershirt. Customers around me take it in stride, so I'm trying to do the same. Anyway, pretending that my life is normal has become part of my daily routine. Yesterday I received a notice that my free pap smear is December 14 at 10:34 AM.

10:34. In a country where a two-hour wait for a scheduled appointment is standard fare. Part of me wants to show up to see what time I'd actually get in, and also to get a glimpse of the workings of socialized medicine. A bigger part feels so exposed on a daily basis, I don't want to feel exposed while actually naked.

Measurement is another point of discombobulation. Helping Siena with her homework of converting liters of wine to decaliters has made it clear that the metric system is far more sensible than our Imperial system. Even so, we continually run into problems. Last week, Keith and I went to Casa delle Tagliatelle, and while I browsed the jars of chestnut cream and truffle paste, he ordered two kilos of *tagliatelle*. I looked up as the vendor fed sheets of pasta into the slicer, and stood mesmerized as the yellow squares became twirling strands of *tagliatelle*. We only came out of our trance when handed a package of pasta as big as a bed pillow. At which point, Keith realized that he'd mistakenly used the ratio for kilometers to miles instead of kilos to pounds.

Toiletries, too, require adjustment. I often look at our contact solution and get confused as to why it's called American Fare. *Fare* means to make or to do. It takes me a minute to realize the label is not in Italian. Also, the priciest shampoo at the grocery store is around two euros, and it is drying out our hair. Siena and I have taken to treating our ends with olive oil, like ancient Romans, while Keith quips, "Do you want a little vinegar with that?"

Then there are the details. Like, Scotch tape—just called "Scotch" here, no tape—costs more than a decent bottle of wine. I never thought I'd hoard tape. Also, Thanksgiving is next week and not only do I not have any lists, I've given it no thought. And then there is the fact that whenever we decide to take the car somewhere, we have to stop and try to remember where Keith parked it—gone are the days of parking in front of our house. In fact, those times when Keith bypasses the parking spots at the top of Spello to drop us off at our door are so delicious, the children burst into a song they've composed to celebrate, "Daddy! The handsome man, living in his waffle van! With all his bountiful hair!" Keith conducts with one hand while easily navigating the tiny, steep streets he inched along just a few months ago, before he lets us out, then drives back up the hill to park.

Speaking of Keith, we're learning to acclimate to the fact that no one can pronounce, let alone spell, Keith's name because "k" and "th" aren't used in Italian. So the Spellani call him "Kit." Naturally, though, "Damiani" trips off the tongue without a questioning eyebrow, and Siena's name is spelled correctly every single time. It wouldn't occur to anyone here to add an extra "n." Just like it wouldn't occur to anyone to refrain from reprimanding her when she tosses off her shoes at the park or wears a tank top in 75 degree weather. After all, it's not like she's the baker.

The biggest places of adjustment are probably found within the shape and structure of our lives. I don't think of making dinner until around 6:00. I have spent more time contemplating gelato flavor combinations than I ever would have dreamed possible. I'm constantly on the prowl for seasonal treats like *pane di mosto*—a bread that the baker tells me is made with wine must, so its season is short. I'm sad to only have this bread for a few weeks, but satisfied to be able to have had an actual conversation with the baker. Then there are *fave dei morti*, cookies made with almond paste found around the Day of the Dead. I love those cookies so much Letizia finally just gave me the last of them, and waved away my attempts to pay.

On a more emotional level, I spend inordinate amounts of time reassuring myself that it is beneficial for children to experience "stuck places" so that they can become strong individuals. Rather than dashing to work each morning, I linger over coffee with Keith and wonder what I'll write about today. But perhaps the biggest shift is that here I'm utterly aware that nobody owes me anything. And so I'm perpetually caught off guard with gratitude at any scrap of interest or kindness. It's this last one that I'm hoping to bring home with me.

15 November

I hate the remote past tense. Many regions of Italy don't even use this way of discussing long ago events, but Arturo believes I need to learn the tense since it's often used in books. He's right, but nonetheless, I'm loath to take on what seems a Herculean task. The third person remote past conjugation of *essere*, to be, is *fu*. That doesn't even make sense. And so it's with dragging feet that I walk to my lesson.

Luckily, Keith, who is accompanying me on his way to go grocery shopping, distracts Arturo for me. When he and Arturo share pleasantries, Keith mentions that he's going to the bakery. Arturo wishes him good day, Keith leaves to do the marketing, and Arturo and I talk about tasty finds at the bakery. This prompts Arturo to ask what foods I miss from home, and when I tell him Vietnamese food, he expresses surprise. He thought Americans didn't eat Vietnamese food because of the war. I find this amusing, until I remember when Americans ate Freedom Fries. Since Arturo's familiarity with Asian food is slim, he wants me to describe dishes and write down ingredients. He's particularly curious about coconut milk. I make a mental note to invite him for an Asian dinner one day. I've heard that Italians are dismissive of non-Italian food, but the way he describes Mexican food makes me think he'd be a receptive audience.

We discuss diet trends, and I tell him that there are some people in the United States who limit their bread and pasta. He placidly informs me that the United States doesn't have a wheat culture since it was founded by the potato-eating Brits. I suppose he's never heard about "amber waves of grain." We agree that everyone knows about the benefits of olive oil. He describes olive oil as a *"spremuta,"* freshly squeezed juice.

The real surprise of the conversation is that I'm able to have it. I don't pause to consider and translate each word. Arturo uses an unfamiliar verb to describe my Italian, *"sciogliere."* Which I think means "melt," based on his demonstration of butter in a pan. I'm going to enjoy it while I can—feeling like my Italian is progressing is the surest sign that I'm about to hit a language wall that will make me feel like I know nothing and will never know anything and I should probably just give up.

Eventually we get around to conjugating, but soon after the bell tolls the hour. I leap up, *"È ora di andare!"* Time to go! He laughs, then orders me in Italian, sit down, we have time. He then comforts me by sharing that 85% of Italians don't know the remote past. Good. That crap is hard. I have grown comfortable with the fact that if I belong in Italian society at all, it is on the margins, but I'm happy to be mainstream in my complete disregard for the remote past.

16 November

Stumped for how to stretch my Italian cooking repertoire, I decide to make a soup recipe on the bag of *borlotti* beans. There are two ingredients neither I nor Google Translate recognize—*cotiche* and *cannolicchietti,* but I figure *cotiche* is a kind of meat, so I can ask at the *macelleria.* Over my morning cappuccino, I ask Letizia about *cannolicchietti.* She takes my empty bag in her hand, pulls her glasses to the bridge of her nose and carefully reads the instructions. Handing it back with a smile, she tells me it's a kind of pasta. Problem solved. Even if I can't find that specific pasta, I know I can get *ditalini*, a short pasta that I'm sure will be fine in bean soup.

At the *macelleria*, I ask the butcher for *cotiche*. With what seems to me a stunning display of clairvoyance, he asks if it is for bean soup. When I say yes, he nods and goes to the back room. I figure he's fetching me what are probably ribs, but it seems he's gotten distracted playing with curling ribbon. That's odd. But I enjoy watching him toss strips around his twirling knife, like an Olympic rhythmic dance contestant, only without slicked back hair and red lipstick. Then he brings out a tray of…what? No idea. *Cotiche*, one can only assume. Hesitatingly, I ask what part of the pig is *cotiche*, and he looks at me curiously and answers "*Pelle.*" It takes me a minute to translate in my head.

Oh. The skin.

I'm not sure how good a job I do of not wrinkling my lip in disgust, but I suspect I don't mask my horror very well. But I'm undaunted. Sort of. Surreptitiously wiping my sweaty hands on my pants, I squeak out a request for pork fat.

At my Italian lesson, I tell Arturo that I'm going to make *cotiche*, but the recipe on the bag was sketchy on how to prepare skin. I neglect to mention that the butcher actually gave me instructions, but I couldn't hear them through the threat of my breakfast rising in my throat. Arturo clarifies that this is for *fagioli e cotiche?* I nod, and he says that he has a friend who is an excellent cook, he'll call her. I focus on taking deep breaths while he talks on the phone. He settles himself back in his seat, and tells me to take out my *quaderno*, for notes. The recipe is fairly straightforward, a three step process. Cook the beans until they are tender. Make a tomato sauce. So far, so good. And then place pig skin in a pot of boiling, salted water for hours until it's tender enough to slice into slivers. Oh, man. My thoughts turn toward the plate of pig skin and the bag of pig fat sitting in my fridge, which now resembles nothing so much as Hannibal Lecter's pantry on Thanksgiving. I grip the table and try to listen as Arturo instructs me to combine the beans, sauce, and *cotiche*, and stir the soup carefully, as I'll want to avoid bursting the beans. I love the verb he uses, it sounded like "*apoptare.*"

After lunch, I plunge the ribbons of skin into a pot of boiling water to cook during *pausa*. After reading sandwiched between Gabe and Siena, I cautiously approach the burbling pot. It smells like slightly bacon-y water, not too alarming. I boil the beans, being careful not to apopt them. Then I make the sauce. Tasting it, I'm surprised at how the lard creates a richer sauce. The tomatoes sing. When the skins are what looks to be tender, but it's hard to tell since I can't bring myself to really manipulate them, I remove them from the water. Following Arturo's directions, I cut the cooked skins into slivers, kind of like pasta, and combine them with the sauce and the beans. Then I ladle the soup onto *bruschette*. And prepare myself for what might well be some serious disgust.

To my amazement, I actually enjoy it. The *cotiche's* texture is somewhere between bacon fat and a cooked onion, and it has a mild, meaty taste. It adds a minor flavor dimension to the soup, but a major textural one. Gabe insists he doesn't like it as he polishes off his bowl. Nicolas says it's okay but the taste might be the same without the skin and so it was therefore not worth the psychological agitation. Siena tries. She eats almost the whole bowl without a peep, but claims that the mental image keeps her from enjoying it. Keith loves it, and suggests we use the boiled but unused skin to make a football.

17 November

At dismissal, Anna Maria invites us to join her at her mother's house in the *borgo* this afternoon. Gabe is thrilled at this unexpected opportunity to play with Lorenzo. While the two boys run around the yard, I sit at the table with Anna Maria, her parents, and Stefano's parents. I exhaust my food vocabulary praising the chocolate and vanilla bundt cake. But I probably could sit in silence, as Anna Maria's parents seem to delight just in patting me like a beloved puppy. I find this level of intimacy moving, even if it's not emotional intimacy, just a habit of an affectionate people. The parents want to know how the children are adapting to school, and talk among themselves in words slow enough for me to understand, about how age and gender matter for assimilation.

Anna Maria takes my hand so we can go outside to watch the boys play, and we talk about food and life, and how for her, the lessons of parenting are about being present. The conversation is mostly in English, though once in awhile she'll ask me to supply the word for *freddo* and *piangere,* and I delight in offering cold and cry. Keith arrives from his trip to Perugia, where he met with the translator he's hired to certify his citizenship documents, and gratefully accepts a slice of cake. As we're leaving, Anna Maria and her family insist that we not only leave with half of the cake, but also a jacket for Gabe. No one believes Gabe when he insists, *"Non ho freddo!"* so he is forced to submit to taking the jacket home. I suspect that his indignation is all pretense, and he's as elated as I am at the care of this family that we never knew existed just months ago.

18 November

A few weeks ago, while Doreen and I were having coffee in the garden of Bonci, she casually mentioned that she had plans to help friends with their olive harvest. I immediately asked to come along, shamelessly ignoring social niceties. I had already missed the *vendemmia*, the annual grape harvest, not having had an inside track. I'd be damned if I missed out on the opportunity to be part of an olive harvest because of a fear of inserting myself. Food trumps anxiety, I am learning.

Doreen obliged, and here we are, driving with the mountain range on our right, before we cross the valley to Bettona, where her friends live. We knock, only to discover that last night's rain has made the hillside perilous, and thus today's harvest has been canceled. Sante and Conci speak of their fear of people breaking their legs so fervently that the word, *scivoli*, slips, burns into my brain. In lieu of the expected harvest, Sante gives us a tour of the garden, fig trees, grapevines, chickens, the crates of already picked olives, and the cantina. He proudly gestures to the barrel where their wine is blissfully aging, as well as the bottles waiting to be filled. I ask about the curious screen-sided cabinet, and Sante tells me that it's for protecting drying sausages from flies. From the corner of my eye, I see something swaying from the ceiling. When I look up, Sante tells me that those are bits of pork, and that they'd take a *noce*, nut, from the fat for cooking all winter long.

Sante and Conci speak less English than Arturo, who works the words "underground" and "slow" (pronounced with an improbable "v" at the end of the word) into every conversation. Those are the only English words he knows, despite the fact that at every lesson he jots notes on my words into his own *quaderno*, complete with phonetic pronunciations. Even with Sante and Conci's lack of English, I don't need Doreen's help to understand their magnanimous invitation to come back for lunch. We accept, and the two of us decide to walk around Bettona in the meantime. It's a sweet town—quiet, save the music coming from the church. We stand at the doors, listening to the unfamiliar melody. As we step away, the music awakens one of my favorite songs from Quaker Meeting, and I sing under my breath—

Spring forth the well, inside my soul
Spring forth the well, and make me whole
Spring forth the well, that I might see
The light that shines in me.

We're hardly across the *piazza* when Doreen's phone rings. It's Conci, asking Doreen to make sure we invite the rest of my family for lunch. When Doreen hangs up, we look at each other, stunned. How can people be so lovely? We call Keith, who, as expected, is happy to bring the children and join us.

We convene at our hosts' house, and I feel an upswell of tenderness watching Keith climb out of the car and move toward me with a grin of anticipation. The children unbuckle themselves and bound to the gate, while I consider how bizarre it is that we are this excited about dining at a stranger's house. Strangers who don't speak our language, no less. Back home, if I told the family we'd be lunching with strangers I'd get dragging feet and questions about how long we'll have to stay. Here, it's just another patch of unknown to throw ourselves into, to see if anything wonderful is to be found where the current leads.

As soon as we enter, Sante and Conci introduce us to their son, Silvano, and his wife, Roberta. We're quickly seated, and begin our meal with Sante's home-cured *prosciutto* and humble wine. Conci then serves us bowls full of pasta *alla Norcia*, with homemade sausage, mushrooms, and cream. We're so busy getting to know about our hosts' lives in Belgium years ago, the work they've each had, their process of making food, that we don't notice that Nicolas is eating one bowlful of pasta after another. He finally declines a serving, in deference to Conci presenting a roll of veal filled with frittata and olives, as well as a platter of pan-fried chicken pieces—not excepting the head—with rosemary. These are followed by a salad of fennel and oranges as well as grilled eggplant marinated in garlic and herbs. We are all stunned, at both the profusion of dishes, as well as their unpretentious deliciousness. Keith comments, "No wonder Italians don't go out to eat." Our hosts guffaw when Doreen translates, but I just nod, contemplating the layers of flavor in each bite. If I didn't know better, I'd think Conci had some vat of "secret sauce" that she sprinkled over everything to heighten each flavor. Maybe it's her olive oil.

Then comes the tart that Doreen brought, and coffee and *grappa*. At which point Nicolas sheepishly asks for another bowl of pasta. Conci squeezes his cheeks and praises him loudly, as she not only serves him another bowlful, but packs him up the leftovers to take home. Then she turns on cartoons for Gabe and Siena, who blitz out to Italian Bugs Bunny. Sante and Conci lean in and ask if we're sure we really need to leave in July. Why would we do that? We'll come back in September, won't we? That would be best. Nicolas bites his lip and says, "*Preferisco rimanere.*" I prefer to stay. Sante's eyes shine as he reaches to clasp my son's arm. I watch as Keith sits back to observe the interaction with a contented air. My own heart is overwhelmed.

Before we leave, Sante hastens to the cantina to fill a bottle of wine for us. The same wine we'd had at lunch, which Sante had written it off as just home-made, but I'd loved every sip of its ruby currant flavor. I'm torn between reluctance to take anything else from these generous people and utter gratitude at a gift of this wine. I land on the side of gratitude, especially when presented with a double-sized bottle that looks like it belongs in a comic strip. Keith laughs aloud and praises the bottle with every Italian compliment he knows.

We part from our new friends with kisses and promises to see each other soon. As we drive back across the valley, my hand over my straining belly, I observe that my well is certainly full. Keith tells me that I should get ready for my gratitude well to overflow, because he has a story for me. When he and the children were on their way to the car to drive to Bettona, they were stopped by Arturo's brother, Marcello. Marcello and Keith did their customary greeting, in which Marcello shouts at Keith, "*Obama!*" and Keith responds, "*Io non sono Obama!*" I'm not Obama. Keith always chuckles when he describes this daily interaction, sometimes varied by his telling Marcello that he can't stop to chat because he has to get to the *Casa Bianca*, White House. Growing serious, Marcello asked if Keith was aware of Umbrians' love of *lumache*, snails. Keith said yes, he's seen a sign for a *Sagra delle Lumache*. Marcello said that he heard we had enjoyed *cotiche*—this apparently amounts to news in small-town Umbria—and he wants to invite the family over for a *lumache* dinner. Then Marcello called out to Giorgio, our neighbor who helped when we lost Juno, to ask if he wanted to come to a *lumache* dinner. Giorgio gave an enthusiastic affirmative. Keith asked if he'd be cooking the *lumache* in tomato sauce, rather than the French butter preparation, and Marcello looked at him like he was nuts. "*Certo!*"

> *Spring forth the well, inside my soul*
> *Spring forth the well, and make me whole*
> *Spring forth the well, that I might see*
> *The light that shines in me.*

19 November

When Keith's phone rings this morning, he misses the call and has to check voicemail. It's the school, reporting that Siena has a sore throat. I walk down to collect her, and the door opens immediately in answer to my buzzing. This time, though, the secretary looks confused by my presence. She leaves to fetch Siena while I read the notices hung in the foyer. Finally Siena appears with her superhip English and Italian teacher, and, for reasons passing understanding, Gabe. She runs toward me with a big grin and asks, "What are you doing here?" I tell her that we'd gotten a call that she was sick. She laughs, "That was last week!" Last week? We got no such call last week. I ask why she has Gabe with her, shouldn't he be in class? She laughs again, easily, and says that Gabe always has snack in her classroom. Gabe helpfully adds, "I wander the school a lot."

This is news to me. In my bewilderment, I turn and tell her *maestro* that somehow the school's call just registered. He nods politely but may well think I'm nuts. I don't show up when my child is ill, and then show up a week later for no reason. I walk home trying to figure out why a voicemail would take a week to register. I know cell phones don't ring if they are too far within stone walls—which is why Spellani windowsills are pockmarked with cell phones—but this doesn't explain why voicemail is unreliable. The best I can do is chalk it up to Italy.

After *pausa*, Nicolas stays home because he has his piano lesson, while the rest of us leave for a local *agriturismo*, a farm-based lodging. Our friends Kathy and Dave are arriving from California and we've agreed to help them check in, since their hosts speak no English. This is a task that should only take one of us, but we haven't seen our friends in years, so all four of us bundle into the Fiat Punto to zip through the countryside to the *agriturismo*. We arrive a shade before our friends, and leap to hug them when they pull up between our car and the open field. To have a piece of home, here, it spins my world. In our jubilance, we bungle the check in to no small degree, but no matter. They are here.

They unpack and wash off the travel dust, and then we head to Spello, stopping briefly at the store for their morning provisions. We park our cars at the top of the hill, and I spontaneously hug them again, before we walk down to our house, chattering continuously. Chattering, that is, until we reach the *piazza* in front of the chapel of San Martino, and an alley lady stops us to tell us something with great seriousness. My brain is firmly in the English zone, so I can't make out one word except *bambino*, child, and so I assume she's chastising our ill-clad children running ahead of us. Only when we see Nicolas jogging out of the alley toward us and his story tumbles out do we realize that he's been locked out. He'd forgotten his key, and had been sitting on the stoop since his lesson ended, to the deep distress of the huddled old ladies. Nicolas had reassured them that he was fine, we'd be home soon, but this was most definitely not okay with them. Not only was he all alone, he was *all alone in a T-shirt*. Anathema. He was eventually forced to borrow a jacket, which he ran to return when he saw his siblings approaching.

It gives me a moment of pause, particularly when Nicolas asks if he can write a guest post for my blog about his experience waiting for us—was this really so noteworthy? But all of this is forgotten in our sitting down to a full table. Particularly when Kathy and Dave pull gifts from their backpack. Gifts that combine home and Italy and the abstractness of my words into the internet's ether, all together in one heady moment. One by one, they present us with Christmas stockings. Kathy whispering in an aside that when she read about Siena's longing for a traditional Christmas she grew determined to bring stockings. Actually, another one of our friends told her she'd best be bringing stockings, and Kathy had told her she was already on it. And those stockings are full of the very items each of us had dreamed we'd want in a shoebox. With games for Gabe since he he'd been stumped to remember the advantages of home. We are uniformly speechless at their thoughtfulness, when we are not exclaiming over rice noodles and Sculpey clay and sour candy and a cocktail shaker.

Over *vin santo*, we hatch plans for meeting in the morning, going to the Sicilian bakery, then to Antonelli for wine tasting. Then Bevagna! Then L'Orlando

Furioso! My life all of a sudden feels full of plans and shared joy. I'll relish it until I have to relinquish them to Venice on Friday. I wonder if I can convince them that the Topino river that runs around Foligno is pretty much just as good as the Venetian canals.

20 November

Sharing the thrills of our adopted home with friends proves as delightful as we had hoped. While the children are in school, Keith and I take our friends to the Sicilian bakery in Foligno and order a cavalcade of pastries to sample. We tour a vineyard in Montefalco and pretend to be refined as we taste wines. A refinement which is shattered when we convulse with smothered laughter at Kathy's pinched expression at the *grappa* she finds too similar to nail polish remover. Afterwards, we head toward Bevagna, sighing together at the patchwork of golden and red vines draping the hills. And then, reunited with the children who have been collected by Keith while I gave our friends a walking tour of Bevagna, we sigh again as Gabe has a spectacular tantrum while we are attempting to enjoy our *gnocchi alla Sagrantino*, pillowy gnocchi in smooth and creamy wine sauce. But soon we are laughing again as we notice that Gabe, who has excused himself to go to the bathroom, is singing "Call Me Maybe" so loudly that we can hear his echoing voice in the dining room.

The day culminates with pizza at L'Orlando Furioso. Siena and Keith suggest the pear and gorgonzola pizza to our friends, Nicolas advocates for the pizza with tuna, black olives, and sweet *cipollini* onions that he orders so often we're pretty sure the chef pops open a can of tuna whenever he sees my son. Gabe champions his favorite, *prosciutto* and mushroom. I like them all. We make short work of our meal as we discuss Kathy and Dave's trip to Orvieto tomorrow, while we prepare for Thanksgiving. I still haven't given the holiday menu any thought beyond applauding when Doreen told me she'd ordered the turkeys from our butcher.

Kathy and Dave repair to their *agriturismo* while we walk up the hill, discussing Thanksgiving. Alessia has asked us to come in and explain the holiday to the students on Friday, and it occurs to me now that this requires some thought. Certainly, we'll talk about being grateful, and celebrating a gathering of friends and family. But I'm stuck on the history. I can't tell these children some Pollyanna version of the Indians and the Pilgrims becoming friends, when I know for a fact that their history books will have no such glossing of the truth. Shouldn't I tell them about the blankets full of smallpox? The Trail of Tears? The venereal disease?

Keith thinks I'm making this overly complicated. What? I never do that. He adds, "Are you planning to teach these first graders the word for 'genocide' in a lesson about Thanksgiving? Have them act out dying of influenza and draw the signs of syphilis alongside their hand turkey? Just give them the rosy version and be done." This, even though he knows perfectly well that the rosy version involves planting a fish with each corn kernel, which will undoubtedly lead these impressionable youth to believe that we plant peaches at Thanksgiving.

I don't want to be an ambassador for my country, and I don't even know the word for pilgrim. When it comes down to it, I'm not sure I fully understand the definition. What is a pilgrim? Am I a pilgrim? Are we all pilgrims, in some way? I don't want to educate when I feel like I'm still deep in the process of realizing how little I know.

22 November

It's funny. When we thought about our year abroad, we expected we'd glide over Thanksgiving. Until we met Doreen, who convinced us that celebrating our national day of gratitude and gustatory excess with expats and Italian friends was a rite of passage. Now I get it. There is a richness to celebrating Thanksgiving on foreign soil. Every step requires more thought—from trying to make sure the rangy Italian turkey can fit in the tiny Italian oven, to hunting for unscented garbage bags for brining the bird, to asking friends from America to smuggle in canned corn and cornbread mix to make our traditional "corn dingo," to serving wine made by the winemaker, to explaining what cranberries are. And the mix of languages, the staccato of English interwoven with the melody of Italian, is music. Keith and I pause in the kitchen and look at each other, silent. I incline my head toward the burbling voices in the dining room. He nods, and we listen for a moment, smiling. I touch his hand and then return to the dining room with a fresh platter of turkey.

The meal is served in fits and starts, thanks to our recalcitrant oven. Sometimes I wish that oven would embody American ideals of over-achievement—hotter is often better. But I discover, thanks to Brenda and Graziano who bring a selection of wine from Vinosofia, and their friend Dwight who owns a vineyard in Le Marche, a well functioning oven is less important than free-flowing wine.

Arturo is thrilled to share the bounty of our holiday table, suggesting that Doreen and I open up a restaurant in Spello and call it Thanksgiving. Then again, he arrived ready to admire—as soon as he handed me his hat, he put his hand over his heart and raved about the jar of *cotiche* I'd given him. "*Mamma mia,*" he sighed, before telling me that he'd shared his portion with his friend Giuseppina, who had provided the recipe. She tasted it and told him I cook like an Umbrian.

At Kathy's suggestions, and with Graziano's help, I explain to our Italian guests that it is customary to go around the table and say what we are grateful for. Brenda begins by saying she is grateful for this holiday and the opportunity to celebrate with new and old friends. A few tears, as we repeat the toast into Italian and English, and her words resonate across the table. Gabe offers that he is grateful for "aminals" and this life where everything is good. Doreen is grateful for celebrating together and having children to celebrate with, and we toast her daughter who is getting married next month, and the passage of time that turns babies into adults. Then Arturo speaks. The table grows quiet as he slowly says that he is grateful for our hospitality and the opportunity for cultures to come together and learn from each other. That this sharing makes our world richer, and more meaningful. Particularly now, he continues, when a troubled Middle East is making small steps to broker peace, he is grateful for the extended hand of friendship between people. We repeat his words in English, giving them more weight by the repetition, and since it's a difficult act to follow, we fall onto the desserts.

It's complicated to describe those desserts to Loris, Patrizia, and Paola. They clearly think I'm kidding when I described a *crostata* with pumpkin. I'm sure they want to tell me that pumpkins are vegetables, and therefore don't belong in a *crostata*. They politely take a little, but are truly curious about the pecan pie, which they taste and then can't stop talking about. After dessert, Loris and Patrizia's son, Filippo, reads *Pimpa* with Gabe and talks virology with Nicolas, while his parents chat with Arturo, who tells them about my *cotiche*, with a teacher's pride. They ask for the story of how we found Spello. Keith tells them that the other towns were too small, or too quiet, or too filled with English speakers. Arturo adds, plus, in the other towns, there are no Spellani. And we all nod. So true.

There is a passage in *A Tree Grows in Brooklyn* where the main character, Francie, talks about when her diet of stale bread and potatoes begins to feel flat, she takes her allowance and buys a pickle. She works on that pickle all day, and relishes its sourness. Then the bread and potatoes taste good again. This Thanksgiving is our pickle. It has shaken our frame for Thanksgiving, what it means, how to think about it, and how to celebrate it. We had to let go of some things we always do, and in doing so, the things we've kept felt all the more special. We didn't plan our menu in October, so we weren't tired of the meal before we even began. We had no assumptions about home, no expectations of how we should feel or how we should create the day. Instead, we were fully present, and appreciated what we had. Corn dingo tastes incredible when that box of Jiffy traversed an ocean to arrive in the suitcase of a friend. We searched for flavor differences in Canadian cranberry sauce. Graziano asked me if the Italian turkey tasted different, forcing me to stop and think about what I was eating. In our dawning awareness of how important traditions are to Siena, our customs feel newly beloved, and our decision to balance our old Christmas celebration with where we are now seems wise. Clinking glasses the Italian way, holding eye contact to see and feel seen, with people I've known for twenty years and people I've known a few months heightened our connections. And I felt the divine that glows within all of us. How unexpected to feel so deeply the spirit of Thanksgiving on Italian soil.

23 November

The benefit of celebrating Thanksgiving in the States is that everyone gets to sleep late the next morning. Here, we have to send our children yawning into school. Over coffee, Keith spots an ad in the paper for a Black Friday sale. It's bad enough that Italians are adopting American convenience foods and video games. Must Black Friday tinge these ancient Umbrian hills? Black Friday without the benefit of Thanksgiving?

I groan at the ad, and we return home to finish making the mini-apple pies I've decided to bring to Gabe's class. Max, our neighbor Giorgio's tabby cat that frequents Marcello's art shop, catches a whiff of our *dolci*. He follows us down the hill, meowing plaintively. We leave him at the door of the school, and he sits to wait. Much as he waits for the alley lady when she goes shopping at the *negozio*. He stares as we move farther away. Farther away...with pie.

As it turns out, my internal machinations for how to explain Thanksgiving were unnecessary. Alessia tells the story, and turns to us when she lacks a detail, like how long the pilgrims were at sea and if Thanksgiving is a bigger holiday than Christmas. I'm as rapt as the students, listening to Alessia's handling of the less than savory aspects of the narrative. She simply tells the children that just like all people, some of the pilgrims were kind, and some were not; some of the Indians were kind, and some were not. But most had love in their hearts. The truth of this strikes me. I love Thanksgiving's modern emphasis on gratitude without gift-giving, but I'm bothered by the level of fear and suspicion that existed between people sharing a land. So to meditate on the fact that some of those early settlers actually were receptive and grateful to the Indians, and some of the Indians took the trouble to help the settlers, even knowing the risks, I feel my own heart creak open a bit wider. Listening to Alessia tell the children about this encounter makes it feel more human, and less like a tragedy in the making.

Alessia asks me what the settlers learned from the Indians, and I tell her about how the Indians taught the pilgrims about soil cultivation. She translates, and then asks me *sotto voce*, what the Indians got from the settlers. I refrain from answering "smallpox" and shrug my shoulders. She turns back to the class and suggests that the Indians got the joy of helping those in need. Which reminds me of Arturo's Thanksgiving toast, about cultures extending the hand of friendship to each other. This expat experience is giving me a whole new way to appreciate Thanksgiving—to embrace newcomers, and offer support. What a notion to celebrate.

We show Alessia Gabe's hand turkey, and she immediately claps her hands for attention. When the children quiet, she instructs them to take out their *quaderni* and begin drawing hand turkeys. Then she crouches next to Gabe and asks him to get his sister. He dashes out, with a sense of ownership over this space that still feels foreign to me. While the children draw their hand turkeys (and the teacher's aide asks us earnestly how to properly color in the fingers—one color? rainbow colors?), Keith and I pass out mini-pies. Gabe arrives back in the classroom, leading Siena by the hand. She's happy to get out of geography, though she whispers it was a more interesting lesson than usual, since they were talking about immigration and the teacher had many questions about her home. Nicolas later shares that he had a similar conversation with his Italian teacher, who took him and a classmate from Morocco aside to ask them about their homelands. He recounted his classmate's descriptions of how school in Morocco is segregated by gender. It seems a day for underscoring a message of cross-cultural understanding.

Pies eaten, turkeys drawn and colored, we say goodbye to the *prima* class. Alessia kisses the three of us and thanks us for coming. Siena returns to her classroom, and we are left to the care of Max, still patiently waiting. We try to ignore his increasingly piteous meows, and conference about what we should do with the extra pies. An idea glimmers, then bursts upon me fully formed. I decide to distribute the pies throughout Spello. One to the school secretary walking up the hill, one to Letizia, one to Marcello standing outside his art shop enjoying the sunshine, one each to Assunta and Gianni, one to Giorgio who is sipping an *espresso* at Tullia's bar. And one to an alley lady making her way down the hill as we're heading up. Keith holds out the tray and I explain that yesterday was Thanksgiving and we want to offer her a pie like we eat in America. While she peers at our platter, one eyebrow furrowed, Max twines himself around our legs, meowing with his nose twitching. The alley lady looks up into my eyes and asks, *"Chi l'ha fatto?"* Who made this? I tell her that I did, and she blinks at me curiously. And then follows with, where had I made them? I tell her I made them at home. She delicately lifts a pastry off the tray and thanks us with a nod. We hear her muttering, "mmm... mmmm..." as she continues down the hill. As she enters the pedestrian tunnel we hear her shout, *"Deliziosa!"* The word rings through the street, amplified by the stone arch over her head. We turn and see her tottering form still moving downhill, one arm raised in exultation. I'm glad she trusted me enough to try one. In the sharing, the connection across the divide, I feel closer to my homeland, and also closer to my foster country. I give thanks, indeed.

25 November

There are disadvantages to being a psychologist. Nicolas would agree—he's tired of my diagnosing him with prodromal OCD because of his fixation on keeping his fingernails "even," and because of his pathological aversion to eggplant. (I still think I'm right about the eggplant.) Often I'm grateful for my training, but when it comes to parenting, it constrains me. Parenting Siena has become a challenge I feel ill equipped to face. She has long runs of expressing nothing but contentment and gratitude, and I'll start to exhale. Then, seemingly out of nowhere, she's miserable again.

She's miserable again. I think because it's Monday, and she realizes that the weekend is over. At breakfast, she starts to panic, and I ask her to state one specific worry. When she thinks about it, she realizes that she's worried that her teachers will be angry with her. Which is not uncommon, particularly in math, but when I press her for more information, she leaps up, remembering that she hasn't finished her homework. She races to her backpack to fetch her math, and while she's furiously working on it, I suggest that during recess she can do her Italian homework that she's forgotten to bring home. She looks up, horrified. "No one *ever* does their homework at recess." I shrug. If it's not allowed, a teacher will tell her and she'll apologize and have new information. This is a pill too large and bitter for my daughter to swallow. In her eyes, a doling of information is a reprimand, and a reprimand is as good as a beheading.

By some divine intervention, she finishes her math quickly even with her panicked breathing. With the extra time, I ask her to make a pie chart for what overwhelms her. The biggest piece of the pie is "not understanding," followed by a large chunk of "teachers being angry or disappointed" when she's not able to follow along with lessons or move seamlessly to the next task. The rest are small bits of "bored," "tired," and "recess troubles." Seeing the pieces of her anxiety on paper eases some of the weight from her shoulders.

Conferencing over coffee after we drop the children off, Keith muses that Siena hasn't changed much from when she was a toddler. In her curly-haired, tutu-wearing days, she was a child of extremes. Totally ecstatic...until she wasn't. And then you could hear her three blocks away. Her more dramatic corners have softened over the years, leaving her joyful soul intact. And so we've forgotten about her tendency to overestimate the negative, until now, when she's taken to making statements like "I'm weary to my bones." I think Keith is right, this is just her pattern—when she feels low, which is rare, she perceives the situation as irreversible.

I can see that now, and it helps. But the difference between Keith and me is that he sees this as just another phase, while I see it as possibly splintering her fragile sense of competence. I try to borrow some of his optimism. It's a challenge, but attempting a long view helps soothe my frayed nerves.

Feeling slightly steadier, I meet Paola at the top of Spello. Over the last of the pecan pie at Thanksgiving, she offered to take me for a country walk to collect wild greens. Yesterday, stopping by her shop, I'd confirmed, and it's a relief to now see her sunny face, welcoming me with an extra bag to fill. She's brought her dog Shiva, so named for his uncanny ability to destroy his environment, though without the Hindu god's promise of recreating his world in stronger ways. Paola, more than her dog, sees the value of destruction to gain clarity. Shiva the dog just wants to sniff and run and chew. We walk from Piazza Vallegloria through the olive groves, with a view onto Spello rising from the mists. I talk to Paola about Siena, and she offers to teach her macramé. The offer arrives like a godsend—handicrafts are meditative for Siena, and the chance to be independent and walk to the shop on her own, and connect with someone kind and gentle—may be just what the heavens ordered.

We turn back toward Spello and breathe in the scent of warming dew-covered olive leaves, Paola continuing to point out greens while we talk about what we each find centering. Really, though, I'm finding Paola centering. Her face is open and she has a smile that not only lights her face, it makes me forget that there was dimness before. Plus, I enjoy hunting for greens. Paola points out *crispigno* (a kind of dandelion), wild garlic (the bulb is excellent in salads), *finocchio* (fennel, which one can dry upside down to release the seeds), ortica (nettle), *rapastella* (with white flowers, best picked before those flowers form), soft and verdant *cicoria* (chicory), and *borragine* (borage). She tells me to cook all the greens together, as the combination of the sweet leaves with the more bitter ones make for a complex and delicious taste. Especially with copious amounts of olive oil, she laughs, her round face beaming.

Her advice sticks with me the rest of the day. The bitterness and difficulty—they create the layers, the complexity. It makes me wonder if perhaps Siena's hardships, combined with her capacity for joy, are what make a real and connected life. Yes, it pains me to imagine my child's heart shattered, but I wonder what will happen if she rebuilds it while braced by the gleaming gold of olive oil, the pink stones of Spello, the care of Arturo (who tells me he found her a violin teacher), and the guidance of Paola, modeling how to braid disparate strands into something beautiful.

26 November

Siena and I spend a quiet hour washing greens. It's like only this kitchen exists, as we glide each leaf through water and place it in a colander. She tells me about how she's feeling a little more stable. Not only did yesterday go better than anticipated, but Chiara has written her phone number on Siena's hand and ordered Siena to call. Siena is nervous, but also flattered, and besides, she has the excitement of her first day at Paola's shop to look forward to.

At 3:30 she bolts like a pebble released from a slingshot, down to Paola's shop, La Bottega Degli Intrecci. By the time I meet her later in the afternoon, she has learned how to make several knots, which she holds out for me, her eyes shining. Paola and I applaud her progress. Then she braces herself to call Chiara on Paola's shop phone. My daughter has done many things in her short life that have filled me with pride. Watching her tremble as she dials, yet steadfastly continue, tops the list. She tucks her long dark hair behind her free ear, and stands tensely, one hand on her waist, staring fixedly at the wall. Chiara picks up, and they make what sounds like small talk. Siena answers that she's doing well, and no, she hadn't done her homework yet. Then Siena gives Chiara our phone number, exchanges goodbyes, and hangs up with a smile. Paola and I cheer. And the two of them get back to work, Siena bouncing a little in her seat, while I loiter and listen to them shift easily between Italian and English as Paola teaches Siena to move the threads to create a bracelet. As I run my hands over the lovely shawls in Paola's shop, I remember the lines of a Wendell Berry poem:

> *It may be that when we no longer know what to do,*
> *we have come to our real work*
> *and when we no longer know which way to go,*
> *we have begun our real journey.*
> *The mind that is not baffled is not employed.*
> *The impeded stream is the one that sings.*

I mull over the words, until my reverie is broken by a gentleman entering the shop. Paola gestures for me to come closer and introduces us. When she says my name, he clasps my hand and chortles, *"Cotiche!"* While I'm pleased that my culinary efforts have preceded me and have earned me cobblestone street cred, I wish that I had been making rosewater or something. It's disconcerting to be known as pig skin. But maybe that's the bitter I can take with the green. Paola introduces the man as Angelo, and explains that he is married to Giuseppina, who gave me the *cotiche* recipe via Arturo.

While we tuck into our dinner of bitter-green-laced pasta, Siena expresses amazement that the greens were "found food," a gift. Little knowing that she is a gift. When life is bitter, when it's sweet, when she baffles me, when she provides challenge that keeps me moving barriers aside to get to the center, when her laughter lilts like birdsong and makes us all notice the exact moment that we're in. Siena keeps me deep in my heart.

27 November

Ho hum. I'm going to Florence today.

Not to sightsee. Not to go to a museum. Not with a map. Not with a Baedeker. For possibly the first time in my adult life, I'm going to a world class city for no better reason than "why not?" Doreen wants to Christmas shop at the open stalls and has invited Paola and me. So I'm going to Florence today. It's one of those sentences that reminds me that I really am living abroad. *I'm going to Florence today.*

We take the train, one of my favorite modes of travel. Our journey to Tuscany is full of stories. Doreen tells us about adopting her daughter from a Mexican orphanage and the earthquake that threatened to prevent her from claiming her baby. We all sigh, remembering that that very daughter is getting married soon in England. Paola describes her time with the Hare Krishnas, which was not always smooth, though there were years in Sicily that sound dreamy in their simplicity. She had difficulty leaving the faith, and struggled raising her son as a single mother. We arrive in Florence far too quickly, and immediately reach for our umbrellas to protect us from the drizzle. I spare a moment to bless Letizia who, when I saw her at the bakery this morning, pointed out the sky that prophesied rain.

Of our time in Florence, there is not much to say. Because Florence is the backdrop to our day, rather than the pivotal focus of our attention. We shop at the stalls around San Lorenzo, before ducking out of the rain to have lunch of *ribollita* and a pasta with pesto made from Tuscan cabbage and a crisp piece of *guanciale*. Thus fortified, we step back into what is now pouring rain.

Strangely, the lack of perfect weather heightens the experience. The stone streets are black and shiny, a counterpoint to white and blue Christmas lights twinkling against the swirling grey sky. The air smells oddly of waffles, and I find myself lagging behind, swept up in the hidden corners and vivid details. On our walk to the covered market, we cross the Piazza del Duomo. Brunelleschi's dome looms into the roiling clouds. Tourists gather, guidebooks open to the deepening rain, furtively glancing up to note features highlighted in their texts. We don't stop, or even pause. And there is this sense that we are living our lives, and this massive, glorious tribute to those that dedicated themselves to the construction of this dome is just here. Like a heartbeat. Always here, while we're shopping for scarves and purses. And because I haven't already pictured the dome in the process of mentally preparing for a vacation, the grace and beauty enter my core more easily. My heart swells and I feel tears pricking my eyes as we return to the honking streets of modern day Florence. To the covered market, where vendors shuffle with their hands in their pockets, as the rain beats a steady clatter on the roof, and odd rays of light catch the blowing mists of rain racing down the street.

Our train ride home is mellow. The rain lashing against the train windows is soporific, and our damp bodies sink into the seats. We perk up when we walk into L'Orlando Furioso to meet Keith and the kids. Neither Doreen nor Paola glances at the menu before Doreen orders *pizza margherita* with one lone anchovy, and Paola orders a pizza with red peppers and arugula. While we wait, Doreen asks Keith about the mindfulness work he's found useful for decreasing stress and increasing focus. They discuss the difficulty of being present and slowing down one's train of spinning thoughts, while Paola breaks in with questions. As they talk, Doreen and Paola flip through the children's sketchbooks and turn aside to comment on the drawings. The children make a real effort to speak Italian or slow down their English for Paola. Paola wants us to explain the word "silly." Siena thinks for a moment, and then suggests that it's like *buffo*, funny, with a little *pazzo*, crazy. Paola mulls over Siena's explanation, while she braids Siena's hair and I finish the wine.

Gabe, Siena, and Keith want to walk home. Which was *buffo* as far as Nicolas and I are concerned. *Pazzo*, too. We accept a ride with Doreen. On the drive, Doreen asks Nicolas about his piano lessons. He says that his current teacher's spare praise and exacting standards have made him realize that he wants to be pushed. His teacher has torn down his notion of piano playing as a way to be the best, and replaced it with solid technique and a drive to improve.

As I tuck Siena in bed, she tells me, a huge smile lighting her flushed face, that when we were back in Virginia, she hadn't realized what it would really mean to live in a foreign country. When she thought about it, she pictured speaking Italian in our hometown. She adds that she was stuck at picturing only one way of living. It reminds her of the model river she used to play with at the children's museum. When she was small, she loved closing the locks and making the toy boats float high. Then she'd release the locks and the water and boats would rush forward. Siena announces that she feels unlocked. Now her understanding of what living abroad means is rushing forward. She sighs that it feels amazing. That might be an even better expat experience than *I went to Florence today*.

28 November

As I walk Siena to meet her new violin teacher at the *scuola media*, I'm reminded of her first day of school, when not one face was familiar and she could barely introduce herself. This meeting feels less alarming, but I'm grappling with confusion. Are we just organizing lessons? Or is she going to have a lesson? For how long? Is the lesson under the umbrella of the community music program? Do we pay the teacher or the school?

The violin teacher meets us at the door, and introduces herself as Mara. She ducks into the school, and Siena and I follow. When Mara sees me tagging along, she startles. Then she turns to the middle school secretary, and it becomes clear to me that I'm not allowed to accompany Siena. I can tell that Mara is pleading with the secretary, who is adamant that I am absolutely *not* allowed to enter the school. Maybe I shouldn't have arrived in fatigues, wielding my bayonet. I interrupt to tell Mara that I understand. Then I turn to Siena and try to make my eyes convey a world of support and positive feeling. Siena frowns slightly, but she nods and follows Mara, who asks me to return in an hour, her voice ringing with apology.

On my way back to school, I pass an alley lady, who asks me if my children are all in the house. I explain that Siena is at a violin lesson. She nods and asks if they've done their homework. No, not yet. She reminds me that it's a good idea to keep track of my children. Thanks a lot, Nicolas—I sure hope those M&M's you ate on the stoop waiting for our return when you were locked out were worth all the flack I'm getting from every concerned octogenarian in town. Keith insists that the questions are sociable; to me, they seem pointed. Earlier today, I helped this same alley lady get her cat Achilles back in her house, as she couldn't wrangle him with her umbrella and her bag. If this is just good conversational fodder, maybe I should ask if her cat is in the house. Wait, I did that, and she asked me the same thing. Okay, I suppose it's possible that Keith is right.

I continue down to the school and wait outside. Mara exits, followed by Siena and two other children. Oh! It's a group lesson. When I ask about paying, she takes me to the office where the pieces slowly come together. This struggling along, knowing that clarity may be around the next corner or the one after that, is a sensation that's become all too familiar. By the end, I learn that the lessons are through the community music school, and we pay €30 a month for a one-hour group lesson a week.

Siena skips home, telling me that Mara was kind and a gifted violinist. I ask her if having the lesson in Italian was as exhausting as she'd expected. She thinks about it—"Actually, no." It was easier since, as a group lesson, she can watch the students if she doesn't understand. But also, she's been taking music through school, so she's picked up more terminology than she'd realized. The Italian didn't faze her.

We've come a long way. Today was nothing like the arresting anxiety of the first day. Plus, she seemed actually happy, rather than simply relieved, when I collected her. And even happier when Doreen drops by later and succumbs to our begging her to stay for dinner. She joins me in the kitchen while Siena does her homework. The kitchen is warm from roasting the rosemary-covered pork loin and the patter of animated voices. Siena periodically puts down her pencil with a grin of pleasure to be sharing our table with Doreen.

29 November

My Italian lessons have grown increasingly complicated. One, because I'm pushing myself to use the imperfect and future tenses. Two, because our discussions have taken a turn for the philosophical, which is difficult enough in English. I can't remember the last time I had a conversation with anyone that includes the word pedagogy (I admit I don't actually understand what that is—it's a little like the remote past tense, it makes vague sense, but it's blurry and oddly lit).

Arturo and I discuss Siena's transition. He's visibly relieved that she's finding her feet. He offers this assessment—he suggests that our family is transparent. All of Spello agrees that we are open and accessible. In fact, he suggests, we are like a clean mirror. The trouble with a clean mirror is that if a fly lands on it, you can't see anything else except that blasted fly. Whereas a fly on a dirty mirror is easily overlooked. This rings true for me. Particularly this year, when there are fewer distractions to muck up the mirror, and I'm more able to sense and respond to the subtle struggles within each of us. It's easier to inhabit Siena's painful place.

I'm still considering Arturo's idea when I take the children out to the hills to collect greens. Without Paola, I can't distinguish good greens from bad, except *borragine*, thanks to their huge size and purple flowers calling like signal flags. From a distance we spot those flowers dotting the grasses under the olive trees. Siena is part wood sprite, climbing hills, darting through the trees, making a quick fairy house, pulling up wild garlic, and harvesting *mentuccia*, the wild mint Italians say is fabulous with artichokes. I haven't tried it, but I love the smell of the mint when the children scamper over it.

As Siena ranges up and down the hills, and Nicolas and Gabe keep closer to me, I walk slowly. My collecting bag hangs empty, as I'm fixated on the views over the valley. The air is so crisp, I can see that the distant mountains are newly flocked with snow. As the light shifts with the sun's weaving behind clouds, the olive trees glitter. Every few steps, the view changes. I continually stop to take it in. To allow myself to feel the cool breeze against my cheeks, and then alternately notice the change in tone as the wind fades away. I notice the shadows slip across the valley. The light playing between the trees is beautiful and true.

30 November

This was not supposed to happen. Not today. Not any day. Ever.

Today was supposed to be about secretly shopping for a Christmas tree while the kids were in school. The main event was supposed to be finding a tree for €25, which seemed a steal until we spot identical trees at the Coop for €12,50. That was supposed to be today. A day for finding ways to amaze our children—where overspending for a Christmas tree is the most dramatic part of our day.

Apparently, the expat gods did not get the memo.

When we collect our children from school, I imagine the expression on their faces when we walk into the house, fragrant with the spicy tangerine scent of a good Christmas tree, and sparkly with lights winking within the branches. I'm so distracted by the tingle of our secret, and by Siena's animated voice chattering about her day, that I don't notice how wan Gabe is as he slips his hand in mine. Finally, I realize he's trying to tell me something quietly, *sotto voce*. I duck down to catch his words.

"My math teacher spanked me today."

The world tilts. What was that? Start again, say it slower, and take breaks between words because my heart isn't beating while you are talking. *What was that?*

"At math, some kids and I were standing on our chairs. And then I fell off and hurt myself. My teacher came toward me and I thought she was going to comfort me, but instead she shouted my name and hit me."

The earth seems to slide from underneath me. I don't know what to think, or even what to feel. Corporal punishment does not rhyme with my world view, and I'm more stunned and confused than angry. I try to stay measured until I have time to think. Before even figuring out what to do about this, I need to figure out how to approach it with my son. I don't want to overwhelm him by exploding, though as the shock melts a bit, exploding seems like the only sensible option. I settle for validating his feelings, telling him that must've been scary, particularly since he knows that there's never an occasion for hitting. I call to Keith, who has walked on with Siena, while I've stopped in the street with Gabe. "Keith?" I try to sound casual, but my voice comes out strangled. "Keith?"

Keith has been married to me for 15 years, and he knows when something is gravely wrong. He doubles back, concern etched on his face. "Are you okay?"

"Yes, I'm okay. But Gabe just told me that his math teacher spanked him." Keith recoils a touch before catching himself. I can see that he is as invested in communicating care without panic to our son. "Whoa, Gabe, that must've been a shock." Gabe nods and bites his lip. I smooth his cowlick and we continue walking up the hill. I search for consoling words, "You know it's never okay to hit. How upsetting that your teacher would break this rule. Does it hurt?"

Gabe nods again. "Yes, a little. But mostly it hurts my heart."

Our conversation stalls as we enter the house. Gabe races to the Christmas tree, spins in circles, shouts when he sees three mini-trees and pastries on the dining room table. I smile as I watch the children's joy, but then move into the kitchen, my thoughts returning to the red light flashing in my mind. Keith and Gabe follow me while I make the worst *frittata* of my life. My mind is clearly not on my hands. We ask Gabe more questions, but don't learn anything more than after his teacher spanked him, he went to his desk and put his head in his arms. I tell him that there are many natural reactions—anger, sadness, betrayal, confusion, embarrassment. He ruminates and says, "I think I'm feeling all of those things."

We sit down to our mostly-scrambled-eggs-but-nobody-cares-because-we-hardly-notice lunch. Siena admits she feels unsafe entering a place that would hurt her brother, and she'll never complain about her math teacher again. Gabe, head leaning heavily on his hands as he pushes the food around his plate, wistfully says that he thought the teacher liked him. Pragmatic Nicolas wants to know what we're going to do. Keith and I fall into a matter-of-fact approach. Hitting children is unacceptable. Today happens to be parent-teacher conferences, where we'll find out if hitting is an aberration or part of the school culture. If it's the latter, we can't send Gabe to school here. *Punto e basta.* Full stop. Even if kids here are used to this, I can't send my child into a building where he knows he might get spanked.

Armed with this plan, Keith and I leave for the conferences, while Nicolas hovers over his siblings as they decorate the house with the ornaments Doreen brought over. Our first stop is Siena's classroom. We sit outside the door along with parents who are catching up like they are meeting for coffee. I want to go home. How can I do this? Any of this? How can I talk about the emotional state of my children in a language that is not my own, or a language that is not the teacher's own, in a place that I am not sure is committed to protecting the well-being of my babies? I want home, where I know how egregious it is to hit a child, where I am confident in my ability to finesse difficult conversations, and where we sign up for conferences rather than descend *en masse* with all the other parents and wonder how we figure out our place. I just want to go home. I've never felt so alien.

All I can do is sit on the hard plastic chair and wait, as the line grows and the confusion of who is next increases. I try not to cry. Finally, it's either our turn or we unknowingly cut into the queue. We sit ourselves in front of Siena's teachers. They both tell us that she is *"brava"* and *"creativa."* They observe that everyone wants to be friends with her, but she has a hard time connecting. The refrain from both is *piano, piano. Piano, piano* she is coming out of her shell. And *piano, piano* she will grow more engaged. The English teacher adds that it's hard to make this transition at this age. He remembers that Siena hid her face in her hands on the first day of school, and then later hid herself in her work, but now she is slowly opening up.

Walking to Gabe's conference, Keith and I agree that the meeting was beneficial. Not that we learned anything about our daughter, but it helped to meet her math teacher and see that though she is distant, which perhaps translates to irritability in the classroom, she seems to empathize with Siena's situation, at least in the abstract. Even more than that, the meeting helps prod us toward the idea of suggesting to Siena that she have one goal for this year—to engage. Division and grammar be damned. Maybe making that goal explicit will free her from the expectations she labors under.

Our wait for Alessia is interminable. Finally, she pops out of the door, and waves us in with a smile. Alessia gushes about how everyone loves *Gabriele*—the boys, the girls, and the other teachers. She shares that his reading is excellent, though his writing could be straighter. Her eyes full of merriment, she tells us that Gabe is speaking half in English, half in Italian. She adds that it's still tiring for him to function in another language, so she lets him meander the school when he needs a break. She thinks it's good for his geography as well as his happiness. She sits back with satisfaction as she adds that everyone reports that he is unfailingly polite in his forays through the hallways, and he always comes back feeling ready. This explains his story of wandering the halls—it's like a self-imposed time-out, to give himself space to step away and get his bearings.

So we affirm, he behaves well in school? An emphatic *"Sì."* I look at Keith, who hesitates and says, "Because Gabriele told us that his math teacher hit him today." Alessia is caught off guard, and asks Keith to repeat what he said. Clearly, she thinks she's misunderstood his English. Her normally bronze complexion turns ashen, and her ebullient voice grows hushed and serious. She assures us that hitting is unacceptable, completely unacceptable. She offers to talk to the math teacher, unless we'd prefer to do it? Seeing as the math teacher doesn't speak English, and our Italian vocabulary doesn't extend to the nuances of corporal punishment, we gratefully accept her offer to talk to the teacher for us.

Alessia asks about Siena and grows even more still when we tell her that Siena is scared to come to school. She understands. Her expression grows closer to its usual liveliness as she describes how much she loves watching Siena help her brother hang his backpack and take out what he needs for the day.

We all stand, the meeting over. Alessia reiterates that she is sorry that this has happened. I feel heard by her, but I admit I would've preferred a touch more outrage. Which is American of me, I suppose. It would have been relieving if she'd grabbed our hands and marched us to the director's office in a "heads will roll" sort of way. But, as long as it doesn't happen again, I suppose that's all that matters.

Gabe comes running as soon as we open the door. "Did you talk to Alessia about the spanking?" We tell him that Alessia had said that spanking was not allowed, and not okay, and that she'd talk to his math teacher. "But if it's against the rules, why did my teacher hit me?" Oh, child. I'm not sure I'm rugged enough to dive into the mind of an adult who can spank an earnest innocent who is already outside the mainstream. In a glimmer of what feels like prescience, I tell Gabe that we are grateful that he told us what happened, and if people ever hurt him, we need to know. Even if his teacher orders him not to tell. Gabe frowns. "But then I wouldn't be listening to my teacher's words." I go on to explain that more important than following directions is doing what's right. And what's right is for us to know if and when a person is inappropriate toward him.

Gabe nods thoughtfully. Then he leaps up to show us the monster head he'd made from the box Doreen brought with her Christmas decorations. Doreen, we owe you a new box. He puts the box on his head, chasing Siena, and collapses into helpless laughter when she thwarts him. Bedtime finds him reflective but calm, which is certainly better than I would've predicted a scant five hours ago, but still I want to cradle that sensitive soul of his. I worry that this will rock him in some indefinable way. But I'm also hoping that his natural resilience will armor him, protect him, and return his faith in humanity. That he will continue to smile at the world.

Bitter Greens

greens, more than you would imagine as they shrink to nothing
(at least the equivalent of three bunches of spinach).
Make sure to have a combination so the flavors marry and blend.
Mustard, chard, spinach—or, better yet—wild greens.

olive oil

garlic, chopped

red pepper flakes (a small amount if you object to
spice, but otherwise, the more the merrier)

salt

---

1. Bring about two inches of salted water to boil in a pot with a tight fitting lid. Once the water is boiling furiously, add the greens, and put the lid on the pot.

2. After a few minutes, stir the greens, and replace the lid.

3. After a few more minutes, check the greens. They should be soft and tear easily. If they are not ready, cook them for a few more minutes.

4. Drain them, reserving the cooking water for soup.

5. Heat olive oil in a pan, and add garlic. Toss in the cooked greens, sautéing until mixed well and heated through. Add salt and pepper.

Serving alternatives:

1. Boil pasta and add about a cup of the pasta cooking water to the greens. Once pasta is cooked, drain and add to the sautéed greens and toss, serve with feta chunks on top for brightness.

2. Skip the sautéing step, and instead melt some butter with a clove of garlic and let the garlic seep into the butter. Drizzle the garlicky butter over a plate of greens.

3. Mix the greens with white beans and cooked sausage for a soup.

DECEMBER

BREAD AND OIL

1 December

What does a mother want to hear the morning after her child is spanked at school? "I slept so well, and had such lovely dreams all night." I fairly float through the routine of making breakfast and seeing the children off to school, Gabe clutching a branch of our Christmas tree for Alessia. Siena's steps are bouncy after our conversation last night about her progress and goal setting. She's cheerful enough to point out that we have five Christmas trees. "Remember, Mommy? When I was upset about not having a Christmas tree and you said not to get upset, after all, maybe the custom here is to have five Christmas trees?" And here they are—our family tree, our three mini trees, and Doreen's tabletop tree wreathed in lights.

My Italian lesson is solemn, as I tell Arturo the spanking story, and he talks about how difficult it was for him to teach alongside colleagues who would similarly break Italy's law against corporal punishment. We sigh together. He confesses that he's worried Alessia won't talk to the math teacher. Maybe it's foolish of me, but I don't share that worry. It's a subject that Keith and I considered long into the night. I know that if we were at home, we'd storm the director's office. But the rules just seem different when we are transients on foreign soil. First of all, I'm not sure I could pick the director out of a lineup. I must have seen her, but she's not standing in front of the school greeting children. Since she is the head of both the lower and middle schools, I'm unclear on how we'd find her. Does she have an office in one of the schools? I've never seen it. Anyway, she might be cold and dismissive. Maybe not, but we don't know. But we do know Alessia, and we trust her. Not only does she seem to hold at least a nominal administrative role, I believe she wants to protect Gabe, and when the ground is tenuous beneath my feet, it feels like trust is my only option. Her love of Gabe feels real enough to count on. Keith and I agree that we are confident that it won't happen again. And that's what matters. If it does, then that's when we'll seek out the director. I try to explain at least some of this to Arturo, who spreads his hands on the table and considers me for a moment. Then he clasps his hands in front of him, leans forward, and says that if it does happen again, he would like to accompany us when we confront the school. My eyes sting as I tell him that being separated from our people makes us feel alone, and so his offer and Paola's similar offer help us feel safer. He says that he knows that with three children, life can be challenging, and he wanted us to think of him as *parenti*. Kin.

Usually the time that the children are in school flies swiftly. I am so engaged with lessons or marketing or writing that I don't spend time thinking of what they are doing. But the spanking has set me back. Now, as I sit writing, the sound of school children outside reminds me that the older students, including Siena and Nicolas' classes, are drawing outside today, creating their submissions for the *L'Oro di Spello* art contest. The festival of oil and *bruschette* begins tomorrow, and I wonder if my children are feeling a part of it. And my mind returns, over and over to Gabe, and how it will be for him to see his math teacher.

The streets quiet, and I walk to the school for dismissal. I peer around shoulders for a sight of my boy, and he comes zooming out of the doors, weaving around parents to stop still in front of me. He drops his backpack to the ground and tells me in great seriousness that his math teacher apologized. She told him that she hadn't known it was against the rules to hit children. I muffle my impulsive snarky remark that perhaps the handbook for being a decent human should be ingrained in one's brain. I try, instead, to be where Gabe is—encouraged that she apologized. In English, to make sure he understood. He told her that he forgave her. Thus making him a better person than his mother.

With a lighter heart, I make *arancini*, filled and fried risotto balls, which are devoured with great enthusiasm. Nicolas wants to know if we can have risotto every week so I'll make *arancini*. The children are in great moods, each with a tumble of stories to share. Siena is puffed with pride that she demonstrated a math problem on the blackboard, Nicolas tried joking in Italian with his friends in the olive orchard, and Gabe describes his conversation with Alessia about our Christmas trees, including telling her that he wound red thread around his little tree. How does he know the word for thread?

As evening closes in, Keith and I decide to take a *passeggiata* to see if the town is decorated for the festival. Gabe asks to join us, and I warm to this unexpected time with my baby. He squeals with delight at the olive branches decorating the walls of the town and the bakery display of a giant loaf of bread formed into a *presepe*, nativity scene. Even the misty rain is pronounced a work of staggering beauty—neither too heavy to be disruptive nor too light to be considered mist. I lift my face as we walk, allowing the rain to fall clear and soft against my cheeks, as I breathe in the scent of mist covered stones and smoky meats. We follow the sound of music, and drift down the hill to the open doors of Sant' Andrea. We creep into the church and stand in the back, listening to a small orchestra featuring an accordion. Gabe begins dancing. His eyes are closed, and his flushed face is lifted to the lofted blue ceiling. He sways and his feet carry him around in circles, as the stately space lightens into something almost whimsical.

As the orchestra prepares for another song, we tiptoe out to Vinosofia. Keith and I have been spending entirely too much time here, sampling wines from all over Italy, under the patient tutelage of Brenda and Graziano, but this is our first time here with just Gabe. He sits primly on his barstool and studies the menu. By the time he recites every item, including *decaffeinato*, we realize that he is really reading. In Italian, anyway. When he tries to decode the English translations, he gets stuck on "th" and the sound of "i." Brenda asks what he would like, and he sits up taller and simpers a little before ordering *succo di frutti di bosco*, wild berry juice. His erect posture gives a bit when he confides that he feels just like a grown-up. But he sits tall again when he sips his juice, and chatters to Doreen and Brenda with as much Italian as he can. Keith's and my vestigial tensions are eased with a plummy red wine from Lago Trasimeno served with a mellow Tomme cheese from the Piedmont. Brenda excitedly shows me little fondue pots she recently purchased, to fill with melted fontina cheese. She thinks it will be perfect for "your next *aperitivo lungo*." I've never heard this phrase at my Italian lessons. I'm so convinced it means a long cocktail hour that it becomes my new favorite phrase. *Aperitivo lungo.*

We leave when Gabe decides to turn the coat rack into a fort. Collecting Nicolas and Siena, we head to the *taverna* for dinner, eager to try our neighborhood's contribution to the festival's pop-up restaurants. Entering the tent draped over what is usually a small parking lot, we notice picnic tables decorated with olive branches, and wine waiting in rough earthen pitchers. We're seated and immediately served an *antipasti* plate with cured meats and a variety of *bruschette*— new oil, concentrated tomato sauce, persimmon. Persimmons are everywhere right now, like orange Christmas ornaments on trees barren of leaves. Simply diced, they melt into instant jam. These are sprinkled with pecorino crumbles, which brighten the flavor with a hit of salty contrast.

Our *primo* is a warming chickpea soup drizzled with new oil. Then the *secondo*, a beef and olive stew with a *chili verde* savoriness. We are surprised by the presentation of another plate of *secondi*. This one more…peculiar. Braised *erbe di campagna*, wild greens, served alongside crackling *cinghiale* bits, like grilled riblets, And tiny birds. Literally. Not quail. Not sparrow. Two tiny birds per plate. Nicolas speculates they are hummingbirds, but I remind him there are no hummingbirds in Italy. Only hummingbird moths. For a moment I fear these are moths, but then I note the endoskeleton of toothpick size bones. They are absolutely minuscule birds. Gabe promptly sticks his finger inside a bird, and uses it as a finger puppet. He sticks the other bird on the index finger of his other hand and proceeds to act out a play of his own devising. He delicately nibbles one bird and pronounces it "pretty gross." Nicolas takes a tiny piece of "breast" meat (one can only assume) between his teeth and slowly chews. He swallows with greater effort than such a tiny bite would demand. He observes that the bird is "stringy and oily." I have zero motivation to taste these little bird corpses.

Over slices of Spellani *rocciata*—apples and raisins rolled in a tube of pastry crust then formed into a circle, kind of like a wreath made of pie—I ask the family if we should try a different *taverna* tomorrow night. The menu changes every night, at every *taverna*. Keith is curious about the *taverne* in the other two neighborhoods. But the children like eating in our neighborhood. I vote to make the decision based on who is serving little birds. Let's avoid the little birds. Our laughter joins the cadence of voices crowding the tent, now full and lit against the deepening rain.

2 December

Nicolas tells me that in a Facebook conversation with his friend Luke, he mentioned that he has the day off of school. Luke wanted to know why, and Nicolas told him it was for the town's festival. Prompting Luke to comment, "That must be a pretty big festival, what's it celebrating?" Nicolas paused.

"Oil and toast."

I suppose in the land of million-dollar Superbowl commercials, oil and toast may seem too humble to celebrate. To which I retort, "Oh, but what oil, and what toast!" And what a brilliant day, with air clear enough to discern the line of trees across the valley, and a scent of bubbling *ragù* arching over filling streets. We follow a band as it weaves through town, its vibrant music resounding off the ancient walls. Before heading home, we stop into Paola's shop to buy bracelets for birthday gifts. Siena is invited to a party on Monday, and we are all invited to a party tomorrow for Gabe's classmate. I can feel my heels digging in. I'm shy by nature. Add in language dysfunction, and it makes anticipating a party rather unpleasant. I'm determined to accept the risk as sustenance for fully living our lives here, but I'm pretty sure I don't have to like it.

We wander to Vinosofia, startling at the sudden addition of Christmas lights strung across the road. The lights winking as the slanting afternoon sun illuminates the town's pink stone leads Siena to sigh, "My dear Spello." As we point at shop windows and new lights, I reflect on the easy joy derived from starting Christmas in December, rather than at Halloween, as we're used to in the States. Instead of over-stretching Christmas merriment, spirit arrives full force, all of a piece. Undiluted by time and acclimation.

Graziano stands outside Vinosofia, turning *bruschette* on a fiery grill. He removes five pieces from the coals for us, drenches them in new oil, and sprinkles them liberally with salt before handing the *bruschette* to us, cradled in stiff paper. Keith and I also have a cup of *vin brûlé*. The wine is an irresistibly sweet and pungent accompaniment to the *bruschetta*, which has cooked up soft on the inside, but the oil crisps the outside so it offers a sensation similar to a donut. Only peppery and salty and completely addictive. As we linger in the waning sunlight, oil-soaked *bruschette* in our hands, we remember how important this simple food has been to the history of the town. Oil and toast.

3 December

Nicolas doesn't join us for Gabe's classmate's party, and I envy him as we walk out the door, leaving him in his jammies with cans of tuna for dinner. But as we walk, I'm surprised out of my ill humor by the sudden hush and delicate drift of snowflakes. Even though it's hardly more than a whisper, the air feels stiller somehow. More three dimensional. In the distance, we hear the festival band suddenly break off their music and begin playing "Jingle Bells." The children skip and twirl, lifting their upturned faces to feel the cold dusting their eyelids, a gentle suggestion of divine approval.

The party is at Terme Francescane, a spa just outside of town. It seems like half of Spello is clustered in that room, brimming over with burbling enthusiasm. Siena even finds a classmate of hers. Elisa invites Siena to play *"Lupo mangia frutta,"* The Wolf Eats Fruit, and Siena appears on the verge of a panic attack at the prospect. She protests that she doesn't understand the game! She's sure she won't like it! This is like recess when people pester her, only inside a big fancy room instead of on the playground! No! *No! NO!*

Meanwhile, Elisa looks on with a befuddled smile. I tell her that it's a little hard for Siena because Siena doesn't understand the game. Elisa laughs that she'll help, and then she holds her hand out to Siena. A brilliant move, because Siena can't refuse an outstretched hand. She allows herself to be led into the group. Every child is assigned the name of a fruit. The child who has been designated as the wolf calls out different fruits. If she calls out a fruit that no one has been assigned, the children chant, *"Non ci sono!"* There aren't any! If she calls out a fruit that one of the children has been assigned, then that child has to run away before she's tagged by the wolf. Only one round of fruity mayhem, and then dinner is served.

Trays of cured meats, slices of turkey covered with slivers of radicchio and drizzled with aged balsamic, *arancini* (which may be my new favorite food group), Ascolane olives, a salad of arugula and mozzarella balls—I'm dazed by the variety. As we're sitting down, Anna Maria, Stefano, and their boys arrive, and in a sea of unfamiliar people rapidly speaking a language we can barely understand even when the words are spoken slowly with crisp edges, these people radiate comfort. Gabe and Lorenzo run off together to play the children's games. While Siena stays steadfastly beside us at the table. I watch Elisa watching Siena, but Siena refuses to notice.

Our conversations with parents other than Anna Maria and Stefano are limited, but everyone is friendly. And they've all embraced Gabe, evidenced by the number of adults who pretend to chase him and the number of children who grab his hand and pull him toward new action. While I'm thrilled at their ready acceptance of my foreign boy, it doesn't escape my notice that it's not just Gabe who is embraced here. I witness how the group adapts to incorporate a bossy boy who yells at rule-bending children, and how the children sit with the girl with Down syndrome.

During the cake cutting, the birthday girl's father places Gabe directly in front of him while he lofts his daughter in his arms. He keeps one hand on Gabe's shoulder as everyone sings, planting my son as one of the group. During a stirring rendition of *"Tanti Auguri a Te,"* I spy Elisa in the next room, alone. I mention to Siena that perhaps she can tell Elisa that there's cake, girding myself for the familiar huff of "I don't know how to say that" or a whine of "That's too awkward." Instead, Siena hurries to Elisa without debate or commentary. And I watch, my heart in my throat, as Elisa and Siena sit down on the couches and talk. Animatedly, for quite some time. Other girls drift toward them. And then they all play a game together, Gabe too. I watch, feeling glad that I overcame my reluctance and joined my family at the party. Yes, I felt self-conscious when I noticed curious eyes on me and when I bumbled even simple introductions. But it was ultimately worth it to be present—to be part of a little girl's celebration, and to witness my children engaging with their community.

Siena holds my hand and skips beside me as we walk back to the car. Pride tinges her words as she describes her conversation with Elisa. She wonders aloud at how kind Elisa is, and how easy she is to understand. Fifteen minutes later, we are tumbling, exhausted, into the house. Nicolas greets us with a complaint that he doesn't want to wake up early for tomorrow's parade. Keith quips, "To experience life, sometimes we need to get out of bed."

More oil and toast tomorrow.

4 December

At the culmination of Spello's *Festa dell'Olivo e Sagra della Bruschetta* I took over 500 photographs. Those pictures are far more effective than my writing at conveying the depth of feeling that surrounds this festival for native Spellani. It's so clearly more than a celebration of foods, it's a celebration of village life, of colorful country ways, of honoring ancient traditions. And so the photo journey of the day can be found at *www.ilbelcentro.com/olio*. If a picture is indeed worth a thousand words, then this will be my longest post to date. Note the hanging hams.

6 December

These Umbrian December mornings are wreathed in darkness. Waking up at 7:00 AM feels like 3:00 AM. Which is unpleasant enough, but nudges into tortuous when my "*buongiorno!*" is met with screams of protest as children burrow deeper under fuzzy blankets. Three such stubborn souls are more than three times as bad as one. But today, I learn that when I nudge them awake with promises of *panettone*, poof! No fractious children—only children who race to make their beds. How lucky that Brenda gave us this wedge of soft, yielding *panettone*, a rich sweet bread, studded with raisins. This morning's revelatory Christmas bread is flavored with candied orange. I suspect more varieties are in our future.

The light never gains full strength nowadays, but my afternoon Skip-Bo game with Gabe is suffused with a warm glow. The Aperol spritz and salami help. Unfortunately, as the sun wanes behind the hills, Siena's mood also fades. Despite the fact that her afternoon was marked by her spontaneously remarking how lucky she is to live here, she is now moaning about doing her math homework. I attempt to set the table for dinner around her cloud of petulance. That petulance suddenly stalls at the startling sound coming from the street. She stops, we all stop.

The sound is eerie, thin, but gaining power. We throw open the windows and lean over the sill to peer down into the darkened street. Below is a man clad in a festive hat and cape playing what looks like a wooden, two-pipe bagpipe. He is casually standing below our window, facing down the hill playing haunting music that reverberates through the silent, darkened town.

Arturo appears, and when the song ends, he approaches the piper to talk for a moment before shouting to the five of us hanging out of the window that the man is a *zampogno* from Abruzzo. He adds that it is a Christmas tradition to have these pipers come into the towns and play Italian pipe Christmas music. The man takes off his hat and holds it out to us, which cues us to the other aspect of this tradition. Keith gives the children coins and they hurry down to hand them to the *zampogno* who has added this moment of unexpected light to our time of vanishing sun.

7 December

I'm beginning to suspect that our language acquisition has more to do with our attitude toward being foreign than it does any innate language ability. Each of us has a different progress curve. The state of my Italian is uneven. Sometimes I surprise myself by what I'm able to communicate, like when I tell Anna Maria that I'm taking the children to make fairy houses, prompting her to cheer at my successful retrieval of the word for "fairy." But five minutes later I get tangled trying to say something as basic as "how are you?" In general, I'm consistently more fluid in my speaking when I'm relaxed. Which is why I think I can have conversations with Arturo about self-esteem or gun control, but if a stranger asks for directions my mouth flops uselessly. I've started dreaming in Italian, but not how I expected. Mostly, I'm translating in my dreams. So the dream unfolds, and then the action stops and waits for me to describe it in Italian, and then starts again. Repeat.

Keith is the one who knows the verb tenses that I'm pretending I'll never need. Who needs future conditional? He's devoted to the study of Italian, to the point that he reads Italian books, a dictionary propped beside him. Since he likes murder mysteries, he's the one to ask if you want to learn the Italian for "rigor mortis." He's like Nicolas in that he's fearless. He'll talk to anyone, and push himself to stretch his abilities. Keith estimates his comprehension is about 50%, and his speaking depends on how much he has to think. So he can chitchat with fluidity, but if he has to say something thoughtful, he gets stuck.

That lack of fear of looking stupid is definitely helpful for both Keith and Nicolas in terms of language acquisition. Nicolas is all in, all the time. He doesn't freeze, and he doesn't second guess himself, he just speaks. And I think this approach, coupled with the immersion of school, is why he's the one among us who catches himself thinking and truly dreaming in Italian. In fact, today in French class, Nicolas was asked how to say 1974 (the year) in English to demonstrate how different languages structure the words for years. He couldn't do it—all that came was Italian. When he first arrived, teachers gave him simplified versions of tests, but now he takes the same ones as his peers. His grades are dismal, but he boasts that he's gone from being the foreign kid who required extra support, to merely being the dumbest kid in class. He tells me that if teachers don't lapse into dialect, he understands about 90% of the lessons. This increased language fluidity has translated into a rewarding social life. His peers no longer hold him at a respectful distance but shove him right along with the rest. He's getting closer with two of the boys, and at a recent assembly sat between them. He informs me, beaming, that doesn't happen when you are a social liability. Only when boys actually want to be with you.

It's funny because he was the one I was most worried about, pre-arrival. Not because I thought he couldn't learn language, but because I knew his academic demands would be the greatest. I remember recoiling at the image of him laboring to write essays in Italian while he still had American soil clinging to his Keens. I predicted he'd be overwhelmed and perpetually lost. I didn't count on his thirst for mastering challenges and his need for social relationships. Because I didn't know those needs existed. To watch him throw himself into the language fray, making mistakes, set goals for himself, meet them with pride, comfort himself when he errs, and celebrate when he's successful has all been new to me. He can even roll his r's now, which he'd previously given up as impossible.

It's been a harder road for Siena. She's shyer by nature, and I hadn't realized that being a people pleaser monkeys with language learning. She's hesitant to try for fear of make mistakes. Even so, she's learning. She can string together Italian sentences with fragments of phrases she knows. So instead of saying, *"Io ho perso il mio quaderno,"* I lost my notebook, she may just say, *"Perso mio quaderno."* It's like the Italian words she needs to express a complete sentence are in a sifter, and only some of them are shaken out, without their accompanying words or helping articles. She tells me about conversations she has with classmates, and while it's certainly bungling, I'm surprised by what she's able to convey. And though grammar and verb tenses are in their formative stages, she has a wide vocabulary. She's the one to ask if you want to know how to say "shadow." *Ombra*, by the way.

Piano, piano. Today Siena shares that in religion, after learning about the symbolism behind monk's clothing, the teacher asked what the colors on the Italian flag represented. A student answered that green was pesto, white was parmesan, and red was tomato sauce. And everyone laughed. Everyone, including Siena. It was the first time she was able to laugh along with the class because she got it, not because everyone was laughing. Which, she adds, is always awkward, because what if they are laughing at her? These are the self-doubts that freeze her, and she clearly just needs to get over herself and dive in. Hello, pot. Have you noticed what color you are?

And then there's Gabe. My American boy is prone to muttering *"mamma mia!"* with his hands pressed together in bobbing, prayer position. He also tries to pepper his sentences with Italian words he often hears—*"guarda," "aspetta," "pronto,"* look, wait, ready. He'll often mull for a minute before producing a sentence with as many Italian words as possible. This morning I heard him practicing upstairs before he came down the steps and announced, *"Tutto finito!"* I finished everything. In essence, he's always practicing. And it works—more and more, those Italian words are instinctive, rather than deliberate. In fact, some words are now easier for him to retrieve in Italian, particularly food and classroom-related words. He's forgotten the English word for ruler. And when I notice a red mark on his forehead, he tells me that he knows it's there because one of Siena's classmates pointed it out. I ask him if the friend said this in English or Italian, and he's stymied. Siena clarifies—Italian.

10 December

The children were given safety brochures, the kind that illustrate how to proceed in the face of various disasters—extreme heat, earthquake, flu epidemic. And a volcano eruption. I'm struck by how far from home we are. After all, my childhood did not include learning volcano preparedness. In case you are ever in need of this information, the safety booklet suggests that you don't attempt to approach the burning lava. Consider this my public service announcement for the day. *Don't approach the lava.*

I think there is a metaphor in there somewhere.

I had another moment of appreciating our geographical distance while Christmas shopping. This whole Christmas experience is new and miraculous, when it's not new and confusing. But the biggest shift is my husband. I am historically the parent in charge of holidays, because Keith worked an astounding number of hours, both for his business and also on the house. So in the past, I did the planning, preparation, and juggling that went into the holidays. Which was fine with me. I like having utter control (insert maniacal laugh here).

Keith hadn't planned on working this year, but the way the financial *biscotti* crumbled, he's been working part-time. More than he'd like, but so much less work than he was doing pre-launch that he feels pretty lucky. But here is the critical difference. Even when his work load is heavier, as it is now, he's able to walk away from it. Back at home, we could rarely get him to join us for walks or trips out for ice cream. Here, he rarely declines any proffered suggestion. So yesterday, I asked him if he wanted to go Christmas shopping with me. And he said yes.

Walking through Spello, we discuss gifts for our children. Keith spots *Cinghiale International* at the newsstand, and I giggle at the idea of getting Nicolas a subscription. I particularly love the "International" part. After picking up a few gifts, we stop for a cup of coffee. The fact that Keith can take this time, that he has the space to join me for a walk to the bakery, to keep on top of forms the children need to turn in, to help the children with their homework, to make a calendar of happenings in December so we can keep them straight, to walk the children to school and pick them up every day and remember to ask Siena if she has her math homework, to sit with me while I cook dinner, to be present and available for all of us. It's astounding. Before, there was no balance. Now there is. Before, he was so underwater with work, he wasn't able to follow his own leadings. Now he can. He's even breathing differently. Before we left, it sounded like he had a chronic cold. And now. Now, breathing is easy. Fluid.

I guess he walked away from the burning lava.

See? I knew there was a metaphor in there somewhere.

11 December

I've grown increasingly uneasy playing the blithe, mild-mannered American tourist by day, when in reality I'm chronicling a narrative of everyone I meet. A subversive, if you will. A blogging mole. And I feel like my secret is interfering with my personal connections. So today I decide to come clean to Arturo. About everything. I upload a few of my blog posts to my computer as visual aids, and walk to my lesson.

I tell Arturo that I am not just a psychologist. I'm also a writer. His eyes light up. What kind of writing? Unable to summon the word for "short story" or "fiction," I say, "Poetry." Given that I've written two poems in as many years, this isn't strictly accurate. I struggle to add that I write short stories. "*Piccoli, piccoli libri?*" Little books? "*Racconti!*" he supplies. He leans forward...*go on*. I take a breath. How to explain a blog to a man who makes copies of his handwritten assignments at the Vodafone store? I tell him that I am writing the story of our time in Spello. Pause. And right now, that story is being told in blog form. He looks at me with complacency. Yes, he affirms, he knows what a blog is. *Continue.*

So, I cautiously tell him, I've written about our lessons. But I didn't want to use his real name without his permission, so I've given him a false name. I pause to let this sink in. He smiles, and helpfully offers, "*Arturo.*" What? He already knows? Yes, he already knows. I suppose I shouldn't be surprised. It's small town Italy, after all. My face flushes in shame and awkwardness. I try to explain that I hadn't told him about it because I hadn't known how. His face stretches in a grin, and he waves away my apology. He understands. But, he adds, growing serious, he doesn't like the name Arturo. He wants me to use his real name.

Angelo.

He instructs me, "*Adesso, Arturo diventa Angelo.*" Now, Arturo becomes Angelo.

And then Angelo (as I can now joyfully call him) brings out his own book of poetry. He suggests that we work to translate his poems into English, and mine into Italian, and appears undaunted by my confession that I have a bare handful of poems. We read through one of his pieces together, discussing the importance of cadence and rhythm. Then I show him the header of my blog which quotes

Thoreau, "Only that day dawns to which we are awake." Translating the quote is daunting, but it prompts him to run to get a book on American authors from his shelf. We talk about Walden, and transcendentalism, Thoreau's beliefs that "most men lead lives of quiet desperation" and how much this thinking has influenced me.

The rest of our lesson is spent discussing writing, art, and music. He gives me a copy of his book of poetry, and writes on the flyleaf, *"Michelle, carissima amica, una poetessa e autrice."* I fear the man is way overestimating my powers of the written word. I hope he is never disabused, but maybe he'll chalk up my writing's narrow appeal to translational difficulties. Angelo tells me about all the published poets living in Spello, including Paola. In fact on Sunday he's organizing a poetry reading.

And he sends me off, telling me, *"Io preferisco Angelo."*

I assure him, I also prefer Angelo.

12 December

Like many small Italian towns, Spello is home to a tiny theater. Both locally grown and traveling performances are held on the small stage, and Doreen tells me there are movies shown during the coldest months. Keith and the children have already visited the theater for a two-person performance of Peter and the Wolf, and they raved about its charm. Gabe and Siena recently saw another show there as a field trip. They loved that performance as well, and Siena told us that during the time for audience feedback, Gabe raised his hand and asked a question in Italian. I've never been to Teatro Subasio, and so have been looking forward to tonight's middle school poetry project.

From the outside, the theater blends with the line of shops and homes. But once in, and through the lobby, the space opens into a surprisingly grand little theater. It's four stories tall, in an almost oval shape, with boxes lining the walls all the way up to the painted ceiling. The four of us fill a box on the third tier, and recline on the red velvet cushions as we admire the simple intimacy of the theater. Humble fancy, Keith calls it.

The show begins. Some of the students read poetry, with photographs of their artwork projected onto the screen behind them. Student musicians play between the readers. I'm surprised by the feeling in the students' words, and the momentum in their phrasing. The students do a marvelous job, even the boy that Nicolas confided has such severe stage fright that he appeared close to panic at the dress rehearsal. When he concludes, his classmates leap to their feet to give him a standing ovation.

Nicolas, wearing his dad's black shirt, walks onto the stage toward the end. He's played piano in front of an audience before, but not like this—where he is entering a world that's not his. And so his ease catches me off guard. He plays two songs, one a four-hands piece with another boy, and then he closes with a solo of "Jolly Old Saint Nicholas" (chosen with a conspiratorial wink by his music teacher), accompanied by ten violins. The music is better than I would have expected; two hours of violin training a week have made for some excellent string players. And Nicolas looks almost at home.

The performance over, all the *ragazzi*, teenagers, fill the stage for a photo, and now Nicolas looks uncomfortable. Take away his instrument, and it becomes a relational endeavor, and he's not sure where his place is, and his shirt sleeves constantly slide over his wrists. My heart clenches a little when I see him so on the margins, but he assures me that in these situations, such as school snack when people congregate and he is left to his own devices, are more boring than they are awkward or sad. It's still hard to watch.

The photo is taken and I see Nicolas' piano teacher approach him. I'm rooted to the spot, watching. She's speaking quickly, and Nicolas is nodding along, and answering her without pause. Nicolas has talked about how much he likes his teacher, despite her not pulling punches, but this is the first time I understand that she cares about him, too. Tonight, she tells him he was *"bravissimo."*

After an evening of music and poetry in a hideaway theater, Italy is in all of our senses, surrounding us, lifting our hearts and our joy and our connection to each other. There is a sense of vulnerability, yes, in our fragile place here, but that vulnerability is real and vibrant. It hums.

It hums like poetry.

13 December

Over pizza at L'Orlando Furioso, Nicolas tells us that he's noticed that his Italian classmates don't take things personally. One boy in his class is academically behind, and this is just part of the classroom narrative. Another friend has the nickname, "*Ciccia*," Fleshy, and he just nods along. He knows he's overweight, why bother pretending otherwise?

It reminds me of when I visited a kindergarten class years ago and witnessed a boy's rage get the better of him. The teacher spoke to him, and in an aside told me, "He's working on his anger." I wish all of our internal struggles should be so well defined and publicly sanctioned. In fact, I wish we could all have T-shirts that pronounce what we are working on. We are all working on something, or we should be, why not be candid? Buried demons create pain, insecurity, and fear of exposure. If we can say aloud what we know to be our own limitations, we can celebrate our progress together, we can humanize each other, we can feel the divine in our vulnerability.

So I ask my family, what would be on your T-shirt? Nicolas suggests that Siena's T-shirt should have a picture of this strange half-wave she does with her hand clamped against her ribcage, as though she doesn't have enough power or privilege to wave with liberty. Her laugh is initially reproachful, but she rallies and suggests that the back of her T-shirt would declare that she's working on her spaciness. I'm on board with that, I can't count the times I call the children to put on their shoes, and walk downstairs five minutes later and see her with one shoe on, and one shoe held in her hand while she gazes off into what must be a captivating world.

Nicolas offers, "My T-shirt would say, 'I'm too handsome.'" The table erupts into laughter. Okay, but really now. He confesses that he thinks his OCD tendencies are a problem. *Not* his fingernails! Those are fine! But he has a need for evenness and balance that he thinks is probably not exactly healthy. Thinking about all the times he grows cross with me when I grow cross with him, I suggest that the back of his T-shirt would read that he's working on his defensiveness. "No I'm not!" he quips. And smiles. He's actually come a long way.

My T-shirt. The front would likely be the same as Siena's. I also struggle with timidity. The back of mine is related—I'm working on my fear of failure. Just yesterday, I completely forgot to take Siena to her violin lesson, and I have been self-flagellating ever since. I'd like to say I forgot the lesson because of the show, but in reality, I forgot because my brain is turning to mush from a lack of structure and an excess of *grappa*. It's a problem. And I beat myself up for it. Past the point of comfort. Then I realized how damaging this was for Siena. I know she also struggles with a fear of making mistakes, if I call myself an idiot in her presence, what message does this send her?

So, yes, allowing myself to fail occasionally is definitely on my T-shirt.

Keith is curiously mum on what would be on his T-shirt. Nicolas suggests that being too sarcastic is his challenge. I add that I'm not sure if it's sarcasm exactly, but that thing he does when I say something like, "I'm not telling anyone else what's for dinner, I've explained it enough!" and he responds, "Oh! I have a question, what's for dinner?" It's true that I laugh every time, but sometimes there's a grumble with that giggle. Keith agrees that his sarcasm could be on his T-shirt, but points out that we wouldn't know what to do with him if he wasn't sarcastic. Meanwhile, Gabe looks around the table. "Are we going to make T-shirts?" We concur that Gabe could work on his sensitivity. "*Hey*! Wait, am I in trouble? I'm okay, right? Did someone say something bad about me? Guys?"

And now the pizza crusts are cleared from the table. And it is just you and me—what's on your T-shirt?

14 December

Earlier this week, Chiara once again charged Siena with calling her, going so far as to write the request in Siena's planner. When Siena hung up the phone, she said with a laugh that Chiara had invited her over. They would ride the school bus together to Chiara's on Thursday. Siena can hardly contain her excitement, though waking up this morning, she admits that she's equally nervous. I insist that she call us when she gets to Chiara's, and after mild protestations that calling would be perceived as weird, she agrees.

At my lesson, Angelo (Angelo!) and I translate a poem of mine into Italian. I sink into our conversation on words and cadence. I learn that there is no word for the noun "blossom" in Italian. At one point, Angelo asks that I close my eyes to listen to the way the words sound in order to choose a possible phrasing. I let myself float on the words, and then respond, opening my eyes to see him beaming at me. And then he points out that my poem is about a moment of change, and adds that I'm like a student of Emerson and Whitman. The laughter rips from my core, unbidden. I suppose this is one of the few boons of cross-cultural poetry work.

Angelo asks if I would be willing to read my poem at the Poetry Society's performance on Sunday. He would introduce me and my family, and after I read my poem in English, he would read it in Italian. He further suggests that Nicolas could play Christmas music while everyone eats *panettone*, and Keith could take pictures for me to post on my *"blog."* Or is it *"blob?"* No, no, Angelo, it's definitely *blog*.

At 1:00 Keith and I collect Gabe from school. We stand and wait for Siena, who emerges hand in hand with Chiara. They are both carried like leaves on a river, surrounded by other children, rushing toward the bus waiting in the *piazza*.

As I'm preparing lunch, Siena calls. She laughs as she reports that she'd been accosted by children on the bus. Many wanted to hand her candy, and some asked if she spoke Italian. To which Chiara scoffed and demonstrated Siena's Italian prowess by asking her questions *alla* game show format. A little overwhelming, but Siena describes the incident with bemused steadiness. She also says that she's been invited to stay for dinner, and she'd like to. We agree, a little confused by this sudden confidence.

Nicolas' friend Mario joins us for lunch. He's eager to greet us all and shake our hands. When he sees me setting the table, he picks up the silverware to distribute around the table, shaming Nicolas into helping, too. He raves about the *zuppa di farro*, the recipe Angelo and I spent a lesson on, which is just meat sauce mixed with cooked *farro* (plus enough of its cooking water to make a broth) and a splash of milk. But his biggest contribution is conversation. He makes jokes in English, casually quotes Dante, forgives our battering of his language, and easily joins in our lunchtime banter. He even shows us the book he's reading about apartheid. I think I love him.

When Keith steps out for his afternoon *espresso*, he runs into Angelo at Paola's shop. Angelo excitedly describes our lesson to Keith and Paola, and laughs retelling the part where we both got goosebumps at the same time. Keith and Angelo have worked out the details, and apparently, I'll be reading my poem at the poetry reading. Luckily, Nicolas agrees to play piano, so I'll have company on stage. But I can't help startling at the incontrovertible truth that I'm not a poet. I'll do it, because, how can I not? How can I say no to an opportunity to connect with creative townspeople in a quaint church, introduced by my Italian teacher, and supported by my family? Plus, I really like *panettone*.

16 December

It's an evening of Spellani poetry at the tiny Chiesa Santa Maria della Consolazione di Prato, built in the 15th century and since converted to a center for medieval music. The event features five poets; their poems are read aloud by members of the poetry association. Angelo then asks questions of the poet, and a discussion about the poetry follows. All of these participants are deeply familiar to each other. As an American visitor, and non-poet, with three young children in tow, I feel like an interloper.

I had expected that I would read my poem at the end, followed by Nicolas playing piano during a reception. I'm wrong on both counts. Though nowadays, being wrong is like salad after pizza. Just part of the scenery. Nicolas is on the stage in front of the packed church, and plays Christmas music between each poet's presentation. I can tell the hardest part for him is projecting rapt attention, when he would prefer looking as bored as his siblings. And these are two *very* bored siblings. Two hours of poetry discussion in English would be onerous for a child, but in Italian it's torture. They are only engaged during Nicolas' musical interludes, particularly when Angelo asks Nicolas to play "Jingle Bells," and then my *maestro* can't contain his enthusiasm and breaks out singing. In English. Within moments, the entire audience is clapping and singing along. Not excepting Gabe who leaps out of his seat to sing with *gusto*.

Paola has come to witness my debut, and seeing how fidgety Gabe is, she offers to take him for a walk. I sag with relief. She confirms that I'm not reading until the end. Yes, yes, I'll be last. She takes Gabe's hand and they sneak out. I have a moment to breathe in the freedom before Angelo calls me to the stage. I can't refuse, but I regret that Gabe and Paola aren't here. However, there's nothing I can do, so I embrace what's before me and try to let go of what is missing. Angelo introduces me, describing me as an American poet in the tradition of Hawthorne and Thoreau, joking that luckily neither of these poets is here to listen to him butcher their names. For the record, I cannot recite one line of poetry by these men. But I trust there will be no pop quiz and play along.

As I stand to Angelo's left, I have a revelation. This experience is my one opportunity to read a poem of mine aloud, to a willing audience, in a beautiful church, in an Italian village. My *one* opportunity, and I need to soak it up in its entirety. I straighten my shoulders, allow the anxiety to slip out of me, and taste the moment. Angelo guides me to the podium. I open my folder, look up at the audience. And begin:

THE CROW

A crow sits in the plum tree
Its black body an echo of the shadowy branches
That linger in white blossoms.
All at once, the crow takes flight
Loosening a fall of airy petals.
Something hard and shiny is in its beak.
I don't know what it is
But I want it back.

It is exhilarating. There's a buzz at the conclusion, which I'm guessing is audience members muttering, "Did you catch any of that? No, me neither...." Then Angelo reads the Italian translation, while I smile and look on.

IL CORVO

Un corvo siede su un albero di prugne
Il corpo nero è nell'ombra dei rami
Che indugiano in bianche efflorescenze.
All'improvviso spicca il suo volo.
Sciogliendo una pioggia di petali leggeri.
Nel becco un oggetto duro e lucente.

Non so cosa sia
Ma voglio fortemente che tutto ritorni
Lí come era prima.

When I return to my seat, Siena is jumping up and down as much as one can on a hard chair. She throws her arms around me, and it isn't until this moment that I realize what this must mean for my children.

Gabe and Paola return shortly after, disappointed to learn that they've missed my recitation. Paola asks if I will read my poem after the event, and I readily agree. That afterwards takes some time in coming. There are three more poetry presentations, then Angelo reads another lengthy poem by one of the featured poets. I've stopped listening by this point, and am just trying to keep my children as still as possible, and failing in spectacular fashion. Despite offering them five cents for every minute they sit still. Then there are closing remarks, and then a man takes the podium to offer insights into the history of the church. Which drags on so long that when it's finally over, a man bolts out the door, muttering, *"Mamma mia!"* There are even more closing remarks, in which I am thanked for bringing an international tone to the event, and Nicolas receives zealous applause, and then it's over, and everybody moves into the front room.

Once the church clears, I do my private recitation for Gabe and Paola. I mug for my small but rapt audience, and relish Gabe's laugh of appreciation at the end of the poem. I curtsy, and Paola places a congratulatory rose in my hands, while I blink back tears of astonishment.

We join the rest of the crowd for *panettone* and *spumante,* and Angelo introduces me to his friend who read *The Scarlet Letter* in college. Then we dismantle the keyboard to bring back home, and walk back through the dimming streets, giggling about how surreal the evening has been.

This concludes my first poetry reading. Which will no doubt be my last poetry reading. Thus, it will live as a cherished event in my career as a writer, and erstwhile international-tone-bringer. And while I want to linger in the memory forever, what I really want to hold dear is the dawning awareness that my anxiety has kept me from putting myself forward. But taking a risk is an opportunity to tap into my vulnerability and my strength. To feel the cadence of poetry in the proffered rose, the sideways smile, the bubbly *spumante*.

17 December

At the poetry reading, Paola introduced me to her artist friend Susan. Susan comes to Spello twice a year, and stays with the nuns at the monastery across from Santa Maria Maggiore. This morning Susan and I meet for coffee at Bar Bonci, and in the course of the conversation about why we moved to Spello, she tells me that when she was young, her mother packed her and her sisters into a Volkswagen bus and they camped through Europe for three months. Susan chronicles stories about how they ventured into countries with newly opening borders, like Romania. It was a pivotal experience for her, and in fact has influenced her art, which focuses on the experience of immigration across the Mexican border.

I'm inspired by her mother's grit. I tell Susan about how Siena recently observed that, "Brunelleschi and Galileo were great thinkers, and also rebellious in some way. I wonder if to be a great thinker, you have to break rules." Susan nods, and adds that she believes that we need boundary pushers in our midst, to show us where the boundary is.

My brain crackles, and I find myself thinking about great boundary pushers. Those determined people who have shown us the possibilities by illuminating uncharted pathways. I feel an upswell of thankfulness for those who struggled for equality among people, swimming upriver against a current of intolerance and fear. I'm holding in my heart Martin Luther King, Jr., whom Nicolas is studying at school now, and because of this he is learning the Italian words for "discrimination" and "freedom." I'm holding in my heart Quakers like John Woolman who traveled across the country urging an end to slavery, and Lucretia Mott who championed women's rights in a time when such a notion was a contradiction in terms. Both of these Friends suffered abuse by those around them, but they knew their hearts did not lead them astray when they asserted that every person holds the flame of the Divine, and is no less or more worthy of rights and privileges as anybody else. I am breathless in the face of these heroes who slid underneath the rhetoric of the day to feel something much, much greater.

And I feel this in the everyday, here in our little town. A town that could have ignored our presence but instead has embraced us. Despite the fact that we don't speak the language. Despite the fact that our children cause extra work for the school. Despite the fact that we'll be leaving after a year. They've embraced our difference and our humanity. Not in ways, perhaps, that deign them a designation of heroes in the history books, but in ways that have changed us and our understanding of what it is like to be on the other side of different. They've invited us to their New Year's dinner when they don't know us, they've given us boxes of treats through Angelo, they've complimented us on everything from our beleaguered Italian to our children's music. These gestures of kindness and solidarity can mean the world when one is outside the sphere of the expected.

It is a small boundary, perhaps. But it is a boundary. And I wonder what slight borders I can nudge to put more Light and love in the world. Because Light is stronger than darkness. Every single time.

18 December

Italy doesn't have a separation of church and state, and so the school's holiday concert is a Christmas concert, and it is held in the town's largest church, Santa Maria Maggiore. Besides being roomy enough to hold the families of the all the school's students, the church features a painting by Pinturicchio, relics of St. Felice, and a storied past—it was built in the twelfth century on what is thought to be a ruined temple to Juno and Vesta. Those ancient Romans pop up everywhere.

The concert's singers are students from the 5th and 6th grade, and the musicians are 7th and 8th graders. The concert starts at 8:45 PM, but the performers have to be there at 8:00, so I accompany Nicolas and Siena to church. Nicolas swaggers directly to the orchestra. You see, this time he's not wearing his father's too-big shirt. Instead, he's wearing a new black button-down dress shirt. What's more, he's just discovered he has the beginnings of a mustache. The child (man-child?) must never look in the mirror, because I spotted that embellishment a month ago. He's full of wild schemes for waxing it into innovative designs.

Siena and I hesitate in the doorway, until a little girl rushes to give her a hug. At which point, the teacher calls the students, and I have time to sit quietly and marvel at my surroundings. On the heels of my poetry reading, I've advised Siena and Nicolas to be fully aware of this moment. I take my own advice. I soak.

Keith and Gabe arrive as the concert is beginning. When Siena sings, her face is aglow. Nicolas looks more bored than steeped in the moment, though he lights up when goofing around with his friends. The evening is also remarkable as Nicolas' percussion debut. As there aren't enough pianos, Nicolas is assigned the triangle for one of the songs. The triangle. Keith tells Nicolas that we'll get him a "Best of the Triangle" CD for Christmas. Nicolas doesn't bother to feign amusement.

My favorite song of the evening is *Pastori e Pastorelli*. The melody, lit with childhood innocence, sweeps me into moonlit meadows. But the whole concert is rousing, and when Gabe isn't asking irrelevant questions, I really enjoy listening to the variety of music, including a Christmas song from Spain and a Hanukkah folksong.

At the close of the concert, the streets swell with parents and children returning home. We file out with the others, under the Christmas lights of Spello. Gabe stops at the door of Bar Bonci to wave furiously at Letizia, who's playing cards with friends. She waves merrily and calls out, *"Ciao, Gabriele!"* Gabe informs me that on their way to Santa Maria Maggiore, he and Keith stopped for a *espresso* and a piece of chocolate. I ask Keith if he told Letizia that they were on their way to the performance. He answers, "She already knew."

19 December

My morning Christmas shopping includes a candy spree at the Superconti. I'm sure if I lived here long enough, the stocking stuffer options in Umbria would grow as tired as those in Virginia. But this year, I pick up every item on the shelf to decipher the labels, chuckling to myself. Laden with purchases, I run into Angelo, who hails me from his brother Marcello's art shop. He tells me that tonight there's a neighborhood dinner at Il Trombone, with pizza and a Christmas party game. He and Paola think our family will enjoy it, and I readily agree. After all, Italian Christmas party games are the exact thing I've been missing that I didn't know existed.

When I pick the little ones up from school, I offer them a trip to Olive Wood to select Christmas ornaments. They each choose one, and we exit the shop just in time to see Nicolas starting his way up the hill. Gabe flies down the street into Nicolas' arms, Siena following closely behind to embrace her big brother. Nicolas wraps his arms around his siblings, then looks up at me with shining eyes.

And that, Charlie Brown, is what Christmas is all about.

During lunch, Siena tells us that for religion class, they are cutting out paper monks and paper clothes. Nicolas says that his English teacher asked him about Christmas traditions in America. He confesses that he didn't tell her about stockings. He doesn't know the word, and was worried the class would assume we fill our dirty socks with candy. Well played, young sir.

When we step into Il Trombone, the restaurant is overcrowded and boisterous. All eyes turn toward us, and I immediately empathize with microscope slide specimens. A waitress approaches us with confusion, and I'm too rattled to be comprehensible. As a consequence, she thinks we're there for dinner, not for the party. Finally, by telling her that Angelo invited us, we're able to communicate that we are, despite all outward appearances, part of the neighborhood celebration. She finally understands, but since Angelo hasn't reserved a table, there isn't room for us. She begins to set a solitary table on the elevated platform at the entry of the restaurant, next to the table piled with prizes. Thus moving my feeling of being on stage from the figurative to the literal. Luckily, Angelo and Paola arrive just as the table is being arranged. Angelo is apologetic, he hadn't known there was a need for reservations. He and Paola settle it that the seven of us will sit in the room adjacent to the dining room.

We have the room to ourselves, which allows us to hear Angelo as he describes the game *tombola*, which sounds like Italian bingo. Players receive a card, and numbers are read randomly. Whoever first gets two numbers on the same line, calls, "*Ambo!*" and gets a small prize. The game continues. The person who matches three numbers on the same line, calls, "*Terno!*" Up until a lucky participant fills the card, at which point the winner calls out, "*Tombola!*" and receives the main prize, which tonight is a painting from Marcello's shop. We wriggle with excitement as we wait for our pizza.

It's a long wait. I try to keep Nicolas from gorging on *bruschette*. A colossal task, since Angelo keeps fetching him more from the kitchen. Finally, some pizza arrives, but after a wait of another ten minutes, we're informed that that's it. No more pizza. Keith and I order pasta, and Angelo insists on sharing his pizza with

Nicolas. Soon it is 10:00, and I can't linger to find out if the pasta will arrive. Gabe and Siena are exhausted from last night's concert, and we reluctantly admit there is no way they'll be able to stay for the game.

Worse than leaving hungry is leaving hungry with Gabe crying bitterly all the way home. Rarely have I seen him this disappointed. Finally he swallows his distress, and crawls into bed, yawning audibly. I sing to them, and Siena pipes up, "I feel homesick." In this moment, my daughter does not get the supportive parent she no doubt deserves. Instead, I remind her that she has been begging for the last half hour to go to sleep, so *go to sleep*. In a tone of exasperation I either express or just think really loudly. Not a fine parenting moment. Gabe is asleep in 30 seconds.

I stay awake, waiting for Keith and Nicolas who return home at 11:30. As it turns out, they had played our *tombola* cards for us, and none of us had won a thing. It's comforting to remind myself that Gabe's disappointment at leaving pales to what we would've gotten an hour later at losing. Also, Angelo told Keith that we'll be playing *tombola* on New Year's, as we've been invited to his friends' Angelo (another Angelo! This one I met in Paola's shop) and Giuseppina's. So we will have another chance at *tombola*. Though if Gabe doesn't win something, I predict 2013 will begin with a wail of anguish.

20 December

As Keith and I enter Bar Bonci this morning, the room is filled with laughter. Letizia explains that everyone is discussing the end of the world, slated for tomorrow, according to yet another Mayan calendar. In response, I think for a moment of the future tense of "to be" and then I crack a joke, in public, in Italian. "*Se il mondo non sarà qui domani, cappuccino oggi!*" "If there will be no world tomorrow, *cappuccino* today!" Letizia guffaws, and repeats my attempt at humor to the rest of the bar, who fill the room with their laughter. Letizia says that I'm absolutely right, and since the world may not be here tomorrow, I should have extra cocoa on my cappuccino.

My work here done, I tune out while I sip my coffee. But Keith is listening intently to the conversation at the bar, and jumps in to ask about the upcoming Italian elections. Which makes Luciano, the retired gentleman who rides the *navetta* for much of the day to chat with the driver, go off on a tear. I have zero idea what he's saying, but I know he's demonstrating at least four different emphatic Italian gestures.

At 11:00, Keith and I walk to the *scuola elementare* for the *prima classe* Christmas performance. Gabe practically falls on the ground when we enter, such is the force of his smiling and waving. I'm sure he doubted we'd attend, but this time Anna Maria reminded us twice and Gabe himself has been talking about the show daily. Alessia begins the Christmas program by saying that Christmas is about more than *panettone*—news to me—it's also about love and friendship. The class then tells a story together, with each child jumping into the center to announce his or her part, accompanied by the whole class shouting lines in unison. Gabe keeps leaping in facing backward. Alessia patiently turns him around each time. His directionality may be flawed, but he recites his lines effortlessly. I'm taken aback. It's at this moment that I realize how he has risen to the expectations placed on him. To go from a home-based preschool with eight children to an elementary school of 24 Italian-speaking children in a labyrinthine ex-seminary. That can't have been easy. But here he is, surrounded by a classroom of Italian kids who have accepted him, and he's adapted.

Song finished, Gabe and a little girl stand in the middle of the circle, and the girl sings the first verse of "We Wish You a Merry Christmas" in Italian, and then the rest of the group repeats the stanza. Then Gabe sings the same verse in English, and the rest of the group joins in, singing in English. My heart hurts, it's so dear. We all clap and are instructed to move to the gym, and so we move *en masse* past the *presepe*, nativity scene, made from old textbooks, down to the basement. As we near the gym, I whisper to Keith that it smells like *panettone*. He says, "That's probably the scent of sweaty Italian children." Luckily, I'm right. There's a table loaded with various kinds of *panettone*. We sample *pandoro*, a tall *panettone* covered with powdered sugar and lacking candied fruits, and watch the children run around like maniacs. I admire the gym—its arches are left over from the building's seminary days, and glass sections of the floor allow a glimpse of the Roman ruins beneath.

Alessia instructs the children to gather against the wall. As soon as they quiet, the peal of bells rings through the space. In walks Babbo Natale. He gives each child a bag of treats to gasps of awe. From across the room, we can see Gabe's wheels turning. Turning. As we walk home, he asks if that was the real Santa Claus. I don't know, Gabe, what do you think? He mulls it over. "I don't think that was the real Santa Claus because Alessia acted like she knew him. And besides, it was daytime." I'm surprised that he didn't mention that the beard was more similar to tightly packed white Cheetos than anything found in nature.

Babbo Natale lives on.

22 December

What can a person say about Venice that hasn't already been said, a hundred different ways in a hundred different languages? Better writers than I have been inspired by Venice, prompting them to write their worst books. Why? Because Venice is too layered to capture in language. The words are trite and hackneyed before they even rise through the mind to animate the pen. Venice is elusive, it tingles the imagination with a world apart. It breathes in grandeur and breathes out improbability. It lives on the edge, between the past and the present, between real and surreal, between haunting fragile beauty and enduring vivid opulence. How can one capture such a quicksilver of a place? I can't. All I can do is feel it. Venice lives on, against the odds. It's sinking, it's overpopulated with tourists, its language is vanishing. Yet it lives on.

I think December is the city's hidden secret. The tourists are so few, you can see in a straight, unpopulated line clear across Piazza San Marco. The air is mellow. Even the pigeons are manageable—a flock rather than a horde to walk on those tourists crazy enough to feed them. The Christmas lights strung around buildings and across streets and canals make this fairytale city utterly spellbinding.

This trip to La Serenissima is marked by spellbinding moments. The lunch elevated by a customer belting opera. Airy ricotta desserts with hot chocolate to warm up from the chilly streets. The placemats with amusing Venetian sayings that we decipher with difficulty since Google Translate doesn't have an Old Venetian option. Hints of Middle Eastern spices in our linguine and clams. The morning *pandoro* in its old world paper box—the Veneto is the birthplace of this sweet, after all. Marveling at tangled radicchio that looks like it belongs with the marine wares, as the tendrils of fog weave between the arcades of the Rialto market. The opulence of Ca' Rezzonico, a *palazzo* on the Grand Canal. The surprise of realizing our Italian is coming easily, as we ask for water or directions. The cuttlefish in its own ink. The fear when we briefly lose Gabe, and just when my knees are growing weak, he appears running out of the fog, clutching one rainbow mitten to his chest.

Then there is the gondola ride as twilight swells into evening. The children are bundled together, wrapped under a blanket, leaning back with loopy grins of bliss as they gaze ahead at the lights on the water. Our gondolier regales us with stories, and wants to know how the children know Italian. We banter, and even Siena joins in, putting together sentences that surprise me. Gabe, though, takes the *pandoro*. After getting support from Nicolas on verb choice and tense, he turns around to ask, *"È divertente essere un gondoliere?"* Is it fun to be a gondolier? The gondolier comes from the back of the gondola to perch directly behind the children. He answers that he loves his work, adding that he needs the open air. Gabe sagely nods, and adds, *"Anche, essere un gondoliere è fantastico."* Also, being a gondolier is fantastic. The gondolier's laugh rebounds off the crumbling walls and still canal waters, filling the dusk with gladness. They continue their conversation, the gondolier saying that he should ask his boat builder friend to make Gabe a little gondola so he can learn to be a gondolier. Gabe asks, *"Domani?"* Tomorrow? The gondolier decides that Gabe is a *piccolo* James Bond, and that's what he calls our son for the rest of the ride.

Nicolas asks the gondolier if he's ever fallen in the water. The gondolier says he hasn't, but it's only a matter of time. He just hopes that when it happens, it's in summer. A little more chatting, and then the gondolier rises from his seated position, and resumes his gondoliering. The ensuing silence fills me—skimming through the darkened canals, past Christmas lights around Byzantine archways, accompanied by the sound of the oar dipping in and out of the water. As we approach an intersection, the gondolier's unearthly call *"Oeh!"* resounds off the ancient *palazzi* and rippling water, and we hear a muted echo. *"Oeh!"* Gabe practicing in response.

We leave the next morning, passing the Rialto Market with our rolling suitcases. I feel a magnetic pull, tugging me closer to the stalls, as I want to be part of the glory of canalside marketing once more. But at the same time, it's a strange sort of comfort to know that as I move toward the train station, the market continues. Next month, when I'm slicing unsalted bread to spread with Nutella, the market will be humming and thriving. Next year, when I am filling water bottles for soccer games, the market will be bustling with activity. Wherever I am, the Rialto Market is constant, every day. Oblivious to my small life far away, moving to a rhythm it has been scribing for generations. Venezia—forever and ever.

24 December

Christmas Eve begins with boiling an octopus. I've never had "boil an octopus" on my to-do list. The task itself is simple—stick the octopus in boiling water. But it feels bizarre hefting a creature that I've only ever seen alive at aquariums, and unceremoniously sticking it in the same pot I use for boiling pasta. After it's boiled and cooled, I chop the octopus into bite sized pieces and combine them with two yellow potatoes (boiled, cooled, peeled, and cubed), two tablespoons finely chopped red onion, two sliced celery stalks, extra fabulous olive oil, a pinch of dried oregano, salt and pepper. While the flavors marry, I try to figure out how to make Christmas cookies. Our Spello kitchen boasts a postage-stamp-sized oven, but the greater issue is that of loft—I can't find anything with names that translate to "baking powder" or "baking soda." So, no leavening. And I don't have beaters, so the critical first step of creaming butter and sugar is impossible. I'm not buff enough to whip air into my batter with a wooden spoon, no matter how filled I am with Christmas spirit.

I look through recipe after recipe, ruling out each one because of ingredients I can't find or don't understand. I am so tired of feeling stupid. Finally I opt to make what is essentially tart crust with the addition of ground hazelnuts and orange zest. I suppose I should feel victorious, but instead I feel sort of vanquished. Then I taste the broth for our Christmas day *tortellini in brodo*, and shudder. I've over-salted it. The only sensible thing to do seems to be to have a meltdown. Stretched thin with too many tasks, missing my standing mixer and tidy boxes of leavener, I'm all too hollow and fragile.

Keith doesn't mock my total lack of self-control, and instead scoots me out of the kitchen telling me that he'll dip the cookies in chocolate. I find my center with a few minutes on the *terrazza* looking out over the Umbrian valley. Stepping away, I realize how little salt and leavener matter. Calmer now, and ready, we all leave for an evening *passeggiata*. Being out in town and connecting with both place and people completes the restoration of my equilibrium. This makes sense, after all, the highlight of my day thus far has been a trip to the bakery. I had listened and smiled as a customer and the baker discussed Babbo Natale and La Befana, the Italian Christmas witch who visits children at the Epiphany. And when I ordered my customary *filetta*, the baker asked me if I'd rather have a *fillone*, since they'll be closed Christmas and the day after. I opted for the larger loaf and left feeling pleased that I'm known enough in town now to merit a kindly reminder.

I felt the same yesterday when Keith returned from shopping for the holidays, with an extra bottle of wine from the butcher. An *"omaggio,"* gift, which they gave to their regular customers. He said that before he was handed the wine, the butcher looked around, to make sure the room only contained other regulars. Keith told me more stories of the easy banter while shopping yesterday, like the *nonna* at the fishmonger who assured Keith that a frozen octopus is actually preferable for octopus salad. Shopping is fodder for conversation here. Connecting is the main objective to most transactions. And so moving our holiday to the street drastically increases my merriment.

As we walk through town to hand out cookies, we see *presepi*, nativity scenes, in little alcoves and spread out in open garages. Some look like a Middle Eastern Dickens village, and one is modeled after Spello. We deliver cookies to Angelo who hands us a box with a *pandoro* and a bottle of *prosecco*. We give bags of cookies to the alley ladies chatting and enjoying the unseasonably warm weather. We stop by Paola's shop and give her cookies and holiday hugs. And, as all good *passeggiate* do, this one ends with a trip to Vinosofia. The children play "mutant checkers" while Keith and I enjoy a glass of *prosecco* with Brenda and Graziano. We chat about Venice, Christmas, and family traditions. I feel warm and bubbly and quite Christmas-y. Vinosofia is the only place we hear Christmas music. It's hard to leave, particularly with Brenda topping off our glasses. When we finally say goodbye, she hands us a bag with two beautiful Vinosofia wine glasses. A bit of Spello to bring home.

Filled with the animating cheer of the streets, we return to put together our feast of the seven fishes. Initially, I was overwhelmed by making seven fish dishes, but that's before I knew that landlocked Umbrians cheat. Like Graziano's family, we have packaged smoked salmon and swordfish as two of our dishes. And one of our "fishes" is a *crostata alla marmellata* with peach jam, as an homage to our inability to keep peaches and fish straight. Our courses are small, in deference to the number of them, but we all take seconds and thirds of the octopus salad and the tiny clams bursting with sweet, briny flavor.

Satiated and a little drowsy, we begin opening presents while nibbling the *crostata alla marmellata*. It's too sweet, but the day has been rich and I'm full of octopus and good feeling, so I can't bother caring. Siena gives Gabe a stuffed *cinghiale* with a scarf she knitted. We give Siena a *presepe* of her own. Gabe gives Nicolas a Nutella cookbook. For Keith, a wine decanter from Vinosofia. For me, *grappa* glasses. The children don't tuck in until past 11:00. So we yawn wearily as we fill stockings. And finally we turn in, under a Christmas star.

25 December

Gabe wakes us up to tell us he heard bells in the night. Bewildering, but par for the course. We used to run around the house with sleigh bells in the night, but the kids never heard them. So we stopped. Since then, invariably, at least one child wakes to bells. Turns out, imagined sleigh bells are more resonant than actual ones.

We venture downstairs, and the children discover their Santa gifts. Gabe and Siena each receive a simple digital camera and Nicolas thrills to his first cellphone. I haven't wanted to give him a phone because I place a value on boredom, and phones impede one's ability to stay open and receptive, but he's fourteen, and it's time.

We all linger over stocking opening, and then the Christmas presents are over. Usually we have friends and family gifts to open well into lunchtime, but this year we've asked everyone for a year off. At dinner, Nicolas and Siena express surprise that they feel perfectly satisfied with having the whole day to tinker, read, and play. In fact, they predict that it will make the Christmas denouement less anticlimactic. Now they have time to make even more movies of the cats cleaning themselves.

26 December

We received a letter in the mail today. It was from Gabe, sent by the school.

> *Cari Genitori,*
>
> *Per questo Natale, vi ho scritto la mia prima lettera! Voglio dirvi che vi amo un mondo!*
>
> *Io sto sempre molto bene con voi!*
>
> *Io vi amo.*
>
> > *Vostro figlio,*
> > *Gabriele.*

Dear Parents,

For this Christmas I wrote you my first letter! I want to tell you that I love you the world!

I am always very well with you!

I love you.

> Your son,
> Gabriel.

27 December

Spellani are looking at us differently. Five months ago, their eyes slid over us. Three months ago, they looked at us with frank curiosity, "Are you still here?" Last month, they nodded and smiled, we were about as interesting as new potted plants in the alley. And now? Now we are stopped for conversation. Last week, an alley lady stopped me to ask *"Ti piace Spello?"* Do you like Spello? It took me a minute to understand, even though *"ti piace"* is right out of the first page of an Italian language book. I was too thrown by her stopping to talk to me, with an expectant smile. I took a breath to formulate my words, and she leapt in with a concerned look, do I hate it? No, no! I love Spello! I love it so much! She nodded, adding, confidingly, that it's a steep town. I agreed, but suggested that the exercise is good for legs. She repeated this with her eyes rapt, and walked away chortling.

Oh, no. I hope I didn't say shrimp instead of legs.

A few days later, I was stopped by another alley lady who informed me she hadn't seen me in awhile. Had I been inside? Once again ill prepared, I had to ask, "*Come, scusi?*" so she would repeat herself while I listened more carefully. I told her that we'd gone to Venice, and she nodded. *Sì*, she thought we'd been gone. She hadn't seen our lights on.

Then, yesterday, Keith and I stepped out for a cup of coffee, leaving the children home playing Legos. What is usually a ten minute break took much longer. Marcello stopped us by calling "Obama!" and then running into his shop. He brought out our plate from the cookies we'd delivered on Christmas Eve. And then he asked questions about how our food had turned out, where we had celebrated, how the kids enjoyed it, if we'd seen Angelo today? I told him that I accidentally over-salted my broth, and his face fell. We commiserated about how frustrating that can be. Keith asked how Marcello's Christmas was, and he talked about his son's visit and dreamily remembered his *agnolotti* in capon broth. I bet its salinity was perfect. We waved goodbye, and then had a similar conversation with Letizia, who also wanted to know our plans for New Year's Eve. We told her we're going to Angelo's friend's house for New Year's, for a *cenone*, a big dinner. She wasn't surprised, *cenone* are quite routine for New Year's Eve.

These moments of interaction have made me realize both how bad I am at small talk and also how much that skill matters in small town Italy. Small talk is a marker, a hum, of Spellani street life. I'll need to brush up on phrases I can fashion for any situation. Like, "*A posto?*" Literally, this means "in place," but I hear it all the time from waiters coming to check on our meal, to neighbors calling to each other. Is everything in place? Yes, yes. Everything is in place.

28 December

Warm sunny weather in December is cause for celebration. Not *pandoro* and *spumante* celebration perhaps, but the everyday kind. Like a stroll to the park, with a stop at the *rosticceria* for a slice of pizza. Once their feet hit the playground, the kids fling off sweaters and unfold limbs that have been hunched into indoor shapes.

In the evening, Keith and I take Siena to hear medieval music at Sant'Andrea chapel, while the boys stay home and watch a movie in Italian. They both attended the same performance with their classes, but fifth grade hadn't. We leave a little early for the concert so we can stop into Vinosofia and say hello to Brenda. When we walk in, we see Doreen, home from London! We linger over glasses of wine with our friends, Siena contributing to the conversation with an ease she sometimes finds hard to muster when she's with her brothers. Brenda tops us off with an extra splash of wine, claiming that it will make the concert more enjoyable.

The church resembles an architectural tapestry—every inch of the walls and ceiling is painted. The ancient music matches the walls, full of curlicue instruments and zigzag tempos. My favorite songs are reminiscent of the olive oil festival, when the men gathered to sing spontaneously created lyrics that seemed bawdy given the amount of guffawing. The curious music fills the curious chapel, and it is magnificent. Yes, that extra splash of wine probably helps, but so do a friend's return and the grace that warm weather brings.

29 December

For months, we've been hearing that we must meet Barbara and Mario when they next visit from their home in Virginia, but when our buzzer rings this morning, I'm unprepared to meet with an accent both familiar and now strange. Barbara whirls in, her thin blond hair coming loose from the myriad clips scattered around her head. In a rush, she tells us that she and her husband return to Spello whenever Southern Virginia University, where she is an art professor, is on break. Barbara entreats us to come to her cocktail party in the afternoon. We don't need convincing.

I make *arancini* for the party, and carry a tray of the fried rice balls through the street to Barbara and Mario's house. Barbara throws open the door and jokes that in America, our homes are 100 kilometers apart, and here they are 100 meters. We enter the house and hug like fast friends. She introduces us to her husband and shows us around the house, which she says was once the servant's quarters of an old *palazzo*.

The party is spirited, a mix of people we know—Paola, Doreen, Angelo—and many we don't, mostly Italians from the neighborhood. Barbara tells me that she met these neighbors years ago, when she joined their *Infiorata* group. Though the Italians don't speak any English, and Barbara's Italian is limited, they communicate without hiccup to tell us about *L'Infiorata,* an annual holiday when townspeople gather to make carpets out of flowers on the street. Riccardo declares that we will join his *Infiorata* group, *Pochi, ma Buoni.* The group's name seems to mean "The Few, but Good," which makes bystanders laugh when they hear it. A man reminds Riccardo that our children will be participating in the *Infiorata* through school, but Riccardo waves this away. It is nothing compared to his group. Barbara agrees. She says though it can be difficult to arrive early enough in the summer to participate, they haven't missed a year. I can't imagine Riccardo will actually remember this invitation, but I'm flattered that he thought to include us in what seems to be a point of civic pride. In any case, I look forward to seeing the town in a bustle of flower-carpet making.

With more than a little satisfaction, I watch the Italians devour the *arancini*— had I really made them? I confess to Angelo that I had tried to form them smaller than baseball size but just couldn't. Paola assures me that these are the size of typical *arancini*, and Angelo retorts that he can make them much smaller. *Davvero?* How? Easy, he smiles. He demonstrates by taking theatrical bites with an impish grin. Silly Angelo.

I realize that it's not that the Christmas season is shorter in Italy, it just starts later and doesn't end until the Epiphany on January 6, when La Befana arrives. It's a celebratory season. And we have something new to celebrate—Gabe just lost his first tooth.

30 December

Siena concludes her midmorning trip to the bathroom with a sigh of contentment. She flops on my bed, looking up at the ceiling with a smile playing about her lips. I look over the top of my Kindle. Seeing my curiosity, she sighs again and says it's nice to use the bathroom in the morning. This is not helping my confusion, and at this point, I'm wondering if I really want to know. With a shiver of distaste, Siena tells me that the bathroom at school is a simple hole in the floor. She would prefer to hold it thank-you-very-much. Ah, this explains her daily rush to go the bathroom when she gets home from school.

It's odd that every day I'll ask the children about their day, and they'll say it was regular, which seems a statistical improbability. But now that they are on holiday, I'm hearing about all these oddball details. I can't fathom why this is the first I've heard that the *scuola elementare* has squat-and-aim toilets. And just the other day, Nicolas told me that teachers periodically ask students to run down to the lobby and fetch them a cup of *espresso* from the machine there. Siena laughed, adding that along with the euro the teacher will give explicit directions for their desired additions, like milk, cream, or a jot of ginseng.

When Gabe wants to play soccer at the park but lacks a ball, Siena suggests that they use a water bottle. I look at her quizzically. She explains that at recess, there isn't any playground equipment, so the kids hunt for a used water bottle and play with that. I wonder if one of these water-bottle soccer players will find their way to the soccer world stage. Nicolas speculates that hill towns make for great soccer players—all that calf exercise. In any case, Siena's recess story reminds me that children without handheld devices really can make their own fun.

What teens do for fun remains to be seen. Nicolas just got an email inviting him to a girl's party. Using Angelo's gesture, I ask Nicolas if the girl is "*bella.*" He blushes faintly, and says yes, but then, that is true for all the girls in his class. I ask why he thinks that is, and he shrugs, and informs me, "It's just part of the Italian condition." Apparently, one of his classmates asked him if Italian or American girls were prettier. Nicolas answered, "Italian" to much cheering from his friends. I ask Nicolas, "Did you also tell him that you had no girls in your class back home?"

31 December

Happy New Year! Cue the fireworks! Shake the *tombola* tiles! Raise a glass of bubbly! If it's true that the way one rings in the new year is how one will spend the coming 12 months, then I'm going to be about 30 pounds heavier when 2014 rolls around. And I'm going to spend an entire year saying *ano*, anus, when I mean *anno*, year.

Our evening festivities begin with a small party at Vinosofia. The champagne flows freely, and it's delightful to have Brenda in arm's reach. Since the shop is closed, she swaps roles with Gabe who has been begging to get behind the bar. He smugly doles out bread that he has authoritatively buttered himself. Graziano places an apron over Gabe's head and ties it securely, the final feather in his *cappello*. Thus initiated into the wine bar staff, my son is instructed by Graziano on how to uncork a bottle. Francesca, the artist with a shop by the *piazza*, calls to him *"Sente il tappo!"* and he obediently smells the cork like any professional sommelier. Brenda pours us champagne while we luxuriate in caviar, smoked salmon, and bread spread with creamy French butter and topped with velvety, briny anchovies. To his bewildered joy, Brenda hands Nicolas, my slightly mustachioed son, a quarter glass of champagne to join in the toast, while the little ones loft grape juice from Montefalco. A *cin! Auguri!* to the new year, and it is hard to believe there is still more celebrating to come.

Ten minutes after kissing everyone goodbye, we present ourselves at the door of Angelo's friends, Giuseppina and Angelo. Two Angelos can get confusing, so we call this Angelo "Sicilian Angelo" in deference to his birthplace, which we're repeatedly told we must visit. Giuseppina is the author of the *cotiche* recipe that won me local acclaim, and at my Italian lesson weeks ago, Angelo told me that she was probably already planning and preparing for tonight. He says that when it comes to cooking, Giuseppina is *brava*. Before we can knock on the door, Sicilian Angelo throws it open, laughing as if we've arrived at the moment of his favorite punchline. This is pretty much Sicilian Angelo all the time. Every time I've seen him since we met in Paola's shop, his eyes are creased with laughing, and I can't stop smiling in response to his effortless jubilance. I'm glad he's stopped calling me, *"Cotiche."* Giuseppina emerges from the aromatic kitchen to clasp our hands and kiss our cheeks. Gabe makes everything easy by being charming and chatty. Paola and Angelo enter soon afterwards.

As soon as we are all assembled, Giuseppina directs us to the table, already set in anticipation of our *cenone,* with pitchers of a neighbor's fruity red wine and bottles of *prosecco* and a flowery Sicilian white all marching down the center of the table. Giuseppina begins immediately, by handing us each a plate of *antipasti*, so complicated and varied that Nicolas tells me that he can see why this is called a *cenone*, what a filling meal! With so many delicious tastes—octopus salad, smoked salmon, shrimp wrapped in prosciutto, *chouquette* filled with tuna purée and an olive, and truffle-sized balls of ricotta and green onion rolled in chopped hazelnuts. Everything made by Giuseppina, down to the mayonnaise and the brioche. No wonder Giuseppina plans far in advance. And no wonder Sicilian Angelo is such a happy man.

Nicolas sits back, satisfied. And then looks up confused when Giuseppina brings out bowls of homemade pasta in cream sauce with baby shrimp and flecks of zucchini. It is then that he realizes that that was the *antipasto*, not the meal. Sicilian Angelo pours him a glass of *prosecco* and continues his story of leaving for France as a teenager to work in the mines, where he met Giuseppina at a May Day celebration. She is originally from Spello but had moved to France as a toddler.

Giuseppina distributes glass goblets of lemon *sorbetto* doused in *prosecco*, and we sigh at the refreshing end of our meal. Until Giuseppina returns from the kitchen with a platter of unbelievably light eggplant parmesan. This time both Angelos laugh at our surprise that the meal is still continuing. Our Angelo still chuckling, Sicilian Angelo goes on to say that it was working in the mines, and seeing how workers were treated as machines, that turned him toward communism. Growing up, I was taught that communism was a dirty word, for reasons that have never entirely made sense to me, and so I watch with interest as everyone nods along. Turns out, the whole table is filled with communists.

When Giuseppina passes a platter of lamb and turkey, we try to squelch our bewildered expressions. And the bewilderment grows when we're served bowls of Umbria's standard New Year dish of lentil soup with locally raised *zampone*, seasoned ground pork, stuffed in a pig's leg. Each lentil is perfectly tender and intact, in savory and clean broth, with earthy undertones thanks to the *zampone*. We eat as many lentils as we can hold—since each lentil represents money, according to Italian tradition. Unfortunately, I can't manage half my bowl. But who needs wealth, when we have such blessings?

Earlier, I had peeked in the kitchen and saw a waiting platter of meringues. So when the soup bowls are cleared, I'm glad that the dessert will be light. I was right about their lightness—each one perfectly swirled and faintly tinged with vanilla (the secret, Giuseppina offers, is vanilla sugar). But I'm wrong about that being dessert, as the meringues are followed by cannoli. The shells were made by Giuseppina days ago, and then filled this morning with airy ricotta filling. Oh, they are incredible. Wow—a perfect end to the meal. But then comes the *semifreddo*, layered with chocolate and cognac-soaked raisins. We burst out laughing when we see Giuseppina carrying it to the table. Three desserts? Unbelievable.

And then she nonchalantly carries in a chocolate mousse.

How can this woman look so calm and serene, with her sparkling eyes and sprinkling of French in her sentences, when she must not have slept for a week? I decide I want to be Giuseppina when I grow up. I bet Giuseppina never wastes too much time on the internet.

Four hours after we sat down to dinner, we clear our plates and fill our glasses for the countdown. The children are thrilled to have their own goblets to participate like grown-up Italians, as we count down from ten to *Buon Anno! Auguri!* The popping of the fireworks impels us *en masse* to the garden, where we watch the *fuochi artificiali* up and down the dark folds of ancient hills. Sicilian Angelo tries his first English word of the evening, pronouncing the show "beautiful!" and takes a small, almost-serious bow when we applaud him. According to the others, the fireworks are less spectacular than previous years—the economic crisis hits in unexpected, though not illogical, places. But to us, it is a wonder.

Back inside for *tombola*, which our Angelo captains. I can barely keep my eyes open enough to follow the Italian numbers, to Nicolas' disgust as I confuse fours and eights. But each of our family wins a round. Thankfully, there are no prizes, as Nicolas, who shouts *tombola*, would have won the grand prize, and our depleted Gabe would have lost it. Angelo prepares for round two, but we bow out. During our goodbyes, Sicilian Angelo realizes that Keith has inadvertently put on *maestro* Angelo's coat. There's a mad search for Angelo's hat and scarf to complete the look, and Keith walks and gestures like our Angelo. A simple thing, perhaps, but at 1:30 in the morning, even algebra is hilarious. Giuseppina presses a bag of meringues and a tray of cannoli into our hands, and we leave with Paola. I barely remember the walk home, such is my haze.

I send a wish for a happy new year, out into the universe. That all those within the reach of my words will feel their manifold blessings. Those blessings are the center of everything. And so I raise my glass and hope that this new year dawns a little more centered, a little more peaceful, and a little more kind. *Buon Anno!*

Arancini

leftover simple risotto

about a cup of *ragú*

about a cup of fresh mozzarella, in small dice

two eggs, whisked

breadcrumbs or panko

frying oil

• ✳ •

1. Oil your hands to keep the risotto from sticking. Take a spoonful of risotto and place in one hand, forming it into a cup shape.

2. Place a teaspoon of *ragú* in the cup, then a few cubes of mozzarella.

3. Take a bit of risotto to top the cup, pinching the seams together and rolling it to create a uniform ball.

4. Heat oil until the tip of a wooden spoon inserted into the oil bubbles.

5. Roll each risotto ball in egg, then breadcrumbs.

6. Fry until golden brown on all sides. Watch the heat. If they fry too quickly, the mozzarella inside won't have a chance to melt.

7. These make great party food, because you can serve them at room temperature. And they are a food that looks like good fortune on a plate.

JANUARY

BRAVE. BRAVO. BRAVA.

1 January

My sleep is fitful after the *cenone* that was really three *cenoni*. When my eyes sluggishly open, I have only one breakfast on my mind—a meringue, a *caffè*, and two Advil. There's a concert at Teatro Subasio of the Spello Philharmonic at 5:00 PM, but the children and I are too listless to think about venturing out. So Keith goes with Doreen. The music was rich, and he knew many of the orchestra members. The baker was playing the French horn—Doreen didn't recognize him, and Keith told her that was probably because he was wearing pants. Siena's history teacher was playing the baritone. Gabe's friend's father, who works at the bank that wouldn't give us an account because I suppose we are some sort of international risk, played the trumpet. These people spend their days at their jobs baking and teaching and banking, then create music together in the evenings. There is a commitment to artistic expression in Spello that constantly surprises me. Since I can't imagine that more raw talent exists here than it does at home, I suppose that people appreciate poetry and music and painting more, and so there is support and avenues for practice and performance.

After Keith returns, the children and I put on pants and follow Doreen to Francesca and Alessandro's house for "just a *bruschette* dinner." We enjoy our crab lasagna followed by a *piccante* pasta, and sausage cooked on the fire, and then something indescribable. I ask Alessandro, who tells me that it's pork. When I look down at my plate with incredulity, Alessandro laughs and goes on that it's the part of the pig used for *capocollo*—the cured meat that is my favorite at the *macelleria*, for its silky texture and almost grassy tones. Sliced fresh, this was marinated overnight with garlic and salt, and then grilled and drizzled with Alessandro's family's new olive oil...eye-rollingly tender and delicious. We eat at the long table, with their friends bantering Italian on either side of us, as the 800-year old-olive trees continue to grow outside the door.

3 January

The city of Gubbio lies north of Spello. It was once inhabited by Romans, who built a theater and mausoleum that still stand, though the town is more well known for its record-breaking giant Christmas tree of lights. I'm picturing a wooden tree form covered in lights dominating a *piazza*, but something about this image seems wrong, so I'm not sure what to expect.

Our visit begins oddly, and only grows odder as the day progresses. The first oddity is a traffic light. Italy loves its roundabouts, and we've grown accustomed to constant flow. I wonder if traffic lights contribute to American road rage. After the long wait for traffic to proceed through the intersection, I continue to feel strange, and realize that the landscape is peculiar after the gentle greenness of Umbria. These hills resemble shrunken mountains, brown and prickly and severe. Plus, as we begin walking through Gubbio, I notice that it feels shadowy. Walking along the base of the *palazzo*, with its cavernous arches, a dark, almost foreboding breeze twists through me. There is beauty here, but it is a moody beauty. On one of our walks, we pass a plaque with a quote by Hermann Hess that describes Gubbio as "disquieting." I think that part of that disquiet comes from the curious doors. The old houses have a door at street level, and then an extra door, narrow and a foot or two higher. Some say that it was for carrying out the dead. Some say it was an easy door to defend if strangers came midnight calling. It is a little unsettling to be surrounded by doors with no known purpose.

We walk to the Roman theater, situated next to a playground, and the children swing, toes pointed toward the crumbling ruin. More wandering, around the Palazzo dei Consoli to an expansive *piazza* overlooking the valley, marked with intricate ironwork. I look around for a Christmas tree, but there isn't even a small specimen, let alone one worthy of record books. Maybe they take it down after Christmas. We take an elevator up to a street higher on the hill to a church with more than one rotting saint. I don't understand the fascination for saint remains. Staring at decomposing bodies does nothing to heighten my spiritual enlightenment. It just makes me queasy.

As we search for the funicular to the top of the mountain, we pass a crane, ubiquitous in these towns that seem perennially under renovation. I confess aloud that I fear the funicular will be like the crane—a basket for people, with an arm that swings patrons up the mountain. We laugh at my silliness. After all, a funicular is a tram. Right? *Right?* As it happens, my fearful imaginings were dreamy compared to reality. Gubbio's funicular is a series of birdcages shooting people up the mountain on ropes the width of Siena's embroidery thread. My palms start sweating. It occurs to me that no one in the world knows we are in Gubbio.

Boarding the lift is panic inducing. Actually the panic begins just watching Keith and Gabe scuffle to clamor aboard their cage. Then Siena races to the first orange dot, and I move to the second. When the green steel basket swings around from its descent, Siena leaps in, and then I leap in, and the attendant shuts the carriage gate behind me with a clang both final and flimsy. I shakily turn around to make sure Nicolas boards successfully and then inch my body straight to focus on gripping the sides of the cage. The ride is harrowing, particularly when the basket bounces over transitions at the towers. I imagine the little hook that holds us popping clean off the cable, sending us to our demise. At one point, we seem to stop, and I'm afraid we'll never get off, or worse, slide backward. When we exit, safe and mostly sound, my children's proud hugs warm me. I look back and am doubtful I can manage the ride down without serious *grappa*.

We walk along the windy ridge of the mountain and enter a grand cathedral which houses three gigantic octagonal wooden pedestals, each topped with a statue of a saint. Apparently, once a year, these are lofted by burly costumed men and raced up the hill for what passes for a sporting event in Gubbio. The church is also notable for a centrally placed and well-lit glass casket with the remains of Gubbio's own Saint Ubaldo. A sign informs us that he was originally interred in the normal fashion, then exhumed at his canonization and found to be uncorrupted. I am here to say, he is plenty corrupted now. Gross.

The chilly twilight forces us to stop stalling and return to the funicular station. After clarifying with Keith that Gabe did not make the cage swing erratically, I agree to ride with my littlest. But actually, the ride down is much more pleasant than anticipated—like flying at sunset.

We reward our bravery in the face of mostly imagined peril with hot drinks all around. And then back through Gubbio, now bright with illuminated stars strung across the darkened street. We also notice colored lights dotting the mountain, but it's not until we drive away that we see that all those lights form the shape of a giant Christmas tree, stretched across the surface of the mountain. On the highway, we see flashes of light in the cars ahead, as passengers try to capture Gubbio's claim to modern fame.

4 January

The gentle sun calls me into the groves. Nicolas has gone to Mario's, and Keith needs to call the consulate in Los Angeles to get a document required for his citizenship application, but Gabe and Siena cheerfully join me. We leave the cobblestones behind to set out on a dirt road through the trees. In the course of conversation, we talk about New Year's resolutions. I suggest to Siena that since her shyness dismays her, perhaps she can make some small, observable goals in this area—after all, shyness is my problem, too. Which is why one of my resolutions is to speak in Italian every day. My daughter is not best pleased at this conversation. As I can tell she's beginning to prickle, I aim to keep it light. Unfortunately, I stumble on the dismount and she runs off, crying.

Once she allows me to hug her, she confesses that she thinks of shyness as a disease, that there is something terribly wrong with her. So the fact that she is not easy or comfortable is emblematic of her dysfunction. And she *can't* be Italian. And it's too *hard* to try. And she *hates* talking about her faults. And it feels like I don't *love* her.

Well, this is a bony and malodorous kettle of fish.

I hold her and assure her that my love for her is endless. She quiets, and I add that she's not expected to be Italian. I am concerned, though, that if she defines herself as shy, she'll stop trying to engage with her life here. The reason I suggested a small goal was so she could practice stretching and begin to see herself differently. Much like I'm trying to prod myself out of my own patterns of camouflaging against Spello's stone walls. I want her to see that shyness isn't a disfiguring mantle she wears, it's a way she feels under specific circumstances, and that it is flexible. For instance, she feels shy at school which is natural, but as she's grown comfortable with Chiara she's less shy with her. The shyness isn't black or white, and she can start wading into the gray when she's ready.

She grows thoughtful and stops crying, and I close my eyes in relief. As she wraps her ams around my waist, I think about how my own shyness has shifted over the years. My memories of childhood and adolescence are scarred by a belief that I was not as good as everyone else. Not pretty enough, not gifted enough, not worldly enough, not talented enough. And certainly not socially skilled enough. I was chronically uncomfortable, and spoke hurriedly so I could get my entire thought out before the person I was talking to lost interest. Going to college and learning to make friends with people who didn't have preconceived notions of me helped, but it was probably Keith that triggered the turnaround in my insecurity. I couldn't understand it, but he thought I was fantastic. And seeing myself through his eyes increased my confidence. Then came other experiences that changed my self-perception—backpacking through Europe on my own, which cemented a sense of self-sufficiency; becoming a therapist, which forced me to practice and grow comfortable talking to people in authentic ways; having children, which filled me with a love that changed me. By the time we left for Italy, I thought of myself as more introverted than shy. I don't like parties and I don't like meeting people and I like my alone time, but my world had grown so comfortable that I could float through it without triggering my insecurity. But when it comes to devising unsettling situations, Italy pulls out all the stops. The composure I once counted on has proved to be illusory. In fact, five months in, and I still can't walk into the *negozio* without feeling like it's the seventh grade dance all over again—everyone knows and likes each other, and I'm this odd little specimen hiding in the corner. Wearing all the wrong clothes and saying all the wrong things.

I can't stand the thought of my daughter similarly riddled with insecurity. Part of me knows I should back off and let her figure it out. But part of me feels like I need to bully her into seeing herself without the blinders of self-doubt. As I watch her and Gabe collect flowers to make fairy houses in the olive orchards, I fervently hope she holds onto the message that shyness is a flexible construct, and that she learns to see and appreciate the beauty of her spirit. While I'm wishing, I notice that she's frozen in a hunched over position. My heart skips a beat as I rush toward her, sure that she's having a seizure. But then I see that her face is silently wailing, and she holds out a small blue viola. To my questioning expression—I thought she liked violas?—she gasps, "It's a flower I used to find at home."

I wish Siena's points of grief could come one at a time. Struggling with feeling shy is hard enough, but add in homesickness, and it is overwhelming. I'm powerless, and that makes me ache for her, but also angry at myself for not protecting her. Sometimes the obvious right thing to say seems just around the corner if I can just push my thoughts forward, and sometimes all I have is the darkness of my own inadequacy. Right now, it's the latter. I simply feel like at some level I've failed her. Maybe if we'd never come, she wouldn't be struggling and falling and doubting. Without words, I look into her tear-filled eyes and wish I could take some piece of this away for her.

Gabe breaks the still tautness of the moment, "If the flower makes you homesick, you should just let it go." He shrugs his shoulders and shakes his head while raising his hands, repeating, "If it's making you sad, and it's not helping you, just toss it over your shoulder and walk away." Siena smiles faintly, wipes away her tears, and takes my hand. Gabe takes my other hand, and we begin walking home. After a few minutes, Siena muses that she'd like to meditate more. She thinks that will help her homesickness. And then she laughs that she's spent so much of the walk in tears.

I smile, but really I can't help but wonder what she did with that small blue viola.

5 *January*

Before Italy had Babbo Natale, children waited for La Befana, the Christmas witch. She was outside sweeping when three wise men, lost (really lost if they were in Italy), asked for directions. Intent on her work, she shooed them away. After they left, she noticed the star, and realized where those travelers were heading. Feeling terrible, she hopped on her broom to try to find the wise men, to have them give Jesus a present. She never found them. Now, every Epiphany, she flies throughout Italy bringing candy to children, treats she'd wanted to deliver to Jesus. There are as many variants to this story as there are Italian dialects. The darkest one tells that La Befana was mother to a child that died, and she went mad with grief. When Jesus was born, she sought him out, under the delusion that he was her child. By the time she found him and gave him gifts, he was no longer a baby, and graced La Befana with the designation of mother to every child (which I suppose means that every child in Italy has a mother who is a crazy witch). In any case, as a Quaker, I like the idea that in La Befana's quest to find Jesus, she delivers treats to every child, acknowledging the Light of God in every human.

Somehow, La Befana finds us on our overnight trip to Lucca. The children wake up to shoes overflowing with treats. Yes, tomorrow, school is starting, but for now, we begin the day with magically delivered chocolate before breakfast.

6 January

I hate waking children the morning after break. They are stones in a river of slumber that I have to push out of the water with brute strength. Of which I have none, since I'm groggy myself. I hate having to say goodbye to them, all at once. Sure, it gets on my nerves when they make forts in the hallway and create art that leaves shreds of cardboard and clay scraps all over the floor. Still, I love having them home. Particularly since Gabe and Siena, despite their periodic bouts of squabbling, have discovered that they actually make good companions. They have spent much of this break orchestrating a show, which included drawing tickets, rehearsing, and making props.

So after two weeks of day trips and Legos and reading piled like puppies on the bed, the spoiled five year old within me contorts her face into an unhandsome scowl and shrieks, "More! More!" A morning walk through the fog to the *forno*, feeling the mellow resonance of Spello's pink stones and seeing both bakers in underpants, helps. By the time we're eating breakfast, I feel relatively peaceful. Until Siena realizes she hasn't started her Italian homework. *Dejá vu.* We race around unsuccessfully trying to find her worksheet. I try walking her through the worst case scenario—her Italian teacher asking her to pay more attention to her assignments. I'm sure Siena can handle that. But she doesn't believe me. She walks into school, eyes still wet with tears.

The day is better than expected. She didn't have Italian, as her teacher was absent, so instead she had religion with the rest of the class and spent an hour coloring pictures of the Virgin Mary in different poses. Besides that reprieve, she reports, her posture tall, that in math she successfully demonstrated a problem on the board. This isn't new, except that this was a *word problem*. Nicolas chimes in with his success of the day—he'd asked a friend to repeat himself, and realized it was the first time in a long time that he hadn't understood someone. Not to be outdone, Gabe said that he spoke *and thought* in Italian all day.

Seeing all three of them so proud of their level of mastery on their individual trajectories made the sting of losing them all day more bearable. If I have to say goodbye to them for five hour stretches each day, at least I can know they are gaining something valuable that I can't give them. A sense of their own power in the world. I know I am too apt to take over and make everything easy for them, to catch their elbows before they fall. But I'm beginning to wonder... does this prevent them from learning to get back up on their own?

7 January

To our intense displeasure, Keith and I discover that our butcher is closed for holiday. We try the other *macelleria*, but it smells funny—not "ha-ha" funny, but "*eeeew*" funny. Though I guess there is no "ha-ha" funny when it comes to butcher smells. And so we walk to the fish market. We decide to go out on a culinary limb and buy whole fish. I find the prospect intimidating, but our calamari victory has emboldened me, and we purchase two *orate* for €12. I only wish that our experience with calamari would have taught me that seafood in Italy isn't sold sanitized.

It doesn't occur to us until the afternoon. Wait, the fish is *cleaned*...isn't it? Keith checks... Nope. Alarmed, I plead with him to check again, maybe they pull the innards out in a creative way. To placate me, Keith investigates more closely before announcing that these fish had all the parts they were born with. Gills, scales, guts. All of it. Oh...no.

When Doreen stops by for a cup of coffee, I offer her the opportunity to gut a fish, but she bizarrely declines. We work on a puzzle together, but then she skedaddles when the five o'clock bells chime. She claims she needs to pick up supplies to make Paola dinner, as Paola is feeling under the weather, but I know better. She beat it out of here like a woman about to be asked to wield a butcher knife against a hapless whole fish.

I summon my courage and search for how-to videos, which has become our usual mode of preparing for cooking nowadays. I watch several intrepid chefs gut grouper, trout, some nameless large fish, and feel gradually more and more queasy. Plus, I get a cramp in my face from grimacing and cringing. Any cooking step that involves blood clots is really not the cooking I like to do. Pig skin was bad enough. But this? This isn't just gross in the "I know what this is, and my mind is making my taste buds shrink." No, this is a horror movie on my cutting board.

The work begins as all dismembering of sea creatures should begin, with Keith offering me a cocktail. Make mine a double...knife skills be damned. Hurry up with that *negroni* before I lose my nerve. Then begins the scaling. This is surprisingly meditative. *Scrape, scrape, scrape...*little clear scales gather on the side of the knife. Rinse, *scrape scrape scrape*. The children watch in awe. Their chance comes on fish two. *Scrape scrape scrape*. Nicolas dashes out of the kitchen, hand clutched over his mouth, but the younger two dive into descaling their fish. Siena studiously experiments until she finds a way to increase the tension on the fish by pulling the tail as she scrapes toward the head.

The next step is complicated by the fact that no video chefs gutted *orate* specifically, so I can't tell which fish gutting technique is appropriate. Plus, people who gut fish on YouTube have incomprehensible accents. And thrill to the job with an exuberance that is unbecoming for a task that involves trying not to puncture a bile sac. So I do the best I can. I use kitchen scissors to make a cut under the chin of the fish (incidentally, do fish have chins?), then dig around, and pull out the gills. This is just about as gross as it sounds. But really not as bad as the next step, which includes making a cut from the anus (fish do have anuses, I am surprised to learn, though I suppose that makes sense) to the chin, lifting the side of the fish, recoiling in horror at the variety of brown curly entrails, and then sweeping it out, face pinched in disgust. Ta-da! And also, *ew*.

But now I have two, home-cleaned fish. And that is kind of neat. In a "when life gives you lemons, gut a fish and stick them inside" sort of way. Which is what I do, along with chives, olive oil, and salt. I lay our little friends on a bed of peeled and sliced yellow potatoes, tossed with leeks, rosemary and more olive oil and salt, and then drizzled the—I must say beautiful—platter with olive oil and white wine. In to bake, and a half hour later, I pull the dish out of the oven. The fish is delicately delicious, and the potatoes have a nuanced, bright flavor.

Keith must have had the *orate* on his mind when he does the next day's shopping. As I'm unpacking groceries from the reusable bags, I'm surprised to find a *baccalà*. I hold the dried salt cod out to Keith quizzically and he shrugs that he thought he'd pick it up just in case. *Baccalà* is popular in Italy, especially around the holidays, but I've never made it, so Keith's "picking one up just in case" is the equivalent of bringing home a tub of chicken livers, just in case one feels inspired to make *paté*. But once I get over the shock of holding a piece of fish as stiff as a plank, I'm game. I stick the fish in water. The nice thing about *baccalà* is that since it takes so long to reconstitute, you have days to figure out how in the world you are going to prepare it.

I decide on fried *baccalà* balls...because in my opinion, just about everything is palatable when fried. They are astoundingly good. So good that we've added them to our next Christmas Eve menu, no matter how many fish we are having. Provided we can find *baccalà* at home. I serve them with mayonnaise mixed with smoked paprika. But they'd be otherworldly with a honey aioli.

Massacring marine animals and frying balls of reconstituted fish. Yep, that's what I do. Hand me my *negroni*, won't you?

10 January

In the wake of the fish hacking, I have a conversation with Siena about bravery. Because she not only threw herself into the task of ripping out organs, she also asked to taste the fish cheeks. She's not a particularly squeamish child, blood doesn't bother her. Blood bothers me. The fear that I might see blood bothers me. Talking about the possibility of blood bothers me. I am just that delicate. But not my daughter. Calamari on the cutting board? She wants to yank out its beak and pull out the ink sac. Whole fish in the sink? She wants to scrape off the scales and inspect the gills, to get a sense of the their texture ("feathery," according to Siena).

So her comfort in wielding a knife wasn't necessarily surprising, but because she has a history of rejecting meat that is remotely odd, I was startled by her request to taste a fish cheek. I had been similarly startled when we had lunch in Lucca and she asked for a bite of Nicolas' beef tongue. I tell her that I've noticed how much more adventurous she is lately, and she brushes me off. She says that since she's hesitant, she's not really brave. Nicolas, who is irrepressibly eager to try culinary oddities, is the brave one.

No, no! I smile. Getting ready to hit her with a whopper of an idea, I tell her being brave doesn't mean not being scared. Being brave means being scared and doing it anyway. She smiles right back. And tells me that I'm dead wrong. Because in all the books she reads, the brave character is never scared. Okay, I tell her, but that's fiction, not real life. In real life, if you have two people jumping out of an airplane, and Susie is excited to jump out of a plane and jumps out with no problem, while Mildred is scared and pushes herself to jump out, it doesn't mean that Susie is braver. It means Susie is sensation-seeking. She is not realistic about the dangers. If she were, she'd be scared. So it's Mildred who is brave.

Siena will have none of it. She insists Susie is the brave one. I'm reminded of my lesson with Angelo earlier this week. He told me that in World War II, his family hid two Italian government resisters who were fighting against Mussolini. Right there in the house where I was sitting. It was scary, he said, but they felt they had to do it. Does the fact that they were scared mean they were brave? I think so. I'm reminded that on that trip to Lucca, the children were playing a tag game in yet another *piazza,* and Siena noticed a little Asian girl watching. The child was standing in between her parents who were weighed down by cameras and guide-books. Siena paused and considered the girl, and then ran over to ask her to play. Turns out, for Siena, compassion overrides shyness.

So does bravery mean initially being scared, but having other feelings triumph? Like loyalty, compassion, love, justice, adventure? I offer Siena another example. This morning, Gabe skipped into school, as he usually does, with a laughing wave. Keith and I went for coffee, and on the way back up the hill, we saw a boy from his class standing in the road weeping while his mom cajoled him to enter the school. Assuming he did go into school, who was braver—Gabe (who went in with enthusiasm) or the boy (who had to muster his courage)? While the story makes Siena's chin quiver, she maintains her line. They are both brave. Gabe may have been braver, since the boy might have been dragged in against his will.

Curious. I hadn't thought about Gabe as brave. To me, he is just a boy in love with his life and in love with people. Tonight, we had Paola and Doreen over, and he was excited all day. When they arrived for our impromptu dinner party, he told them "*Tu sei qua, tu sei qua, e io sono qui.*" You are here, you are here, and I am here—plopping between them. He is so vivid and engaged, he hurdles across obstacles. He asks the wait staff in every restaurant we visit where the bathroom is—even if he's been there before—just for the fun of asking in Italian. Is that bravery? Or is that something else? Does the fact that he goes into school so willingly speak to his bravery? Or his openness? Or are those connected concepts? Does being scared and doing it anyway actually mean that you are open to accessing emotions other than fear?

I have been using this example in therapy for 15 years. I've never been challenged. Who knew Siena would be the upstart to complicate my conception of bravery. One thing is for sure, I think it's time for her to read books with more complicated heroes. Perhaps the child needs a little Katniss.

11 January

I'm still mulling the concept of bravery. Perhaps between Siena's belief and mine lies a firmer truth. Maybe brave is rising to a challenge. No matter how easy it looks to an outside observer.

It's not an irrelevant consideration, as we've impulsively decided to go skiing for a week. Keith loves skiing. Nicolas loves skiing. Siena loves skiing. Gabe loves the ski lift, which at his age probably amounts to the same thing. I don't love skiing. I hate being hot and cold at the same time. I hate the feeling of slipping. And I really, really hate the panic-inducing sensation of dangling from the sky by a thread (I see you, Gubbio funicular). I also lack any sort of grace or coordination that would make skiing enjoyable. I have childhood memories of repeatedly falling when trying to extricate myself from ski lifts. Followed by fifteen minutes of untangling my skis, while I tried not to cry. As an adult, I've skied only once. That trip was notable for Keith skiing behind me and shouting, "Tips!" as my skis kept crossing and sending me sprawling across the ice crusted snow. I doubt my athleticism has improved.

I was never tempted to try skiing again until Keith took Siena skiing in West Virginia, and they came home glowing with stories of tranquilly gliding past pines. I had always imagined skiing as racing down a barren, slushy mountain with 1,500 other people. I hadn't pictured quiet, with dappled light and the smell of trees.

That whispers to me. Besides, in order for the trip to work, I'll need to ski. I can take lessons with Gabe while the rest of them whiz down black diamond slopes (even Siena, my child who tells me she's not brave), and then take him back to the house while the rest of them stay on the mountain.

So we are leaving tomorrow for the Dolomiti. We found a house in Moena to rent cheaply, and since we'll have a kitchen, it won't be much more expensive than being home. I'm trying to wrap my mind around the fact that we are going, really going. Tomorrow. The gauntlet is thrown. I'm scared, but it's time for me to put on my big girl snow boots. It's on. Wish me luck.

I'm pretty sure I'll need it.

13 January

I fight valiantly to think positive thoughts on our drive to San Pellegrino, rental skis secured in the trunk, chains on the tires. But the dread keeps rising. Keith gets Gabe and me ready, and we meet Stefano for our lesson, while the rest of the family hastens to the ski lift with goofy grins of anticipation plastered across their faces. Gabe had insisted he wanted an English-speaking instructor, but as it turns out, he speaks almost exclusively in Italian to Stefano. In Gabe's world, they form a deep and instant bond, and Gabe asks that I take a photo of him *con Stefano.*

We begin at the training ground, where I am surprised my body remembers what to do. Stefano tells me it's like riding a bike. I don't tell him that I find bike riding fearsome too. Instead, I allow myself to be distracted by the stunning beauty of the Alps, stretching high above me. I enjoy the gentle swish, swish of skiing down the mild incline. Meditative and barely thrilling. As we move to the slopes, Stefano tells me that he is from Moena, and when he's not ski instructing, he's leading naturalist hikes in the Alps, or biking tours of Tuscany. I later relay this to Keith who retorts, "Jerk." It is, in fact, Keith's dream existence. Imagining I could ski, and replacing biking with goat herding, I'd sign up, too.

Off the training ground, the slope is serene. The path takes us over a bridge, where we watch a horse-drawn sleigh glide into the distance, and then ski beside a rippling stream, bright within its snowy banks. The run includes only one slope of any difficulty. Stefano attaches a spacer to Gabe's skis and takes him down, then *runs* back up the hill on his skis to guide me down. All is fine until we reach the lift. Lift alert! I swallow my fear and realize that lifts are now only terrifying when it comes to my children. I can trust myself to stay vigilant and ramrod straight, clutching the side of the lift, skis properly placed. But I'm not convinced that my kids won't impulsively lunge like zombies in search of brains, and consequently tumble headlong into the yawning stretch of ice below.

After completing that run again, we move to the disk lift. Much less user-friendly (though less panic inducing), it's a plastic disk on a pole, with a stretchy cable connecting it to an overhead line. You get in place, the man hands you the disk, you put it between your legs with the disk behind you, and let the disk pull you up the hill. Stefano is very clear that I must not sit on the disk. I will be tempted, but I *must not sit.* Easy breezy. I will not sit. Except that I sit, and immediately the cable releases all the way down and I'm on my rear, trying to scramble back up. I crawl off the path, terrified of someone crashing into me from behind. I needn't have worried, the disk distributer knows better than to let anyone else on while I'm flopping like a landed fish.

The next time I don't sit. We allow the lift to scoot us halfway up the hill, and then Stefano exits the lift by easily skiing to the side with Gabe held in front of him. I follow with considerably less grace. This run is steeper, and scarier, but still pretty fabulous. I enjoy a few more runs, then excuse myself, as my legs are growing quivery. Gabe most definitely does *not* want to take a break, so he and Stefano continue. Keith and the big kids come swooping down the slope with admirable elegance, and when they see me leap up to greet them with a smile, they rush toward me eagerly. Gabe and I have had a blast, and we are now officially a family of skiers.

14 January

Day two of skiing and the snow feels different. It's actively falling, which doesn't bother Gabe, who is improving with every run, but I find it harder to stay in control. The feeling of spinning out of control is my ninth circle of hell. I fall. A *lot.* With each fall, I grow more unnerved. At the end of our lesson, Gabe stumbles on the disk lift, and in my trying to exit the lift before I careen into his little body stretched on the snow, I let go of the disk, timing it so it doesn't hit Gabe. Only I don't count on the disk dipping before rising, and it hammers him on his helmet with an audible thwack. He pauses, ducks his head and starts to wail. Stefano swoops in to carry him off the path, and I hobble to my baby, and pull him close while he sobs. And I sob, beside myself with guilt and the sickening sound of the disk hitting his helmet stuck on replay. We finally make it down the hill, me visibly shaking.

After lunch, I reluctantly agree to allow Keith to take me skiing. A well-placed reluctance, as that run is not only a low point in the trip, it is a low point in our marriage. Keith says we'll take the disk lift to the top of the hill. I mutter that I never want to touch the disk lift again but then chide myself that it will be okay. We get on the lift, but Keith exits to the right, not the left as I had with Stefano. All the same mountain, I would've guessed the runs would be roughly equivalent. I would have guessed wrong. This run looks terrifying. Like a roller coaster dive. Keith insists it's fine, I can do this. I don't believe him, though I can't really answer him when he asks what I'm scared of. Death seems melodramatic, but also kind of accurate. Only later do we find out that the run is designated red, one notch shy of a black diamond. I had been sticking to the baby runs. And those demarcations matter.

I wipeout, quickly and surely. That's fine, I can handle a fall. But then I crash again. And again. Each time the hill looks steeper. I don't see how I can make it down, and I grow worried about my children, waiting for us on their own at the bottom of the mountain. Keith assures me that the children are fine and tries to give me instruction, but all his words seem irrelevant. He might as well be telling me how to sail. He moves toward straight support, telling me, "Your body knows what to do, but your body is getting in the way." This also seems irrelevant, and in my wobbly state, feels downright insulting. On my next fall, my fragile resources snap. Imagine the most high-strung toddler in the circle of your acquaintance. The kind that falls apart when you cut her banana in half, and spends twenty minutes sobbing on the floor trying to put the banana back together. Now imagine that that person is actually a grown woman in ski clothes bulky and tight after six months of living on pasta and unsalted bread with Nutella. Make sure you include much pounding of snow with furious fists and tears that freeze instantly and you are pretty close to the disaster on the mountain of San Pellegrino. I yell at the mountain and I yell at myself, but I save my best yelling for Keith. For taking me on a difficult run when I insisted on needing to feel competent. Keith keeps his cool, no mean feat. Finally, he asks, "Do you want to walk down the hill, while I carry your skis?"

Yes, as a matter of fact I do. I gather the scraps of my pride, fleeing like marbles on a slanted floor, and I walk until the slope gentles. Then I put my skis back on, and I fall another time or two. But because I know I can handle the slope, the falls are more inconvenient than a sign of imminent doom. I swoop down the final incline, and the children run toward me, wondering why it's taken so long. I hedge. And send them off so they can ski once more with Keith.

My anger with Keith melts with the snow on my boots, leaving me feeling ashamed of my outburst(s). I still think he should have listened to me, but I know he believes that I could do it and that I was my own obstacle. As is common in our history, he trusts me more than I trust myself. Without fear obscuring my vision, I can see that my husband was trying to facilitate my seeing how strong I actually am. I remembered his insistence that I was much improved from 20 years ago. Once we reached the bottom of the mountain, he'd requested that I look up and see that the slope I descended with relative ease was actually not much different than the one I walked. I wouldn't acknowledge it. He wanted me to take pride that I made it down the mountain, I refused. It felt better to be mad.

In retrospect, it would have been wise to just to walk down the mountain as soon as I realized that trying to ski down it involved not a stretch of my tender abilities, but instead a snap of my sanity. I wish I had rejected the mountain, rather than being ripped bare by it. If I had, I wouldn't now be struggling to reconcile my outpouring of panicked anger. I try to forget it. I try to justify it. But, it's too deeply humiliating to wave away. I like to think of myself as capable. A tantrum on the mountain doesn't fit with that narrative.

Early evening finds me bundled on our porch while Siena paints the view. My eyes drift up to the towering peaks. It occurs to me how small I am. Truly, very small. My highs and lows will pass unrecognized, not even a flutter in the space of the existence of these mountains. I'm human, no more, no less. I have human frailties and human weaknesses. And that's my narrative. Feels pretty good, actually. For me, and for Keith and me. After being so exposed on the mountain, I am more vulnerable with him. I'm able to tell him that I need him to accept where I feel weak, rather than always spinning it to see my strength. I don't need to be fixed so much as held where I am. And he's able to tell me how much he wants me to believe in myself. I can't yet say that the tenderness we're sharing was worth the pain of the stormy outrage on the mountain, but it does put it in perspective.

15 January

It's the last day of my three-day ski rental. After a night of never wanting to ski again, I really want to slide down those slopes once more with the Alps soaring above me. To say goodbye to the Alps with a smile on my face. A migraine, unasked for but perhaps not surprising, stymies my desire, with its persistent throbbing. We decide to go to a different side of San Pellegrino. I'll sit quietly in the café while Keith takes the kids skiing. He'll check on me after an hour, and if I feel better, I'll join them. And if I don't, I'll take the ski bus back with Gabe.

I have a cup of *biancospino* tea that's described as being good for stress. I will myself to feel better. When Keith and Gabe arrive, their cheeks flushed with cold, my head feels only marginally improved, but I can't refuse Gabe's request for one more run together. So we all go up the disk lift and gather at the top of the mountain. Siena chatters about how nice it will be to ski with her Mommy before she promptly takes off, with only her snow dust as a reminder of her company. Nicolas, ever the nervous old lady, follows hard on her heels, keeping her in his sights. Keith, Gabe, and I tip our toes over the mountain. At first I'm distracted, watching Gabe's little body zip around as if he's being controlled remotely. And then I fall. I get up quickly and with a smile. Keith, despite my protest that I can manage on my own, stays with me and calls down to Gabe, "Do five turns, and then stop." A minute later, we realize Gabe is shooting down the hill like a bullet. Keith muses, "I bet he thought I meant 'Do five turns and then stop *turning*' rather than 'stop *skiing.*'" This is precisely what happens. Our Gabe has skiing in his blood now. "My legs just want to *ski!*" he keeps insisting. I'm glad the big kids are at the bottom of the hill to receive him, as he reaches the base considerably before me. I only fall once more, and then, listening to Keith's instructions, vary the arc of my turns as the terrain shifts, ending with shorter turns and more speed.

And a big grin.

I did it.

I smile up at the mountains. They couldn't care less. But I'm human, and I care. More skiing is impossible, since the adrenaline sends my migraine into full tilt and my pounding head and nausea compromise even my ability to shepherd Gabe home. I feel grateful that Gabe is, despite his outrage that his skiing was done, patient and gentle with me all day.

Skiing no longer looms as a thing I tell myself I don't like. If I can take it slow, I'd like to continue to learn. My children had dazzling experiences, driving home the point that skiing is about the flying, sure, but it also gives you access to places that a shivering pedestrian can't go. I love their stories as they come home every day high on arresting natural beauty and unbelievable runs, thrilled and exhausted as only an adventurous day in the outdoors can bring. I've dusted the snow off, and now I can see—skiing is actually amazing. As long as I do it my way. Slow and steady. And mindful of the power of the mountain.

17 January

Moena doesn't even seem possible. Huddled deep in a valley framed by Alps that break the surface of the azure sky, it combines the free spirit of Italy with Austrian sensibilities to realize a village both vital and whimsical. The architecture is alpine, stirring thoughts of roaring fires and creamy hot chocolate and woolen slippers embroidered with reindeer. And the lights—lights on all the buildings, lights around giant Christmas trees, lights in shop windows decorated with gnomes and mushrooms and felted birds with ski hats. To round out the charm, there are festive flourishes in every possible space. From an antique carved sleigh, hitched to beautiful wooden reindeer, to a besprinkling of realistically-painted forest animals in a pocket park. And, our favorite, wooden structures erected in the river with water gushing from the top. As the water freezes, it creates a stunning array of icicles. Because it relies on organic processes, the ice towers change constantly.

Our apartment is a five-minute walk up the hill from the center of Moena, and I never fail to catch my breath as the main *piazza* opens up in front of me. In the day, without snow, when I can really appreciate the clean lines of the architecture and the buildings painted with elegance and charm. In the day, *with* snow, when a white blanket softens the blunt edges and the town seems sprung from a dreamer's vision of the quintessential winter village. At night, when the lights twinkle against the deep velvet of the sky, the Alps around are felt more than seen, and the village is trimmed with lights.

Despite the heavy tourist action, the shopkeepers are friendly. Primarily because of Gabe. I walk into the *macelleria*, and the butcher is polite. But then Gabe speaks, and all heads swivel. How does your son speak Italian? And then there is dialogue. I'm surprised by how routinely this scene replays, and then I realize that the places we frequent in Spello are used to us, and our language progression is under their watchful eyes. But in Moena, we're novel. We are Americans working to communicate in Italian, rather than the usual tourists from Germany and Russia.

Gastronomically, Moena is a fascinating area. This is dairy country, and there is much cheese. Beautiful, ripened, stinky, barny cheese. Moena actually has a cheese named after it: *Puzzone di Moena*, which literally translates to "the big stinker of Moena." It is pungent with a round creaminess and a mellow paste. And so achingly strong that although we store it in a sealed bag, in a closed drawer of the refrigerator, every time we open the fridge Nicolas shouts out from across the apartment in dismay. We also discover speck, which we've had before, but not like this. Here, it is cured meat nirvana. It's salty like excellent *prosciutto*, but with a faint smoky flavor and a juniper greenness. We eat a lot of speck in Moena. Speck on pizza, speck on pasta, speck on bread with pickles. Speck speck speck speck speck. Another surprise is the beautiful pastries. The *cornetti* are much closer to croissants, buttery and rich. Strudel figures in every restaurant and bakery, and in fact, apples are everywhere. Particularly apple fritters, which I find a way to delight in almost daily. Sometimes with an apple *aperitivo*, tart apple juice mixed with *prosecco*.

Gabe and I had three-day ski passes, so we spend a lot of time in Moena. We gather *würstel*, sauerkraut, and smoked pork chops to make warming dinners for the rest of the family, who grow lyrical in their descriptions of not only the alpine skiing, but also restaurants at the top of the mountains serving *pappardelle* with deer, pork wrapped in speck, and Black Forest cake—with a 360 degree view of the Alps no less. I'm unable to sample any of those wonders, though at the little ski café at the baby slopes, I did sample sandwiches with locally sourced ingredients like sausage and pickles and fondue-like melted cheese with grilled field mushrooms. On our last night, we feast together in Moena. For me, polenta with wood mushrooms and a slice of cheese grilled to melty decadence. Nicolas, who has grown fond of game, praises his *spaetzle* with deer *ragù*. Keith's alpine country dish of *pappardelle* with speck, arugula, and parmesan is delicately warming, and Siena and Gabe have pizza. Siena's is covered with *puzzone* and chanterelles.

It will be a struggle to leave. It's revitalizing to be in nature. And nothing says nature like Alps in your backyard. Those peaks wreathed in clouds are a constant reminder of the power and vividness that is our world. Plus, I delight in the creek that tumbles by our house, chattering. And the trees on the surrounding banks dip their limbs into the swirling waters, and became entwined with brilliant snow. If only I can figure out how to strap a container of *puzzone* to the top of our car, it will be a little easier to tear myself away.

19 January

Confession: I am a small, insecure person. And despite my professed disregard for people who grate on my nerves, I secretly want every single person to like me. (This is all leading to something. Treat it with delicacy, it's not used to being outside. It's used to being shoved into a hidden crevice where I can try to ignore it. Or, as Gabe says, *ingore* it.)

But first, some background. Given our living in Italy, I've formed some opinions about travel in Umbria. Opinions I've been sharing on TripAdvisor. I've been contributing mostly with suggestions, sometimes with a link to my blog. Knowing that some websites frown upon posters linking to their blogs, I read TripAdvisor's guidelines carefully, and understood that as long as there weren't any links to advertisements, it was fine. I also poked around previous threads and found many links to blogs. So I felt secure in posting mine, and even more so when I received positive feedback from forum members.

Now I find that all my posts on TripAdvisor containing links to my blog have been removed. In their place is a notice from TripAdvisor that the post was deleted because it was inappropriate. It's the internet version of a public shaming.

But I can't imagine that with the 20 Italy forum questions that are posted every 90 seconds, a TripAdvisor employee would have the time to read all the threads looking for where contributors posted to a blog. And besides, immediately after my removed posts are other responses linking to responders' own blogs—those are still standing. And then I realize. Someone has systematically reported all of my posts as inappropriate. Someone out there who doesn't like me, or doesn't like my blog, or doesn't like me posting my blog.

I've gone back and forth on how to re-right my tipped equilibrium. I've tried telling myself not to let the actions of one mean person make me feel less than myself. I tried telling myself that maybe what I did was wrong, and so it's okay to accept that I made a mistake and didn't read the guidelines properly. Clearly, the fact that no one else was "caught" has nothing to do with my error. Nothing really works. Then I remember what I have been telling Siena. She was playing basketball in PE, when she got "out," and joined the group of children climbing up a pole. The PE teacher looked over when Siena happened to be climbing the pole and yelled at her. Siena felt so terrible, she cried as she told the story. She had done her best, observing others to figure out the rules, but her strategy didn't work this time. It was painful enough for her that she started to resist going to school the next day. Afraid the teacher would see her as a troublemaker and would single her out. I cajoled her to go, and it was fine.

But now it makes me think that perhaps when we protect ourselves from the needling discomfort of small-minded people, we wind up losing our ability to tolerate their jabs. It's like snake phobics. The way to cure snake phobia is to encourage the phobic person to get close to the idea of snakes, then closer to actual snakes, until they are holding a snake, and have mastered the anxiety by realizing the anxiety is just anxiety. It swells, and then it dips, and then it's gone. I am holding out hope that this year helps Siena learn to approach the snake of imperfection.

The savvy will notice what I did there. Started talking about my daughter instead of me. It's just so much easier.

In any case, this is clearly my work, too. When I think someone is angry with me, disappointed in me, or just plain can't stand me, my own self-concept rocks. I lose all sense of my center, and my inner Light becomes damp and hazy. My mind keeps returning to "why?" and "how can I make it better?" When the underlying truth is actually easier to bear. There is a person out there who just doesn't like their perception of me. And in their dislike, they have created a difficult space. My power lies in what I do next. This is my work. To increase my comfort level with being found wanting, knowing that I'm never going to please everyone.

How much time and energy am I going to expend trying?

22 January

Siena and I talk about the trauma with her *ginnastica* teacher. We talk about it, process it, and move on. But it turns out, that was a loose "we," because Siena most definitely did not move on. Only I have been blissfully unaware. On Tuesday, when I realized that since it was Tuesday and so there was a 50% chance of having *ginnastica* (January, and I'm still unclear on the schedule), I reminded Siena to wear *ginnastica* appropriate pants. She refused. Instead, she stood there just shaking her head at me. She was sure the teacher will hold a grudge against her. I tell her that that's not how teachers operate. Though I really should resign myself to the truth that I'm no authority on probable teacher behaviors in Italy. When that doesn't work, I tell her that if she isn't ready to go to school when we are, she'll have more trouble than the *ginnastica* teacher. Let the hate mail begin—all I can say is that when faced by the prospect of sudden school refusal, all my positive parenting flies out the window. She goes to school.

While I can almost forgive myself for my parenting fail in the face of her sudden resistance, I cannot forgive myself for being so stupid as to not follow up with her fully before the next possible *ginnastica* day. I had this coming. And it's bad. When it's time for school, Siena starts shuddering, telling me it's impossible. Last time she resisted, but it turned out she didn't have *ginnastica*, so now she will, and she just can't face that teacher. Somehow we convince her to put on her shoes and walk to school. But once outside the door, she locks her feet and won't move. I send Gabe in without her. And now my panic is matching hers. She has to go to school. I can't let her stay home because she's scared of her *ginnastica* teacher. Then I'd have to keep her home two days a week. She needs to go in and face her fear and get over it. We have a stand-off. I say, "You need to go to school." And she answers, "No! I won't!" I grit my teeth and repeat myself. She grits hers harder and repeats herself. I can't think of what to do, and in a fit of exasperation, I toss her backpack to her feet. We both stare aghast at that backpack. My tender daughter looks up at me, stricken. Wordlessly, she picks up her backpack and turns into school, biting her lip to keep from crying. I instantly see my behavior in the context of her pain and I'm furious at myself. I reach out and grab her hand to turn her back to me. I murmur words meant to be comforting and supportive, but I can see in her eyes that in the face of my actions, my words don't matter. She blinks back tears, ducks her head, and silently walks into school.

I walk to Angelo's and spend much of the lesson sniffling as I tell him what happened. So much has evened out, it surprises me that these moments still send my mind wondering about the feasibility of getting us home. He sympathizes, and we talk a little about the teacher and how to help Siena. Then he asks, *"Che fa Siena a casa oggi?"* What is Siena doing in the house? I sniffle and answer, sort of confused, *"Lei non sta a casa, è andata alla scuola."* Oh, she's not home, she went to school. And Angelo breathes a huge sigh of relief.

He tells me that an Italian mother would have kept her child home, comforting her with *caramelle*. I tell him that I wouldn't want to reinforce a message that a child was unable to manage. I want Siena to believe that she's strong enough for anything. Angelo smiles knowingly, and tells me that this sentiment is uniquely American. Americans believe they can overcome any obstacle. Whereas the Mediterranean way is to shrug and give up. *"Boh."* He uses my recent *gnocchi* experience as an example. *Gnocchi al Sagrantino,* a local dish with a wine-laced cream sauce, has become a family favorite. We order it whenever we see it on menus, so I decided I wanted to learn to make it myself. The first time I made it, the taste was amazing, but the texture was off. The second time I made it, the texture was right, but the flavor wasn't there. While we were eating it, I told my family, you better be okay with eating it again next week because I'm going to master this dish no matter what. He laughs that an Italian would have said, "You want *gnocchi*? You better go to a restaurant, because I'm not making it!"

As a former teacher, Angelo says that kids often refuse school. And when their parents keep them home, children become *"furbo,"* clever like a fox. I admit that I actually did want to keep Siena home and baby her. He assures me that this is because part of me is her *mamma* and part of me is her *maestra*. The *mamma* part wants to hold her close when she is in pain, the teacher wants her to strengthen her muscles. To learn to let other people's words go in one ear and out the other (so they have this expression in Italian, too). Because when she gets to university or has a job, she will undoubtedly run into mean people, and she needs to learn to learn to put an *ombrella* up in the rain.

I'm on pins and needles at dismissal. My heart catches when she flies into my arms. Once home I put her in my lap, big as she is. She apologizes for her resistance, and tells me it was the right thing to do to make her go to school. She admits that when I tossed her backpack, it made her feel alone. I apologize, saying that the gesture came out of reaching a mental impasse. It was wrong, and I feel terrible. She forgives me. It'll take much longer to forgive myself.

Siena says that though they didn't have *ginnastica*, the difficult morning and the fear of having *ginnastica* had been exhausting. We settle on a plan. Siena agrees that she needs to go to school, so she's just going to do it. But she's not going to like being yelled at by teachers, and she'll feel tenuous about going on *ginnastica* days. Deal. I assure her that any day that includes being yelled at by a teacher will also include copious amounts of loving attention when she gets home. I know that she needs time to recover from these threatening experiences. My fervent wish, formed while she is giggling, practicing the dismissive Italian hand gesture she'll do in her head the next time a teacher snipes, is that this makes her confident in her strength. That from this place of vulnerability in the face of others' negative perceptions of her, she'll discover wings she never knew she had.

23 January

I have received many gifts in my life. But not until today have I received a gift of snails. A pot of snails made by Marcello's wife, delivered to us by Angelo, whose mouth is watering as he instructs me on reheating and serving *lumache*. I learn more than strictly necessary about where snails store their poop. He brings us his snail forks, rolled in a paper towel, asserting that while toothpicks are serviceable, snail forks make it feel like a *festa*. He admits that he filched a snail from the pot and ate it cold. He is downright hyper, but grows serious as he insists that if we don't like them, no problem. But with his descriptions of sauce sopped up with bread and lots of red wine and a mess that sounds reminiscent of crab parties, I really want to like them. Marcello really wants us to like them, too. He stops Nicolas ("*Obambino!*") on the street to ask if he knows about the pot of *lumache*, and reverentially praises snails in his zero personal space way that we've grown fond of.

At dinner time, despite Siena and Gabe taking turns insisting they are absolutely not eating snails, then relenting, then re-insisting, I put the pot of snails on to heat, per Angelo's explicit instructions. The sauce smells sweet and rich. Nicolas says the aroma reminds him of graham crackers. Which is true, and mildly disconcerting. Snails, to my mind, don't go with much besides garlic. Certainly not graham crackers. We sit down, check to make sure bread and wine are in place, and begin.

Gabe is the first to dive in. He initially pronounces the *lumache* de-*li*-cious, but after his second snail he decides they are really kind of gross. Siena put hers on a piece of bread sandwich style, and then eats all the bread around the snail until the bread disintegrates and she's left with a cold, crumb-covered snail. I give her a fresh, hot replacement. She falters, and swallows it seemingly without chewing, shivers in distaste, and chases it with her tablespoon of wine. She announces that she could eat snails the French way, but not the Italian way. I don't know how she can come to that conclusion, having eaten neither before, but I secretly agree. I need my mind altered to overcome the instinctive repellent reaction. Altered by vast amounts of *grappa* or toxic levels of buttery garlic. One or the other. Preferably both.

But I try, I really do. So does Nicolas. We eat them with and without their tails. We eat big ones and small ones. We eat them fresh out of the shell and on bread. And we decide we just don't like them. Our minds are never able to forget the image of slick snails with their antennae pulsing in and out as they leave trails of mucus. Springing them from their shells is hardly helpful—there is far too clear of a view of innards that should really stay innards. Plus, they taste sort of liver-y. Keith's end of the table is quiet, so I look toward him. He chews one slowly and thoughtfully. And another. And another. With growing wonder and delight. He remarks, smacking his lips, that each one tastes different. "One tastes like grass, another like meat, another like clams, and another like…like," he pauses to find the right words. "Like a Wint-O-Green Life Saver."

Really, Keith? A Wint-O-Green Life Saver?

"Yes." He stands by his declaration. "A Wint-O-Green Life Saver."

Looks like he'll be invited to the snail party. As for me, I have to figure out how in the world I'm going to look at Angelo's eager face and tell him that for four of us, well, we found the snails less than a refreshing romp through verdant fields of mint, and more like an exercise in controlling the gag reflex.

Wint-O-Green Life Savers.

Honestly.

24 January

I arrive at my lesson as Doreen is packing up. She pulls me aside and whispers that today is Angelo's birthday. She asks, "What do you think? Should we take him out for dinner?" We conference quickly, and then she turns to Angelo and tells him we'd like to take him to pizza tonight. He beams, and asks if it will be an elegant occasion or casual. *"Come vuoi."* Whatever you like.

At dinner, Angelo insists on sharing the wine with the children, and we toast to our friend's birthday, *"Tanti auguri!"* Best wishes! We clink our glasses, and before we put them down, Angelo has us in his thrall with a story of a woman in Napoli who, after two *baba*, rum-soaked pastries from southern Italy, was arrested for driving under the influence. We talk about what makes an excellent pizza, the delights of *piccante* oil, the combination of pears and gorgonzola, and the blandness of the American dollar Gabe pulls out of his pocket to Angelo's curious delight. But Angelo never stops being *mio maestro*. Mid-story, he addresses me in an aside, informing me that he's using the conditional tense.

After dinner, Angelo offers to drive Nicolas and meet us walkers at home. Nicolas readily agrees. The rest of us walk, enjoying the still night air. Still, that is, until burst by chirpy honking as Angelo's car races by. We laugh and wonder why he's going in the wrong direction. Twice more, Angelo's car whizzes by with exuberant pips. Then, as we walk past a covered walkway, Angelo pops out with a "boo!" and doubles over laughing, telling us that it's just like "allowy." Allowy? What's allowy? You know, he persists, that American holiday with masks and candy. Oh! Halloween!

We continue up to our house together, pausing to say goodbye at our front steps. Once there, Gabe shrieks, "Somebody stole our poop!" And we English speakers smother our laughter and feel thankful that our neighbors won't understand Gabe's outburst. We quickly explain that Daddy cleaned up the squished pile of dog droppings on our steps that we'd been studiously avoiding all day. And now it's time to say goodbye to Angelo. I look at him with a mixture of joy and regret that, like the *pan di mosto* of olive harvest season, these moments are over so quickly. A year here means we have bursts of revelatory delight, and unlike at home where we can count on apple cider donuts again next fall, the experience is *finito*. Done. And now that we have as much time behind us as we do ahead of us, I'm particularly mindful of these fleeting and exceptional occasions.

And I wonder, how many of these moments do I miss at home? In my distracted existence and assumption that everything comes back again, do I neglect to notice the lilac that blooms fleetingly on the street corner? The evening smell of bacon-wrapped dates from the Spanish restaurant in my neighborhood? The joy of finding nectarines at the farmer's market?

Here, I am always aware. When I walk to the bakery in the morning, I notice the nascent light warming the rosy Subasio stones of every wall, the fog that makes the narrow alley ahead veer toward *sfumato*, the instant smell of comfort when I open the *forno* door. But Italy doesn't have a monopoly on charming moments. The question is—can I feel the beauty of those moments, even when I'm not constantly reminded that they are evaporating?

As we kiss Angelo goodbye, I muse that he was born in Spello, yet he never stops *seeing* it. He is of the old guard, and still he embraces the newness and novelty of a transitory American family. He creates his own variety, his own fleeting moments by living with vibrancy, following challenges, intentionally learning. Maybe there is something there that I can adopt when we are back. So that I can keep this sense of the fragility and the power of every moment.

Buona notte, Angelo. Il mio maestro. E tanti auguri.

25 January

My butcher has just returned from vacation. He is full of descriptions of beaches, and laughs as he relates stories of his and his wife's attempts at English, which are limited to pronouncing wine "veeeery goot!" Customers laugh with him, tossing in comments. I want to participate, but I hang back. Until I remember my resolution of speaking Italian everyday. I take a breath and ask the butcher, "*Dove siete andati per la vacanza?*" Google Translate tells me that this way of querying "Where did you go for vacation?" is incorrect, but the butcher understands me and gives me a wide smile. He tells me they went to the Canary Islands, describing how warm the weather was. As I walk home with a bag of meats both fresh and cured, I consider that asking a question, prompting someone else to start talking, allowed me to have a different sort of conversation, with different vocabulary. Unlike when I am asked a question, even a simple one, as I have a tendency to drop into my deer-in-headlights masquerading as an ostrich-in-the-sand routine. "Ack! I don't know! What is my name? Where am I from? I have no idea! I pass! I forfeit!" When I ask a question, I'm only really expected to nod and smile. Without the pressure of having to respond, I actually enjoy the conversation.

Once home, I look up the Canary Islands, and I'm floored. Holy cow, that's a beautiful spot. I think of Paola, who is preparing for a month in Thailand, and her son who just returned from South America. I remember Loris and Patrizia are going to Burma in February, and Gianni from Bar Tullia is preparing for a trip to Mexico. Europe has always been our destination spot, and that of my social circle, so I assumed that Italians felt the same and would vacation in Paris or London or Vienna. I didn't expect Italians to have a culture of grand adventures. It's making me wonder how different our own country would be if there was a national impetus to travel regularly to places so different, they seem shrouded in mystery. Places that challenge our assumptions about what daily existence looks like, what comprises breakfast, and what one can learn from a butcher.

26 January

Angelo's fascination with Asian food motivates me to invite him for dinner. Working with spare supplies is a challenge, but there is a power there, a feeling of creation, that rivals the dynamism of executing a painting and getting an A on a trig exam. Combined. My bean sprouts are out of a jar, limes and basil and ginger are slightly complicated to come by, but cilantro is impossible. The meats, however, are easy. At the *macelleria* there are no trays of steaks or hamburger meat.

Instead, there is a side of beef, off of which I can order my meat however it suits. For today, I order a half kilo, thinly sliced. The butcher slices one piece, and asks my approval on the thickness before trimming the fat. I sigh with contentment.

The menu: Shrimp Korean pancakes, spicy eggplant and ground pork, beef and cabbage with shittake mushrooms, steamed rice, and *pho*. Not real *pho*. Fake *pho*. *Finto pho*. Chicken broth with rice noodles, jarred bean sprouts, chives instead of green onions, and a generous dash of fish sauce from the Asian market in Perugia. Served with condiments of Sriracha, chilies soaked in fish sauce, basil, and limes. I fairly dance as I prep the ingredients, flush with the joy of cooking Asian food for Angelo and Doreen, and the quiet to focus. Keith has taken Siena to a birthday party, and the boys to the hair stylist. I look forward to them coming home neatly shorn. I look forward to it for nothing.

When they walk in, Gabe looks fairly normal. A little dopey with a slight mushroom shape to his head, but fine. And then Nicolas leaps out from behind the door. With a *cresta*. Oh, my! A *cresta?* A *cresta* is a toned-down Mohawk. The hair is short at the top, and styled so that the edges swoop up toward the middle. The result is a bit like a rooster. It's a hollow victory that it's not an actual Mohawk, which is also popular here, a fact that inevitably makes Keith comment, "Italy is where the 80s went to die."

I grow acclimated to my son's strange head shape. It helps knowing that it's not a true *cresta*, but rather a *finta cresta*. If it's not styled into a *cresta*, it's rather innocuous. It does mean that Nicolas will now have to spend time on his hair in the morning. But, fourteen is probably a good age to start paying attention to one's personal appearance.

I try to stop being distracted by my son's resemblance to Astro-Boy—or maybe Bob's Big Boy?—as I welcome Doreen. Angelo arrives soon afterward, with a plastic bag, an eager grin, and loud praise for the cooking scents wafting into the street. From the bag he produces three heart-shaped boxes of chocolates, and presents the first to Nicolas with a well-rehearsed, "I...love...Nicolas!" Which sounded more like *"Ay loff Nicolas."* Then another for Gabe, "I...love...Gabriele!" Gabe runs to show me his chocolate box, before running back to throw his arms around Angelo as he murmurs, *"Ti voglio tante bene, Angelo."* And Angelo smiles and smiles. Siena, returning home from the party is charmed when presented her chocolates with Angelo's love.

I serve the Vietnamese soda I made from *acqua frizzante*, simple syrup, lime juice, and mint. And then we dive into the Korean pancake, which Angelo loves so much he drinks his leftover dipping sauce straight from the cup, exclaiming "*Che saporito!*" How flavorful. We talk about the mushrooms in the pancake, and Angelo tells us a story about people in Spello who had gone mushroom hunting, and fed a mushroom to the cat to see if it was toxic. As the cat continued in good health, they ate the mushrooms. Soon after, the cat began writhing in pain. The family frantically took medicine to vomit, and then noticed that the cat had delivered a litter of kittens. Burst of laughter from the table, and a worried, "Is that a true story?" from Gabe.

Then comes the *pho*, and Angelo exclaims that it's both *gustoso*, tasty, and *leggere*, light. He ladles in the condiments, with extra fish sauce with chili. He tells us about the intense spices in Baghdad. It's stunning to me that this man of such modest means somehow found a way to visit Mexico, London, and Baghdad in his lifetime. He tells us that while his countrymen shirked the regional foods, he sampled every Iraqi spice lined up before him. They didn't always agree with him, but he felt compelled to try them all.

The rice is already cooked, so I quickly sautéed up the last few dishes. *Mamma mia!* More food! Angelo is curious about the rice. Just boiled, not made into rice salad or *risotto*. Doreen explains that the rice serves as a component that flavors can be added to. And I tell him about *congee*, a little rice cooked for a long time in abundant chicken stock until it's like pudding. His eyes shine.

Our guests leave, amid hearty goodbyes. And tomorrow, Keith is going to show Nicolas how to shave the fuzz on his upper lip that is darkening from peach fuzz to soot fuzz. Oh, how I wish that that, too, could be *finto*. That we could stall this growth, and return to the days where "shaving" for Nicolas meant him lathering his cheeks with bubble bath, gleefully swiping the soap off with the back of a red rubber pick-up truck. Time, no matter how much I want it to pause, to slow, strains ever onward. Tomorrow my boy will have both a *finta cresta* and a real shave.

27 January

Over breakfast, Siena remembers her art project is due today. The panic begins. She wails that she can't find it. I groan inwardly. Organization has never been Siena's gift—she's such an "in the moment" child that she has a hard time thinking about what's been requested of her and what will be required of her in the future—but this year it's been obscene. She insists that she has so much in her head trying to keep up with the day, that she can't remember everything. We come up with systems that seem to work, and then here we are again. Wailing. Over her crying, I suggest, "Just start something, anything is better than just crying." She's too hysterical to settle down. I find the sketch upstairs, and when she sees it, she wails anew. There's no way she'll be able to finish coloring it in time.

Okay, she'll have to tell her teacher she'll turn it in tomorrow. Her face flares with hives. And I remember that her art teacher is also her math teacher, of the sarcastic, biting style. Recently, this teacher berated Siena for not moving on to a new problem with the rest of the class. The teacher yelled that Siena was rude and needed to keep up with the class. I try to convince myself that it is important for Siena to practice brushing off ill-placed judgment. I tell myself this, but secretly I have inappropriate fantasies of violent acts that fly in the face of my Quaker faith. I struggle to find Light in someone who once asked my daughter a multilevel question in rapid-fire Italian (a question that she eventually asks the whole class, but began with Siena, giving the non-native speaker no chance to watch others respond or have a moment to allow comprehension), and when Siena responded, "*Come?*" mocked her with "*Good morning, Si-e-na!*" Bless Chiara, who leaned over and "translated" by using simpler and slower words, so Siena could respond, her face flushed in shame. People say that children can be cruel, but it is this big-hearted child who is helping Siena cope with her teacher's cruelty.

Once I realize why Siena is so terrified, I don't know what to do. I can't send her to school with her work unfinished and hives on her face—that would break her. She's been cheerful about school lately, but it's a fragile peace. I can't walk her in and deal with the teacher myself because parents aren't allowed in the school—besides, this isn't Alessia who I can count on to be empathic. I would worry that she'd nod to us and then increase her ire to Siena when we walked out the door. I can't keep Siena home for the day, as that would send a message that if you don't finish your work, you get to stay home. Given how tenuous Siena's cheer is regarding school, and how often she forgets her work, this would be setting a dangerous precedent. I just hold her and try not to cry myself.

Keith approaches the two of us, huddled together. He's looking at the schedule, and proposes that Siena miss the first hour of school, and go in at the transition to the second hour. She shrieks, "*No, no, no, no!*" Her teacher would berate her for being late. We tell her that people are late all the time, back at home, and here. I see kids walking in to school at all hours. Eventually, she agrees.

I sit with her while she spends the next hour on the most inane art project I've ever seen. That's not bitterness talking. Her assignment is to draw alternating geometric shapes on three lines across the page, connect them with bands of colors, and then color in the shapes, bands, and background with marker. It stuns me that the country that houses the Sistine chapel would have an art program this irrelevant.

But coloring is meditative, and her breathing and skin tone return to normal. She thanks Keith and me for our patience, and apologizes for not remembering the assignment. She agrees that it's important to hold up a wall between other people's opinions and the center of her heart, but confesses that she'll never be okay with people being mean to her. I'm not okay with people being mean to me, or even deleting my posts on TripAdvisor, and I'm 41 years old. But I'd like her to get to a place where she doesn't have a phobic reaction about the *possibility* of people being mean. That she trusts in her own resilience.

The quiet time, with only the sound of her marker filling in every white space on that paper, allows me to reflect. Over the weekend, Keith pushed Siena to redo her math homework, past the point that I would have said, "You're tired, go do something fun." He pushed her with a jovial tone that suggested she was capable of doing it and didn't falter when she resisted. And she kept working. Understood the material, and then stood tall with pride. Taking his cue, I then told her it was time for violin. She started to sag and tell me she was too tired, and whereas I usually would have said, "Well, it's true, you've been working hard, just do a few minutes extra tomorrow," I told her she was strong enough to practice her violin for ten minutes.

And she did. Not only did she practice, but she practiced a challenging new piece. She talked about how hard the piece was, with a thrill rather than a moan. It's clear to me, I hold my daughter with kid gloves. Children rise to the level of their expectations. Make things too easy, success is meaningless. Give a child a challenging task and mastering it is meaningful.

Her coloring outlasts my reflections, but as I watch her finish, I understand that sending her to school when she was in utter panic would have been a snap, a break. Keeping her home for the day would have been coddling her. Between the two extremes lay the option of allowing her to stay home for an hour, and then have to go in late with her homework done. A stretch.

On the walk to school, we discuss how to say, "I didn't feel well this morning" in Italian. She rehearses with a smile. Siena gives us each a fierce hug before walking in with her shoulders back.

Brava, Siena. As it turns out, she does get a sigh and an eye roll and a remark she doesn't understand from her math teacher when she walks in late. But she tells us about it with an eye roll of her own and a dismissive wave of her hand.

Brava, indeed.

29 January

Not all gifts look like gifts when they are put into our trembling hands. Siena tells me that she wasn't able to finish copying an *avviso* from the board to her planner before the teacher erased it. Since she's been yelled at for holding up the class, she opted for coming home with half a message, rather than telling the teacher she didn't catch all the words. "Well," I tell her, "the upside is now you have a reason to call Chiara and while you are at it, you can invite her over." She hems and haws. I drop it. And then, at dinner, I bring it back up in a matter-of-fact/ we-need-the-*avviso*-information sort of way, and her response? "Okay!"

Wait, where did Siena go?

"I'll call."

"Do you want to talk about it first?"

"Nah."

"And you'll invite her over?"

"Sure!"

She smiles. Finishes dinner. When the kitchen is empty, she comes back and modestly asks if I know what spurred her sudden willingness to call her friend. I confess that I have no earthly clue. While she has called before, it was only under Chiara's marching orders—she can't bear to let a friend down—and never without reluctance. "Well, I realized that this year isn't just about getting to live in a house in Italy and have great experiences like skiing in the Alps. It's also for trying new ways of living. So if I really want to get all I can from this year, I need to find new ways to make friends and new ways to see the world. I'm not going to learn anything by coasting." That's literally what she says. I know because I am so dumbfounded I beg her to repeat it.

I ask if she is actually ready to invite Chiara over. And she says, "Well, I'm going to do it someday, so I might as well begin now." And then she calls Chiara. Bear in mind, Gabe has been asking me to call Lorenzo's mom all week, and I keep finding a good excuse to put it off. And Anna Maria speaks English. So I understand just how hard this is for Siena, and how much nervousness she has to overcome to make that call. When I see my girl on the phone, voice quivering, but still pushing forward, my heart just bursts. She hangs up, and says she feels like she ran a marathon. My daughter, with more resolve and tenacity than I've seen in her, made the call with confidence. And it only took six months. And so much angst on my end, so much guilt for putting her in this seemingly untenable position. It has been a rough ride.

But I have learned my lesson—let her figure it out. Me shepherding her through the process only results in her focusing on my feelings. By allowing her to sit with it and feel her way forward, she taps into something much deeper. So I guess I let her go to it, my job here is done. If you need me, I'll be on the *loggia* with a chilled glass of limoncello.

Gnocchi al Sagrantino

roughly one pound of *gnocchi*

2 tablespoons fabulous olive oil,
or 1 tablespoon olive oil and 1 tablespoon butter

70 grams guanciale or pancetta, chopped

1 yellow onion, chopped

1 ½ cups Sagrantino wine (or another robust wine, such
as Australian Shiraz or Italian Barolo)

1 ⅓ cups heavy cream

½ cup grated aged pecorino, or parmesan

⸻ ● ✦ ● ⸻

1. Warm fats in a sauté pan over medium heat. Add pork and cook until crisp. Add onion to the pan, and cook until golden. Add wine, and scrape up the fond from the bottom of the pan. Cook gently for about 20 minutes, until the wine is the consistency of syrup. Add cream, then salt and pepper to taste. Let simmer gently while you boil batches of *gnocchi* in boiling, salted water.

2. As each batch of *gnocchi* floats to the surface, remove from the water with a slotted spoon, and then gently lay in the sauce. Once all the *gnocchi* is in the sauce, add grated cheese and serve, flourished with another fall of cheese and cracked pepper.

FEBRUARY

SAVORING

2 February

As I walk Siena to her violin lesson, I spot Sicilian Angelo in the *piazza*. He laughs when he sees me, opens his arms, and calls across the *piazza*, "*Cara* Michelle." I wish I could always hear my name in an accent so lilting and affectionate. I confess to him that I'm going to the *negozio* to buy chocolate for Gabe. He tells me, his faced creased in his permanent smile, that chocolate isn't part of a strictly healthy diet. I nod, and say, "*Io so, ma un pezzo di cioccolato è sempre perfetto.*" He howls with laughter and agrees, yes, a piece of chocolate is always perfect. His warm brown eyes look directly into mine before he kisses my cheeks goodbye.

My spirits warm further at dinner. It's a rare quiet moment when Nicolas sneezes. Mid-bite, I don't manage to bless him before Gabe pipes up, "*I baffi!*" We all swivel toward him. "*I baffi*, Gabe? Why are you talking about mustaches?" One of his eyebrows pulls up toward his forehead, and he answers, "I heard someone say it at school when someone sneezed. *I baffi.*" I am pretty sure that "the mustaches" isn't the Italian version of "bless you." Gabe must have misheard and filed away this little nugget for future use. Unless it hasn't been filed away, and he's congratulating his classmates on their mustaches whenever they sneeze, to their perpetual confusion.

3 February

Blustery days blow the grey residue clean away. Leaving a morning that is so brilliant that only the Italian word *chiara* seems to express the fresh lucidity of the air. The downside is that the wind wreaks havoc on my carefully constructed hairstyle. The one where I brush about half my hair and than have to rush off to find Nicolas' missing shoe and therefore neglect the rest. The wind is probably an improvement.

It's so windy that a cypress is knocked across the road to Sante and Conci's in Bettona. I clutch the pastries on my lap, careful lest the battering wind buffet our light car, and thus knock away our thoughtfully selected Carnevale treats from the bakery.

We're greeted at the gate like long lost relatives, the Abruzzese mountain dogs leaping exuberantly. We hug and kiss Sante and Conci and Silvano and Roberta. They lead us to the table, and stop to point out the pasta drying on the huge wooden tray. Everyone jokes that this is Nicolas' portion. And then we find our seats in front of the cutting boards loaded with home-cured salami. I use my new technique of asking Sante questions about the curing process, which allows me to enjoy his animated recitation of salami making. After our *antipasti*, Conci serves up the pasta with a sauce made with browned *pancetta* and garlic, sautéed with a jar of *tartufata*, a mixture of truffles and mushrooms, and finished with cream and a generous handful of grated parmesan. Nicolas hates mushrooms, but polishes off his plate. When I question him, he whispers that he would eat a block of cheese if Conci gave it to him. A way with pasta seems to be important to secure my son's unswerving loyalty. As I wonder at the creamy, earthy pasta, Conci offers me a serving suggestion for the leftover dried pasta she's going to send home with me. One is to briefly cook finely minced onion and zucchini in butter, then add a jar or two of baby shrimp. Cook for a few minutes, then add cream, or a cube of *"Philadelphia."* Another is to sauté chopped broccoli and once it's tender, add a cube of that Philadelphia. Doreen tells me in an aside that here, Philadelphia (there is no other word for cream cheese) comes in easy-to-use squares—half the size of American packages—perfect for whipping up a pasta sauce.

I struggle not to lick my mushroomy plate clean and prepare for our next course: Thinly sliced roast beef with a light sauce. I recognize mustard seeds, but little else. Conci says the sauce is juice from the roast beef, a little mustard, and a cooked carrot that has been whizzed in the blender. Nicolas has five slices. The table erupts in laughter when he takes his final helping, but Conci just sits and beams. She and Mario's mother seem dedicated to fattening up my beanpole of a son. Every time he returns from Mario's, he tells stories of the number of servings piled on his plate.

For *contorni*, Maria brings out *melanzane sott'olio* and a huge, gorgeous salad. When Sante gets up and moves toward the other end of the table, I ask if he's getting salad. Everyone cackles as he answers that he will have salad later. I suggest that maybe "later" means "tomorrow." And he clasps my arm and laughs until I think he might cry. I can't understand why he doesn't have the salad—it's like a salad miracle. Crisp, slightly bitter lettuce, radicchio, pieces of red orange, chunks of apple, and cubes of cheese. Siena asks if the cheese is provolone, and it's not. Siena and I tell them about the fabulous cheeses in the Dolomiti, and how the boys had a seizure every time I opened the fridge. Conci tells me about a special kind of refrigerated box you can buy just to keep cheese.

Before *dolci*, Silvano runs out and comes back holding high a small bottle of dessert wine so red it approaches black. Keith asks if this is something *particolare*, the common way to describe local delicacies and special rarities, and receives a serious nod. I settle in. This ought to be good. Silvano tells us this is *amarena*, wild cherry dessert wine with a perfume so decadent I want to fall in my glass, Alice in Wonderland style, and curl up in it. The children get a splash. Nicolas wants more than a splash; he is taking to this "Italian children drink wine" thing with a bit too much *gusto*. I'd offered him *"un po' di vino,"* with lunch and he'd been incensed by the *po'*, which hardly moistened the bottom of his glass. Glaring at his inadequate serving, he'd turned to Sante and sweetly asked if he could have a glass of wine. *"Certo!"* boomed Sante, and filled my newly-shaving boy's glass dangerously full with homemade red wine. Which I sip covertly.

Over the trays of *dolci* and that heady *amarena* wine, we talk. I'm more comfortable than I expected, and everything is more understandable than last time. Nicolas is cracking jokes to wild applause and consistently assuring our hosts— who cannot stop patting him—that he plans to stay in Italy with them. Siena translates for me when I get stuck answering questions about my progress cooking Umbrian food. The table at large argues the relative merits of *cotiche, lumache*, and Texas BBQ, and the family looks at Keith with amazement when he states his love for *lumache*. I ask Roberta about her upcoming course on mushrooms. Later, I'm able to bring my hosts to giggling tears with my insistence that there is no maple syrup like Virginia maple syrup. And all six of us Americans sit back with satisfaction and watch, as a bona fide Italian family heatedly argues remote past tense conjugations.

We leave when nothing but crumbs remain on the *dolci* trays, standing together as Conci packs us eggs, bread, and pasta, engaged in an earnest discussion of the importance of friends and warm attachments, *soprattutto*. Above all. Above money, Sante adds, which just fades away. My heart swells, appraising this family that has embraced us. They have fed us the fruits of their land, with methods that have been passed down through generations. Their warmth fills me with a sense of the divine grace within the human spirit. At their table, I am taught to sip, to taste, to savor.

6 February

Gabe invites us into his room, where he's displayed the gifts he made for us, hid, forgot, and recently discovered. What are these treasures that he ducks his head with pleasure to present to us? Typical re-purposed "gifts" from a child who has no income. A shiny red and gold "silk" bag he had asked his teacher for because he liked it so much, which he had filled with... a paper clip he'd bent into the shape of a house. A wealth of Christmas wrapping paper from the other *prima* classroom that he had asked for, which he used to wrap... a folded piece of card stock with images of colorful European houses. Also from school. A stubby pencil he'd found and wrapped with red and white tape, along with one of his socks decorated with the same tape, to assuage Siena's grief after she broke down in L'Orlando Furioso about losing Christmas. Gabe's teachers must think he is some sort of magpie.

Stumbling over forgotten gifts is an inherent part of living with children. I have been known to take a trip to the attic and happen upon discounted dresses I ordered for Siena but forgot when dress season rolled around again. Or toys I purchased at a sidewalk sale so long ago that the boxes are barely familiar. Our lives are lived half in chaos, and as such, our loving gestures are sometimes shelved behind the more immediate necessities of finding music books and packing lunches.

When I was arranging the house for our tenants before we left, I found a packet of papers underneath the bookcase. The children gathered around me as I unfolded the papers one by one, until Siena shouted out, *"Oh!"* It was the Christmas cards she had made for us years ago. The cards that she labored over for days, and had decided would be safest, apparently, under the bookcase. But then she had moved on to making doll dresses from silk squares, and had completely forgotten about the cards. When Christmas came, she had no recollection of where she'd stashed them, and her grief had been terrible. Finding these tokens, when each child was a good several inches taller, my crow's feet were a fair bit deeper, and mellow summer sunlight was streaming in the window…well, it was a whole different kind of gift.

Better than finding coins under the couch cushions, stumbling over forgotten gifts is a profound reminder of the love that binds a family. Even here, our lives are busy enough that we lose track of that love; unearthing evidence of it makes us stop and recognize how lucky we are. The gifts are everywhere—behind the radiator, tucked into the salad spinner, beating in the hearts of our babies snuggled under their fuzzy blankets. Gifts are everywhere. Unseen, sometimes unfelt, waiting for us to remember, and gape, and stand in awe of the power of a love that compels a five year old to create treasures from refuse to express his connection and devotion to the people that matter the most to him in this world.

The gifts are everywhere.

7 February

We gather around Gabe's sleepy form to sing him "Happy Birthday." He holds his fuzzy blanket tight against his chest as he looks around at us with shining eyes, tousled and red cheeked. He opens his presents in bed, and then opens his armoire to bring out a box. He hands it to me, saying that he'd prepared a thank-you gift for all of us. It's a barn made out of cardboard and tape. I know it's a barn because there is a sign above the door that reads "barn."

Keith and I join Gabe in his classroom at 10:00. Gabe has told us that for students' birthdays, parents bring pizza and juice and cake, so our arms are laden with pizza from the *rosticceria*, juice boxes, and a chocolate cake. I'm glad Gabe asked for this particular cake from my repertoire, as it blessedly uses whipped eggs instead of leavener. We walk in as the students are describing their dream gifts for

Gabe, just in time to hear Lorenzo wish for Gabe a *quaderno* with all the Italian words. Alessia asks Gabe if he prefers English or Italian. He answers clearly, *"Italiano!"* to mingled shouts and cheers. Gabe dances jauntily as the class sings him *"Tanti Auguri a Te,"* and then he blows out the enormous candle I'd jabbed in the cake in lieu of cake candles. A huge inhale to blow that candle out, surrounded by his friends. I love each of them for opening their hearts to our son. When the *festa* ends, two of the girls join Gabe to walk us to the school's front door.

After school, we take the train to Perugia, and then ride the Minimetro to the National Archaeological Museum of Perugia. The porticos of the monastery-cum-museum are lined with Etruscan funerary urns. I linger, trying to make sense of the writing and philosophy, since Angelo had just told me about the Etruscans, who arrived in Umbria from the Middle East. The newly arrived Etruscans and the native Umbri got along fine. The Umbri, as a largely agrarian society, had nothing worth stealing, and the Etruscans were too intimidating to consider attacking. So the Etruscans stayed to the west of the Tiber, and the Umbri stayed to the east. While the Etruscans were busy being happy and productive, other fortune seekers arrived in Rome. They developed into the ancient Roman culture we think of today when we hear "toga" and "forum." Those Romans eventually conquered the Etruscans, and incorporated their civilization into that of Rome.

Because of that lesson, I am particularly interested in the museum's Etruscan and Umbri artifacts housed in a long, lofted room, with a wide, central aisle. All the cases to the left are filled with items found on the Umbri side of the Tiber, and all the cases on the right are filled with items found on the Etruscan side. I'm captivated by the curious metal statues, as the Umbri examples are stylized, whereas the Etruscan examples are rounder and more realistic. On our way out of the museum, we stumble upon a sign that leads us to an actual Etruscan burial ground, unearthed during construction. After seeing exhibits that displayed Etruscan life, pots they used for cooking, a rock carved with writing that indicated property agreements, this ancient people suddenly feels *real*.

After meandering through history, we find modern Perugia disarming. I catch myself tiptoeing lest my steps disturb an underground Etruscan tomb. We wander to the cathedral, per Gabe's request. He loves cathedrals, maybe because his attention span for them is the same as ours, so he never feels restless. This time, he asks to pray. We leave him kneeling in a little chapel, framed by ethereal light and the lingering scent of incense. When he rises, a priest offers him a bookmark with an image of the church's prized Madonna. We close our tour of the cathedral by making six offerings so that six candles light and quietly singing "Happy Birthday." This moves me, but Keith worries it's sacrilegious. Gabe asks to pray again. We remove ourselves a bit and watch while he kneels, piously clasps his hands under his chin, and closes his eyes. When he dusts off his knees and rejoins us, we step outside. He slips his hand into mine, and comments, "Even though my body is cold, my heart is very warm."

The rest of us didn't pray, so we are still cold enough to seek out a café. Our drinks arrive with a tray of savory snacks, but we're unable to enjoy them because Gabe starts complaining that he feels unwell. I hope it's just Etruscans and Catholicism mixing unpleasantly in his system. We leave, and I cross my fingers that the walk will revive him. We stand outside Ristorante Tokyo and ask him, "Do you really want to have sushi? We can always come another time." He's adamant, sushi is what he wants for his birthday dinner. We go in, a little tentative, but hopeful. Gabe still looks a little peaked, but shows signs of rallying. So we order. And then he throws up.

Keith gets him to the bathroom in time, but we are made aware of the vomiting at the earliest possible moment because Gabe announces it to the restaurant at large when he exits the bathroom. Charming. My mind is scrambling like a lab mouse. Do we ask them to stop making our sushi and leave? Do we ask for all of it to go? Do we eat and hold back a portion for Gabe that he can have tomorrow?

Gabe makes everything easy with his casual happiness. He would *love* some sushi. And he eats one, and another. And looks okay. My shoulders relax, and tighten again when he starts rejecting the tuna sushi. Nicolas is full tilt into his camp counselor routine, trying to cajole me to stop worrying about Gabe, trying to convince Gabe that he's having a marvelous time, trying to pull the energy of the table up to dizzying heights. I tell him, "Honey, I don't need you to fix anything." This falls on deaf ears.

We order another two rolls of the simple sushi that Gabe prefers tonight. He smiles around the table, admiring the restaurant, the food… right up until he excuses himself to throw up again.

Time to go!

We leave, Keith and I strategizing how to manage the possibility of Minimetro vomit. It's hard to conference because Nicolas is interrupting to express his vehement cheerfulness. Everything is great! Gabe looks great! Aren't we all having a marvelous time? Isn't this all wonderful?! Which finally rankles me until I rankle out loud. And Nicolas deflates. I feel terrible, but his veneer of enthusiasm is only making the rest of us feel weird. So I apologize, but advise him that no good happens when he takes responsibility for how other people feel.

We make it home without further trouble. Gabe chattering happily—talking about what a great birthday it was, how much he loves Perugia, and how much he loves birthdays, and he can't believe he's *six*, and he can't believe he's so lucky, and how happy he was that he only threw up before and after eating the sushi—as opposed to which less optimal alternative? I silently wonder.

Even though this birthday is far from perfect, there is an overarching appreciation of how fortunate we are to have this little boy in our lives. Throughout the day, we'd all turn to each other and gesture toward Gabe with an expression of wonder that this little five year old—excuse me, *six* year old—is part of the fabric of our days. A boy that constructs a barn out of cardboard in advance of his birthday in order to have a thank you gift prepared, that prays without training, that finds the blessings in a birthday that involves vomiting.

I often feel that with the age gap between our children, our family is a cult into which we are indoctrinating our youngest—like our rituals of having cardamom-flavored Christmas cookies when we trim the tree, our predilection for making our own cleansers from baking soda and whatever essential oil strikes us, our insistence on pronouncing *mangos* the Spanish way and saying *choneys* instead of underwear, and our pattern of making every vacation center around food and markets. We've spent years considering that our job is to bring our youngest into the fold. Little realizing how much of the tapestry of our family is designed by him.

9 February

Here's what's hard about having sick children in a foreign country. Everything. Everything is difficult. You can't help but be on hyper-alert for fear that symptoms will devolve faster than you can manage, and since you can't mentally draw a map between yourself and the hospital, you're pretty sure the building of bustling white coats will fade into the Umbrian mists like a mirage the moment you need it. You start looking on the internet for crazy remedies, throwing everything you can at your eldest child in the vain hope that if the inhaler doesn't do the trick, perhaps breathing the smell of honey from the jar or hot showers or ginger tea will ward off the dreaded pneumonia.

Sure, back at home your mind would create catastrophic pathways at any odd sign, but now it's taking exponentially more pathways at record speed. *"What's that my baby, you say you have fatigue in your knees?"* And the mind starts to race—maybe it's mold or a fungus taking over his fragile body, maybe a lack of oxygen from his ragged breathing is resulting in cell death at the farthest joints. And the voice you used to count on—the one of reason that would say "Humans have weird symptoms all the time, they are often innocuous "—that voice no longer seems to speak the same language. That voice is quiet. That voice has left the building. And, by the way, *what is that red patch on your child's face?*

You argue with yourself. What right did you have taking your children from the germs they had learned to tolerate and the doctors you could trust and the community that would gather if you needed to dash to the doctor with your sick child? What if something terrible were to happen here? You would never forgive yourself. You would never go on. And the effort to escape these thoughts is exhausting.

When your mood lightens, just a touch, you catch yourself. Wrong, wrong, *wrong!* Smiling means letting down your guard, and only constant vigilance can prevent the worst from happening. Insane, yes. But impossible to feel otherwise. And so in place of trusted rational thought, comes the voice of looming catastrophe. Tragedy is just beyond the next wheeze, just past that vomiting episode, one degree higher in fever, the next wracking cough.

And when evening comes, and you have the joy of sitting across the table from your eldest while he eats a bland, but at least full, bowl of food, and you cannot hear his wheeze while you pretend to eat, and you are hold your littlest two in your arms reading *The Wonderful Wizard of Oz,* and they are smiling, and breathing regularly, with no cough, and no rattle, it will feel like a reprieve. A reprieve that, in this novel sense of being stranded in newness, feels far too fragile.

11 February

To my mind, *Carnevale* began weeks ago with intriguing pastries gracing display cases all over town. But it kicks off in earnest with a school-wide *festa* in the *borgo*. Siena, who shrugged off the virus as easily as she shrugs off her sweater at the playground is fully recovered. Gabe is wan, but symptom free, and I'm relieved he's able to participate. Unlike Nicolas, who really needs to kick his wheeze and find his energy.

On the eve of the party, Chiara comes for her first visit to our home. Siena is trepidatious—I know the foggy tendrils of Halloween silence with Amalia linger damply in her consciousness. We are not prepared for the beam of light that is Chiara. First of all, Chiara talks. She has opinions and ideas about what to do. Also, she is skilled enough to figure out what we're saying, even if we're saying it wrong. She even seeks us all out for conversation. The two of them get candy at the *negozio*, go for a walk together, and make *carnevale* masks from felt.

I watch my daughter turn a corner. Chiara asks to go to the grocery store with Keith to help Siena pick out a costume for the *festa*, and when Keith calls from the store to tell Gabe the costume options, I can hear the two girls collapsing in giggles in the background. I'm surprised by the relief that washes over me as I listen to that laugh—I haven't realized how much I've been carrying a sense of bleakness for Siena, that her life lacks a critical piece of joy. The afternoon is a balm on this *mamma's* heart.

With the power of that playdate, Siena borders on ecstatic at the prospect of getting ready for the *festa* at Chiara's. We walk into Ca' Rapillo without her, Gabe dressed in his Indian costume, with no idea what to expect. The music is too loud for talking, which gives me permission to sit and observe from one of the tables surrounding the dance floor. It's akin to a giant Halloween party. Mostly store-bought costumes, some with a homemade flair. Four little girls—a lady pirate, a ladybug fairy, a ballerina fairy, and a witch—run up to us to ask where Siena is. We tell them she's on her way with Chiara. And I am filled with thankfulness that these little girls somehow look past Siena's incomprehensibility and tendency to distance herself, yet still want to befriend her.

She arrives in her princess costume, hand in hand with Chiara, and surveys the room with a grin of anticipation. And thus begins her coming-out ball. She wanders the room with a group of girls, has confetti fights with them, checks in with us, races off again. Gabe enjoys how Siena's friends take him under their collective wing, until he becomes exhausted. Keith takes us home, leaving Siena with Chiara's parents. After he drops us off, Keith returns to the party, while Gabe and I snuggle and he recovers his equilibrium. I offer him a game, and, mindful of his disappointment that he couldn't fully enjoy the party, I cheat to give him the Skip-Bo hand of a lifetime. And I watch his eyes gleam as his turns grew more and more successful. He lays down his winning hand with a flourish, his face alight. It's so easy to make a six year old happy.

Siena comes home, breathless with exhilaration. While she laughingly removes the crown from her confetti-flecked hair, Keith tells me that when he returned to the party, he couldn't find Siena. The room was completely full, and he struggled to make his way around groups, and over children's costumed heads, trying to find our daughter. She wasn't in the bathroom, and he began to worry when he didn't see her with Chiara's parents or on the dance floor. And then he looked up and saw Siena. On stage. Making up dance routines with her friends, being merry little girls.

I smile as I listen, and Nicolas enters the kitchen with nary a wheeze. Gabe is aglow from his card playing triumph, and looks forward to Tuesday's school *carnevale* party. He excitedly tells me that the *prima* class will be making masks and parading through school. *Carnevale* sure is handy for stacking the deck toward joy.

12 February

Nicolas tries to go to school today. He walks down the hill, looks at the building, and finds he can't do it. His wheezing is gone, but his energy is still low, and periodic bouts of nausea slay him. He spends the rest of the day in bed, and so therefore, sadly, misses whatever celebrating happens in the middle school. Including the march of the *prima* class through his classroom.

Thus, he has no concept of the holiday that Gabe and Siena are smitten with. I overhear the two of them discussing *Carnevale* at bedtime, agreeing that it is right up there with Christmas. Siena says that though the holiday has religious roots, it feels like a holiday that's just about fun. For the school celebration, she and Gabe dress in their costumes, and enjoy a whole day of hedonism. Everyone brings treats, so I send Siena and Gabe with orange bundt cakes, since Google tells me that orange cake is a common *Carnevale* dessert. When they come home, the children can't wait to tell me about all the different treats—fried dough soaked in berry syrup with a bit of rum, sheets of fried dough called *frappe*, and pastries filled with Nutella.

Besides the fun of a *dolci* smörgåsbord, Siena reports that her class spent the entire day outside, playing games like "*Strega commanda colore*" and Italian clapping games. There's a lightness to my daughter, and I credit *Carnevale*. Chiara tells her to call later, and when I ask if she wants help preparing translations, she brushes me off. She wants to do it all. During the phone call, I hear Siena laugh and speak with confidence, rather than breathlessly ending every sentence with a question mark, and constantly apologizing, "*Non ho capito.*" She hangs up with a surprised smile, "That was fun!"

Under that princess costume, her skin fits again. She clearly feels part of the class, of the school, of the experience. She relates an incident with her impatient math teacher with the following commentary: "My job isn't to learn perfect Italian. My job is to learn what it's like to live in Italy for a year." And so she refuses to let the teacher dictate her self-concept.

Carnevale is emblematic of her transformation. Of embracing growth, of removing barriers of self-inflicted expectation and diving headlong into happiness. *Carnevale* is supposed to be a last hurrah before the stringency of Lent, but for me, it seems like a beginning.

14 February

Valentine's Day is one of those holidays I was looking forward to leaving behind. When I was new to parenting, and committed to making every moment whimsical, I would decorate the table with treats and love notes each Valentine's Day. I did it because I enjoyed the surprise for my children, and liked having an opportunity to create a space devoted to loving each other. I didn't even notice I did this from year to year. Until Gabe was born. A few days after his birth, Keith and I overheard 7-year-old Nicolas talking to 4-year-old Siena and reminding her of how much fun Valentine's Day is. "Remember, Siena? We come into the kitchen, and the table is pretty with treats and decorations? I love waking up on Valentine's Day." Crap.

I looked at Keith with alarm. I hadn't changed out of my jammies in days, I was rank with sour milk, and I was still getting used to having one more human in my family. I had zero energy to create a special, festive display of my overflowing love. Keith mouthed, "Don't worry, I'll take care of it." And he did.

Ever since, I've resented the expectation. Not enough to back out of it, but enough to heave a sigh of begrudging aggrievement at the realization of another Valentine's Day. I've made the dreadful mistake of creating too many expectations, and I'm enjoying a year liberated from Valentine's Day, birthday parties, or filling hundreds of plastic eggs.

Valentine's Day in Spello is as mellow as I'd hoped. I yawn and stretch in the morning, and curl against my husband without racing downstairs to put out the final bits of flair. I tussle my children's hair and tell them I love them and Happy Valentine's Day, they respond with dawning understanding, "Oh, right!" When I come home from the *forno*, I find that Keith has adorned the frothed milk in my morning coffee with a cocoa heart, and I'm moved by the simplicity of the gesture.

As I do my marketing, I pass my neighbors, with perks of awareness of the hidden holiday. No one notices me secretly sending love to passersby. I'm a reckless love vigilante. I have a conversation with the butcher and his wife, who want to know if we are staying in Spello, *"Per sempre?"* For always. And I love them. And the Moroccan produce vendor sells me one more *etto* of olives than I ask for, and I grumble, shrug, and love him. And on the *navetta* Luciano, without my mentioning it, offers to tell the driver to stop at the *forno* so I can get off closer to my house, and I love him. And Siena calls from Chiara's house, asking to stay longer because Chiara wants her to stay as long as possible, and I love them both. And I send Nicolas and Gabe to the *piazza* together to buy chocolate, and they leave hand in hand and I love them. Nicolas comes home and tells me that the owner of Bar Cavour complimented him on how polite he is and apologized for being out of the Milka bars he usually buys and I love her. I see Sicilian Angelo in the *piazza* and he hugs me and calls me *cara* and I love him. And in the evening, we stroll down to Vinosofia where we enjoy a fabulous Montepulciano d'Abruzzo that tastes of blackberries and caramel, and spirited conversation, and Brenda's gift from Graziano—her favorite *Carnevale* treat of a ring of small, fried balls of dough mixed with hazelnuts, bound with honey and a little orange. I love them both, and I love the way my senses sing.

As we walk home, Gabe assiduously lugging his precious bag of *pandoro* for tomorrow's breakfast through streets that are mellowed with fog and tender with starlight, I can feel in my bones how much I love it all.

Love—sans candy hearts, unadorned with plastic roses, without a Hallmark card. Whimsy-free. Just a simple, vigilante valentine.

15 February

I am not a communist. Never have been, never will be a member of the Communist Party. But I will go to any communist party, at anytime, anywhere. Because communists? They are the happiest bunch of people. Though perhaps this is only true of Umbrian communists—those comrades in the habit of ingesting fine wine and salami with their radical ideas. It may be different to party with Marxist-theory-quoting communists that smell of borscht and decaying fur hats.

I didn't know it was a communist party when Angelo told me about it, just that it was a dinner at Il Cacciatore, €20 a person for a complete dinner. Belatedly I learn from Doreen that it's a communist dinner. And then I have to rethink my whole outfit. Unnecessary, as it turns out, as communists are a very casual crew. For the first time in our sojourn in Italy, I feel overdressed.

When Keith and I arrive, we are met with smiles of welcome from Angelo, Sicilian Angelo, and Giuseppina. I haven't seen Giuseppina since our New Year's *cenone*, and I'm thrilled when she approaches me with arms open and eyes alight. She praises me for the thank you letter I sent, and then ushers us to her table. Doreen arrives soon after, and then the speeches begin.

I don't understand much of the oration, but I enjoy the challenge of trying to decipher bits and pieces. I know one of the presenters welcomes the *"tre americani,"* and our end of the table helpfully shouts and points at us. As if anyone in the room is unclear as to who are the Americans, in this roomful of people who have known each other since they were babies waving hammer and sickle flags. I don't think we'll ever stop being conspicuous, even with my new Italian haircut.

But I must pause a moment and mention my new Italian haircut. Siena and I had our first haircuts in eight months this afternoon. Siena's hair is silky and gorgeous, with layers framing her face that are so flattering, even her clueless elder brother complimented her. As for me, my hairdresser asked me if I wanted my hair *naturale* or some word that I took to mean a curling iron. I said, "*Naturale.*" In the States, natural means I leave the salon with wet hair. In Italy, *naturale* means a ball of mousse the size of a small melon, the hairdryer, the hairdryer with diffuser, and then a straightening iron to relax the front curls. And then a super-model-size dose of hairspray. That's *naturale*.

Enough of my capitalist haircut, back to communism. One of the speakers bemoans the amount of money being paid for interest rather than education or infrastructure. My country would kill to have such a tidy little debt. The speaker goes on to say that in Italy 25% of people have 50% of the wealth. Their indignation, compared to the resignation of the much more dramatic disparity in the States, strikes me. One of the speakers apologizes to us three Americans that they don't approve of Obama, as Obama doesn't endorse their communist choice. I can't imagine Obama ever throwing his weight behind a candidate who would serve to confirm the far-right's assumption that he's a secret Muslim communist. I suspect Obama is most likely to support the viable candidate that is not Berlusconi. Who is narrowing his lag, for reasons I can't understand because every Italian I know can't stand the man. Can't stand him to the point of trotting out all their angry and insulting hand gestures.

Perhaps it is the communists' fervency in their beliefs, their commitment to every person, and their complete isolation from actual political power, that makes communists so fun. Plus, they eat well, if the dinner is any indication. My favorite is the *antipasto*—a plate of sliced meats, cheese, a thin *focaccia* with sausage bits, *bruschetta*, and grilled mortadella drizzled with aged balsamic. We enjoy *tagliatelle alla regina* as *primo*, a dish Angelo tells me the restaurant is famous for. Google tells me that this dish usually has zucchini and tomatoes, but Giuseppina (whom Angelo calls Giussi, sounds like Juicy) tells me that the Il Cacciatore version always has peas, mushroom, and *prosciutto*. It has a deliciously deep, woodsy flavor, but the server spoons so much of it on my plate, I can't finish it. I'm glad I don't, because it's followed by a dish I like even more, *rigatoni all' amatriciana*. I've made *amatriciana*, but I can't get it to taste like this. A perfect layering of savory flavors. *Secondo* is a *spiedino* of grilled meats—cooked in the ancient fireplace which has point of pride in the newly remodeled kitchen—with roasted potatoes, and a salad passed around the table. Dessert, during the longest of the speeches, is *biscotti* and *vin santo*. Angelo joins our end of the table and whispers that Doreen is eating her *biscotti* all wrong. He takes two *biscotti*, drops them into the *vin santo* and then swats Doreen's hands away while he covers the glass with a napkin. Later (speech still going), he waves off the napkin and orders Doreen to take a now sodden *biscotto*. And then offers one to Keith and me. I am stuffed and decline, Keith takes a piece and then tells Angelo it will be good when he's toothless. To much muffled snickering. The speeches are still continuing after all.

Though I don't think communism is a workable option, the dinner does prompt me to wonder what a society would be like where teachers are paid the same as bankers. It really doesn't make any sense to me that we value commodities brokers, basketball players, and movie stars so much that they accumulate vast sums of wealth, where those who educate our next generation, those who provide health care in rural towns, those who preserve our open spaces, have to struggle to get by even though they work just as hard, or harder.

Better than speeches is Giuseppina's recitation of different recipes. I suggest to her that she teach a class, especially to Doreen and me. But the two of us have a pasta making lesson with Conci tomorrow and we should share the culinary wealth. In addition to food, Giuseppina also tells me about the asteroid that's going to narrowly miss the earth. Keith offers that if the projections are off, our world will be no more. Thanks, Keith. So comforting. I think I'll go home and take all my children and curl up in bed together. We walk home with Doreen, who asks if there's an asteroid strike, could we come check on her?

Of course. That's what comrades are for.

16 February

Learning to make pasta with Conci is a revelation. From the first moment, when she asks if Doreen and I want to learn to make it with a machine or by hand. We choose by hand, to the delight of Sante who insists this is the traditional

Umbrian method. When I express surprise, Conci adds that pasta rolled on a wooden board adopts the texture of the wood, which creates pockets to hold sauce. Unlike machine rolled pasta, which is *come vetro*, like glass.

And so we begin. Much of what I learn is unlike what I've read in the past about pasta making. But I remember once when Conci packed me home with leftover pasta, I made a simple sauce of zucchini and onion and cream and my family was moaning about how good it was. Was it because of my deft hand with the cream? It was not. It was because of Conci's way around a pasta board. So though her methods seem contrary to popular opinion, I'll never use any recipe but hers. The woman is a pasta genius.

* ※ ·

1. Crack 3 fresh eggs into a bowl. Conci's eggs are laid by her hens, with cohesive whites and vivid orange, or practically red, yolks. If you crack an egg and the white is watery or the yolk is pale, that's a bad sign. Since pasta is essentially eggs and flour, the eggs must be excellent quality. Glossy cookbooks insist on making a pile of flour, creating a well in the middle, and cracking the eggs into the well, and then mixing from there. But this is an exercise I find frustrating because inevitably my "volcano" springs a leak, and I'm left racing to catch the egg before it splatters my floor Jackson Pollock-style. Nice to know there is no magic in the frustrating process. Ignore Food Network, and use a bowl. Just incorporate the flour slowly, lest the sudden influx of gluten cause the eggs to seize.

2. Add a spoonful of olive oil to the eggs and beat them with a fork. I know, I know— olive oil in pasta is not done. Do it anyway.

3. Sift in about 4 cups of flour and begin to mix it into the eggs. This is where it gets tricky, because Italian flour is not like American flour. First of all, it's different wheat, so the gluten level is not the same; and second, it comes in various grinds. Some people believe that the 00 and 0 refer to gluten levels, but they don't. All Italian flour is different gluten-wise from American flour, and the 00 or 0 refers to how finely that flour is ground. Popular pasta recipes call for 00 flour, which is ground so finely it's like talcum powder. For pasta, Conci uses 0, but she considers the quality of the flour much more important than the grind or the gluten. You must use excellent, excellent flour. One more note, Conci often mixes in a little bit of whole wheat flour into her pasta. Not so much that you taste it, but

enough that when you look at it, you can see brown flecks, and when you eat it, it has a bit more power and heft. As for amounts, don't stress. Pasta dough is like a baby—if it needs more, it will ask for more. For now, just slowly mix in about four cups with the aid of a sifter. If the flour gets stuck to the sides of the bowl and you can't free it, you can add a little water.

4. Remove the dough onto your board, making especially sure to get every egg bit back into your dough. Scrape the dough off your fork with your fingers. The egg is precious!

5. Begin to knead. Have that sifter at the ready, as you will be flouring the board and the dough frequently. Also, keep a scraper handy, as you will need to scrape off the stuck bits from the board. Knead in the flour until you have a supple dough, turning, pushing, flouring, turning, pushing, flouring. The finished dough will be only slightly sticky.

6. Roll into a circle. Your cooking show experts will tell you to let your dough rest in the refrigerator or on the counter, well-wrapped in plastic wrap, before rolling it out. Conci doesn't do this—and I'm not sure if it's because our flour is different so it needs that time to relax, or if it's a step that someone did long ago and we continue to do so because we assume that's the way to do it.

7. Rotate the dough, flip the dough, still continually sprinkling it with sifted flour. You want to roll it to the size of a round serving platter. Make sure you scrape consistently; you want zero tackiness on your board.

8. Now comes the tricky step, both to describe and to master the technique. It will take some practice, but pasta is more patient than you think it is. Just keep flouring it, and it will hang with you until you get it. This step is all about stretching the dough evenly, so you get a circle of uniformly thin dough with the diameter of your rolling pin (which is why, in Italy, rolling pins come in various sizes, indicating either one-egg, two-egg, or three-egg pasta). Here are the steps: Place rolling pin at the top edge of dough, lift dough up and toward you, wrapping it over the rolling pin. With your palms, roll the pin toward you while you roll the pin back and forth against the palms of your hands, while simultaneously moving your hands from the middle of the pin toward the edges. It's several motions at the same time. One, roll pin toward you, essentially creating a burrito with the pin as the filling, and the dough wrapped around the pin. Two, use short rolls

(bearing in mind step one, so it's almost a two-steps-forward, one-step-back rolling) using the palms of your hands. Three, sweep palms of your hands from the center, where you begin, to the outer edge, where you will finish.

Once you feel the dough slipping outward as you roll the pin toward yourself, you know you've got it. Just remember to sift flour over the dough once in awhile to prevent the dough from sticking to the board, the pin, or itself when it is rolled.

9. When the dough is wrapped around the pin, use the rolling pin to alternatively flip the dough over, or rotate it sideways, so it you are continuously flipping it and turning it. Once you've released it, roll it out the traditional way with the rolling pin, taking care to get those edges (which have a tendency to fatten), nice and evenly thin.

10. Once the dough is the correct thinness, lay it out on a tablecloth or on the pasta board. Let it dry, flipping it once in awhile, so it dries evenly on both sides. The speed of this process is depends on the weather and how wet your dough is; we wait about a half hour. If you cut it too soon, it'll be too sticky and gummy to cut. If you wait too long, it'll be too brittle and the sheet of pasta will break. Err on the side of too soon, you can stop cutting if you realize that the dough isn't ready, but you can't go back in time and moisten it. My suggestion? If you realize you waited too long, and you can't cut it into the strips you'd planned, cut them in squares the size of your lasagna pan and make lasagna. With these fresh lasagna pasta, you don't need to cook it first, and there are all sorts of lasagna variations that can accommodate the ingredients you had planned for pasta.

11. Cut the pasta into ribbons: Fold the bottom of the pasta up two inches, repeat, repeat again. Then do the same for the top down, until you have what looks like a tea towel folded longways. Pick it up, and place the end on a cutting board. Cut the ribbons carefully to regular widths. After cutting a few, use the point of your knife to pick them up from the middle, and lift the ribbons (shaking them out as you do so to help them unfold) and remove to another board. Sprinkle with *grano duro,* or semolina flour. Repeat.

12. That's it! Your pasta is ready. Cook it in boiling, salted water (as salty as broth) for just a few minutes. Pour your sauce on, and serve. And when you eat it, you'll realize why in Italy, the sauce is a side-note for the pasta. Because fresh, homemade pasta is a thing of beauty.

18 February

At the communist dinner, I noticed a literal pain in my neck. The left side of my throat tugged with an electric pang. I felt twinges on and off after that, largely ignored in the service of enjoying myself and laughing at Keith's joke about the sodden biscotti being a nice treat if he were toothless. Ha, ha. Since then, absent the copious quantities of wine, the pain has moved beyond twinge. I wonder if I've scratched the inside of my throat, and the pain is radiating out. I even feel radio waves of pain in my ear. Luckily, Advil helps.

But the pain gains momentum, and now I'm miserable. I have no energy, and my throat aches even when I turn my head. Advil doesn't touch it, which is unfortunate since this means I wasted two of our €9 pack of 24. In any case, my throat still feels as if I have a burned or abraded a spot. I decide it's probably a tumor. Keith mocks me with an Arnold Schwarzenegger impression, *"It's not a toom-ah,"* but when I only smile wanly, he grows serious. He consults "Dr. Google" and determines that I have an infected abrasion or a virus. I am too flat to care anymore.

The pain grows until I have to hold my cheek to speak, and feel like I'm going to lose my mind when my children require goading to get out of bed. Keith goes to the health food store and brings home a spray. I love the word spray in Italy. There is no Italian equivalent, so they say "spray" but it sounds more like *"spraii."* And at the *Carnevale* party, there was a sign that forbade any *"bomboletti spry,"* silly string. I find the word charming.

But my *spraii* is more than charming, it is wonderful. It contains propolis, a bee-made product that is sticky and useful for plugging up little holes. Also, Wikipedia informs me that it is an antimicrobial and antiviral compound that can reduce inflammation. I instantly feel a little better. With increased energy, and poking my tongue around my mouth, I notice that my molar is chipped. A piece of it is just gone, a piece that is adjacent to what looks like a filling. I become concerned that perhaps a piece of the filling fell away, along with a tooth fragment and that is what I swallowed, slicing my throat and creating an infection. An infection would be bad, but the thought of possible consequent dental work to repair a filling sends me into a panic. I'm sure I couldn't convince my dentist to fly here. Remembering my dentist, I wonder if I can email the office and ask how to proceed. I'm shocked to get an almost immediate response that says that the dentist looked at my films, and that filling was originally a small circle. Which it still is, so the filling is intact. And that if the jagged tooth bothers me, I can file it down with a nail file.

Now I just have to hope that the jagged tooth continues to cause me no pain. I categorically do not want to go to a dentist here. Heck it took me months to get my hair cut. Thinking about that aversion makes a cloudy observation clearer. We didn't go to the doctor when the boys were wheezing, I didn't go to a doctor with my throat was hurting so badly I took to my bed, and I am digging in my heels about seeing a dentist. But why this aversion to medical professionals? I'd rather research "pneumonia" online to make sure my boys didn't have more symptoms than just the wheezing. I'd prefer to wait for the pain to recede.

Which makes me feel, for lack of a better word, toothless. I don't feel the power and resolve that comes from a settled existence. I'm transient. Aspects of permanent residency don't apply to me. We are supposed to pick up the kids' grades tomorrow, and my feeling is "why bother?" Yes, we'll collect the grades, and if Nicolas had blue lips or if I developed a fever, we'd find a doctor. But it's easier to skid along whenever possible. I'm missing the power that comes with permanence.

Our stay here is limited, so I won't be able to find out if there would be a point where I'd feel that I deserve a piece of the *torta*. As Don John says in *Much Ado about Nothing*, "If I had my mouth, I would bite. If I had my liberty, I would do my liking." As a transient expat, I don't have my mouth or my liberty. Not truly. The ground underneath me is too tenuous for me to stride with purpose. Things are too complicated, every step involves questions. At home, it's easy enough to pick up the phone and dial my pediatrician's office. Here, I'm playing a complicated game without a rulebook. So until I know something is necessary, I proceed with caution, and focus on the optimism and joy that drive me most of the time.

I suppose the moral of the story is that in being here, I feel less capable. And that is an unpleasant surprise. I consider myself a tenacious person, but here, unclear of what's around the cobblestone corner, I'm muted. The flip side is that I'm rarely angry or sad because no one owes me anything. I feel the gentler, more gracious, aspects of myself. It's a trade-off. Usually, it works in my favor, but in these moments of fragility, it's a challenge. Thus far, the odors of tragedy in the making—the spanking, the lungs unable to take a full breath unaccompanied by albuterol, the pain—have been few and far between. Thus far it has been okay, because teeth are unnecessary for joy. Joy is just easy.

For man is a giddy thing, and this is my conclusion.

— Shakespeare, *Much Ado about Nothing*

19 February

We are initially stymied by the *avviso* that states that grades will be processed February 19, from 16:30 to 18:30. Does this mean teachers are working on grades, we have to go pick up grades, our children have to do some sort of test? We finally realize it's the time for us to pick up *pagelle*, report cards. First stop, Gabe. Alessia kisses us in greeting and introduces us to the newly returned math teacher. It turns out the one that spanked Gabe was a long-term substitute. Alessia informs us that Gabe is fully integrated. She and the math teacher regale us with stories about our son, and we laugh, gratified. It helps that he's learning the Italian words for concepts alongside his classmates. So the difference between his knowledge base and theirs is much smaller than the difference between our older children and their classmates. His first ever report card is a successful one.

Next, we collect Siena's report card. No gushing. Or commentary of any kind, they just hand us the report card. I ask how she's doing, and her teachers immediately launch into how *timida* she is—the Italian/English teacher with empathy, the math/science/art teacher with scorn. She adds that Siena is so scared to make a mistake that she rarely participates. I am stunned to silence by the preposterous absence of insight inherent in this sentence; how can you one minute yell at a child for making a mistake, and in the next minute criticize that child for fearing to make a mistake? The Italian/English teacher breaks in with a joke I didn't get because I am still staring in disbelief at the math teacher. They don't get Siena at all. I understand that she holds back, so they don't see her wise compassion and ability to draw connections that her previous teachers have acknowledged. And they haven't noticed the shift just since January. She's making friends—with

Chiara, with a girl she met on field trip to Perugia, with the girls she danced with at *Carnevale*. Seeing this turnaround makes me dismiss the opinions of these authority figures. Which, I admit, is a huge shift for me. It's becoming clear to me that as she is being challenged and strengthened, so am I.

The *pagella* indicates her grades are better than expected. In the comment section, the math teacher writes that Siena doesn't respond to teachers in a satisfactory manner, but she admits that this is because Italian isn't her mother tongue. That this is what the teacher chooses to focus on in the comments of her report card appalls me. Really? The teacher doesn't want to note that Siena's solving word problems on the board? That she is kind and creative? That she has a heart big enough to hold the whole world, even the people who yell at her? Instead, the focus is on the fact that *she doesn't respond in a satisfactory way to teachers in a language that is not her own.* I'm floored.

And then to the middle school. While waiting for our turn, I meet Mario's mother, who asks if Mario has been behaving himself at our house. I have so many words to say, they form a logjam. Finally, I garble that Mario is *molto educato*, well behaved. I want to tell her that Mario is welcome at our house any time, that he folds into the fabric of our family with ease, but I can only easily envision the first few words of the sentiment. In any case, I'm glad to meet her, as Nicolas has said such nice things about her. And her cooking.

Nicolas' grades are given to us by his Italian teacher. She laughs at how Nicolas is one of the strongest students in Italian grammar, which she attributes to the fact that he's thinking about grammar all the time. On the walk back, we realize that Nicolas' grades are identical to Siena's, and he is also described as holding back in class, but the feeling behind that observation is completely different. His teachers love him for trying, and celebrate each step of his progress.

It's pure luck that Nicolas and Gabe were blessed with loving teachers this year, and Siena was not. I like to tell myself that this absence of external gardeners for her heart is making her more responsible for the care and management of her spirit. That she will learn a truth more important than how to locate Greece on a map. I hope, I hope. That what she gains is an ability to look at herself without flinching, to see what she wants, and what she needs, and who she is. And see the holes in her skill set as opportunities for growth. And that in this way, the grades she gives herself are the ones that matter most.

20 February

Angelo and I are having a marketing lesson. Yes, Spello's Wednesday market is humble, but since I purchased eight extraordinary artichokes there last week, I realized that you actually don't need 15 fruit vendors. Just one good one. We stroll to the market together, and my first lesson is "how many people Angelo knows." At every turn, he's entangled in a new conversation. My second lesson is at the *salumi* stand, where Angelo explains why some salami sticks under my tongue. I had suspected fat content, but Angelo says it's caused by lack of temperature regulation during the curing process. Then he points out the *salumi* vendor's vats of anchovies packed in salt. He tells me that when friends gather for a snack, they select an anchovy, shake off the salt, and wash it down with a glass of wine. I don't buy any anchovies, but I do purchase *guanciale* for *amatriciana*. Angelo smacks his lips as he recounts how much he loves *guanciale* placed atop toasted bread, so that the fat melds into the bread, topped with a sage leaf and a sprinkle of vinegar.

As we pass the fruit stand, the vendor calls us over to give us each a French walnut. Angelo and I munch our walnuts, and I mention that the walnuts at the *fruttivendolo* are from America. And he responds, "*Chissà?*" who knows, It's not like you hold the walnut to your ear and it speaks French. I realize I just assume that the ebullient vendor is honest. Angelo doubts it all. I whisper to Angelo that the fruit vendor claims that his *mandarini* are special, maybe we should buy some of the tempting little oranges? He looks at me aghast. Of course the vendor says the *mandarini* are special! What is he supposed to say, I hiked up the price because I want more money? I giggle as I toss away the walnut shells.

My eye is caught by *ravanelli*, radishes. Like jewels, they radiate their own light, glowing in the darkened corner of the truck bed. I must have them. I buy two bunches for a grand total of €1,20 and delight in the perfectly smooth surface and the young, springy leaves. Angelo instructs me to order them by saying "*Io voglio comprare ravanelli.*" Really? It sounds so leaden and egocentric. "I want to buy radishes." Not, "May I have some radishes?" Or, "Can I buy some radishes, please." Like my daughter, I suppose I struggle with accepting who I am and what I want. To say it aloud, so baldly, it feels strange.

It reminds me of *Howard's End*, when Margaret is frustrated by Henry's inability to use "I." She wants him to peel off his outer layer of motorcars and cricket scores and get to the vulnerable man underneath. The man who is flawed, and has made mistakes, but is still worthy of love. Using the word "*voglio*" here, the simple "I want" means much the same. I may be American on Italian soil, I may use the words with a flat inflection, but nonetheless, I want the radishes. And they are handed over with a smile. And a *mandarino*. A *mandarino* that is juicy and tart, so decadent I go back and buy a bagful. Turns out they *are* special.

I tell Angelo that I'm going to eat the *ravanelli* the French way, with butter and salt. He clucks in disbelief. I must eat them the Italian way, dipped in good olive oil. Yes, I tell him, *pinzimonio* is delicious. But I will eat my *ravanelli* the French way. Butter to mellow out the peppery bite of the radish and salt to lend a briny flavor. That's what *I* want.

Later, E.M. Forster hums in my mind while I walk to a dance performance at Teatro Subasio with Doreen and Paola. Much of the performance goes over my head, but I do understand that in the first act, a woman talks about her history of wanting to be a dancer, in deadpan narration. Interspersed in her recitation, she dances. Really dances, with grace and talent. The second act is sort of a parody of the first, with a man charting his love of dance, only without any dancing skill whatsoever. It's amusing, but the people behind me are laughing so hard I fear they might hyperventilate. Paola tells me it's because the actor is known for his serious demeanor, so to see him exposing his vulnerability in this kind of comedic way is particularly amusing. As I walk home, I think about vulnerability and the pathway it creates to the artistic spirit. These were performers who put all their essence on stage to be judged, mocked, damned. What strength comes from connecting to vulnerability, to the "I" within.

> *Only connect! That was the whole of her sermon. Only connect the prose and the passion, and both will be exalted, and human love will be seen at its height. Live in fragments no longer.*
>
> —E.M. Forster, *Howard's End*

19 February

I first went to Tuscany over 15 years ago. I found the food pleasant, but I couldn't quite get what all the hoopla was about. I remember eating *ribollita* and thinking, "Okay, I *almost* love it…" and being hesitant to admit my lackluster opinion, so ingrained was the notion that Tuscan food is the epitome of Italian cuisine. Now I'll have a chance to try again.

The five of us are going with Brenda and Graziano to Da Muzzicone, a restaurant in Tuscany that they claim makes extraordinary *bistecca alla fiorentina*. Leaving our cars parked outside the walls of Castiglion Fiorentino, we take a *passeggiata* to breathe in the clear air. Unlike our pink stone Spello, the town is glowing yellow stucco, with Medici crests and a stunning arcade overlooking the surrounding countryside. We continue to the top of the hill and enter the old castle yard. I look around and realize, there's nobody there but us. The walls whisper—of battles where bows were propped through those tiny arrow slits, of cultivating castle gardens against a siege.

Hunger propels us back down the hill toward Da Muzzicone. Graziano opens the door to a large room with nondescript décor, but an energetic vibe and intoxicating smell. Brenda reserved a table in the back, closest to the open grill set into the wall. A grill that is merrily cooking the most enormous steak I have ever seen. I sink into my seat with a definite thrill. Brenda plucks the wine list off the table and asks if Keith and I want to pick the wine. I laugh aloud. Why would I pick the wine when I'm hanging out with two sommeliers? Brenda selects a Morellino from the Tuscan coast that she knows will be new to us. It's followed by a Vino Nobile di Montepulciano, both fabulous. I'm assuming. I'm drunk with steak by the time the second bottle arrives.

There are no menus. We request *antipasti*, and they bring us a board with a preposterous variety of delights. Cured meats including *prosciutto*, *capocollo*, a pale fennel salami, and *coppa*—a head-cheese-like meat that I avoid, but which Keith reports is wonderful. Plus, *bruschette* unlike any toasted bread I've ever had—some topped with vivid tomatoes cooked down to sunshiny sweetness, finished with a touch of spicy heat, and others topped with an earthy and clean *paté* that forces me to sit back and ponder. The liver is ground, and flavored with briny capers. Also gracing the *antipasti* board is a salami and half a fresh pecorino to slice as desired.

While the rest of us perseverate on the *antipasti*, the owner and Graziano talk beef. The owner describes the beef he has available, and Graziano turns to us to explain that a *bistecca* has a buttery filet—our filet mignon—on one side of the bone, and a beefy contra-filet on the other. To illustrate, the owner brings us a steak. It's cut from the end of the tenderloin, and therefore the filet side is narrower, but it's perfectly aged. If we want a larger filet, the chef could get another side of beef and cut from that, but it's less aged. I have no opinion to offer, as I'm rendered mute by a process that takes meat so seriously. Graziano opts for more aging and less filet.

I'm not sure if it's the quality of the beef, the aging, the preparation, or more probably all three, but the steak is exquisite. Perfect flavor, silky roundness, with caramelized grilled edges. Graziano laughs at how easily two steaks disappear, but he didn't count on how much our children love steak. Nicolas particularly is taking his place at the head of the table as a sign that he should be eating a man's helping of beef. Brenda orders a *tagliata*—a boneless piece of beef, gracefully grilled, then sliced, drizzled with olive oil, and scattered with green peppercorns and rosemary. Not as astonishing as the *bistecca*, so only the second best piece of meat of my steak-eating career.

For *contorni* we order a plate of *spinaci* and a plate of *fagioli*. Humble, yet the spinach is satiny and tender and dressed with peppery olive oil. Sweet and glossy greenness. The cannellini beans are creamy, with a delicately round nuttiness. I'm confused. This is not the Tuscan food I've had before. This meal is a *magnum opus*. The answer, I suppose is simple. The presumption about Tuscan food is that it's all about excellent ingredients. I've known this, but I don't think it sank into my culinary soul. I assumed that if I use a second-rate carrot in my *sofritto*, it will be less carrot-y. But it's not just less carrot-y. It's less exceptional. This beef is just beef. These beans are just beans. But the owner handpicks the beef daily and ages it carefully. It is seasoned with nothing but salt. It is clearly excellent beef, prepared in a way that brings out the illustriousness of the meat. I have no idea what they do to the beans, I suspect they simply boil them. But they are beans of unsurpassed quality. I wonder if Tuscan food earned its reputation from restaurants like Da Muzzicone, but then the hype of Tuscan food increased traffic to touristy places, while local institutions like Da Muzzicone remain with the Tuscans. Tuscan food is a revelation. And savoring it together is a gift.

Dessert is traditional *vin santo*, a dessert wine, and *cantucci*, almond cookies. The owner grabs a bottle of *vin santo* and plunks it on the table with four short glasses, and then cuts a plateful of *cantucci* from a log of uncut cookie under the clear dome of the *cantucci* cart. We are to help ourselves to as much as we want of both. *Vin santo* with *cantucci* is common all over Italy. But this time I finally understand why this dessert has gained a place of prominence in Tuscan cuisine. The *cantucci* are baked once, rather than the more common *biscotti*, which are baked in a log, sliced, then baked again. Baking just once shortens the shelf life of the cookies, but ours last mere minutes. They are a little eggier than usual, with a soft bite that I thought would fail to stand up to dipping in *vin santo*, but on the contrary, it soaks it up with alacrity. Brenda notes that the *vin santo* has aromas of acacia honey and golden delicious apples. I close my eyes and breathe in my glass. All of a sudden, those flavor notes are heady, beautiful. The dessert, with *caffè* and followed by a *bella grappa* (as requested by Graziano, looking a bit like the cat about to relish the canary) is a sublime end to a meal that will live in our memories always.

Hours later, we're home, and trying to figure out what to make for dinner. Which is shocking because I thought we'd never eat again. Gabe tells me that all he really wants is steak. And I laugh aloud—he should have had enough steak to last a month. But then I think about it... and I ask myself, "What sounds really good right now?" And I realize...

All I wanted was one more bite... to close my eyes...

And savor.

22 February

Something is different.

I can't quite put my finger on it, but something is different. We seem to be more...here, now. When I wait outside the *scuola elementare*, other parents nod and smile and greet me. Whereas for months they have looked at me with confused stares. I guess they have grown used to me. So when I'm strolling through town, fellow parents acknowledge me as if they know me. I don't know them, because it's still a sea of unfamiliar adults, whereas my identity as the "American mom" has been clear to them since day one. But slowly, the fog of humanity is clarifying. It's making the whole foreign landscape feel a bit more knowable.

Nowadays, I feel like we stand on the margins rather than on the outside. This shift was brought into focus when Nicolas went to a party at L'Orlando Furioso. Over the summer, we saw a party of high schoolers sharing pizza at Orlando, and we imagined how wonderful it would be to reach a point where he could be part of a group of teenagers, dining without supervision. But we reluctantly agreed it was sort of impossible. One, middle schoolers would probably not have the same kind of freedom to dine *sans* adults. And two, we just couldn't imagine Nicolas being part of such a group in the space of one year. And then he was invited to this gathering of 15 of his classmates. Picturing him eating pizza with his friends, it occurs to me that he has reached a level of arrival that we had thought was beyond dreaming five months ago.

He comes home radiant, and he comes home late. When we have pizza at Orlando, we are there for about an hour. This dinner didn't end until the restaurant closed at 11:00. I guess the kids are in training to be the kind of adults who can sit at the table for hours. Pizza, followed by fries, then cake, with vast quantities of tangy Fanta. Nicolas said he understood all of the conversation, it was easy to participate, he felt like one of the group and he even made jokes. And amid all the teenage mischief, the waitress called him "*caro,*" and smiled at him conspiratorially.

Wow.

Or as they say here, *Uaou.*

23 February

Keith and I are walking home from our morning coffee, when his attention is caught by a sign in the *comune* window. The movie-size poster declares that water to many municipalities in our valley will be shut off on February 26 into the morning of February 27 as the aqueduct is being repaired. Huh. No water. It doesn't really occur to me to think too much about it until later. Much like the pope abdicating didn't strike me as odd until I said to a friend, "Does the pope wear a funny hat?" and stopped to realize—not for much longer.

The children bring home notices that the school will be closed during the aqueduct work. No water means no radiator heat, no flushing toilets. Wait, this means *we* will be without heat and flushing toilets. Oh, no. Doreen comes up with the idea of a Spello exodus. We can migrate for two days, to a land of milk and honey. Or at least a land of running water.

So on the 26th we will leave for Le Marche where Dwight, from Thanksgiving, owns a winery and *agriturismo*. The road through the wilds of the Apennines goes through the town of Norcia, home of Umbrian *salumi*. Perfect for a lunch stop and a pantry stocking.

Provisions in tow, we'll land at Dwight's with Doreen and Paola, relax and go for wanders if the weather is decent, and then make unleavened *gnocchi* together. It will be a triumphal sleepover party. And there will be sweet hot *and* cold running water.

Now, is that not the promised land?

26 February

We are surprised by the still having of water. Look! I turn it on...water! I turn it off. I turn it on...*Eccola!* Water! Only when you are in danger of losing something does its excellence shine. And then begins the exodus of the waterless Spellani refugees.

We stop in Norcia, which is Disneyland for *antipasti* lovers. Notably, me. Racks of *prosciutto* on display outside *salumi* shops, goofy *cinghiale* heads mounted on colorful walls, a stand of the largest olives I've ever seen, windows filled with teetering towers of cheese. And everywhere, everywhere...*salumi*. This caricature of a town has the gall to be even more surpassingly charming by including a frame of snow-covered mountains, peering down into the main *piazza*. We pop into a shop, and the boys and Paola pop right back out again. None of them are fans of cheese, and the shop is—*sigh*—the shop is ripe with the smell of cheese. We taste a salami, then another, then another—each one better than the last. We taste cheese. And leave, palates satisfied and bags spilling over with treats. The *cinghiale* heads look on in approval.

Lunch, however, is a disappointment. My dish of *tagliatelle ai tartufi* is bitter.

Doreen says that sometimes restaurants use truffle oil that is usually made by adding chemicals to last year's oil. Bitter on bitter. Plus, the bits of truffle themselves resemble shredded cork. The *porcini* on Siena's bruschetta and Paola's *tagliatelle* are slimy. On the upside, we learn how to say "slimy" in Italian, *viscido*.

Back on the road to Le Marche. Past beautiful plains framed by the grassy foothills of snow-capped mountains. Past dun-colored villages so much a part of the landscape that one of the houses is built around a ten-foot-high boulder. Past waterfalls and rushing rivers. And then we enter the Le Marche countryside. Siena marvels, "It's like a giant tossed huge boulders for a game of marbles, and then draped them with a patchwork quilt." She's right—there's an undulation combined with field diversity, which makes for an evocative landscape. My eye doesn't know where to land, and even when I do fix my gaze on a particularly spectacular vineyard, the colors constantly shift as the sun plays Marco Polo with the clouds.

Dwight's home is no exception. His *agriturismo*, Nascondiglio di Bacco, is surrounded by beautiful vineyards, patches of grassland, and groves of olive trees that combine to create a landscape of staggering beauty. We greet Dwight, then we tour the bed and breakfast, and walk through the vineyards. Dwight tells us that the valley's vines are owned by farmers with varying methods of vine training, which explains the textural differences in the fields as one pivots to take in the mesmerizing shifting landscape.

We walk to the cantina of Dwight's Paolini e Stanford Winery, a modern structure, with floor-to-ceiling plate glass windows overlooking the vineyards. After touring the winemaking areas, we decide to cook dinner at the cantina, thus inaugurating the new kitchen. Several trips to and from the house with equipment and supplies and we're ready to begin. Meanwhile, Siena and Gabe build forts between the olive trees and grapevines, decorating their areas with chamomile flowers found everywhere underfoot, pausing now and again to drink in their surroundings.

Keith lays the *antipasti* out to enjoy while we cook, and Dwight selects bottles of his Pecorino, a white grape with a nutty flavor. The moment is only slightly marred by my exclamation of "Pecorino! I didn't know you raised sheep!" The wine is lively and woody, but the best part of this wine is its presentation. I dash to the house to fetch a pan, and loiter in my walk back to the cantina, admiring the sunset through the olive trees. As I walk into the bustling kitchen, full of sunset and cooling breezes, Dwight turns toward me with a grin of welcome and a luminous glass in his outstretched hand.

We cook dinner together, and dine at the table stretched along the wall of window that faces the now shadowy valley. The meal, being a communal endeavor, is fully enjoyed, the more so since it is accompanied by unlabeled wine fetched from the cantina. With our dessert, Dwight produces a measuring cup filled with his *passito*, a dessert wine made from dried grapes. It's nutty, delicately flowery. We laugh at Dwight's description of how he hand pressed the *passito*. The grapes were so dry, he struggled to turn the press, each time releasing just a few drops.

Dinner conversation flows between travel, politics, and even religion. Here, this is the meat and heft of dinnertime banter. It creates a layering with the view and the wine and the food and the community. I float back to Dwight's house and accept a goblet of his homemade white liquor. Clear, with a flavor of anise, it's surprisingly light and sweet.

And sends me humming up to bed—my head light, my heart lighter.

27 February

I wake up in the morning and am drawn to the window where mists shroud the distant hills. Doreen and I meet at the breakfast table, and note that while Spello is quiet, the silence of people being quiet is different than the silence of no people. One by one, everyone gathers for coffee, cakes, jam, cheese. Siena and Gabe quickly finish breakfast in their haste to get back to play among the vines. The rest of us chat, have more coffee, and eventually decide to venture out into the brisk morning. We walk the road until we arrive across the valley from Dwight's. Siena stands still, and says this is one of the most beautiful places she's ever been. Dwight beams, and Nicolas whispers to me that he is worried his sister might explode with adoration.

Keith ask Dwight why there are artichoke plants at the head of each row of vines, rather than the roses that usually front the rows to signal the presence of fungus and disease. Dwight laughs that with organic growing, by the time a blight shows on the rose, there's no possibility of saving the vine. These local growers won't waste the bit of space between the vines and the road with silly roses.

Instead, they plant artichokes. Which require no maintenance, are perennial, plus they are delicious. Have we tried them with wild mint?

We reluctantly stroll back to the house to pack, and rally a little at the prospect of wine souvenirs. One of the benefits of being a water refugee in Italy. Though it's at this point that Paola checks her messages and learns that Spello never lost water. I guess that's the second great thing about being a refugee in Italy—the comical confusion about the whole affair. We say goodbye to Dwight, and drive to Ascoli Piceno. A simple drive, which nonetheless answers our residual question of whether or not we still need to dose Siena with Dramamine for every drive over 20 minutes. And that's all I'm going to say about that.

We walk through Ascoli Piceno, admiring the charm and life of the town, while Siena gets her legs back under her. Once ready to eat, we walk into Migliori, on Dwight's recommendation. I order a grand fried platter of Ascolana olives, artichokes, lamb chops, and even squares of fried custard. The custard confuses me, I thought *"cremini"* would be mushrooms, not cream, but it's always a pleasant surprise to find a little dessert among your meal. I've had Ascolana olives several times, and about half the time the meat filling within the fried olive has the taste and texture of ground olive pits. But this is succulent. As is my *contorno* of *cicoria*, braised chicory with velvety olive oil and pepper flakes.

Rather than our usual bottle of wine, we order two half liters to sample local varieties. In one wine, we note an aroma of horses, nutmeg, and ricotta. Pretty sure those aren't flavor compounds on the quintessential poster of aroma notes in a glass of wine. Neither is smoky banana, which we taste in the second wine. Both of our jugs are complicated and brimming with personality. And inexpensive, at €5 a bottle. Marche wines are something special.

After lunch, we stroll to the grand *piazza* and Doreen, Paola, and Keith enjoy coffee in the grand, historic Caffè Meletti, while I stay outside with the children who play tag with great enthusiasm. The *piazza* is empty, and they sprint wildly, giggling with joy. We wander back out of Ascoli, to part ways from our friends for the drive back to Spello.

If the incomprehensible ways of the Perugian water authority means an impromptu midweek vacation with friends, they can shut off my water any time.

28 February

The cold is less pervasive lately, so we amble to Bar Bonci after *pausa*. Halfway there, I notice that Nicolas has casually reached for Siena's hand, and the two of them walk, linked, laughing at Gabe skipping backward ahead. We step into Bar Bonci with a cheerful greeting, and indicate that we'd like to sit outside. Letizia warns us that nobody has been in the garden for ages, so it needs to be cleaned. Undaunted, we venture forward, and start brushing tree debris off the tables. Our children tackle the task with greater than average vigor, thanks to a tag game that involves throwing pine cones. Nicolas munches an apple at a table with the Bonci cat curled up on his lap, Siena makes a harbor out of boats she fashions with bits of bark and leaves, and Gabe takes pictures of gravel, as we bask in the splendor of having the garden to ourselves.

I sip my Aperol spritz, letting the glow of the early spring sunshine, the gladness of delighted children's voices, and the lively orange cocktail thaw my bones.

It's getting warmer.

Joyful Carnevale Cake

5 eggs at room temperature

250 grams of sugar

200 grams (2 American sticks) of butter, melted and cooled

500 grams all-purpose flour

zest of 1 orange, preferably a blood orange
(carefully remove the waxy orange rind with a knife,
scrape off any white pith, and mince finely)

juice of same orange

250 ml of milk (about a cup), or you may need
more as flour in the States is different

2 16-gram packs of *lievito per dolci*, or 6 teaspoons of baking powder

——————————————— * ❋ * ———————————————

1. Preheat your oven to 180° C/350° F.

2. Beat sugar and eggs together until they are creamy and make a ribbon when you lift the beater(s). Add the zest and continue to beat for another few moments.

3. Add a third of the flour to the egg mixture, beat for a minute, then add another third, and beat for a minute. Add the melted and cooled butter and beat for another minute.

4. Beat in half the milk, then half the remaining flour, the rest of the milk, then the rest of the flour (beating after each addition).

5. Add the *lievito* or baking powder by sprinkling it on the top, adding the orange juice, then beating a bit once more.

6. Butter a large ring pan, then flour it and shake out the excess flour.

7. Pour in the batter, then tap to remove air bubbles. You can sprinkle coarse sugar on the top.

8. Bake for 30 minutes to 45 minutes depending on the size of your pan.

9. Serving suggestion? Excellent with a glass of juniper-infused grappa and a view over tile rooftops.

MARCH

THE WATER IS HERE

3 March

You know what they say…when the cat's away the mice will play. So when Keith and Graziano make plans to go skiing, I'm externally thrilled that he'll enjoy a day of skiing and friendship, and internally thrilled that I'll be able to make the children pancakes for lunch with no one looking at me quizzically. Keith has rules around eating that I find too rigid. He can't eat anything savory (unless it has eggs) before noon, and refuses pancakes past brunch time. To be fair, I have my own eating idiosyncrasies—Keith always grins when he asks what I'm reading while I nibble a snack. Snack time is Jane Austen time. In any case, I enjoy the freedom to go out of orbit a bit. It makes the shift out of line exciting, and the shift back in line feel cozy. The sun feels warmer somehow.

I pick up the kids from school, and make them pancakes and sausage patties I MacGyver by dismantling linked sausage. The three of them are in American-breakfast-for-Italian-*pranzo* heaven. We then catch the train to Foligno. On a school day! The children run around the park like springs suddenly loosed. When the afternoon wanes, we take the train home, chattering about the pope's abdication. As we walk through our door, we find Keith taking off his shoes, his face flushed with his adventures. He and Graziano had a great day, but ski conditions were so challenging that they both were exhausted by mid-afternoon. We feed the children, then tuck the little ones in, and Keith and I go out for dinner, stopping first at Vinosofia for a glass of wine. Keith and Graziano catalogue their various aches, and I luxuriate in the depth and calm of a glass of wine with friends.

4 March

Angelo pops into the *comune* to discuss why Spello never lost water. Raimondo, the man to ask when one has a question about the *navetta,* civil paperwork, parking, or where to find a good *cornetto*, tells him that our sustained hydration goes back to Hispellum days. The ancient Romans built an aqueduct to carry melted snow from a giant cave inside Mount Subasio down to the town. As time went by, and Spello became more populated, this amount of water proved insufficient, so a second aqueduct was created from an underground river that was also fed by water on Subasio. About 30 years ago, a third aqueduct was built to draw water from a river south of town to Spello, Foligno, and Bevagna. This new aqueduct helped meet the increased water needs subsequent to a modern lifestyle that included tourism. It was this aqueduct that sustained damage during the 1977 earthquake, and was slated for repair last week. To repair the line, the Valle Umbra Servizi (VUS) workers shut the water off at that source, but the engineers didn't factor in Spello's other two sources of water. Foligno did lose water, but Spello experienced no hiccup. The unseasonably warm temperatures reduced the use of radiators, and there are few tourists in February to strain the water supply with their water parties and water balloon parades. In addition, at least seven Spellani left town for greener pastures, further lightening the demand on the two older sources of water.

Angelo tells me that the citizens were irate that VUS didn't run simple calculations to judge the impact to the water supply. If they had, Spellani would have been spared the inconvenience and cost of purchasing bottled water, arranging childcare, and the loss of two days revenue for bars and restaurants. I guess it was pretty easy for us to find the whole thing a big adventure, since we had the time and freedom to skedaddle.

What I find interesting is that it was this new source of water that created the disturbance, while the oldest sources of water allowed Spello to continue its operations with nary a wrinkle. The underground cave full of water beat a modern pipe, once again proving that modernity doesn't necessarily equate with quality. Sometimes I think that with our advancing society, we're losing more than we gain. The easier tasks become, the less those tasks mean. With email, the art of letter writing is waning. With convenience foods, children have no idea that chicken comes with bones and people are forgetting how to cook. With computers to run calculations, people stop trying to calculate. With all of our new "free time," are we living deepened lives? Or does making things easy make it too easy to fritter away our moments, letting our lives drift by in a series of status updates and text notifications?

The water is here.

Let's drink.

5 March

Tomorrow we leave for Spain. We're eager for the new tastes, the gracious *piazze* (I must endeavor to now say *plazas*), the *churros* dipped in hot chocolate, the warm weather…eager is probably an understatement. At my lesson, Angelo asks about our plans, and I tell him that I'm particularly excited about convent sweets. I explain that there are cloistered convents in Sevilla where the nuns make sweets to sell via a lazy Susan, rotated one way to give the treats, rotated back to give the money. I've made a map of convents and a list of Andalusian treat names to decipher edible possibilities. My tastebuds are gearing up to be delighted.

Angelo smiles knowingly and tells me that the same system existed in Spello. While teaching me all sorts of convent vocabulary, he instructs me on the life of a cloistered nun. How those *ruote*, wheels, were used to bring supplies to the convent, or to sell goods—such as embroidered fabric in Spellani convents—or for the Mother Superior to leave a key to a trusted woman in the outside world so that woman could accompany a plumber to fix leaky pipes, while the nuns huddled in an airless room. A room that not even the pope could enter. Sometimes unmarried girls would put their babies in the *ruote*, and nuns would wake up to mysterious cries and then have to alert the authorities to remove the baby to an orphanage. All without ever being seen.

Angelo's voice lowers as he whispers further stories of intrigue. I didn't even know there were scandalous convent tales. But he tells me that Santa Maria Vallegloria, which was once cloistered, had prisons built atop the garden walls. *"Per chi?"* I ask, and he answers, *"Per le sorelle."* For the nuns who were punished by the Mother Superior. In fact, the street below these cells is called the Street of Wailing. But it wasn't until recently that the convent's dark stain was truly revealed. Workers were drilling in the yard when they stumbled upon the skeletons of women and babies. Nuns that died respectably were carried out of the convent to be buried. But those that died in childbirth, impregnated by men who scaled over the convent wall, were secretly buried on site. I shiver.

Angelo goes on to say that cloistering as a principle was hard to maintain. What with all the nuns escaping in the night. So eventually, the pope decreed that nuns in formerly cloistered convents could choose whether or not to stay hidden behind convent walls. Angelo relays the story of one Spellani nun who had entered the convent at age 18, and in her 80's decided she would take the pope up on his offer. She walked out of the convent for the first time in almost 70 years. And thought she'd gone crazy.

In the streets where she remembered roaming pigs and chickens and cows, there were now cars. Sure, she might have heard of cars, but she'd never seen them, even in photographs, since television, newspapers, radio, were all forbidden. The world was an entirely different place, with electricity, noise, and women in short pants. The shock was too much for her. She had a heart attack, and died.

The story makes me reflect on technology and modern advancement. Life moves forward. I don't have to be a slave to the advancement, but I can't put my head in the collective sand and ignore that the world is changing. Rather, my job is discernment. To decide with intention what modern philosophies and conveniences I'll incorporate into my life. Neither eschewing all of it, or accepting all of it. But working toward finding my balance, my center. Some nuns could walk out of the convent at 80 and feel nothing but delight in the adventure, some need to stay behind familiar walls. It's not my job to determine an empirical "best," but rather to determine how I open my own gates.

13 March

Sevilla is a moveable feast, a feast for the senses. With breezes that smell of oranges and incense and garlic, and something indefinable that is probably tapas cooking at the neighborhood bar—tapas that you can purchase with just the change in your pocket. The buildings are a riot of architectural styles and colors, tied together with tiled patios to peer in, grassy roofs, Moorish embellishments, and wrought iron balconies that speak of warm nights and tendrils of wind. And from one neighborhood to another, there are glossy trees adorned with vibrant oranges. The early spring light is vivid and shifting as the sun ducks behind clouds, creating a moodiness that is swept clear in the next moment by the sun's victorious return.

A feast for the soul. I'm thinking of flamenco music and dance, certainly, but something more. Everywhere there is the sound of people talking, laughing, sharing, welcoming. The people are casually and effortlessly present to life. English is spoken less here than in any other European city we've visited, and even when people speak English, they answer in Spanish if you begin with Spanish, no matter how bad your Spanish is. They nod like they understand and keep the conversation going past the point of necessity. They are warm beyond reason. Our Airbnb host is our first sign that Spain takes friendliness to a whole other level. Pepe gives us a walking tour of neighborhood tapas, invites us to breakfast with his family, drops by to give us a bottle of his father's sherry when I express an interest. Nicolas is ready to move in. We all are.

A feast for the imagination. We tour the seat of the Spanish Inquisition, and ponder the cracks that develop in a society bent on monoculture. We stroll through the art market in front of Sevilla's art museum and honor people who feel a pull to create. With Pepe's help, we file into convents and whisper the secret code that produces *yemas*, a candy made with egg yolks and sugar whisked in a copper pot. We accept a handful of tiny dried shrimp from a vendor and enjoy their briny crispness, before looking up confused as the smiling vendor has moved away before we can purchase any. We sample *torrijas* from the bakeries, a creamy French toast swimming in a light honey syrup, and imagine the history of this Sevillian treat. We sit with our mouths open during a flamenco show in the long smoky room of La Carboniera, and remark that we couldn't move any part of our body as fast as the guitar player plays or the dancer steps. We wander the royal palace, and feel the rapture that comes from seeing the interplay of history and architecture and landscaping in a setting divinely beautiful (and incidentally, create a useful family rule: No parkour in UNESCO World Heritage Sites). We climb to the top of what looks like giant mushrooms for a view of the city, and remember that this Metropol is built on a bustling market, which is built over Roman ruins, which reminds us of the presence of Greek and Phoenician ruins scattered around the city. We watch our children attempt Spanish with strangers, and are taken aback by their comfort with yet another foreign language.

And Sevilla is a feast in the literal sense. Octopus and paprika tapas on small plates in restaurants, colorful shops of olives and runny *Torta de Casar* cheese aged with thistle rennet, lively markets of fishmongers angling the seafood so our children can get the best photo and then offering a candy, *churros* made in a stand that sells chicken at night, market stalls spilling over with fascinating products like donuts with anise, and stalls that sell nothing but oysters and *cava*, tantalizing scents from open windows. Shopping is a way to connect with the flavor of the city and the people lucky enough to live and work in this vivid place. While I linger lustfully at a cheese counter, a customer starts telling me about her favorite cheeses. She doesn't recoil at my terrible Spanish, but rather keeps sharing and asking questions, as if nothing is unusual. The marketing is the link between Sevilla's dynamic food culture and its incredible warmth.

I come to consider tapas the perfect social food and a clear metaphor for Sevilla. It's so easy to get just one more plate, one more round. So easy to pass around and experience together. So easy to try new things with low risk. And so wonderful to sample the flavors of Andalusia, one little taste at a time.

14 March

Gabe's back on Italian soil. It's taken him about five minutes to start begging me to invite Lorenzo to our house. I still eschew phones, and so I'm gratified to run into Anna Maria outside of school during drop off. I'm also gratified anew that her English is excellent, as my Italian skills upon landing are horrible. Even Letizia has been cracking up at my crazy errors. And my children have turned correcting mom into sport. No, Mom, *como* is Spanish. So is *esto*.

Over coffee, Anna Maria compares the warmth of the Spaniards with how Italy was 20 years ago, and how southern Italy still is. Prompting her to once again insist that we visit Sicily. Lischia, a woman I met on the plane to Sevilla demanded the same. Lischia and I spent the three-hour flight in conversation starting with complaining about RyanAir's crazy baggage system. Turns out you don't need much language to complain about airline travel. Which allowed me to warm up and have a real conversation with her. She told me that she's always wanted to visit Pennsylvania because of William Penn. She finds Quakerism intriguing. My jaw dropped and I stuttered telling her that I was Quaker, and we looked at each other in astonishment. What are the odds? She told me she was Catholic, but *una critica cattolica*. Can't believe I had a discussion about theology in Italian with a woman from Napoli on a flight to Sevilla (where she was meeting her son who is living in Portugal). In any case, she ordered me to visit Sicily. I'm getting worried that we won't get there. The opportunities for travel are dwindling.

Anna Maria agrees that we can have Lorenzo over on Friday. Gabe is thrilled. I am nervous. While older Italian kids can extrapolate meaning from pieces of sentences, young children have historically just looked at me like I have broccoli erupting from my eyebrows when I say something inscrutable. And I'm not sure if Gabe's Italian is good enough to make this a successful playdate. I'm swamped with memories of Halloween, when Siena and Amalia took turns avoiding each other's eye contact for hours. Having Chiara over took some of the edge off that memory, and I should remember that Gabe and Lorenzo have a relationship that somehow works despite Gabe's lack of functional Italian, but still—the memory of that wearing silence is omnipresent as Gabe chatters about Lorenzo's visit.

In the afternoon, Gabe pulls out his school *quaderno* to show me a drawing he's made of the new pope. In 2005, the last time we had a new pope, Nicolas was Gabe's age. The papacy was nowhere on his radar. If I'd asked him, "What's a pope?" He would have guessed a fizzy candy. Possibly cola flavored. It's a real marker of this year abroad to have our Gabe draw a picture of Papa Francesco in celebration of his ascension to the head of the Catholic Church. Gabe celebrates the new pope by making us all cross necklaces. While he cuts the yellow construction paper, he asks if he can send a necklace to the pope. I'm pretty sure the pope has plenty of jewelry. But I do find myself fantasizing about Gabe and Lorenzo spending hours making paper jewelry for the pope. Then, at least, the silence will be less abrasive.

15 March

This morning Gabe cleans his room in preparation for Lorenzo's arrival. After we walk the children to school and have coffee, Keith delivers his now completed application for Italian citizenship to the *comune*. It seems a long shot that the application will be completely processed while we are here, but he's hopeful that at least he'll be available to correct any errors discovered in these next four months. Citizenship feels like a fairy tale to me, but still, when I wave Keith off, I call, *"In bocca al lupo!"*—"good luck," or, more literally, "in the mouth of the wolf." While Keith is gone I make a meat *sugo* and gird myself for a long playdate. But either our Italian has improved or Lorenzo is bright enough to be able to figure out what we mean from what we say. There are no conversational hitches. Lorenzo says, "Thank you very much!" in cheerful English when we hand him his plate, and soon asks for seconds. As they eat their pasta, Gabe turns to Lorenzo and says, *"Dopo pranzo, vuoi disegnare insieme?"* After lunch, do you want to draw together? The four of us look up at each other in astonishment. "Did *you* know he could speak like this?"

Thus begins an afternoon of Italian language euphoria. The four of us keep stopping and gesturing to each other as we listen to Gabe chatter with Lorenzo. Lorenzo is speaking so quickly, we can't keep up, but Gabe answers just as quickly. He uses the past tense. He uses the present tense. He uses unfamiliar nouns. And the two of them play fluidly. Periodically, I hear a bang from Gabe's room and call out, *"Tutto bene?"* And they shout back, *"Sì!"* They find this so amusing that they start to chant, *"Tutto bene!"* whenever they make any loud sound. And then they give way to conspiratorial giggles.

The ease of Gabe's language, the comfortable connection with a friend, the love of the pope marks him as Italian. But then he spends the evening practicing his flamenco clapping to American music playing from my iPod, earbuds planted firmly in his ears. So maybe he is a citizen of the world. That's good, too.

16 March

The essay I submitted for publication has been rejected. I feel like I explicated a piece of my soul, and that fragment was squished like a too-ripe banana. With the same eerily grey color. And a nasty, sour smell. Walk away, people, from the delirious woman yammering about bananas. Keith "helpfully" informs me that writers need to handle rejection. To which I respond, "Fine, I just won't be a writer anymore." Never let it be said that I cope with rejection with anything resembling maturity.

The truth is, I have a toxic reaction to rejection. I have been known to obsessively reword texted invitations so that if my friend declines it won't feel personal or over-read emails declining play-dates by noting punctuation and emoticons. It's not pretty.

It was Siena who helped me understand this neurosis. When she was three, she asked me to play dolls. I declined and she burst into tears. When she'd calmed, she told me, "When you say no, it feels like you don't love me. " That's it. Someone saying "no," couched in regret, feels completely fine to me. Life moves in disparate paths sometimes, I get that. Someone just saying "no" leaves me cold. Alone. And the icy wind is formidable.

As I'm rereading the rejection email, it occurs to me that some people could blow it off. I wonder what that would feel like. I close my eyes and imagine me, reading the rejection email and thinking, "Oh, well, I'll revamp the essay and send it elsewhere." Almost as if the essay is not in fact a piece of my soul, but rather a puzzle piece that doesn't fit. I imagine being over it. And all of a sudden, I am. There's a bit of catch, but it's a mere hitch, rather than a downward spiral of self-flagellation and negative messages.

I hum as I straighten the house. The village priest is coming to bless our home for Easter, a custom in small town Umbria. I'm a little nervous about what in the world we'll talk about with a priest—will he ask us questions we don't understand? I make an apple cake, and can't decide if I'm more excited or anxious. And I wonder if apples are inappropriately symbolic of original sin.

The buzzer rings at 5:00, and I run down to welcome the priest. He looks confused to be greeted by an American family, but once our welcome is clear, he enters. He asks who is the oldest. We indicate Nicolas, who says that actually, I'm the oldest. The priest chuckles and admonishes Nicolas that a woman is never considered the oldest. I tentatively offer him cake and he declines, but hands us a rock embellished with a picture of Jesus. The priest asks where we're from, and if we're Catholic. We admit that we're not. Unperturbed, he smiles and proclaims that we all live under God. He then launches so quickly into the blessing that I'm not sure it's happening until he brandishes a silver shaker of holy water, flicking it in the shape of a cross in our living room. And then I hear him chant, in Italian, bless this house and all who inhabit it. Unsure of the appropriate response, we smile and thank him, and give him an envelope with our donation. This we're sure of, since the envelope arrived in the same package as the information about the timing of the priest's visit. He chats for a few more minutes, and then takes his leave.

After the door closes behind him, I notice that Gabe is dabbing the errant drops of holy water off the chair and smudging his cheeks. The child is blessing himself. I blink back tears as I wish fervently that it could be so easy for me, as an adult, to trust my ability to beatify my own soul.

17 March

This is a hard day. My children are whiny and argumentative, and that probably is part of it. Plus, Siena lost her cool in spectacular fashion—so dramatic that I wondered if she had a twig stuck in her gears. Despite the fact that when I asked her yesterday, she said things were great, thus proving the adage that people won't talk about the hard stuff just because you ask. They will wait until they are ready. Your own state of readiness is rather immaterial.

So yes, my children's moods are depleting. And yesterday's rejection still probably stings at some level. All the turmoil forces the protective layers around my heart to grow wrinkled and worn and weak. Without my usual barriers of optimism and rather hearty denial, the feelings I have kept at bay enter without a "how d'ye do?" And what do I find?

Emotional distance. This year abroad has exposed cracks in friendships that I had convinced myself were functional. Perhaps despite evidence to the contrary.

Looking back, I can see that the fissures began long before we flew the American coop. Separation now shines a blaring light on the yawning rift. I can no longer ignore the breach—dismissive or even irritable responses to my reaching out, and sometimes radio silence.

In short, I feel alone. Tearful, regretful, without the inner power to tell myself that it's natural for relationships to change over time. Instead I felt damaged. There must be something wrong with me that people I love can walk away from the heart I tenderly hold out to them. Yes, I expected to feel a pause in my relationships during this year, but I didn't predict loss. Or worse, compounded loss. And now I'm struggling under the weight of that grief.

Feeling alone and unloved when I am far from those who would embrace me, from those friends who do value me, is painful. So I find myself moving as if through water. Sure, I'll make the beds with the sheets I spent all day washing. Sure, we can go to Orlando for dinner. Sure, I can look at the picture you made. Sure. When really, it's all I can do to stand up straight.

An evening of pizza and connecting with my family (*they love me, right?*), followed by ducking into Vinosofia for a glass of wine with Brenda and Graziano, and sharing their eagerness to gather and connect as much as we can in the next four months, helps. It helps a lot.

But as night closes in, I feel the void again. I know this isn't a problem for me to solve. It's a grief I need to feel, not deflect from or justify. Just feel. Until the pain becomes dull. And turns to resignation. To which I will acclimate until I can accept it. But I don't have to like it.

18 March

Gabe is hidden behind a closed door, and all I can hear is the sound of tape being stretched and torn. Stretched and torn. Finally, he marches out of his room to show me his work, with a grand flourish. A castle! Made from paper! Complete with family crests and turrets. I suggest it might be fun to make a moat with crocodiles. He considers my idea with a furrowed brow.

Five minutes later he reappears at my side with a self-satisfied smile, trailing a long piece of tape from his shoe. He asks if I think anyone would pay €3 for his castle (clearly not understanding that this work of art has used at least €3 worth of tape). The clouds part and I realize what's happening. He isn't making the castle to play with. He's making the castle to sell. As is typical for young children with low cash flow, he loves making and selling. Just last week, I bought a garden he made from paper, despite the fact that I don't have much use for paper gardens. I've "rented" Lego structures, purchased "jewelry" made from toothpicks and rubber bands, and dropped coins into a jar perched demandingly at his side as he alternately strummed his guitar and flamenco clapped with deliberate concentration.

I suggest that perhaps no one will buy his castle. I might as well have told him that not only is the tooth fairy imaginary, we've been grinding up those baby teeth to make cat food. Tears rush down his cheeks, and I'm not sure that bottom lip could really bend down any further. He wails, "Why then did you give me extra work if you weren't going to buy it?" A moment of confusion, and then it occurs to me that he took my suggestion of making a moat, and turned it into a commission.

And then, repeatedly, "You don't like my castle! You think it's ugly!"

There is really no way to backpedal out of this one. All I really want is for him to enjoy the process without getting hung up on the product. I repeat this message frequently, using metaphors, humor, and storytelling. He is most definitely not interested. He needs to sit with his grief. And he needs me beside him while he does so.

I can empathize. I am finding that the pain of my rejections is eased by connecting with people who care about me. It makes me aware of the beauty of the present—the love that is all around, the unerring way the clouds continue to glide across the brilliant blue Umbrian sky. Perhaps part of what makes losing friends hard is projecting my present sadness into the future—imagining the loss spinning out forever. I'm working to accept that I'm sad now, but see that sadness in context. The future will work itself out, and these losses are a confined piece of my current life that is surrounded by a great deal of beauty. That helps. A bit. It's a variant of "*piano, piano*," I suppose. Take the moment as it happens. What I have in front of me is awfully nice.

I hold Gabe while his sobs subside. Eventually even the hiccups stop. And he sits up and announces, "I feel better now." Goodness, how many times this year have I tried actively helping my children in their pain, only to find that just holding the space works better?

19 March

Today is Father's Day, or Saint Joseph's Day. This means that in Italy, Father's Day holds as its model a non-biological father. The symbolism strikes me—to be a father requires not the donation of an x or y chromosome, but rather love and devotion. Fathers come in all forms, some likely, some unlikely. And blessed be to those men who grace others with their care and affection.

I use the occasion to make ravioli. I've been eager to try it, even though it means making pasta on my own for the first time since Conci's lesson, without her guidance or supplies. My board is too small, my rolling pin is standard rather than the long, pasta-rolling variety. Deciding to leap before over-thinking it, I divide the dough to fit my wee board, and use the side of a business card to guide the straight lines of the pasta squares. I notice a real satisfaction in the jerry-rigged process. It is oddly reminiscent of the work Keith did on our Virginia house, figuring out ways around our crooked walls. Now that I think of it, it reminds me of Joseph himself. I'm sure he would have preferred a son of his own blood, as I would have preferred a ravioli cutter, and Keith would have preferred straight walls. We find ways to make it work, and maybe all that intention makes the process sweeter.

Along with the ravioli, I prepare fava beans, which are a common food on the feast of Saint Joseph because long ago in Sicily, there was a drought, and the people prayed to Saint Joseph for rain. It did eventually rain, but the crops were already so damaged, only the fava survived. But fava beans are so packed with protein and vitamins, they supported the population. Keith brought home a bagful of favas, as he's seen them everywhere, along with signs alerting customers to the presence of the beans, since some Italians are highly allergic. Which I find sort of unsettling. Here, make use of this fabulous plant, packed with nutrition—just kidding! Hope you have health insurance!

I start researching recipes for the classic Saint Joseph's treat of *zeppole*, fried balls of dough, sometimes sweet filled with a pastry cream, and sometimes savory with a bit of anchovy. But Siena starts throwing up about an hour before dinner, and so I jettison the *zeppole*. I put some pasta aside for her, thankful that ravioli can hold when circumstances demand a change in plans.

She and Gabe give Keith cards they made at school. Gabe's is a report card, where he gives his father full marks on love and patience, but only rates Keith a 5 for *fantasia*, imagination. Gabe is missing his education on American sugarcoating. But I suppose we rarely get perfect marks in life. The trick is learning to roll on.

We sit down to dinner, sans Siena. The wood and lemon smell of the sage, heated in butter, wafts from our plates. We dive in. The butter-sage sauce works on the eggs in the pasta to explode with rich flavor. Even Gabe, cautious around cheese, loves the dish. I chew slowly, really tasting each decadent bite, and think about all the ways that ravioli should be the emblematic food of Father's Day.

20 March

Siena recovers from her stomach bug, but I keep her home from school, just in case. The boys walk to school on their own, since I'm in the middle of caring for Siena and Keith has no pants on. He must've left a pair of his jeans in Spain, because we simply cannot find them. He tried shopping for new jeans, but realized that Italian pants are not suited for American bodies. I thought it was just me that had a hard time winching myself into skin-hugging Italian pants, but even my lanky husband can't find pants—leaving him homebound in his flannels, since just washed jeans take an age to dry in March.

The day is a blur of washing sheets, washing stuffed animals, monitoring liquid consumption, canceling Siena's violin lesson, and finding new and interesting ways of asking, "Do you want a banana?" I'm just grateful that she's well enough for Brenda and Graziano's *cinghiale* dinner tonight.

We walk through the misty streets to our friends' house, and we enter to a heavenly smell. The *cinghiale* has been marinating in a wine bath for days—first white, then red—and now it's bubbling, beef stew style, in a generously sized enamel pot. Brenda leads us to our seats, and serves us a salad of *puntarelle*. It's a curious vegetable, with the crunch of bok choy and the pepperiness of arugula, dressed with a zingy dressing of lemon and olive oil. I secretly want every savory curl of stalk and leaf. Along with the salad, Brenda has made a braided loaf of bread with walnuts and *pecorino* that's so satisfying, Nicolas tells her that though he favors neither walnuts or cheese, the bread is fabulous. Then Brenda ladles out a silky horseradish potato puree, with ramekins of plain potato puree for our gut-compromised daughter and spice-compromised youngest child. I wiggle in anticipation as the main dish is brought to the table—*cinghiale*. I've only ever had wild boar in the form of *ragù*, so I'm not sure what to expect. My eyes close to savor the stew. The meat is tender, and the broth is luxurious, with a wild, herbaceous flavor. I eat more than strictly necessary, and have to struggle to find room for the dessert of grapefruit and blood oranges with fall of black pepper, which is oddly similar to a zesty vanilla. And then my arm is twisted to accept a bowl of chocolate gelato drizzled with vibrant olive oil and sprinkled with sea salt flakes that are briefly discernible on the tongue, before they dissolve into a delectable memory.

Three red wines accompany the meal, increasing in strength and particularity. Ending with an *amarone*, which has rich, almost bitter notes. Graziano notes a flavor of balsamic, and Keith notes a flavor of tea. Drinking wine with people who take it seriously is a whole different activity than simply unscrewing a bottle to go with a plate of indifferently prepared pasta. Here, it is a process. Drinking in the smell of the wine, and then letting it stir the imagination before taking a sip. And then using that sip to note idiosyncrasies not apparent at smelling alone.

While we linger over the *amarone* and then apricot *grappa*, the children watch Pippi Longstocking, in Italian. Which I find all kinds of funny, but then again, I'm three glasses of wine into the evening. After the sunshiney warmth of the *grappa* has faded, we gather our children to head back out into the fog-blurred Umbrian alleys.

22 March

When we enter Bar Bonci today, Luciano greets us and asks how we are. Keith and I smile and answer that we're well, with kind of contentment that comes from beautiful weather coupled with merrily sending one's expat children off to school, and the prospect of a day open with possibilities. I guess that's known as "joy." Luciano says a run of Italian that we don't catch, so he slows it down, and Letizia helps, and they gesture and mime until we get it. "*Gente felice il cielo aiuta.*" I translate this as "happy people hold up the sky," as in happy people create more space for Light in the world. But when I mull this over later, I realize that the verb is in the third person singular, so it is the sky that helps, rather than people. As in "heaven helps happy people." I can't decide which version I prefer. I like that my mistaken translation means that there is a power and a purpose to happiness. It creates music in the world. But the actual translation has a nice meaning, too. Perhaps akin to fortune favors those that feel fortunate. At bottom, maybe they both mean the same thing.

Joy begets joy.

It's a nice thought. At least when I'm happy. When I'm discouraged or frustrated or overwhelmed, it only makes me feel like I'm in a coffin of my own design. Which is fair, no one can be happy all the time, that's denying the fact that reality is sometimes tricky and painful. Holding up the sky? A big task. But even when life is not painful, how does one find happiness to begin with? When we are trucking through our days without the benefit of a glorious day with the prospect of beautiful wines in our future?

There is another Italian quote that resonates.

"*Chi vuol vivere e star bene, pigli il mondo come viene.*" Those who want to live and be well, take the world as it is.

Notice where you are. What you have. The beauty that fills your senses, the pain that reminds you of the aching vulnerability that comes with being part of humankind. Delight in the violet growing out of the concrete, smell the scents the wind carries, and let your heart bleed a little when occasion warrants. Grounded in the present, that is when we feel our connection to the Light within us and between us and to the world at large. That's where I feel joy. And joy begets joy.

23 March

Nicolas has school today, the last day before Easter break, so Keith and I take the little ones on a walk along the *Strada di San Francesco*, which leads to Assisi. The sunshine flushes the shadows lingering around us like spiderwebs. The children are in an ecstasy of flower picking. Siena carefully constructs many a posy before tossing it into the wind. They race up the terraces of olive trees to the top of the hill, only to fall into raptures at the meadow of flowers and come barreling back down the hill to describe the grasses rampant with blossoms.

Later that afternoon we visit the Franciscan convent with Angelo. Perched at the top of Spello, the once cloistered convent looks out over the valley. As we approach the convent, Angelo whispers that the convent is home to two nuns. I guess there is not much call for Franciscan nuns in these modern times. It's the novice nun who greets us and leads our tour. First we visit the church of San Severino, built in the twelfth century, home to the oldest local fresco. The nun leads us behind the altar to the sacristy, where we admire a huge, letterpressed book that could be read by a roomful of people at the same time. "Early Spellani TV," whispers Angelo in Italian. Then we head to the cloister, where the nuns traditionally took their constrained constitutionals. The children look at the courtyard and suddenly realize that cloistered nuns never left. They ask, why would nuns be cloistered? I answer feebly that they prayed a lot. My children give me a communal baleful gaze, why must one be cloistered to pray?

After purchasing a Saint Francis comic book, we leave the convent, and lean over the town walls over the surrounding countryside. Angelo points out the secret doorway that leads out of Spello. When Spello was under siege, a runner would dash out through the tunnel to fetch provisions to wait out the enemy.

Siena and I walk to a talk at the Palazzo Communale on the representations of women in art through time. It's probably fascinating, but Italians don't believe in quiet during performances, and the ambient muttering makes it exhausting to decipher the lecture. We duck out and celebrate our lack of attentional skills with a *panino* from the newly opened *panini* shop on the *piazza*. *Capocollo* sandwiches in hand, we join the people standing in the street, happily munching. We notice Siena's friend Elisa across the *piazza*. Siena initially leaps to greet her but then cozies back up the wall. I can see she's once again trapped by a fear of the awkward situation, which I find exasperating, as Elisa is holding a puppy. What's a better conversation starter than a puppy? Siena steadfastly ignores my nudging to go talk to Elisa.

Instead, we head home, with me trying to swallow my annoyance. Just when I feel like she's pushed through her insecurity, she freezes in the face of what seems to me a simple situation. If someone were saying cruel things to Siena about her competence, I'd be angry with them—it's complicated when the person telling her she's deficient is herself. And possibly me, what with my pointing out how easy it would be to talk to Elisa. I realize that I'm pushy, but all I want is for her to not be as riddled with inadequacy as I have been. It would behoove me to remember that my own path out of insecurity is not a straight line. But it is hard to keep that in mind when all I can focus on is wanting her to not be like me. Come to think of it, thoughts like these are probably depleting to my own stores of burgeoning self-confidence. There is a paradox here that I'm struggling to untangle.

We peep into Tullia, hoping for gelato. Assunta spies our peering into the echoingly empty case and calls out that she'll start making gelato next week. We smile in anticipation, and step into the street in time to see Nicolas and Gabe racing down the hill, hand in hand. They eagerly shout that they are on a candy run, their faces aglow with cheer—a spot of brightness in an increasingly glowering pall.

A pall that becomes a deluge at homework time. Siena insists that she can't write a journal entry, it is *impossible,* and she point-blank refuses to try. Even if she could do it, the teacher would read it aloud, and everyone would laugh, and there is no way she's putting pencil to paper. Keith and I argue with her for a solid hour. This is not hyperbole. An hour of my tossing out every clinical tool in my arsenal, all while my head is filled with fearful imaginings of my daughter's present and future marred by her intractable belief in her own inadequacy. Plus another half hour where she and I abscond to the darkened *loggia* so she can calm herself down. Finally, she agrees to write five sentences, and we can decide later whether or not she'll turn them in. I hope this demonstrates to my daughter that she can do more than she thinks she can.

My friend Sophia had emailed me that she wished Siena could "see herself as a miraculous fava bean—feeding others, yes, but being able to do that because she's looked after herself well enough to survive the drought and fill herself with protein." Siena is always worried about impeding some social norm that transcends common sense. She needs to take care of herself, and not let the other stuff through her protective skin. Siena had warmed to the fava bean image, to the point that I'll ask her, "How's my fava bean?" and she'll respond, "*Miraculous.*" But on the *loggia,* she admits that she doesn't feel miraculous. She feels weak. Like she is letting us down.

I think I handled this all wrong. Maybe I shouldn't have prodded her to talk to Elisa. Maybe I should've let her fade into the walls of the *piazza.* Maybe I should've shrugged when she insisted she can't write in Italian. I just wish she believed in herself. I wish I didn't have these painful thoughts that maybe coming here has broken some tender part of her. That if she doesn't get to the point where she can revel in her strength while we are here, she'll always see herself as fragile and ineffectual.

I feel that Saint Francis would have something to say about all this. Maybe something along the lines of accepting how it is, and letting her find her way to let her be the Light and prayer of her own devising. Maybe he'd say, as he once did, "True progress quietly and persistently moves along without notice." Or maybe he would take Siena aside, brush the hair off her forehead, look in her eyes and tell her, "Start by doing what is necessary, then what is possible, and suddenly you are doing the impossible."

Or maybe he'd say, "Oh, man, now I remember why I preach to the birds. Ten-year-old girls are a force to be reckoned with."

24 March

Angelo is part of a men's group called *Il Tribbio*. The group's purpose seems to be to safeguard the cultural inheritance of Spello. Rather than accomplishing this goal by becoming insular and clannish, they preserve their town's traditions by sharing them with others. Today, they've invited the smattering of expats living in Spello to a lunch showcasing the Easter foods and traditions of our adopted town.

When we enter Il Cacciatore, scene of our arrival into Spello communist society, Angelo greets us, and gives us a guided tour of the foods spread across the purple tablecloth. He points out the airy cheesebread called *pizza di Pasqua*, hardboiled eggs, *salumi*, sweet *vernaccia* wine, and *colomba*. The latter seems to be the Easter version of *panettone*—a sweetly lofted bread, flavored with amaretto and candied orange, shaped into a dove, and sprinkled with pearl sugar and pieces of almond.

Marcello rushes toward us to tell us the recent neighborhood drama surrounding Gabe's poster. Angelo loved Gabe's drawing of the new pope so much that he'd turned it into a poster that Marcello hung outside the shop. Today Giorgio caught a woman meticulously removing the staples from the poster. Giorgio called out for her to stop, and asked her what in the world she was doing. The woman responded that she liked the poster so she was taking it home. Giorgio was adamant that the poster belonged with the store. The argument was settled by Giorgio plucking the poster from the woman's hands, and handing it to Marcello to re-hang in its rightful spot. We applaud their victory, to Marcello's nodding and bowing.

Don Diego arrives to perform the benediction. The *Tribbio* lines up behind him, and the priest blesses the food with his silver holy water spritzer. We stand with the friends of the *Tribbio*, and the other expats—Doreen, an Australian couple, and a couple from Iowa that returns to Spello annually. We nod to the prayers, and then we tuck into the blessings. I quickly determine that *colomba* is my new best love. While I surreptitiously take another slice, an ex-schoolteacher, whom Angelo describes as his *amica del cuore*, friend of the heart, grips Nicolas by the arm. She pulls him into the seat beside her and starts asking him questions. At the conclusion of the grilling, she pronounces him *molto bravo*. She looks around for our other children, but luckily for Siena, who is across the room trying on the *Tribbio* medal, the teacher is distracted by the burning egg shells.

Since the eggs have been blessed, the shells cannot be blithely tossed into the *spazzatura* with the salami rinds and orange peels. Instead, they are gathered in an iron pot during the meal, and now, Fabrizio and Giorgio light them on fire. Our plastic Easter eggs filled with jelly beans feel a world away.

25 March

When we visited Colleen and Tom in Piegaro last weekend for a celebration of the town's glass-blowing history (while the children made mosaics, we learned that Piegaro is responsible for the glass tiles used in the mosaics on the facade of Orvieto's famed cathedral), Gabe noticed Colleen's Lakota Indian buffalo hide drum. She taught him a hunting rhythm, which he practiced as we walked through the town. Colleen laughed at his brow bent in concentration, and offered to let him borrow the drum. Since that day, he has been practicing daily, and that drum is now the centerpiece of a show that my youngest children are plotting.

So far, their Easter break has been a hum of creating signs, tickets, and scripts for their drum spectacular. The giggling energy is so much nicer than the butt jokes that devolve into toot jokes that sink into screams of disgust and slamming doors. If this never happens in your house, then I'm totally kidding, and it never happens in mine either.

The children take a break from cleaning their room—this is without a doubt the best show ever—to break open their giant chocolate egg, a gift from Paola. There is much debate about how one opens such a large egg. Gabe suggests that he himself karate chop it, and he's mystified when his siblings don't embrace his idea. Finally, they agree to drop the egg as a team. One, two, three! *Crash!* They open the foil to find chocolate pieces surrounding a bundle of little toys and games.

In the evening we drive to Foligno to watch *I Croods*. On the drive, we realize that this is the first movie we've all been to together since Gabe was small and we saw *Mary Poppins*. Though that hardly counts since only the fact that Siena lost a tooth at that show informs us that it was after his birth. I bet it's hard to be the third child and have no one remember your presence. Maybe that's why Gabe makes up for it now with being overwhelmingly present. So we don't forget him.

We park underneath the theater, in the worst parking lot in creation. Columns block the openings to a large proportion of the spots, and the remaining ones require a 95-point turn to navigate in. A process that takes so long, at any given time there are 20 cars wrestling with getting in or out. Add in the frustration that Italians seem genetically unable to form a line, and this is the Boot's inefficiency at its worst. The utter opposite of the theater, where a ticket buys a specific seat. Once in the dark, the cues that mark us as interlopers are blessedly muted, and we are simply a family. Laughing along with the rest of the audience. All present together.

28 March

Charlottesville's annual parade celebrates the Dogwood, with uniformed firemen leaning out of spiffy red fire trucks to toss candy to children, teens in cowboy boots sitting on hay bales and clapping to country music, Shriners looking oddly serious as they drive tiny cars, a band of merry cloggers following a wagon pulled by Belgian draft horses, and a pink float of Misses Virginia/Dogwood/Albemarle/etc. holding onto handles and waving gaily. The procession is an upbeat tribute to small town Southern charm. But here, in the land of the Holy See, the mood is somber as we gather with the rest of the townspeople outside Chiesa Sant'Andrea for the Stations of the Cross procession. Don Diego, regal in a purple brocade cape, uses his microphone to tell the assemblage that we'll be walking through town, stopping at spots marked by artwork depicting a moment in Christ's journey to his crucifixion. The priest and his crew of robed companions, one carrying an enormous gold cross, begin moving through town, chanting Hail Mary, and doing a call and response prayer, with the townspeople following behind, chanting and responding and singing on cue.

Not being an observant Catholic, in that I'm not Catholic, my walk is less about reflecting on the stages of Christ's journey. Instead, I revel in the sense of mystery as we walk through the shadowy alleys. I breathe the smell of candles burning along the road and clustered at the stations. I shiver at the breath of wind that stirs and brings the dust of olive groves and smoke of grilled meat. I admire the evocative paintings, each radically different in style and resonance. A Quaker among Catholics, but trying to be less "chronicling observer" and more "respectful witness," I open myself to what this procession, and really this holiday, can mean for me.

As we walk, I recall that a Hindu friend once told me that many Hindus don't believe in the existence of myriad gods. Instead, those gods personify a constellation of characteristics, and praying to one helps focus prayer and intention. It occurs to me the Catholic stations can act in much the same way. Easter itself is a metaphor, for the renewal or rebirth of connection with the divine. It's a time for reflecting on the challenges to that connection. To strive toward a love that is universal. Gloriously so. It's not always easy to reach out to another, unsure of the reception we will receive. Or to remove our armor to reveal the vulnerability that lies beneath. Or to stand with the marginalized and help those in pain, despite the pressures of our own existence. Or to let go of past hurts to create a pathway to humane connection. When we act in these tender ways, we tap into the divine that lies within us, and revel in the divine in others. In the process, we often trip and fall. We're mocked, we're scolded, we're rejected. And we bruise. And then hold back, so afraid of the vulnerability and its attendant pain.

So, Easter? Maybe Easter is a time to let that pain go. Let go of the holding back, the shielding ourselves from the stirrings of grace, and instead love with all our hearts. Let our souls quiver and plunge back into the Light. Love without reason. Love without fear.

That is a true miracle.

30 March

The Spello bells are pealing merrily as we walk to Vinosofia for Brenda's and Graziano's Easter celebration. We walk in and shout *"Auguri!"* to the friends clustered at the bar—Doreen, Brenda and Graziano, and Francesca and Alessandro from New Year's, who are unpacking *una cesta*, a hamper, of blessed foods. They tell us that the day before Easter, churches have a mass benediction of food items. People bring in their baskets of salami, *pizza di Pasqua*, wine, eggs, even salt, and the priest blesses all the food at once. The food is then considered ready for breaking the fast on Easter morning. I wonder if this is the origin of the Easter basket. I tempt fate by accepting a bubbly but unblessed wine from Brenda, while Francesca and Alessandro continue to place items onto the decorated linen they've spread on the bar. From the *Tribbio* celebration, I'm adept at noting *pizza di Pasqua* and *vernaccia* and a *colomba*, whose delicate orange fragrance seems to be calling out to me. Once all the food, including the blessed eggs Doreen brought and the unblessed cake we brought are stretched across the bar, we raise our glasses to wish one another a happy Easter. And then we dive into the breakfast. The home-raised and cured *salumi* is perfectly tender and flavorful. Alessandro tells us that cured meats are like wine, it's all about the earth and how you feed the animals. I nod as I push my *pizza di Pasqua* to the side in favor of more *capocollo*. Francesca laughs when she sees my forlorn bits of cheesebread, and shows me that eating it alongside the *vernaccia* softens the dry bristle of the bread and brings out the nutty complexity of the cheese. We close with glasses of homemade white wine, lofted high again in celebration.

The sound of a band pulls us outside, where we see a statue of Jesus moving from one church to another. Siena realizes that it's the first statue of a resurrected Jesus she's seen. In fact, the resurrection itself isn't one of the 14 stations of the cross, but an optional 15th. Which I suppose makes sense since the procession is on Good Friday, the day Jesus died. So it's really all about that, leaving the observer in a state of tension for two days until ta-da! He has risen.

We follow the statue until it is placed in the church that is next to the *scuola elementare*. As we admire the statue, and Gabe wonders what kind of flag Jesus is holding, we talk about the story we heard about Pope Francis washing the feet of the juvenile delinquents in Rome. How he flouted church tradition and washed the feet of girls, even a Muslim. And how traditionalists can grumble about how it's not done, but no one can complain outright because he is the pope after all. The Captain of Catholicism.

Siena wonders aloud if the pope is secretly Quaker. In his honoring of the Light in all people, it does feel pretty Quakerly, but I find that the deeper people progress in their faith, the less these distinctions matter. This pope is showing himself to be a man of heart, with an emphasis on a spirituality based on inclusion rather than exclusion. And I'll light a candle for that anytime.

Spinach and Ricotta Ravioli

pasta sheets cut into squares
(I can vouch for squares with a side
the length of a business card)

ricotta
(2/3 regular, 1/3 sheep if possible),
between 1 and 2 cups

1 egg

a handful of grated parmesan

a bunch of spinach, sautéed with garlic and just the water
clinging to the leaves, cooled, then minced.

salt and pepper and a shaving of nutmeg

* * *

1. Combine all ingredients except pasta to make filling. Taste for seasoning.

2. Place a spoonful of filling in the middle of a square of pasta, drape another square over the cheese, and press down starting at the filling and working outwards to avoid trapping air. Then stand back to admire your handiwork. You might not have been born a ravioli maker, but you sure can create some beautiful filled pasta. *Mangiamo!* Let's eat.

APRIL

BLOOM

2 April

Our winter days have been marked by a gathering grey that bullies any attempts at blue sky. Spello has felt damp, quiet. And I have felt much the same. I've been missing home, missing the friends I haven't hugged in seven months. Missing my dryer. Missing my bathtub, so wonderful for winter soaks. I've started wondering if six months would have been sufficient.

And then the sun comes out, and I feel something new. A stirring of warmth. People are venturing out of their stone walls. I find myself remembering the men playing cards outside Tullia, the ladies gathering in the alley, and the streets filling with people. There is rising enthusiasm that I realize faded away when people were trapped under six layers of clothes and hunched against umbrellas.

With our door open to the fresh spring breezes, we hear someone calling from the neighboring yard. Gabe steps onto the *terrazza*, and is hailed by our neighbor Anna to come and play with her grandson. Siena and Gabe dash out, run the 20 steps down the alley, and knock on the door that we've always wanted to pass through. They play soccer with the little boy, and Keith and I listen to catch their combined laughter.

As Siena has her weekly macramé date with Paola, I call down to bring the children home, and we stroll down the street. We step into Paola's shop, and I impulsively invite her to dinner. We stand in a circle and smile broadly when she accepts. Siena stays with Paola, while Gabe and I continue walking. As we cross the *piazza*, we see Brenda, on her way to work. A few moments of chat before we amble through alleys and return home. Keith is unloading groceries, including a tray of strawberries so ripe I smell them before I see them. My husband is animated as he tells me about dropping Nicolas off at Mario's for the afternoon. The boys are going to visit their friend Petrov to play Russian video games.

I call Doreen to join us for dinner, and then start boiling potatoes, defrosting shrimp for the zucchini and shrimp cream sauce, researching rising agents (yet again) to decide how to approximate biscuits, and macerating strawberries for strawberry shortcake. Siena bursts through the door to distribute bracelets and tell us stories about people she met in Paola's shop. She says that Doreen had stopped by and bought tea for the three of them at Bar Bonci, and the barista had walked over with the tea when it was ready, and the afternoon felt *whole*.

Doreen and Paola arrive and keep me company as I roll and boil the *gnocchi*. Over dinner, Nicolas tells us about his afternoon, riding bikes with his friends, learning Russian video games, and playing with Petrov's toddler brother. Plus he was sent home with a huge jar of honey from Mario's beekeeping uncle.

This is the reason I chose a warm country. With people out in the streets, the flavor of a town changes. The energy, the vitality, the openness for spontaneity and possibility and sudden sweetness. Gabe sums it up. "Today smells like magic."

3 April

Now that my children are safely back at school—Siena armed with a five sentence journal entry that she surprised herself by writing—and it is just you and I, I can confess something to you. It's about *colomba*. *Colomba* seems to have been invented for those pining for the end of *panettone* and *pandoro* season. Known to the urbane as December. Despite its peaceful dove-like form, I believe *colomba* is the devil. I can't stop eating it. I seem to have a *colomba* abuse problem. I eat it for breakfast, I take a slice between midafternoon snack and cocktail hour, I'll sneak a wedge to accompany an evening *grappa*. I'm basically on a no-*colomba*-left-behind program. Which explains why we have a tower of empty *colomba* boxes. And Keith just picked up yet another from the aisle of *colomba* that is as long as the canned food aisle back home (much like the *panettone* and *pandoro* aisle back in December). It only costs a euro, so he couldn't withstand the sweet pressure. A euro. What the heck is in this that they can sell them so cheaply? Well, for perhaps the first time in my life, I am an advocate of "don't ask, don't tell." I won't look at those ingredients, and no one tell me what they are. All I know is my favorite brand has the logo, "*Piano, piano, buono, buono.*" Slow, slow, good, good. That's enough for me.

I ask my Spellani friends what the next *panettone* incarnation is. Maybe one with three colors of candied fruits on top to celebrate *Liberazione?* I'm sadly informed that there are no more sweet yeast breads until next Christmas unless I decide to make my own. Which I may try, if withdrawal symptoms prove too agonizing. But in the meantime, I'll try to remember that whenever the pastry gods takes away one treat, they open the window to another. When I was mourning *pane di mosto* is when I discovered *fave dei morti*. When *panettone* season was fading out, that's when I stumbled upon exciting *Carnevale* treats like *chiacchiere*, fried sheets of cookie, and *castagnole*, mini cream-or-Nutella filled doughnuts. So I guess I'll have to watch our *forno* for what our next seasonal delight will be. *Colomba* is gone, but something wonderful is around the corner.

I can smell it.

5 April

Yesterday, Alessia asked Gabe if he plays an instrument. Before he could answer, Lorenzo, ever the loyal friend burst in, "*Si, lui suona la chittara!*" Gabe nodded, adding that in addition to the guitar, he also plays the drum. Alessia suggested that he bring in his drum sometime, and Gabe—presumably before she quite finished the sentence—suggested *domani*, tomorrow. So today he brings Colleen's stretched-hide drum to the *prima* class and plays a Lakota hunting rhythm. When the students sing the national anthem, he plays along on the drum. This may be the first time a Native American drum is used to accompany the Italian national anthem.

In the afternoon Keith takes the boys for haircuts, while Siena and I make crêpe batter. Noticing that I'm low on milk, Siena offers to run down to the *negozio*. I hesitate. I'm not thinking about the distance—after all, it's a scant 30 second walk from her school—which is a one minute walk from our house. I'm thinking about the fact that she'll have to interact with people. Adult people. In Italian. I want to ask, "But what if you freeze and try to hide behind the olive oil?" My better angels keep me mum. I hand her money, which she slips into a purse and dashes out the door. She returns a few minutes later with a bottle of milk, my change, and a wide smile.

We make the batter and curl up to read *Pimpa* together until the boys come home, shorn. I fill the crêpes with ricotta and spinach, and cover them with tomato sauce and a sprinkling of cheese. As the smell of bubbling tomato sauce and cheese fills the house, I remember how I used to regularly make *crespelle,* or dinner crêpes, in the States. Particularly the buckwheat kind I'd fill with goat cheese or melted mozzarella and spinach. I'd bring a basket of them when I was picking up children from one activity to deposit them at another. We'd eat them in the car. This felt normal.

Keith hands me a glass of wine, and tells me that when Gabe was getting his haircut, the hairdresser asked him what he liked about Italy. He said it was *"più libero."* More free. Gabe observed that there are fewer cars and less general busyness. I think about all of our car dinners, and how my children would have to do their homework while they waited for a sibling at an activity. Now I can send Siena to the store, have her back in ten minutes, make batter, cuddle, and then make crêpes while the kids do homework and play music, and then sit down. Together.

Our American drumbeat, on Italian soil.

6 April

Doreen is leaving to go back to the States. It feels like the end of an era. Of drinking *negroni,* while we work on a puzzle and talk about things big and small. Of having her drop by to bring me a book and convincing her to stay for supper, and then all of a sudden, it feels like a party. Of my children clamoring for her attention, and delighting when they get to have Doreen all to themselves. Of Gabe, sleepless with excitement that he gets to have a date with Doreen the next day. Of offers of tea and companionship the day after I publish a blog post that has the scent of sadness. To say it's a loss is putting it mildly.

I'm afraid goodbyes are part of our current condition, and this is one on a road that will have many more. I had envisioned our year abroad as rather solitary, which was fine, as I value my alone time. But Doreen helped me realize that I need relationships in order to thrive. It doesn't usually occur to me to call a friend to get together unless I'm cued by seeing them. Doreen's graceful folding into our family made me realize that though I might have a introvert streak, it's offset by a vivid need to connect. And I need to honor that, or risk feeling shut-down.

It's hard to picture our final four months here without her. I invite Paola and Brenda and Graziano for a going-away dinner. Gabe and Siena—who I overhear discussing how much they're going to miss her—make her gifts of art. I make dinner for nine. And Keith makes Doreen one last *negroni*.

Before our guests arrive, Siena dashes into the olive orchards to collect flowers for the table and wild onions for a salad. She asks to be allowed to go to the *negozio* to purchase more vegetables, and I hand her the money with a smile. When she returns, she tells me that she even asked how much the *radicchio* was, to make sure she had enough money. Siena takes a large platter from the sideboard and creates a festive salad, while I finish making ravioli and a bean and shrimp dish. Paola arrives with gelato, which we will use to fill *chouquette* that Siena and I made earlier. Brenda and Graziano bring wine from Le Marche that lingers like smoky caramel. It's a meal full of talking and laughing and remembering. With children collapsing to sleep, despite their wish to hang on to every last Doreen moment.

7 April

Letizia asks if we celebrate Easter Monday in America. We say no, but mention that this Easter Monday fell on April 1st, which is our April Fool's Day. Of course, my Italian is in no shape to be able to say "April Fool's Day" so I refer to it as, "A grand day of jokes in April." Letizia and Luciano lean toward us to shout that April 1 is a grand day of trickery in Italy, too! They grin as they take turns telling us about the holiday. Luciano laughs aloud, recounting times someone has posted fake death notices on the obituary boards in town. Letizia doubles over with hilarity, then tells us that the more common *scherzo* is to secretly place a fish on a friend's back. I startle, remembering that my mom told me stories of when she was a little girl in France and people put fish on each other's backs. I figured it was a memory born of conflating several holidays, but Letizia's anecdote suggests that maybe I shouldn't doubt my mother.

The origin of a day of jokes may date back to Roman times, but it's more likely that it was born in the 1500s when Pope Gregory the VIII changed New

Year's Day from April to January 1. Thus anyone who still marked the new year on April 1 was considered a fool. Seeing as April 1st falls in Pisces, the foolishness of the mistake was denoted by calling the blunderers April's fish. Which later mutated to attaching paper fish to people's back, a now common custom in France, Italy, and Belgium.

Back home, I never even thought about where April Fool's Day came from, when I secretly removed the bag of bran cereal from the box and replaced it with Fruit Loops for a little morning revelry. But since our conversation in Bar Bonci, I've been reflecting on April Fools. I realized that though we failed to honor this day of ridicule, we probably unwittingly commemorated it. Italy is inoculating me against the fear of making a fool out of myself. In fact, had I known what day it was, and stuck a fish on someone's back, I would probably wind up the fool because I would have surely taunted my victim by saying, *"Pesca d'aprile!"* And they'd wonder why in the world I was talking about peaches of April.

One of the best lessons I'm learning is to embrace my inner fool. I don't have to have all the information. I don't need to always be correct. Heck, I can walk around with a fish on my back. Why pretend I'm impervious to correction, instruction, and improvement? When true engagement happens only in a humble and open place. It can't happen while I'm pretending I have all the answers. I have spent so much of my adult life trying to build a façade of impermeability. Italy is taking it down.

One peach at a time.

8 April

We're at Vinosofia, breathing in a wine from the Langhe, when Graziano remarks that it has the scent of *sottobosco*. He struggles to translate the word, is it woods or leaves? And together we realize that it means smelling of the forest floor. Over an evening of languidly sipping wine and sampling cheese and learning new words, Brenda invites us to join them for a trip to the once-monthly antique market in Pissignano. The plan morphs to include lunch at one of their favorite restaurants, Trattoria di Oscar, in Bevagna.

The drive to Pissignano winds through wildflower—strewn fields, one of which we park in, between sections of the market. Stalls stretch in either direction, so far we can't see the end. We pass tables with tea sets and pith helmets and hand-cranked coffee grinders. Then more tables with old maps and seltzer bottles, one the idyllic blue that matches the dairy store I dream of opening. I buy a scarf, two fanciful Easter linens—to line the *cesta* I don't have—and a ravioli cutter that is so aged it is form fitted to the hand. Siena exerts the power of the purse to buy a beautiful cloth with embroidered violets, and a merchant offers her a little glass butterfly. The same merchant hands Gabe a glass mouse, and he used his *own* money (insert earnest insistence here) to buy an Italian comic book. About a cowboy in New Mexico. Named Tex. A Nutella spreader for Nicolas, and for Keith, we find antique *aperitivo* glasses—Martini, Aperol, and Cinzano. They are all differently shaped with the logo etched in the glass, and I can't believe our luck in finding something so perfect.

We leave the market pleased with our uncommon purchases, and plenty of euros left for a nice lunch. Continuing to Bevagna, we pass green rolling grasses, wildflowers between the grape vines, and shimmering olive groves. A patchwork of green and yellow, all reflecting the brilliance of the sky.

At Trattoria di Oscar we meet Filippo, the owner and chef, and are struck by his ardent intensity as he describes today's menu. As we're debating our choices, we are poured a rustic white wine and served delicious (and salted!) bread with a slight serving of potato skin soup. Graziano walks with Filippo to discuss the wines, and we reap the benefit of his careful selection.

Siena starts with a chickpea flan nestled beside sautéed country greens, and the rest of us opt for the egg. I need to stop here and wipe small tears, remembering that egg. It's poached, and then fried. And then served in a bowl of *pecorino fonduto*, melted pecorino. It's like breakfast. It's like dinner. It's like dessert. Creamy, slightly sweet, crunchy—it hits every possible culinary spot. When I put down my spoon, I glow with the kind of contentment usually reserved for the end of an excellent meal with excellent red wine. Along with our *antipasti*, Filippo brings us a board of *prosciutto* from pigs he's raised on a diet of acorns and proudly slices in the dining room.

Filippo, being from Emilia-Romagna, understands *ragù alla bolognese*. Since I love *bolognese*, and I love ordering the house specialty, that's my choice for *primo*. Particularly after Filippo proudly shows us the certificate for the *Chianina* beef.

The *bolognese* is incredible—succulent yet comforting, deep yet bright.

The children run outside to play while Keith and Graziano consider *secondi* and Brenda and I luxuriate in the last of the wine. Keith finally settles on a *spiedino,* pieces of meat grilled on a skewer, of quail and fennel with orange and honey glaze. And Graziano orders *scottadito.* Both are beautiful works of culinary art. We ponder dessert while being served a lovely *passito,* a sweet wine pressed from dried grapes. We recall the children to enjoy a strawberry *panna cotta,* which they inhale, pronounce delicious, before running back outside. Keith orders an exquisitely silky *budino di latte,* milk pudding, topped with fine olive oil, and sprinkled with feathery anise. The kind of thing you put in your mouth and have to close your eyes to shut out all other senses so you can focus on the heavenly tastebud celebration.

My dessert is a chocolate cake of surpassing beauty. After my first bite, I stare at my cake in wonderment. It has a faint spice, like an unctuous, chocolatey gingerbread. Heart-wrenchingly good, even without the beautiful chocolate flowers and the drizzle of reduced *passito.* Every bite thrills me, while making me sad that I'm one bite closer to finishing. Brenda tells Filippo how enamored I am with the cake, and he smiles and nods before returning to the kitchen. He emerges a few minutes later to hand me a piece of paper. I look at him quizzically, and then scan the paper, on which he has written the recipe for the cake. I can feel my eyes shining, as I whisper a *grazie.* A little coffee, a *bella grappa,* and we float out of Trattoria di Oscar. Is it me, or is the world a little rosier?

We take a *passeggiata* through Bevagna, then realize with a start that it's 5:00. Only in Italy can you walk out of lunch and realize it is approaching dinner time.

11 April

Nicolas has left on a *gita,* a three-day field trip with his class. It's weird to think of him on a boat floating past Venetian summer homes without us. He's texted a few times since he left, mostly checking to make sure Freja is okay without him, or making snarky comments because I made him bring a coat despite the warming temperatures. It's hard to be sarcastic in a text, but he manages. In his wake our friends Stephanie and Gray arrive from California. Walking with them through the streets of Spello lifts a veil that has obscured the colors and flavors of our day-to-day existence. Our visitors stop at every alley to gesture in disbelief at the rampant beauty. They bask in the warmth of a streetside greeting with Sicilian Angelo, or a Bar Tullia patio conversation with our Angelo. Their eyes widen at the gracious beauty of Vinosofia. A simple sandwich from the *piadineria*, the shop in the *borgo* that serves the Umbrian version of wraps, prompts them to pause to taste the freshly made flatbread, crisp greens, and excellent meats. A walk through the olive trees is punctuated by astonished expressions at the loveliness of the countryside.

These are great travelers–open, curious, easily moved to joy, willing to take risks that took me months to manage—so their enthusiasm is infectious. But more than that, I think just moving my angle of observation over a few degrees, it feels like I'm seeing everything again for the first time, but with the added benefit of it feeling like home. I suppose I'm taking on their sense of novelty, and also realizing my own sense of place in contrast with that novelty. So Spello feels at once glorious and familiar.

We walk into the *macelleria* and Stephanie stops still at the display of meats. When the butcher sees her whip out her camera, he begs her to wait, and he trots to turn on the light. Display properly illuminated, he nods for her to proceed. All at once, I notice afresh how lucky we are to have this shop that has become a touchstone. And then, when the shop is empty, the butcher orders me to come behind the counter, and asks Stephanie to take a picture of me between him and his wife. Even simple transactions are amazing.

But here is the thing. Life itself is amazing. Yes, Spello is almost cartoonish in its capacity for charm. But my life in Charlottesville is amazing, too. Different amazing, but amazing, nonetheless. In my old neighborhood, I'd sometimes walk past a friend's house and catch a whiff of her climbing yellow rose, and all of a sudden, a kaleidoscope tumbled my brain circuits and my thoughts stopped, leaving me with pure gratitude. Much like what happens here when I walk home from the bakery while the pink stones of Spello are just lightening, and I'll notice the contours of a stone, chiseled by people 2,000 years ago, and again I'm flooded with emotion.

I'd love to learn the trick for switching filters—from thought to feeling, from having the world around me appear a blur to seeing every corner filled with Light.

Until then, I suppose I can relinquish the need to control my feelings, and just enjoy those moments when my defenses slip and I am transported by taste, smell, sight, sound, love, to a plane of utter adoration for this life I'm lucky enough to live.

12 April

The fortieth birthday is a milestone, and today Keith hits that milestone. After dropping the children off at school, we celebrate with pastries at the Sicilian bakery in Foligno with Stephanie and Gray. We stop first at the Coop to fill a little jar of raw milk. The warm *sfogliatella* makes my eyes roll back in my head, and I offer a taste to our friends. They are just as charmed with the layers of crispy pastry enfolding orange and spice-scented ricotta, and order two for themselves. Keith's *cannolo* makes him beam like a child. His birthdays should always begin with *cannoli*.

With bellies exultant, we continue to Bevagna where we wander into the Roman baths that we've always admired from outside the window. As Stephanie and Gray are not visiting Rome, I'm happy that they get a taste of ancient civilization, tucked away in this quaint town. We then travel forward in time to visit Bevagna's old(e) candle maker and pharmacy. The medieval candle maker rotates a wheel hung with wicks, dipping them into molten yellow liquid, before twisting them into a two wick candle. We walk away with bags of candles and with the combined scent of woodsmoke, wax, and honey clinging to our clothes.

After lunch at home, we make an alarming discovery. Gabe has hives all over his trunk and down his legs. He also sports a stuffy nose, and since he's gotten hives before when he has a simple cold, we convince ourselves that these are virus hives. The itching is manageable, so we continue with our plan to take a *passeggiata* around the walls of Spello. It's one of my favorite walks, as it combines countryside, with its *borragine* and wildflowers, with the protected feeling of town walls. We pass a woman in a flowered house dress collecting greens. When I compliment her on her early spring haul, by telling her "*complimenti,*" she beams a toothless smile.

The walk ends in the *piazza*, where we visit the *farmacia*, and then spot Angelo. He's stricken by Gabe's hives and advises us to go to the *farmacia*. We tell him that we've just learned that we need a prescription to purchase antihistamine for a child. The pharmacist also told us what every Spellani already knows—there is an office called the *guardia medica* behind the *posta* where one can see a doctor, and get a prescription to carry to the *farmacia*. Angelo wonders why we aren't doing that. He says, as we all were conferencing in the *piazza*, you can stand here talking, or you can actually do something useful. I suppose when Angelo said he wanted us to view him as kin, he gave himself the right to boss us. Which is frankly not a bad thing. Going to a doctor has been a hurdle, exacerbated by our relentless optimism that everything will be well. We do as we're told, and visit to the *guardia medica*, but they're closed until 8:00 PM, at which time the *farmacia* will be closed, so any prescription would be unfillable. We decide to give it till morning, to clear astonishment from both Angelo and Paola, who are huddled in consultation in Paola's shop. We assure them that if the hives worsen, or there are any accompanying symptoms, then we'll take Gabe to the emergency room immediately.

Right now though, he still seems like Gabe. So we pat him with cool washcloths, and stroll to Vinosofia, where Brenda presents a beautiful *cinghiale* salami—spicy and perfectly aged. And glasses of nuanced and rich wine. Vinosofia has made me completely reevaluate my lackadaisical just-order-the-house-red approach to wine. So when we enter La Cantina for Keith's birthday dinner, we decide to order a bottle, rather than our usual pitcher of whatever they feel like pouring. Settling into our seats, Stephanie and Gray's heads swivel to take into the cozy and evocative space. Unfortunately, the itchiness of the hives is bothering Gabe, and I'm checking the time every few minutes. Where is Nicolas? I finally turn to Keith and ask if we should be worried that Nicolas is late. At which point, Keith nods his head in the direction of the door and says, "Look who's here." I glance up, and there is my boy entering the restaurant, backpack slung over his shoulder, looking taller and older and more self-assured than I remember. I stand up and move toward him, tears pricking my eyes.

The table feels complete. Our wine is Lacrima di Morro d'Alba from Le Marche. It startles us with its scent of violets and roses and a hint of lychee. But it is also round, and tannic enough to keep it complicated. In honor of Keith's birthday I order *scottadito*. Though I'm realizing that it's what I always order, so perhaps it's time to admit that I am laboring under a lamb obsession. Perhaps because the crispy, salty bits are my favorite parts of most meat dishes, and *scottadito* has the perfect proportion of tender, flavorful meat to caramelized edging.

By the time we weave our way out of La Cantina, we're sated and content. Sending the children outside between courses had allowed us to enjoy our meal without undue squirming, and reminded us what a blessing it is to live in a town this predictable. And when we join them outside into the cool night air, we felt the full weight of our gifts. The gifts found inherent in living, the gifts of friendship, the gifts of good food prepared with talent and sensibility, the gift of new tastes, and the gift of loved ones come home. Though the hives are not the kind of gift one wants sullying a celebration, there is much to celebrate. Turning forty in Italy is not too shabby.

13 April

Waking up this morning with Nicolas in the house feels like a blessing, until we discover that Gabe's hives haven't magically disappeared in the night. Gabe observes that they're better. "But don't get all 'woo-hooo!' because they are not that much better." Though he's developed no new symptoms other than a worsening of his stuffy nose, we decide we'll take him to the *guardia medica* when they open. While he waits, he reads Italian comic books, and his hives grow fainter and fainter. At noon, Chiara comes over, and I take the girls and Nicolas to the park with Stephanie and Gray, while Keith walks a very excited Gabe to the doctor. Gabe has primped like an expat girl preparing for a *Carnevale* party. Keith feels a little foolish walking into the office with his perky and healthy-looking son. They wait ten minutes, then are called to see the doctor. No charts, no forms. Keith tells the doctor about the hives, Gabe pipes up cheerfully when warranted, the doctor asks questions about strep symptoms and allergies, and then writes a prescription on a scrap of paper for the antihistamine. Keith tells her that we are Americans, living in Spello for a year, to prompt our bill, since we don't have the national health insurance. She just smiles and says that's nice, like Keith had told her that we'd had yogurt for breakfast. No bill.

Keith meets us at the park while we're still just getting situated and luxuriating in the warm sunshine. Gabe races around like he's forgotten about his hives, Nicolas jogs up the hill to buy a yo-yo, and we all dine on pizza from the *rosticceria* while Siena and Chiara play hand games with a backdrop of medieval stone walls.

Our only sadness is the impending departure of our friends. After waving them off, I take the girls and Gabe wildflower picking. The stroll is truncated when Gabe leans to pick a blossom and his shirt slips enough for me to see that the hives are making a dramatic comeback. I hate to pull the girls away from the hillside, but I have Gabier fish to fry. Once home, I measure out Gabe's medicine. He opens his mouth like a baby bird and I drop in ten drops of the milky liquid. His eyebrows lift as he tells me that it tastes like chamomile. Then he smacks his lips, and amends that to rotten chamomile. By bedtime, the hives are unchanged. It's hard to tuck him in with his legs looking like I've dipped him in hot oil. He seems awfully little when he is unhappy.

14 April

The hives are better this morning, though still uncomfortably vibrant. More medicine, more crossed fingers, and like the day before, the hives fade within an hour of waking up. At noon we meet Angelo, Marcello, and Giorgio at Bar Tullia to caravan to Collepino. For unclear reasons, Marcello has invited our family for lunch. Though we're confused as to the occasion, we are game for an afternoon with the Spellani septuagenarian card players.

After wandering the tiny town of Collepino, enjoying the crisp air and the neat alleyways, we enter Taverna San Silvestro. Angelo charges Gabe with drawing Collepino. As Gabe is finishing his picture, the waitress brings out a tray of *salumi*, *bruschette*, and *melone* so heaving that we don't finish half of it. It's excellent, as evidenced by Nicolas helping himself to multiple servings of *capocollo*. He's not a fan of salted, cured meats. It is my secret shame.

Next is the full Italian meal—*primi*, which for most of the table is ravioli with an artichoke sauce, *secondi*, which is *scottadito* for the majority (including, and this should come as no surprise, me), *contorni*, artichokes soaked in oil and mint for all. I've decided artichokes and lamb is a sumptuous combination.

Our meal lacks the easy banter borne of speaking the same language, but it's worth it to learn about these men who have been friends for 70 years. Marcello tells us that though he lives in Trevi, he has a house below Teatro Subasio, with a garden perfect for the dinner party he's planning if we'll agree to attend. Angelo and Marcello joke with Giorgio—who is given to arraying his trim frame with purple pants and crisp yellow shirts, and always has his black hair combed dramatically back from his forehead—about his days as a professional soccer player. The men lean forward to ask Nicolas about his *gita*, and laugh in satisfaction when I describe how I've heard Gabe muttering Italian in his sleep.

As we wait for dessert, the men make use of the table's toothpicks as they grumble to each other about the fact the *scottadito* was more *pecora*, sheep, than *agnello*, lamb. It's true that while it was nicely crisp, it did taste like the bright green tones of a grassy lamb were removed, leaving a bitter edge. The men lament that it was *troppo duro*, too tough. I sit back and watch them evaluate their meal, with no need to pretend it's perfect, even though Marcello is treating us all.

Marcello voices concern that the children might be too full for dessert, so Keith shares the oft-used refrain about kids having a meal stomach and a dessert stomach. The adage is novel for the gentlemen, and they repeat it among themselves, laughing uproariously each time. Their *dolci* amusement increases when they notice that Nicolas is trying to convince Gabe that he really doesn't want to finish his dessert. Marcello, wiping tears of laughter from his eyes, calls the waitress to order Nicolas another *tiramisù*. This reminds me of earlier, when Angelo asked the children if they wanted red or white wine. I'm growing more comfortable abdicating my parental responsibility. It's a novel pleasure to have other adults invested in my children's happiness.

After coffee and a round of *grappa* sent over by the owner, we pat our bellies and leave for San Silvestro. As we make our way to the parking area outside Collepino, Siena huffs and pouts that she wants to *walk* to the monastery. She can't understand why she's not allowed to *walk*. The fact that it's miles up the hill, and we have to follow the men to get there seems beyond the point. She's in a snit. Luckily, Gabe has found a giant plant and has plopped it on his head so he looks like a mermaid—a welcome distraction from Siena's stubborn crankiness. Once we're at San Silvestro, Siena regains her equilibrium listening to Angelo tell the story of the monastery's fountain.

Long ago, the monastery had no water source, so the monks had to get their water from Spello's convent. The monk in charge of water retrieval was, by necessity, the youngest and strongest brother, and therefore perhaps it should have come as no surprise when this monk and a novice nun began a clandestine affair that resulted in her pregnancy. The nuns were embarrassed, but the monks were enraged. The senior monk waved his staff and yelled that if there had only been water *here*, at this wall, they would have been spared this shame. He thrust his staff into the wall, and water exploded from the stones. This water took on a mystical aura—breastfeeding women would drink the water to increase their milk supply. I want to know what happened to the monk and nun. To please me, Angelo declares that they got married, had their child, and everyone was always happy. The End, he adds, in English. I applaud. I love a happy ending.

Angelo makes friends with a nun, while Marcello and I talk about Italian humor. Both Marcello and Angelo, when they are walking and have something to say, will stop walking to say it. I thought it was in order to slow down their speech and gesture helpfully for their American friends, but I've noticed them stopping each other. If I try to keep walking, to keep that forward momentum going, they'll throw a hand out to stop me, insisting that the conversation happens face to face. In Italy, forward momentum is less important than looking at each other while speaking.

17 April

I board the *navetta* after marketing at the *macelleria* and the *fruttivendolo*. The *navetta* is full, but the ever-present Luciano scoots over to free up the seat next to him and calls me over with a cheery, *"Signora!"* When I see him at Bar Bonci in the mornings, I find him hard to understand. He speaks in dialect, and anyway, my American sense of personal space starts sending out panic signals that impede my comprehension when he backs me into the wall with his gesturing. On the bus, though, it's surprisingly easy to engage in dialogue. Perhaps because a gentleman from Rome inveigled me into conversation while we waited for the *navetta*, and I have found that language requires either a good warm up or a good wine. Luciano asks me if I like Spello better when it's hot or when it's cold. I tell him hot, because that's when all the people are out, and he laughs.

It's funny because it is true—at home, I look for spring in the leafing of the maple trees. Here though, while we are certainly appreciating the greening of the *piazza* and the poppies that are speckling the countryside, the real sign of spring is the people. The alley ladies have begun congregating again. Sitting on their green plastic chairs, their backs against the leaning stone walls, some with giant bags of greens to sort from a morning spent foraging, some with nothing but conversation and a sauce simmering in the kitchen. They are back. And their presence makes it feel like old times.

So does the reemergence of gelato. In the afternoon, we amble down the hill to Bar Tullia. Gabe races ahead, but the rest of us dawdle, basking in the cerulean sky, the distant chimes of Santa Maria Maggiore's bells, the delicate breeze, the freshly planted flowers all around us, and the warming burble of alley lady chatter. As we approach Tullia, we notice activity and wonder if the card playing men have started gathering again.

We come in sight of the table, and yes, the seats are filled. We smile at the card players and only then do we notice that Gabe is sitting among them. His hands tightly grip his cards as he earnestly speaks to Marcello. What they are playing, I have no idea. Nor does Gabe. He is along for the ride, and he rides it with determination. It seems to be a variant of "War"—or what we call in our Quaker household "Goin' to the Pumpkin Patch"—but with a deck of intriguing cards that I suddenly realize we have in our sideboard. Marcello, Giorgio, and a couple enjoying gelato are at the table, teaching Gabe and cheering when he wins a trick. Marcello pretends disgust when Gabe takes a hand, but breaks character and erupts with laughter along with the rest of the table when Gabe, concerned that he's being allowed to win, asks if this is *uno scherzo*, a joke. Marcello doesn't let on. Despite his constant air of mirth, he has quite the poker face.

To no one's surprise but Gabe, he wins the game. And Marcello treats us all to gelato. He waggles his finger at Gabe, proclaiming that he'll win the rematch, and Gabe will have to buy *him* gelato. To which Gabe replies, "*Ma forse, io vinco.*" But maybe I'll win. The assembled crowd guffaws and proudly argues over how well Gabe is speaking Italian. Marcello and Gabe glare at each other with what I can only assume are their "game faces," and then burst out laughing.

Ante up, Gabe, you've been dealt in.

18 April

Since his trip, Nicolas has regaled us with stories from the *gita*. The stories are mostly of paprika-flavored Pringles and the revelry inherent in 50 eighth grad-ers on the loose, rather than reverence for palaces along the Brenta river. But nes-tled in these stories that animate my boy is a tender discovery that he relates with quiet wonder.

But first, a little backstory. Back in December, during the middle school eve-ning of poetry, there was only one student who struggled with his delivery. He stared at his feet and winced at the words. Nicolas told us later that the boy suffers from severe stage fright. Nicolas wondered why the boy had even been given a poem to recite, since it seemed like torture for him. We didn't know either, but we were moved by how supportive the students were to the one child who hung back.

That boy, Giovanni, is in one of the other *terza* classes, so Nicolas didn't have contact with him before the *gita*. After spending time with him, he's realized that Giovanni suffers from more than stage fright. His speech is hard to understand, and more than that, Giovanni isn't fluent in social norms. In short, he hugs too much. He likes to pet students' hair, and gets closer than is comfortable—even for Italians. He's also distressed easily and requires a full-time aide.

I can picture this kid in the American school system. Or at least the school system where I used to work. There, he'd likely be placed in a different classroom, surrounded by children with difficulties ranging from mental retardation to autism to oppositional defiant disorder. He'd learn academics, but he would learn little about functioning in mainstream society. Or perhaps he'd be deemed high functioning enough to be in a mainstream classroom, but then he would at best be avoided and at worst, bullied.

Here is what is striking about Spellani schools. There are no bullies. *There are no bullies.* There are no Queen Bees. And there are no outcasts. If you have ever loved a child who has been victim of the caste system inherent in American schools, I think you will understand why this is so astonishing, and so moving.

Giovanni is not ostracized. He is not placed into a separate classroom, rather he is with the rest of the class where he is loved and accepted. The other chil-dren—middle schoolers, as into Justin Bieber and their smartphones as kids in the

U.S.—fold him into their lives. They look out for him, they allow him to pet them, they laugh when his awkwardness crosses a boundary, they gently remind him of appropriate behavior when he goes too far.

They give him a place at the table.

And he is not a special case. Gabe's classmate Renata has Down syndrome. She also has a full-time aide, not because she went through a lengthy process that forced the school to provide support, but because she needs it. Much like our children have been given Italian lessons simply because they need them. Yes, Renata struggles with learning academics and also managing social skills, but she is learning all this within the context of being with other children. Who are also learning something vital.

Everyone gets a place at the table.

The child who is reading several grades below average, the child who is atheist in a country of Catholics, the child who was born in Morocco, the child who eats chalk for attention, the child from America who doesn't speak the language. There is an expression in Italian, *"Tutti parlano la stessa lingua a tavola."* Everyone speaks the same language at the table. It's a gift to see this in action.

Because it's not just welcoming for those who don't have their chromosomes lined up like animals entering Noah's ark. It's also relevant for the rest of the class. Students learn that everyone has value. Everyone. Initially, having a special needs child in the classroom proved challenging for Gabe. He would come home every day with annoyed stories about Renata's atypical behaviors and how "if Renata learns anything this school year, I'll be surprised." Now? Alessia tells us that he has taken the lead in showing her kindness. I'm grateful that Gabe is learning to feel good through empathy instead of feeling good through superiority.

And this lesson lasts into adulthood. There is an aged man in Spello who also has Down syndrome. He is a little challenging to understand, even for locals, but no one rushes him. People stop and listen. He comes into Bar Tullia and eats his pastry behind the counter. The owners weave around him to make *espresso* for patrons, sometimes patting his back with a smile. And then he leaves. I'm not sure if he pays. The community takes care of him. And in this way, he helps the community. Folding him in increases the town's flexibility and capacity for care. Everyone wins.

It's a lesson, above all others, that I hope my children take from this year. More important than how to make pasta. More important than how to conjugate irregular Italian verbs. More important than an increased sense of scope and possibility. In fact, it's the most important lesson of all.

We, all of us, get a place at the table.

19 April

One of Spello's manifold attractions is its vibrant bar scene, which is concentrated in the *centro*. This is unlike many towns, where the bars have migrated outside the ring road, pulling life away from the center. Bars are a gathering place, an easy spot to greet and feel greeted. Where men play cards and couples take in an Aperol spritz as the heat of the day begins to wane. You need that in the center for a town to thrive.

There are three bars in the center of Spello. Nicolas enjoys Cafe Cavour on a weekly basis for his candy runs, but I find it a little dark and tucked away. I prefer the jubilant laughter at Bar Bonci and the shyer warmth of Bar Tullia. Recently, we took the children to Bonci for breakfast. Gabe had his heart set on a chocolate *cornetto*, and glared at the display case devoid of his chosen treat. Letizia asked Gabe why he looked so angry, and he said, *"Perché io voglio un cornetto al cioccolato, e non ci sono."* Because I want a chocolate *cornetto*, and there aren't any. Letizia found this hysterical, and in a stream of Italian ordered him not to worry. She went to the back counter and retrieved a chocolate *cornetto* and said that she had been saving it, but wanted Gabe to have it. He refused, and shouted over Letizia shouting for him to take it, *"Ma adesso io vedo altre cose che mi piacciono…io prendo il nido."* But now I see other things that I like, I'll take the *nido*—a round, cream-filled pastry. Letizia laughed and relayed the whole story to the other bar patrons, while calling him her *tesoro*. Her treasure.

Bar Tullia is different. Siblings Gianni and Assunta are quieter, so the energy of the Bar revolves more around the regulars who stop in and cluster around the display case, full of enticing pastries made by Gianni's and Assunta's mother. Though the staff at Tullia are more reserved, they are no less kind. And that kindness feels textured and deep. We felt like we had "arrived" when Assunta started referring to Gabe by name and grinning at any of his attempts at Italian. When the bar is crowded so I can't reach the sugar, Gianni will quietly slip a packet of the raw sugar I prefer onto my saucer. When Keith picks me up a *cappuccino*, Gianni will wrap a spoon and a packet of that raw sugar into a napkin. And he moves with the surety of a ballet dancer—placing a silver spoon on the white ceramic saucer with a twist of his wrist, flicking the stem of the milk frother to crush the plastic bottle with a rhythmic flourish (to reduce space in the refuse bin, I imagine). Assunta serves gelato, apologizing to Keith when she's out of *amarena* or explaining to Gabe that she has yet to make *stracciatella* because her chocolate-chopping machine is broken. Gianni is the expert coffee and spritz maker.

Oh, the spritz. Nowadays, Gianni makes them so full for me that I have to take a few sips before I can dependably carry it to the patio. And I'll risk public scorn to admit that an Aperol spritz is my favorite way of feeding my children. It works like this: It's 4:30 in the afternoon, and the kids start clamoring for a snack. I suppose I could rummage through the refrigerator to rustle something into submission. But really, I'm living my dream, and my dream hums with an Aperol spritz. Besides its being refreshing, and besides the feeling that life is a golden paradise when I'm sipping one on Tullia's patio, facing the street lined with the sunny walls and stone edifices of Spello, the beauty of an Aperol spritz lies in the snacks. Because it is an *aperitivo*, it comes with snacks. Gianni gives us extra large bowls of chips, fennel rings, and peanuts. A little something salty. I feel it rounds out the children's gelato nicely, making for balanced refreshment.

Bar Tullia faces the elementary school, and when Stephanie and Gray were here, we were enjoying the gelato/cocktail hour with Angelo while Siena and Gabe played a game in the space in front of the school. Then suddenly Gabe shrieked. He had leaned down to pick something out of a planter and inadvertently scratched his eye with a stick. Stephanie ran into the bar to get paper napkins for his eye, and when Gianni saw her, he asked if she wanted *ghiaccio*. Seeing her confused expression, he searched for the word for a moment, and then asked, "Ice?" There is really nothing like quiet generosity when the chips are down. It was hard to hold my baby with blood trickling from his eyelid, but better once we knew he'd only scratched the lid, and better still when we felt this seen and supported.

I love our bars so much, I want to start one at home. Because there is no place like an Italian bar. As useful in the morning for a shot of *espresso* as in the evening for a cup of hot chocolate or a more adult-warming beverage. A spot to pick up a *cornetto* to eat surrounded by the banter of locals or to get a piece of pizza to wrap in a napkin and eat while walking. It's the perfect display for seasonal treats (*fave dei morti*, anyone?), or a convenient location for a moment of alone time, or a place to gather with friends and family for a spell and watch the world go by. Where else can you get a treat for children, while having a glass of wine? Where children are allowed to be children in their quest for play and creation in a garden or small adjoining *piazza*, and adults are allowed to be adults in their desire to lean back and let their life stand still for a moment?

The beauty of Italian bars echoes on, like the bells that toll the hour. Assunta waves me over to tell me that she was finally able to make the chips for the *stracciatella*, adding with a smile that she thinks this news will make our Gabri happy.

20 April

Over pizza, Paola's friend asks Siena if she'll be glad to go home. Siena gives a flat "no." Thinking she must not have understood the question, I repeat it in English. Siena assures me that she understands, but there is much about her life here that she loves, and will regret leaving. I nod, turning away so she wouldn't see me blinking back tears. Of relief. Of joy. I have been holding onto the worry that this experience has been too much for my girl. Hearing her describing her experience in such loving terms lifts a huge weight from my heart, replacing it with a sense of liberation.

And she is happy—I can see her radiating enthusiasm. She loves her Monday routine of going to Paola's shop to macramé together. She loves the independence of going to pick up groceries or bread for us and interacting with the vendors. Most of all, she loves her newfound opportunity to get out in nature. As much as she loves the bustle and stimulation and wafting scents of food that embody towns, she is a green girl. Never happier than when she is running through woods, pausing at interesting mushrooms. Now when she notices in herself a need to breathe in the natural world, she asks to dash out for a bit. To pick flowers, stretch, and feel the trees all around her. She always comes back with flowers.

Paola showed me how to hunt for asparagus last week, and Siena's been begging me to teach her. We set out as a family and gather in the lacey shade of olive trees surrounded by brilliant poppies, nudging aside prickly foliage to search for the tips of asparagus gingerly poking into the sunshine, while a rooster crows in the distance and the breeze gentles the warm sun. We look at each other and grin like idiots.

Knowing that we'll stop at Tullia for gelato on the way home, stopping to talk to people we know, and that I'll turn our haul into dinner only heightens the gratitude and contentment. Life is most definitely good.

21 April

I've watched *Friday Night Lights,* so I am familiar with how vital high school football can be to a small town. What I didn't know was that football is to Texas what foraging is to Spello. Take a walk in the countryside around the town, and you'll see a woman in sensible shoes with a knife and a plastic shopping bag staring intently at a patch of green that looks like your basic overgrown grass. But she knows better. She'll squint one eye, then pounce and come out triumphant with a new addition to her bag of vitamin A, C, K, and folate. She's getting her exercise and plotting meals that feature just-picked, wild, organic greens. Not too shabby for a morning's *passeggiata*.

Three weeks ago when we were taking a stroll through the countryside, I noticed a couple returning back to their car from deep within the olive groves. The woman held a large handful of what looked like sticks. My mind spun from possibility to possibility—twigs for a fire? branches for decoration?—before I realized. Wild asparagus. A mental leap only possible thanks to a poster for a wild asparagus festival that caught my eye while I was sipping my *cappuccino* in Bar Bonci. Convinced that what I now saw gripped with a proprietary firmness was asparagus, we dove into the groves ourselves. But having a scarce knowledge base of what we were looking for, we scanned for the familiar thick stalks. With the purple rubber band. Unsurprisingly, we came up empty handed.

I asked Paola, and she confirmed that wild asparagus season is beginning. But one must be careful because this is also the season of vipers, just waking up and eager to make sure their poison sacs are still limber. Lest I think this was just a scare tactic to keep me away from her secret troves of wild asparagus, she invited me to come with her to harvest the green. She showed up with two *bastoni*, big sticks. We'd need the sticks to brush the grass in front of us and clear the area around the asparagus plant before reaching our hand into the grass. All of a sudden, the expression "Walk softly and carry a big *bastone*" is starting to make sense.

Our first trip was a bust, despite the fact that everyone who saw us with our bags offered advice about where to look, and despite the fact that Paola approached the *contadini* working in the trees for guidance. We found plenty of the foliage, but no stalks. Finally, Paola spotted someone she knows who is *bravo* when it comes to foraging, and she entreated him to help us. He sighed that the area was already picked over, but within moments, he'd spotted a stalk of asparagus and plucked it for us before lumbering into the groves. It was to be our only stalk of the morning. We collected *borragine* as a colorful consolation prize.

The following week Paola told me she had discovered a bountiful patch, and on Saturday we tried our luck again. And now that I've found wild asparagus and had the joy of cooking with it, I'm hooked. This is my kind of sport. In trying to get Nicolas to join us yesterday, I told him it was like a riskier Easter egg hunt—perilous with the prickly foliage, the threat of vipers, and the skidding down the hill with arms windmilling, which is funnier when Laurel and Hardy do it. He retorted it was like an Easter egg hunt with asparagus instead of jelly beans. Good point, son. Get your shoes on. Ultimately, he was glad he went, and not just because of our gelato afterward. He realized it is indeed satisfying, and eating dinner that night he kept marveling at the fact that we had just gathered the asparagus. And here it is! In our *tagliatelle*.

Here's how to collect asparagus like a pro. First, get a plastic shopping bag. White, if you want to fit in with the *nonne*. Then, nod and smile at the people you pass with your bag that announces your intentions. When people ask if you are going to pick asparagus, nod and ask if they know any good spots. If you are on the cusp of language learning, you might not understand the particulars of their answer, but standing in the street watching them animatedly describe their favorite areas as the sun streams over the medieval walls, you'll realize it hardly matters. Then head to the groves, as asparagus grow under trees. Keep your eye out for asparagus foliage, which looks like a tangled mass of prickly pine tree. Sometimes the growth is small, just a few viney branches, and sometimes it's huge like a Christmas-tree tumbleweed. That foliage is prickly, gloves can help unless you favor the idea of sporting asparagus wounds, like a varsity jacket.

Once you find the foliage, clear the area around it with your stick and get low. Look for dark green or purple heads of asparagus just poking out of the ground, a few inches high, or even taller than the foliage. Those stems camouflage themselves well, so practice vigilance. Training helps. When I went this morning with Angelo and a friend of his I'd met at the communist dinner—she'd approached me at Bar Tullia to ask if I'd yet been asparagus picking. When I suggested we go together, she willingly accepted—I learned the full meaning of the expression "Asparagus picking is in the eyes." That's a real saying. I'd search a patch of asparagus foliage and come up empty, then Angelo's friend would blithely snap a stalk that was waving right in front me. Luckily, the advantage of collecting with communists is they give you half their haul. Actually, Angelo's friend gave me her entire bag, and resisted my entreaties that she keep some.

No matter how much you find, once your bag contains asparagus, you have arrived. You are one of the Spellani. You can smile knowingly and nod conspiratorially when you see a walker headed out of the Roman archway with a white plastic bag. You know what they are about. You can compare asparagus foliage scratches on your hands with the woman at the bakery. When you hear people talking about where they've found asparagus, you can jump in. You can boast of the asparagus you found on your trail. Now, when people hail you on the street with the oft-used greeting of *"Hai trovato asparagi?"* you can grin and say yes, indeed, you have found asparagus. You can debate whether to toss your asparagus with *tagliatelle* or cook them into a frittata. These are the only two sanctioned ways of preparing wild asparagus in Spello.

And the asparagus tastes fabulous. Like a cross between asparagus, herbs, and greens. And since you expended all the effort to collect them, you can feel perfectly comfortable buying yourself a congratulatory gelato. For the win!

22 April

Siena and I are running late to her violin lesson. She begs to stay home, worried that tardiness will annoy her teacher. I reason with her and she reluctantly joins me in racing down the hill. She grows more agitated with every step closer to the *scuola media*. I tell her, "Siena, I think it would be useful if you could practice letting go of things over which you have no control. You will be late, that's a given. Whatever happens, happens, you'll deal with it then." She responds, "But that's my nature, I want do things right." And I counter, "Yes, that is your nature, and it comes from a good place, but that is why you need practice trying it a different way. Being stressed won't help you get there on time, you might as well practice accepting that you didn't get it perfect, and move on." She's quiet for a few moments, and then says, "Okay."

Wait—what? It's not supposed to be that easy. It certainly isn't for me.

But she noticeably calms. Then she confides, "Since our last walk to violin, I've realized that part of my problem is that because I'm scared of not being liked, I hide. I hide away, and no one can see me. Which means that no one can like me because no one can know me. That doesn't make any sense. So I've decided to work on not hiding."

I make some sort of attempt at responding, garbled and incomprehensible. While my daughter serenely sails down the hill. In answer to my stuttering, she announces, "I love our walks to violin practice. They are just long enough to get me thinking about something, and then I can take my time later to think more about it." I have a moment of wondering what it means for my professional 50-minute hour to have my daughter resonate with five minute conversations. It's obvious that I suffer from over-talking—preventing Siena from doing her own processing. Looks like I have my own practice to do.

We arrive just in time enough for a quick hug before I release her into the middle school. I'd planned to apologize to the teacher for Siena's tardiness, but it's the school assistant who lets us in, and she won't let a parent though the door without a note from the prime minister. So Siena has to walk in, on her own, and face her teacher, on her own. To the assistant's bewildered expression as Siena sidles by with nervous reluctance, I explain that Siena is worried about being late. The assistant guffaws that everyone is late sometimes. Siena pauses to absorb this, before shaking off whatever lingering concern she has and ascending the stairs.

When I pick her up, she reports that the teacher had no reaction to her tardiness. She muses that they must expect students to be late sometimes. So did she nail it? Did she throw off her need to please others in her sudden understanding that the world would continue to turn if she messes up sometimes? She did not. But she did practice. And that's the work.

25 April

April 25 is the anniversary of the day that Allied forces and Italian *partigiani* successfully pushed the Nazis out of Italy, liberating the country from Mussolini's fascist regime and the Nazi invasion. It's a big deal, made more salient living in a town that housed Nazi resisters. In the U.S. we have Veteran's Day and we have Memorial Day, but we don't have a day dedicated to the end of World War II. A day to honor, not just those in the military but the civilians who provided aid to resisters, those who housed victims of cruel and immoral persecution, and the overthrow of oppressive regimes that were based on denying the fundamental humanity of all. It is a day to reflect, so that we can truly make sure that we never forget.

Like many Italian holidays, April 25 carries somber undertones. As we walk to the celebration in the *piazza*, I reflect on Angelo's words, that April 25 is a celebration of liberation, and also of the beginning of a friendship between Italy and the United States. The *discorso* begins with the entrance of the Spellani band. They play "*Bella Ciao*," a folksong re-purposed into an antifascist song of resistance, as they stream into the *piazza*. Nicolas leans to tell me that on his *gita,* the band in Alfonsine played "*Bella Ciao*" while his friends sang along.

The mayor, dressed in his Italian flag sash, speaks about the importance of giving the youth a sense of hope for the future. At the conclusion of his remarks, a trumpeter plays a mournful song as Antonio, the town gardener, climbs a ladder propped against the *comune* wall, to hang wreaths of bay leaves around the plaques honoring the Spellani that died in World War II. Then the band plays the national anthem, and the children release balloons. Not being properly prepared, we didn't attach notes about peace to the string of the balloon, as Nicolas did in Alfonsine (after checking his grammar with friends). When the balloons pop, the peaceful messages drift from the sky.

Liberation Day is a reminder that under Mussolini's rule, Italy was allied with Nazi Germany. That the people overthrew Mussolini, and welcomed the Americans into Sicily, as the Germans were invading from the north. That the country experienced incredible hardship as the battle raged between the Americans and the Germans, with the *partigiani* fighting the Germans from pockets in the north.

Until finally the Americans and Italians, together, pushed Germany out of Italy—marking the beginning of peace and reconstruction. You can't visit an area of Italy without seeing the destruction of bombing, as Allied forces sought to destroy German-occupied areas. It's a day to reflect on the horrors of war, the sacrifice of lives and dreams and souls. And how to create a future defined by peace.

Happy Liberation Day. Though I'm certainly milking it by insisting that it is a day when I am liberated from hearing whining or fixing a proper lunch, I'm also sitting with the deeper parts. I wish for us all a day of liberation from the external and internal forces that stymie our push toward peace, that obstruct our drive for love and beauty, that distort our view of grace. A day to imagine those American soldiers handing out chocolates, and feel that flowers bloom in unexpected places.

26 April

Sante and Conci have invited us for lunch, and I decide to make an apple pie. At one time, I would have tried to mute my American-ness, but I've since realized that our new friends don't expect us to be Italian, and in fact enjoy the background we bring to the table. So I'm bringing apple pie. We walk in, and I begin to wonder if this was a stupid idea. My thoughts are stalled by Conci peeping under the napkin and yelping, "Apple pie?" When I nod, there are delighted cries of "apple pie! apple pie!" intermingled with our greetings and introductions to Roberta's family.

We find places around the table, while Conci and Roberta's mother bustle away in the kitchen. Homemade *salumi*, pasta with a perfectly light *ragú*, platters of pork and *cinghiale* ribs and chops, eggplant, and dessert. Followed by coffee and apple pie and slices of melon from Sicily. I chat with Roberta about her mushroom class, Keith uses unrecognizable verbs in his conversation with Silvano about politics, and we all laugh as Nicolas is plied with plate after plate of pasta. Gabe gets up from his seat to put his hand on Conci's arm, and tells her that everything is *molto delizioso*. Conci wraps her arms around Gabe, and drops a kiss on his cheek. Siena is quiet during the hubbub of the meal but afterward she leaps to join Silvano and Roberta for an asparagus hunt. Gabe and Nicolas play with the dogs while Keith and I opt for the proffered *passeggiata* with Sante. Walking is a great expat activity. It relieves the pressures of a post-Italian lunch, and there is a constant stream of possible conversation topics. Our walk takes us past an Etruscan tomb, complete with funerary urns and dank air. When we return, I open the gate to find Siena teaching Roberta's niece to twist the stems of daisies into a crown of flowers. The two of them present the ring of blossoms to Conci, who pulls the girls in for a hug.

27 April

There are old people in Spello. Everywhere I go, I see old people. When I'm collecting wild asparagus in the olive groves, asking my butcher how to make a robust polenta sauce, picking up bread and pizza at the *forno*. There they are. Stopping to ask if my cats are in the house. Pausing to squeeze Gabe. Sorting greens and playing cards. Really, they are everywhere.

Of *course* they are. The real question is, why am I not used to this? How is it that at home I so rarely see old people?

And let me pause here and talk terminology. Now that I've crossed the line into middle age, I no longer consider 40 to be old. Angelo tells me that I'm in the *adulto* stage, between ages 30-60, which is followed by *"anziano."* I thought that meant ancient, and avoided the word as methodically as I avoided asking for *penne*, for fear I'll not hit that double n hard enough and people will think I'm desirous of penises. But no, *anziano* is a term of respect. Kind of like "seniors" in the U.S. *"Vecchio"* is the stage of life after *"anziano."* So Angelo, as over 60, describes himself as *"anziano."* Once he is nearing 80, he'll take on the mantle of *"vecchio."* And will likely be perfectly happy to wear it.

Because being old here is clearly a different matter than being old at home. I ask Keith where all the old people are in Charlottesville, and he says, "In a nursing home or in Florida." That can't be true. But it is true that 80 year olds in Spello seem really different from 80-year-olds at home. Granted, I don't see any in either place when they are shut in to their homes because of physical difficulties, but in Spello, every time I leave my house, I see a *vecchio* walking with a cane, or dragging a shopping basket on wheels. They have a presence here. And with that presence, they have a community—a vibrancy.

Something is keeping old people in the center of the community, rather than marginalized on the edges. It could be the walking. Living in a hill town necessitates much walking, which translates to heart health, as well as breathing clean air and sunshine. Or maybe it's that people eat close to the ground here. Literally, in that foraging is sport, and what could be more vitamin packed than wild greens that you pick and eat the same day? Or maybe it's as simple as the lauded Mediterranean diet. Coupled with free medical care, which allows for solving problems before they become debilitating.

But I think there is something more. Angelo reminds me that our country is a young one. And yet, in the space of just over 200 years, we've become a superpower. Drive and determination and grit propelled our relatively young country onto the world stage. Which is terrific. *Complimenti.* And now, those qualities that made our country great—relentless energy, productivity, force—are the ones that are prized. Angelo's conclusion is that as Americans age and their energy fades, and they move from a place of powerful execution to softened reflection, they are dismissed as irrelevant. Placed in homes surrounded by other aged people. Where the ease of their lives and the lack of vital stimulation, coupled with separation from loved ones, hastens both their mental and physical deterioration. Decline by bingo, I suppose.

Contrast American retirement communities with a cross-generational community like Spello, where *vecchi* not only have each other, but have toddlers to delight in and *adulti* to argue politics with. Since it is not productivity that is valued in small town Italy (for better or for worse—*see*, economic crisis), but civic engagement, these older people don't lose their value. Their roles shift, but they still have roles. They bookend one end of the human experience, as the baby born across the street bookends the other.

Siena says that having *anziani* and *vecchi* makes Spello feel "real." She's right. When we looked to buy a house, we looked for a neighborhood with "young families." For reasons that make sense—we wanted to be surrounded by people like us. Images of children walking to visit friends and lively neighborhood barbecues were large in our mind. But we neglected to factor in what we'd miss by not living in a multi-generational neighborhood. The quieter energy and the sense of history-in-process that comes with an older population. We got our Disneyland existence. But we forgot that Disneyland gets cloying after awhile.

In America we value youth as the perfect stage, but too much of any "perfection" becomes one-note. Italians are very adept at accepting imperfection, very able to fold the bad in with the good. Like with the differently-abled, the community gains strength borne of incorporating what is less than "perfect." After all, the beauty of life is in the contrasts. The high, perfect, youthful moments are better noticed when arched across the grey clouds of gathering age. And it is easier to maintain a sense of perspective about how annoying it is when the neighbor lets his dog pee on your rosemary, when you are constantly connecting with people who watched bombs fall on Foligno.

We need the striving, but also the resting. We need the youthful energy, but also the frailness of age. We need the enthusiastic productivity, but also the time-worn hand caressing the cheek of our baby. We need the push and the fight to direct our lives, but also the peace of acceptance for what we have. We need the feeling that we are invincible, but we also need the surety that we, too, will age.

I stand on our *terrazza*, and gaze at the grapevine in our neighbor's derelict yard. I'm mesmerized by the contrasts. The tough and gnarled vines sprout tender green leaves, sprinkled with delicate white flowers. Without our older generation, we have no rhythm for our melody, no tannins for our wine, no clouds to establish the blueness of the sky.

28 April

At drop off today, I see Anna Maria and impulsively invite Lorenzo over for lunch, to much cheering from both Lorenzo and Gabe. As I set the table, I tell Lorenzo that I have prepared a *"pasta con tonno nel modo americana."* Otherwise known as tuna casserole. Sounds better in Italian. He is enthusiastic to try what he refers to as *pasta alla Inghilterra*, English pasta. This poor child is going to have a strange conception of English food. Which, perhaps, is valid.

Lorenzo polishes off his pasta, salami, and salad. Nicolas murmurs that the boy doesn't ever stop smiling, even when he's eating. Only once during lunch do I see his face cast down, and that is when he talks about the fact that Gabe is moving. Gabe nods sadly, and then talks about the story the class is writing about his leave-taking. I know it's on the eighth-grade radar as well. Nicolas has told me that he and Mario have come up with a plan—Mario will to visit us in America for two months out of the year, and Nicolas will stay with Mario for two months. I never expected these expat friendships to take root, so it is surprising to watch them blooming into *amici di cuore*.

We take the boys to Bar Tullia, where Assunta is as familiar with Lorenzo's standing gelato order as she is with Gabe's. And then to the park, where Anna Maria meets us with a smile, a gift of chocolate, and advice about our upcoming trip to Sicily—what to eat, where to go, punctuated with the classic Italian gesture of "this thing that I am describing is so wonderful, there are no words." Remembering how during her last visit, she'd been intrigued by maple syrup, I invite her family to come to our house for an American breakfast when we return from Sicily. She is thrilled. Prompting a new resolution—let's cement this friendship by finding some bacon.

29 April

I wonder, in the States, do we celebrate friendship? Sure, we have girls' nights and we have poker parties, but do we celebrate the simple act of loving each other? It's on my mind because Marcello invited us to his garden for his promised *festa*. He'd shown me the garden last week, and when I clasped my hands together in wonder at the view, he'd given me a key. With a smile and an invitation to use the garden whenever I want. Then he told me about the sausages he's going to grill for the party. I smacked my lips in anticipation, then remembered to remind him that Siena and Keith would be tardy, as she is coming from her *gita* to Carsulae.

As I walk with Nicolas and Gabe to Marcello's garden, we see a sign with an arrow that reads, *"La festa è qui,"* The party is here. We giggle, and then notice that the entire route to Marcello's is punctuated with these signs. As if anyone in attendance couldn't find their way to Marcello's garden with their eyes closed. On the gate, a new sign reads, *"Per chi ancora non sa, la festa è qui."* For those who still don't know, the party is here. Once we walk through the gate, we see that Angelo has festooned the olive tree with paper hearts, with "Love" written on one side, and the name of a party guest on the flip side. Keith's name is spelled, appropriately, "Kit."

The party is simple. The boys play in the garden, while the adults talk, and the sausages sizzle on the fire. Umbrians grill by building an oak fire on the back of the grill, then dragging the ashes forward. Then they use a grill on legs, with two grates that sandwich the meat inside, to cook the sausage. The legs allow the meats to sit above the embers, and when the meat is sufficiently cooked on one side, the grill can be rotated to the other side, where there are identical legs. So one can cook meat anywhere there are embers, and turn all the pieces with a simple flip. Meats cook to juicy, caramelized perfection.

The grilled sausage are served with squares of *focaccia* and the *erbe*, greens, that Maura (who made the *colomba* for the Tribbio Easter celebration) had cooked earlier. We each break open a slice of *focaccia*, and fill it with sausage and *erbe*. Nicolas tries to refuse the *erbe*, but Maura overrides him. I love Italy. With his eyes rolling in wonder, Nicolas admits that the *erbe* brings the whole sandwich together. It adds a shot of lucidity to the smoky sausage and highlights the juiciness. Together with the soft and salty *focaccia*, it makes one incredible meal.

Keith and Siena arrive when we're getting seconds. Siena, flushed with sunburn and elation, submits to much kissing and introductions before she sits down with her sandwich, polishes it off, and makes a second. Then we all gather for *prosecco* and *crostata alla marmellata*.

A toast to *amicizia!*

Italians are intent on making eye contact during cheers, a way to affirm seeing and being seen. When we first arrived, I felt exposed and vulnerable at that degree of eye contact. Now, I love it. It feels like a moment when guards come down and kindred spirits are summoned. Cheers to the couple who brought the cheese from Rome, and leap up when I praise its deliciousness, to tell me all about how it's *genuino*, from small farms, where the cheese is wrapped in *vernaccia* (the leavings of the grape harvest) and placed in caves to ripen. Cheers to Marcello, who is so welcoming he created a *festa* that my children rank among their favorite parties. Cheers to Maura with her cooking wizardry. Cheers to Giorgio with his dapper outfit and inability to keep from laughing hysterically when Marcello reads a poem aloud. Cheers to Angelo who has more room in his heart than almost anyone I know. Cheers to everyone. I love them all.

On our walk home, Siena chatters about her field trip. The ruins were inspiring, and she was incredulous that she got to see the Via Flaminia, the ancient Roman road. But what most moved her was friendship. She said she had always thought that the girls wanted to be her friend because she was foreign and different.

She hadn't realized until this trip that they thought of her as more than an interesting side note. But on the trip, she connected with many different girls, and listened in surprise as she was listed as a "best friend" of many of them. Particularly Chiara, who named Siena immediately, and then paused to say other girls as well. My daughter was astonished at this new demonstration of how she is loved.

Angelo's tree of *amicizia* is ripe with low-hanging fruit. All we need to do is gather, and celebrate.

30 April

I feel like a broken record. Each day I announce some variant of "Spring is here!" In my defense, my local residency is in its infancy, so I'm not familiar with the seasonal landmarks. When I see yellow flowers illuminating the ground under olive trees, or the rough grapevines wreathed with tender leaves, or alley ladies and card-playing men resuming their warm weather positions, or the reemergence of gelato at Tullia, or succulent heads of asparagus playing hide-and-seek among prickly fronds, I am liable to leap to the conclusion that this, *this*, means that spring is really here.

But this time, I'm sure.

Because Spello is beginning to hum in preparation for *L'Infiorata*—the annual honoring of Corpus Domini with the laying of flower carpets. The celebration is June 2 this year, and Spello is already ramping up. Nicolas reports that Mario missed school yesterday because he was picking flowers late into the night. We've spied a *cantina* in the *borgo* where a team is de-petaling flowers. And yesterday, when Siena and I were walking to the countryside so that she could paint poppies, we passed the alley ladies removing the petals from yellow flowers. I stop and ask why they collect the petals so long before the *Infiorata*, and the ladies titter at my innocence. There will be many, many petals. The petals from these flowers can be dried, which creates a different shade and texture, and allows some of the work to be done in advance.

Flowers are a major part of the Spellani identity—apparent in the profusion of colorful pots attached to stone walls, framing doorways, lining alleys—and the *Infiorata* is what has put Spello on the world flower stage. I've been told stories of groups working all night to create images in flowers, I've seen books on the splendid displays, I've been warned that moving around Spello on the day of the *Infiorata* is all but impossible. Many towns celebrate the *Infiorata*, but Spello *breathes* the *Infiorata*.

My daughter, with her love of all things floral, is in heaven. Actually, since the first nascent blossoms made their hesitant appearance along the stone walls of Spello, she has bloomed. Gathering flowers, drawing and painting, noticing shifts from grape hyacinths to poppies as the season progresses. I've never seen her so happy. In fact, she recently mentioned that she can't remember why she was ever homesick. After all, she'll be going home soon enough. And living here is a miracle she can't seem to wrap her mind around.

Sure, she grumbles on P.E. days because she still feels nervous around the teacher that punished her so harshly, and she reports school is often boring, and she snaps at her younger brother like any self-respecting older sister. But to balance this, there is a creeping flush of joy. And a burgeoning confidence that we don't remember seeing, even in the States. When she goes to the *forno,* she asks how much the cookies are, and if there is enough after buying bread, she'll bring home treats for the family. Which means more lengthy conversations with the baker, since cookies are sold by weight. When she comes home, paper bag rustling with a *filetta* and cookies or yogurt bread, she announces that she managed the whole conversation without hesitation. And an accent that sounds less and less American.

The appearance of poppies seems to parallel the appearance of Siena's joy. Fields and fields awash with red. I stand, surrounded by the brilliant, nodding heads of the flowers, while I watch Siena leap across the field, determined to not crush one precious bloom. Surrounding herself in the brilliance, and confessing that she feels tearful in the midst of so much beauty. She stands for another moment, long enough for me to notice how tall she's grown, how gracefully she holds herself before sinking to the ground to arrange her pencils. I watch her draw, and when she's done, she packs her bag and finds her own way back to the road.

Dare I say it?

It really is spring.

Tagliatelle con Asparagi Selvatici e Pomodorini

fresh *tagliatelle*, preferably homemade

olive oil, the best you have

1 or 2 cloves of garlic

wild asparagus
(cultivated can be substituted, look for thin stalks),
woody ends removed, broken into pieces

cherry tomatoes, halved

a handful of parmesan or aged pecorino

* * *

1. Bring a large pot of salted water to a boil.

2. While the water is heating, heat plenty of olive oil in a large pan. Add garlic, and swirl to coat.

3. Without letting the garlic brown, add the asparagus pieces. When they are almost tender, remove the garlic, and toss in the cherry tomatoes.

4. Add the *tagliatelle* to the pasta water, and boil for a few minutes until *al dente*.

5. Reserving a bit of pasta water, add the drained pasta to the pan of asparagus and tomatoes, and toss. If it looks too dry, add a bit of pasta water. Sprinkle in the cheese and a fall of black pepper, and toss again before serving.

6. Inhale the aroma of spring, and dive in.

MAY

WITHOUT A MAP

1 May

Loris and Patrizia have planted grass by their pool, and this seems to be cause for celebration. They've invited us for dinner, and though it's strange to be going without Doreen, who always makes everything easy with her Italian fluency and ready laugh, I'm smiling with excitement when we knock on their door. The children walk to the yard, and cheer at the sight of all the green grass. They throw off their shoes and tumble and chase all over the yard. Filippo arrives and brings out a soccer ball, and they play soccer before we sit down to dinner.

Patrizia serves us a *risotto* with speck, fava beans, and saffron, which sings of springtime. As does the rabbit, with its tantalizing aroma of light and herby flavors. Though the meal is extraordinary, the conversation is more memorable. Because for the first time in Italian-speaking history, I cannot shut up. All of a sudden, I feel gripped to try to speak—give me a willing listener, and I'll dive into talking, even without a clear plan of what I'm going to say and how I'll conjugate *avere*. Loris raises his eyebrow at Keith and nods toward me, like "Can you believe this?" Keith, who is mastering the art of gesture, raises his hands and gives the ubiquitous Italian shrug. While I smile and smile.

2 May

Twice a year, in June and September, Foligno celebrates *La Giostra della Quintana*. The celebration is named after the equestrian-training road of the Roman Empire and features a horse race with a dash of jousting. In the *Quintana*, a horse and rider complete a series of figure 8's on a track. A statue of Mars, known as the *Quintana*, sits at the intersection, holding out a small ring. As the rider passes the *quintana*, he must spear the ring, then race back around while a smaller ring is hung and the *quintana* is turned to face the new approach. Three rings total—ten centimeters in diameter, then eight, then six. Each rider is timed, and loses points for missing a ring, hitting a flag, or for going off course.

Similarly to the Palio in Siena (the city), the riders represent districts, termed *rioni* here. In Foligno, there are ten *rioni*, and each sponsors a *taverna* and champions a horse for the event. Brenda suggests that we attend the trials, where riders compete for the privilege of representing their district at the *Quintana* in June. So we collect Siena from Chiara's house, pick up kebabs for dinner, and find seats in the stands, with no clear idea what we are waiting for.

On the field, a rider is warming up. After a few minutes of easy loping around the track, a companion holds up the lance. The rider approaches, and plucks the lance out of the outstretched hands. There is a pause as the rider adjusts the weight of the lance, tossing it slightly, until it is in the desired position. He looks up, and begins trotting, the lance held upright in one hand while his other guides the reins. His pace quickens, until he is leaning over the horse's neck and they are racing along the track at a dizzying speed. The crowd falls silent. In the sudden hush, all we can hear is the blur of hoofbeats, as the horse banks so tightly around corners it looks as if its feet will slide from underneath its body. Horse and rider explode from the turn, and sprint toward the center of the ring. As they approach the *quintana*, the rider stands slightly in the stirrups, raises his lance to shoulder level, and *ding!* spears the ring. My goosebumps stay lodged long after the rider has gone on to spear the next two rings.

As the next rider warms up, we wave over the peanut and vermouth vendor to buy peanuts we don't particularly want, just to ensconce ourselves further into the merriment in the stands. Though we lack district scarves, we feel part of the burgundy *rione* behind us, inexplicably singing "Macho Man." I remember over dinner one night, Graziano told us about growing up in Foligno, and how each *rione* has its own character and civic pride. I wonder what it would be like to grow up like Graziano—feeling a sense of camaraderie with your neighbors around scarves and horses and restaurants. I turn to Keith to ask which *rione* Graziano belonged to, and he points out a child wearing a black and yellow scarf with an image of a sword, *la spada*.

The light shifts as the sky darkens and we inhale sharply with the crowd when a horse goes off course. Angelo tells me that *Quintana* rivalries are more antagonistic than soccer rivalries, and the actual *Quintana* is therefore more intense. Particularly since the participants are fully costumed. I struggle to imagine anything more thrilling than what we didn't know to expect tonight in Foligno—speed and daring under the mantle of history.

3 May

Gabe is up all night, shrieking and clutching his ear. Upon waking, he cries that his ear is saying, "Hey, why are you shooting at me?" We are loath to treat ear infections with antibiotics, but it is clearly time for the *medico*. After dropping Siena off at school, we walk to the *guardia medica*. We wander the building, an ashen Gabe clinging to my leg, until a *nonna* takes pity on us and looks for the *medico*. She regretfully informs us that he won't be in until evening. And so our only option is the hospital. We stop by Angelo's, hoping he can help us. But he's not home, so I leave him a note, canceling my lesson.

When we exit the hospital four hours later, and realize we are in the wrong parking lot, Keith jokes that we'll have to bushwhack. I retort that bushwhacking is what we'd been doing all morning. A morning that begins at prompt care, where we are redirected to the ER. But we can't find it. Signage toward the ER peters out and leaves us in a hallway full of people chatting. We find an information booth, where a woman volunteers to guide us to the ER. Once there, we realize we have no idea how to proceed. There's no counter, just a group of distressed people huddled around a closed door. When the buzzer sounds, announcing the unlocking of the glass door, whoever decides they are next enters triage. Every few minutes Gabe worriedly asks me what's happening and I answer, "I have no idea."

Finally we're buzzed in, and give the triage man our documents. He clicks at his keyboard, asks us bureaucratic questions in a muttering undertone, and then sends us to *Pediatria* with a sheaf of paperwork. As we wander, lost again, we pass Fabrizio from Spello's *Il Tribbio*, wearing a white lab coat. My heart sags in relief to see his familiar face. He starts to guide us, but looking at his watch he realizes he can't. Instead he gives us instructions—follow the signs to OB-Gyn, and through it we'll find *Pediatria*. We follow the pregnant ladies, but once we arrive at OB-Gyn, we are stymied by three branching corridors. We lurk next to a nurse talking to a patient in the hallway, and when she turns toward us, we ask for help. She tells us to walk straight and go through the *"porta blu."* We walk to the end of the corridor, where we are met with three blue doors, two of one shade, one of another. *"Blu"* is a shade of blue, as are *"azzurro"* and *"celeste."* I'm vehemently regretting that I blew off the lesson on colors, under the misbegotten idea that learning to ask for half a salami was more useful than asking for a dark blue crayon. Hubris rears its ugly head. Lesson: Learn your colors.

"What's happening, Mamma?"

"I have no idea, baby."

We finally find *Pediatria*. Only there's nobody here. We stand in front of the nurses' station, helpless. Finally, a nurse directs us to wait, and gestures to the closed doors off the hall. We go through the doors to a small room, lined with fixed stools, that connects to the main bustle of the hospital. Finally, we've arrived. Except we haven't, really. We see people entering a room off the waiting room. Keith peeks in and sees another waiting room, this one designed more like a pediatrician's waiting room, with chairs around the perimeter and magazines on the tables. Which are we supposed to wait in? Divide and conquer. Gabe and I stay in the hallway waiting area, Keith loiters in the second room. And we wait—and wait. We return to the nurses' station to make sure we're in the right place. Vacant, again. A doctor hurries by and we practically lunge at him. He flicks through our paperwork, tells us that he has to do rounds, which will take 40 minutes and then he'll see Gabe. He suggests we wait in the toy room, we nod, and walk down the corridor. Wishing we'd caught him 30 minutes earlier. For example, when we arrived at *Pediatria*.

The toy room is scattered with chunky, plastic toys. Gabe and I sit on small chairs while he plays on my Kindle and I stare at the crucifix over the door. Keith stands guard in the hallway to make sure we aren't forgotten, and a little girl flies out of her room to attach herself to his leg. She looks up, and seeing that Keith is not her father, she scurries down the hall, where her father is emphatically whispering into his phone. I note the girl's socks and pajamas, and realize the obvious. All these rooms are filled with sick children.

"What's happening, Mamma?"

"I have no idea, baby."

An hour and a half later, we're called to the examination room. The doctor speaks in a quiet mutter. We ask him to repeat himself and he looks at us, unnerved. He murmurs an instruction to Gabe, who shouts, *"Come?"* in response. After all, the child's ears are presumably full of fluid. The doctor is taken aback, confused about what to do with us. We ask him to please, just repeat himself. Gabe understands dialect and native speech patterns, he just needs this doctor to speak up.

Instead, the doctor silently put an electronic band on Gabe's finger to test for... I don't know, actually, because a nurse runs in shouting, and the doctor grabs a red backpack, and our paperwork, and is gone. The band still strapped irrelevantly to Gabe's finger. A nurse walks in, speaking so quickly as to make her incomprehensible. She gives Gabe medicine. What is it? I ask. She replies that it's fever reducer. But no one has taken Gabe's temperature. She leaves. We're alone again, in a room filled with the sound of the finger machine unceasingly beeping.

"What's happening, Mamma?"

"I have no idea, baby."

We wait. And then Angelo calls to see how he can help. We ask if we can see his doctor, as it is now 11:00 and our children will be out of school at 1:00, and we have gotten nowhere. Angelo orders us to meet him in Spello in 30 minutes, and he'll walk us to his doctor's office. We decide to alert the staff that we're going. In doing so, a nurse apologizes for the wait, and promises to get us a doctor right away. Five minutes, maximum.

We sigh and call Angelo to cancel our plan. Another nurse arrives to finish the exam. She puts a thermometer under Gabe's arm and sits down behind the desk to flip through papers. The thermometer beeps, and she doesn't react. I ask if she wants it, and she looks up confused, before holding out her hand. Only the reading isn't accurate, so she hands it back to me and asks me to redo it. I'm fairly certain the frazzled mother shouldn't be trusted with any medical device. She makes some notes on our paperwork that has somehow reappeared. In response to her question, I tell her that we'd given Tylenol to Gabe during the night. She looks horrified, and berates me for doing something so dangerous. She leaves.

"What's happening, Mamma?"

"I have no idea, baby."

Ten minutes later, a new doctor arrives. She speaks clearly, and not so slowly as to imply we are idiots. She looks into Gabe's ear and groans, *"Mamma mia."*

She notes his lymph nodes are swollen, and has me palpate them so I can feel it, too. The doctor asks if we'll accept an antibiotic, and we gratefully agree. She's ready to hand us the amoxicillin, but when she realizes we're not on the national health plan, she regretfully tells us we'll have to go to a pharmacy for the antibiotic. That's fine, just give us the script and turn us loose. She pauses, pen hovering over paper to ask what we've already given Gabe. I tense before telling her that we'd dosed him with Tylenol. While she doesn't look like she's gearing to report me for willful child endangerment, she also doesn't look pleased. Clucking a little, she suggests that we give him Tachipirina instead, as it is *"più semplice,"* simpler. It turns out, Tachipirina is acetaminophen, the same medicine as Tylenol. I suppose the nurse thought we had given Gabe aspirin, risking Reye's syndrome, and the doctor understood, but preferred the lower dosage in the packet of strawberry-flavored Tachipirina powder.

And we leave. I'm guessing we'll get a bill in the mail. But that, like everything today, is a mystery.

"What happened, Mamma?"

"I have no idea, baby."

4 May

"What's *that?*" is a continual question in our house. Gabe will ask, "What's a Nazi? What's a Fascist? What's helium?" Then again, he's six, asking questions is part of his circuitry. Siena will ask, "What's a meme? What's Episcopal? What's propaganda?" At ten, she's asking more questions than ever. Then again, we all are. On a daily basis, we run up against the holes in our awareness. Not just the expected gaps in knowledge, like how to brine olives. A novel life, in a foreign country, with different people, raises questions that I'm surprised we've never asked before. Right now, in the wake of Liberation Day, much of our conversation is about World War II. Angelo has been challenging my assumptions about this epoch, making me wonder about issues I've never considered. Why did the English bomb Dresden? Why a reversal of American policy to not use the atomic bomb when the war was drawing to a close? Why did the people of Italy support Mussolini?

The weight of what I don't know makes it impossible to assume that life is a predictable constellation of factors. Instead, the very earth under my feet is in question. It's not dirt after all—but the dust of decomposing civilizations. Part of this comes from understanding the world stage in a way that I couldn't while hoodwinked by American isolationism. Isolationism that prevents my nation from stopping genocides in countries that most Americans can't find on a map. Isolationism that makes natural disasters on foreign soil worthy of no more than passing interest, while natural disasters on our own soil are deemed tragedies. Isolationism that prompts contributors on TripAdvisor to respond with derision when I post a question about non-D-Day centered places to stay in Normandy. Is it so unusual to want to travel for purposes other than exploring how other nations' histories are joined with my own? I think for many Americans, it is.

But it's not just breaking out of American isolationism that is forcing me to reckon the mass of the unknown. There is also a frame shift that comes from switching sides of the earth. Angelo tries to explain a concept by sketching a map of Charlottesville. On it, he draws several *piazze* and at least one *palazzo*. Charlottesville has neither, but it doesn't occur to him that a town could lack these Italian mainstays. We grow accustomed to what we see—when what we see is different, it makes us question our filter.

Just daily living here forces my scope to pry open. Angelo takes us on a tour of two small towns that, like Spello, are built on Mount Subasio. Our first stop is San Giovanni, a town abandoned after an earthquake; most of the damaged houses have been sold to Romans looking for a second home. In the not too distant future, the buildings will be rehabilitated, and the town will be inhabited again, but never as it once was—with life rooted into the seasons, and townspeople cooking in ovens situated in the wall beside the front door. I imagine dusk filling San Giovanni with the smell of dinner, and townspeople chatting as they push the bread or roasting chicken closer to the coals. The town is empty, but the ghosts of what it once was stirs not only my imagination but also my understanding about what a community can be.

Our next stop is Armenzano. According to Simona—the woman we meet on the street who invites us back to her house where she and her husband have created a museum of farming implements found in the fields—Armenzano is home to more cats than people. I'm surprised it's not populated—with the abandoned and unlocked castle in the center of the streets laid out in concentric circles, the town is charming. At the base of the town, with an unceasing view across the valley, we find the old laundry area. Two large stone basins, connected by a channel, fed by the aqueduct. Women as recently as World War II would congregate here to tell stories, sing, and wash their laundry—dirty clothes in the basin furthest from the incoming water.

While our children play in the little park on the edge of town, we talk to Simona. It's easy to meet strangers with Angelo, because in Angelo's world, there are only two types of people. Friends, and friends he hasn't made yet. Simona asks about Siena's name, and tells me that Italians of Jewish heritage often have surnames that are the names of the cities they came from. Her last name is in fact, Siena, because her ancestors fled Siena during the plague. A crevice in my brain creaks open to allow this new image.

As we drive home around Subasio, I realize that I have never thought to wonder what lay across this mountain. How life was lived there 2,000 years ago, 50 years ago, and now. All around, here and at home, there are areas of unknown. I just found out that our little *forno* sells pizza dough, and that if you bring them an uncooked meal in the morning, they'll bake it for you by noon. I knew that this was common long ago, when people didn't have ovens. I had no idea this happens today, around the corner from my house.

A shadowy thought is gaining clarity—Alexander the Great was dead wrong. There are plenty of new worlds left to conquer. You just have to step back and realize the mysteries that are everywhere. Wonder, drive around the mountain, ask questions, turn your map upside down, or better yet, get a new map. The world is a wide place.

5 May

Celebrating Cinco de Mayo is about honoring the power of conviction over might. I love the story of how a ragtag group of shoeless Mexicans defeated a well-equipped and substantially larger French army. Oh, Napoleon, always trying to get his oar in somewhere. Nobody expected Mexico to win—and they did lose the war—but that surprise upset, a sort of David-resists-Goliath, gave the hope of the possible to Mexicans everywhere. It's a story worth celebrating. Preferably with a margarita.

Since both Angelo and Mario have professed an abiding love of Mexican food, I decide to invite them both for a Cinco de Mayo celebration. They both enthusiastically accept. The morning of the dinner, Angelo reads me a report he's prepared in English about the holiday. Later, Mario bounds up our steps. He hovers around my elbow, asking if he's allowed to know the menu, or if it's a secret. I start telling him—and Nicolas interrupts to make sure I don't spill the pinto beans about dessert. Mario then gingerly asks, "Will some of the food be spicy?" I admit that I fear that some of it may be *too* spicy, and he erupts into a dance of enthusiasm. I just want to hug this child. Mario's dance grows more zealous when I send the boys in search of avocados. My regular *fruttivendolo* didn't have any today, but one of the other markets in the *borgo* may prove more fruitful. They return with the last two avocados in Spello, and I offer to teach Mario to make guacamole. He mashes the avocados with determination, but stalls when I ask him to taste for seasoning. Shamefaced, he admits that he's never had guacamole, so doesn't know what he'd be looking for. On closer questioning, I discover that he's never had any Mexican food. His enthusiasm for the cuisine is purely based on his understanding that it can be spicy.

Angelo arrives with candy for the children and a bag heaving with fava beans from a friend's garden for me. We begin our meal with chips with salsa and guacamole, and Mario puffs with pride when I tell Angelo who made it. Mario, seated beside me, whispers to ask if I might write down the recipe for him, as he's afraid he'll forget how to make guacamole. We then move to *sopa de queso*—Angelo delightedly adding cheese, cilantro, and spices to his bowl. Then chicken-chipotle tacos with refried beans that aren't really pinto, but no one is the wiser. The teenagers begin a hot sauce party, burning their mouths until they gasp and need honey, and then reload with *piccante*.

Over warm apple empanadas with cinnamon gelato, Angelo tells us a story. He teaches Italian to the Moroccan immigrants in Spello, and once they complained to him that they were suffering from sore throats. He recommended *miele*, honey, but the Moroccan-language trained ear has a hard time catching the faint "i" sound. So they thought he was telling them to lick *mele*, apples. They next time he saw them, he asked how they were feeling, and they said they were still feeling quite badly, and he asked if they'd been licking *miele*; they responded that they had licked all they had in the house, to no avail. Angelo, with dawning comprehension, asked where they purchased their *miele*, and was told the *fruttivendolo*, of course.

We tell our guests about our trip to the Foligno hospital. When we describe our inability to understand the nurses and doctors, who sounded like they were all chewing marbles, Angelo and Mario look at each other before whooping with laughter. Angelo explains that our language impasse was due to dialectical differences between Foligno and Spello, towns that are separated by five kilometers of fields.

"Okay, Mario, *prima,* finely chop a few slices of red onion and sprinkle them with salt. Then, *poi,* squish? Press? Do you understand press, like push, like this? Good. Press the onion with the back of your fork. So it makes a *spremuta* of onion juice. *Allora,* take an avocado, roughly cut. Sprinkle the *pezzi* with olive oil and the juice of half a lemon. Mash, or mix, it together. *Basta!* Not too much. *Lo hai fatto!* You did it! It's Mario's first guacamole!"

9 May

Keith and I are in indifferent health at the moment. I like to think it's my elevated body temperature that causes me to tell Graziano that I'm *fibroso,* fibrous, when I mean fevered. He is too polite to laugh, but he does look at my quizzically. Luckily, we are well enough to herd our gaggle of children into the car this morning to Città di Castello, home of the fifteenth Annual *Concorso Nazionale "Enrico Zangarelli,"* the national music competition. The *concorso* lasts three days, with competitions for soloists to orchestras, across instruments. Nicolas and Franco are playing four hands piano. Their teacher believes it forces students to work on maintaining tempo, as speeding up or slowing down will throw off the partner. Nicolas has been playing piano long enough that he's sanguine about the process of playing for an audience. This time, however, he's really worried about letting Franco down, and he practiced harder than he ever has.

When we pull up, we see Franco and his mom waiting. The mom observes, "*I ragazzi sembrano tranquilli.*" I agree that the boys do look calm, "*Ma sempre sembrano tranquilli.*" We laugh together—these boys do always wear the same placid expression. She adds, "*La maestra, tuttavia, è molto agitata.*" This surprises me, Nicolas' piano teacher is so unflappable, I have a hard time picturing her stressed. We agree to find the teacher together. Walking into the building, I tell her that Nicolas said that the teacher was quite *calma* at the rehearsal yesterday, and she says, "*Certo, ma era prima del concorso.*" Sure, but that was before the competition. I'm glad my sluggish brain is able to handle the conversation. It's the kind of easy interaction I might have with a fellow parent before an event in the States.

We locate the teacher, and she directs the boys to the competition room. They hesitatingly enter, then sit side by side on the piano bench. They briefly warm up and then begin. For the most part, it goes quite well. The pieces are extremely complicated, and their hands fairly fly over the keys, all the while keeping pace with each other and putting emotion and dynamics into the music. The last song is actually perfect until Nicolas hits the final note—wrong. Particularly egregious since that last note is played *forte*. And if the judges for some reason didn't notice, Nicolas' immediate look of shame, his eyes darting to his piano teacher who's shaking her head, I'm sure alerts them to the mistake. She shrugs when the boys finish and pronounces their performance a good learning experience. No remonstrance. Or warm fuzzies. She's exacting, but she's not doing it for the win. She's doing it for them. And Nicolas loves her for it.

Though he is still ruminating on that last note. He confesses that he was too self-confident as the piece was going so well and they were almost finished, so he was not reading the music and misremembered one of the three notes of the last chord. He blamed the button down shirt that Keith made him wear. Hopefully time will ease his fixation, and help him remember the overall success.

The winners should be announced this evening, but as they post the results on-line, we are free to go. A windfall since we still have to pack for our trip to Sicily tomorrow. We elect to eat lunch in Città di Castello, and then head home to pack. Wandering the decadent streets of the city, I admire the buildings in shades of saffron and coral, with ornate flourishes. The center *piazza* is full of vendors, and we purchase fried seafood in paper cones for our lunch. From a delightful woman in a fish van, who seems to enjoy our coming back for seconds, because when I asked for three *etti* of fried shrimp, she weighs it, and then throws in another few *etti* of the fried calamari we enjoyed so much the first time around.

Our energy flags quickly, so we return home. Mario knocks soon after we arrive, with a bag of candy to tide Nicolas over on the flight to Sicily, and a hug goodbye. I smile watching them embrace, promising emphatically to see each other as soon as we're back. As I put together a simple dinner, I pause to step out to the *terrazza*. I'm grateful that our health has held out, so that we could enjoy the excitement of the *concorso*, and the unexpected loveliness of Città di Castello. And though I have few expectations for the competition, for Nicolas' sake, I can't help but wonder how much that last note will cost.

13 May

Sicily is scented with climbing jasmine and wild herbs—fennel and oregano and something sweet and toasty like fenugreek. This mix of cultivated and untamed is everywhere. Trim lines of grapevines lead to dramatic, craggy mountains. Neat rows of olive trees divided by a riot of shimmering undergrowth. Stately Greek ruins rise from a tumult of colorful, delicate wildflowers. That's just Sicily, or at least the tiny corner of Sicily we are able to explore. Our short stay prohibits our venturing beyond the Trapani peninsula, and our poor health restricts us further. Luckily, we've grown used to ignoring other people's conceptions of what we must see. All those "must sees" do is make me anxious about what we're missing. Raised on a diet of "anything is possible," I think I had developed a belief in "the best, or bust." Now, I've decided to instead enjoy where I am and what I am doing, rather than comparing it to someone else's "best." So the narrowness of our possibilities makes for zeal in moments of grace. The timely bench for repose, the feel of the warm air on weakened skin, the smell of herbs rising from my footsteps. I revel in the grand elegance of Trapani, perched out into the waters stretching out to Africa. I marvel at the dramatic mountains, unexpected greenery, impossibly blue waters, bulbous African trees, and the island glow surrounding our days. With no expectations, I thrill to the incidental adventures alive around every corner in Sicily.

I feel this profoundly on the butterfly-shaped island of Favignana. Once docked, Keith rents a jeep, and the children leap into the back with a bag full of cherries. The day is spent roaming from beach to beach, exploring rocky outcroppings with tide pools the size of swimming pools. We recline with *granita* on the soft sand as the children romp in waters of staggering clarity and wander through towering ruins ornamented with Phoenician writing as the crashing waves sing a soundtrack of timelessness. And, of course, the meals—ubiquitous curled *busiate* noodles, fresh tuna, the wild herbaciousness in every dish, vibrant tomatoes, vividly fruity *granita*, sweet eggplant, African influences of couscous and cinnamon and nuts, *arancini* at every bar, floral and still dry white wine. Plus there is that moment when Keith's phone *bings* and we gather around to read the text from Nicolas' piano teacher. They won first place. Yes, even with that misplaced note. The beach fills with cheering and dancing while Nicolas mostly stands mute with wonder.

As we travel about, sometimes it niggles my brain that perhaps we aren't doing it "right." Maybe we'll find out later that we missed something wonderful. But then the wind lifts my hair, and my children yelp in delight at a patch of brilliant turquoise water, and Keith smiles as he reaches across the white sands of San Vito lo Capo to clasp my hand (the one that's not holding a succulent peach) as we recoup on rented chairs under a shady umbrella—and my spirits soar. Really, what could be more? Getting caught off guard is delicious.

After an impromptu lunch of heavenly *arancini* at a bar overlooking a beach in Favignana, Gabe finds a dandelion as big as his head and holds it out to Siena, prompting her to make a wish. Without skipping a beat she answers, "What is there left to wish for?"

16 May

We're home and our health is flagging. I don't know what we have, but it's a doozy. Some sort of upper-respiratory bug that appears to have morphed into an infection. Keith and I struggle with a periodic fever, plus wheezing that is worse for Keith, and coughing that is worse for me. And pervasive tiredness.

Keith thought he'd shaken it yesterday, but wakes up this morning with a fever and difficulty breathing. So at 7:30 this morning he trudges down to the *guardia medica*. And comes back 15 minutes later with a diagnosis of a mild infection, a prescription for antibiotics, and a strongly worded suggestion that I get myself down there before the doctor leaves at 8:00. I don't want to go, but our friends are coming from Brussels the day after tomorrow, and I need to give myself every opportunity to be on the upswing by their arrival. Plus, my coughing has been so bad that I have to lie down on the ground in child's pose to relieve my rib-cage. I make it to the *guardia medica*, with a brief stop in the street to say hello to Anna Maria, who tells me if I need translation help, I should let her know. I opt to go it alone, but just knowing she is close settles my apprehension about trying to navigate medical matters in a language not my own. Which allows me to communicate more easily than I otherwise would have.

I leave with my very own antibiotics prescription. And the same warning from the doctor—if I don't feel better in 3 days, I need to go to the hospital for a chest x-ray. The very idea of returning to the hospital sends chills down my spine, so I am fervently hoping that the illness gracefully bows out in the presence our matching his-and-hers antibiotics. I don't know what we'll do if we don't both improve, and soon.

17 May

The last navetta ride...

Today we learn that Luciano—our Bar Bonci and *navetta* friend—passed away. Just a few weeks ago we rode the *navetta* together and laughed about the tastiness of the *macelleria's* smoked herring. The next day when I ran into him at Bar Bonci, he talked insistently about kids today. He secretly paid for our coffee and smiled, and waved, before stepping into the morning sunshine. Last week Letizia told us that he was hospitalized after a scooter accident. And now on the obituary boards—omnipresent in Italian towns as a place to hang death notices—I find posters of a younger Luciano effortlessly smiling. Part of me feels like perhaps it's a belated April first joke. After all, it was Luciano who told us about the prank of printing obit posters for people still living. I stand in front of Luciano's poster, the photo of him young and full of hopes and dreams for his future. And I remember his earnest Italian gestures, his smile that brightened the bar when he saw me.

Rest in Peace, Luciano.

20 May

Keith is in the hospital. The antibiotics quickly beat my infection, but Keith was still not better this morning, so he went to the ER. He just called to tell me that he has pneumonia in his upper-right lobe, and the doctor has gravely insisted that he stay in the hospital until Wednesday, for fear it will suddenly worsen. Keith tells me, anxiety lacing his words, that the doctor expressed concern about an attack. I clutch the phone to my ear and whisper scream so the children don't hear, "*What kind of attack?*" He admits he doesn't know. My mind reels while I endeavor to hold it together.

I don't know what these next few days will bring. Much begging of friends to drive us to the hospital (Angelo is on tap first—he's taking us at 4:30), I imagine. We don't know how hospitals work here. Balancing that with keeping the kids humming along without undue anxiety—well, it's a cocktail that I wish I could refuse.

I'm trying to process. And not doing a good job. This fog of confusion is nauseating.

20 May (later)

Our neighbor, Anna, calls to Gabe to come play in her garden when she spots him on our *terrazza*. He dashes out, and a few moments later she's knocking on the door. Gabe has told her his father is in the hospital, and she asks, "*Di che cosa avete bisogno?*" What do you need? I tell her there is nothing, "*Angelo ci porta in ospedale fra un' ora.*" Angelo is taking us to the hospital in an hour. She nods and takes Gabe out for gelato. I watch them walk away with my heart full of gratitude. They return, hand in hand, just as Angelo arrives. Gabe is holding a little bundle of flowers and Anna plucks a few more blossoms from her pot to augment Gabe's bouquet. As Angelo puts Gabe in the car, Anna whispers to me that he's *molto preoccupato*, very worried. I nod and blink back tears. We're all worried. I'm glad at least Gabe has someone extra to tend to his frazzled emotions.

Angelo tries telling silly stories on the drive, but his words, for perhaps the first time, fail to warm me. I'm desperate to see my husband. Without a reality check, it's too easy for my mind to dip into a scary visual place. Our walk to the pulmonary wing is blessedly smoother than my previous trip to the pediatric unit—we have only to follow Angelo, who is parting the sea of humanity before us. At the unit, we are faced with a locked door. Angelo locates a buzzer, and we huddle against the door, willing it to open. Nothing happens. We ring the bell again. *Niente.* After our third push of the buzzer a nurse pops her head out, gives us a once over, and dismisses us. Angelo stops her as she's closing the door by telling her I am the wife of a patient. She pauses, and barks that no children are allowed in the pulmonary wing. Gabe and Siena begin to wail, and Nicolas wraps his arms around them, guiding them to seats in the hallway. I beg them to be patient, we'll try to find a way for them to see their father. They tearfully nod that they'll wait quietly.

Angelo and I follow the nurse down the long hall, and find Keith in the last room on the right. My mind had become blurred with images of Keith with a gray pallor and rattling breath, so my exhale is audible when I see him looking like himself. Angelo goes in search of the doctor, while Keith sneaks out of the hospital wing to hug his children. They cleave to him, curling into his neck and patting his arms. Gabe gazes searchingly into Keith's merry eyes, and my baby's brows slowly begin to unbind. He hands Keith the bouquet of little flowers and Keith clasps it to his chest.

Having Angelo translate from Italian to slower Italian is a blessing. We learn that specialists don't consult on weekends, and the general doctors wanted to wait to talk to the specialists before deciding a course of action. Also, a parade of blood tests is required to determine if the pneumonia is viral or bacterial, and then to tailor the medicine to the strain. Right now they are giving him an IV with a broad spectrum medicine. Angelo also says that the doctors worry that because we are *stranieri*, foreigners, we might not seek treatment if Keith's symptoms worsen, because we wouldn't know where to go. This rings uncomfortably close to home.

Understanding a bit more about why the doctor has recommended hospitalization makes me feel less panicked about his condition. But I still feel helpless. Keith is the one with the driver's license; how can I stay with him, particularly since the children aren't allowed in the unit? How can I offer support? Everyone at the hospital seems to be surrounded by family members. And Keith has nobody. When I give him the bottle of water I'd brought for him, he sighs with relief. He's been thirsty, and when he'd asked for water, the nurse had rustled up a small plastic cup to fill in the bathroom. What if he needs other basic necessities, and there's no one to help? This sense of powerlessness increases when I talk to Keith by phone in the evening. He says that dinner was better than expected, but the hospital doesn't provide silverware. A nurse had located a set for him to borrow. I pack him silverware, along with a glass and a towel.

I'll deliver these to my hospitalized husband after I drop the children off at school, as Alison and Andrew are shuttling me on their way to Norcia. When my introduction to Alison via our expat blogs spurred a friendship that compelled us to plan this visit, my biggest concern was not making good on my promise of warmth to my sun-deprived Belgian friends. Now there's this. In response to my repeated apologies, Alison and Andrew scoff and pour me another glass of wine. Thank goodness they brought chocolates. I need all the stress reduction I can get.

21 May

Along with cutlery, my bag for Keith today is filled with a card Siena painted, a bag Gabe filled with herbs "so he can smell it and remember me," and Nicolas' phone so Keith has something to do. After Alison and Andrew drop me off, I stop in the hospital lobby to pick up a vending machine *espresso*, per Keith's urgent request. Breakfast arrived sans coffee, and Keith is feeling the lack of caffeine. Paper cup of *espresso* in hand, I stand outside the locked door of the unit and call him on my cell phone to let him know I'm here. He opens the door, to cheering from the family members outside the door who have been repeatedly, and uselessly, depressing the buzzer.

Keith looks great. Well, great given the fact that he's sleeping on a diminutive bed in a room with flickering lights and a 5:00 AM blood draw. But his low-grade fever broke in the night. And his breathing is considerably less noisy. He is coughing more, but it feels like a change in the right direction.

As I'm talking with Keith, Fabrizio strides into the room, trailing an aura of Spello. He pulls up a chair and explains that Marcello had alerted him to the hospitalization and my concern that Keith would need something and have no one to help. Hitching one ankle onto his knee, Fabrizio pushes his heavy framed glasses onto his aquiline nose and brushes the silver hair off his forehead while he chats easily about the hospital. Before he leaves, he jots down his phone number and orders Keith to call *"se hai bisogno di qualcosa."* If you need anything. Seeing a familiar smile when I'm feeling disoriented in a place that is foreign from its waiting room procedures to its BYO cutlery makes me feel like I'm in the presence of something akin to divinity—a brush with universal good.

When I check in with Keith later in the day, he's cross. He hasn't been able to get answers to what medicine he's taking, or why he needs to remain in the hospital when he's improving. The barrier isn't language, the doctors just don't seem disposed to give information to anyone. Even Keith's roommate, who ostensibly got pneumonia in Sicily because he went swimming, is left with nothing more than a pat on the shoulder. It's frustrating having him gone when I can't help wondering if he could be home.

22 May

Brenda accompanies me to the hospital and brings Keith a book, an English language newspaper, roses in a wine bottle, and water. She knows from experience what we are just figuring out—water is not part of the protocol here. You can get a cup of water from the tap, just as you can take your temperature if you're interested, but neither are part of the hospital routine. I would have thought they'd be pumping patients with water, but I suppose that's my American love of hydration talking. I also bring Keith water and a bagful of fruit and also toilet paper. There is toilet paper in Keith's bathroom, but I wonder if perhaps it was provided by Keith's roommate's family. No one likes *uno scroccone*, a freeloader.

I stop to get Keith an *espresso*, which he desperately needs, as it was another night of poor sleep. His early morning blood draw schedule combined with his roommate's late night blood draw schedule is wearying. Keith keeps asking why they continue to draw his blood, but he's not getting an answer. Worse, his fever has started creeping back up, and his head has been hurting. He asked for Tylenol, and "the nurse looked at me like I was asking for crack." Finally, she handed over the goods. Which helped.

Midway through my visit, a nurse comes to clean the room, so I leave to fetch Keith another *espresso* and pick up more Pope Francis trading cards from the gift shop. While I'm gone, the nurse yells at Keith for having personal items on the floor. This is decidedly *not okay*. So we stash his suitcase in his locker, and organize his food into his side table. Not *on* his side table, as he was yelled at yesterday for having items *on* the side table. Storing belongings *on* the side table is most decidedly *not okay*. Really, I think the Italian hospital system is useful for surgically removing the American hand-wringing and replacing it with an Italian shoulder shrug, *"eh EH!"* A dismissive gesture that seems to indicate a combination of "whatever" and "what are you gonna do?"

Alison and Andrew bring me back to the hospital in the evening, carting a box of their new favorite Umbrian wines for Keith. When we walk in, Keith is chatting with Graziano, and it all of a sudden seems a little like a party, especially when Doreen calls from California. We all pull chairs around Keith's bed, and talk about how the wine would mix with Keith's IV antibiotics. Begrudgingly, Keith agrees that it would probably be better to keep the wine at the house. He'll stick with the water we all keep bringing him. Keith entertains us with stories of his newfound hobby of doctor-stalking, which has finally yielded some answers. Apparently, Keith's x-ray indicated a pneumonia that looked unusual enough that they wanted to follow it up with a CT scan (called a TAC in Italian, hence our confusion about an "attack"). In the meantime, they have been drawing his blood several times a day to determine what strain of pneumonia he has. They haven't isolated it, which is why they are still taking blood, but since Keith is responding to the antibiotics, the doctor agrees that it's probably bacterial. In addition, some of those blood tests are to assess the functioning of his vital organs, to be sure that he's having no systemic dysfunction.

I assumed that national health care would lead to a perfunctory "get 'em in, get 'em out" approach, so I'm surprised by the doctors' tenacity in tailoring a treatment to a specific cause of the pneumonia and their determination to stay abreast of possible systemic consequences. And if we had the national health insurance this would all come for the price of...zero euros and zero cents. Yes, the taxes are high, but really. I'm willing to bring my own toilet paper if it means thorough care.

Keith says goodbye to Alison and Andrew, and laughs as he vows that our next visit together will be hospital-free. I wish he was joining us for dinner at La Cantina tonight, but the larger feeling is one of gratitude that he'll be home tomorrow.

He looks so well, I feel positive that he'll be released. I superstitiously cross my fingers as we enter the elevator—that 10:00 AM CT scan must come back clear.

23 May

During my morning visit, the doctor comes in to remind Keith about the 10:00 scan. Oh, no worries. He is more than *pronto*. He has taken to standing by the windows at the end of the hall, looking across the fields toward Spello, luminous on the hill. Anna Maria picks me up from the hospital (I ran into Stefano yesterday and he whipped out his cell phone to alert her to the pneumonia), and I leave hopeful that it will just be a few hours until Keith is home again.

But 10:00 comes and goes, and no one comes to fetch him. He walks out to the front desk and gets read the riot act because he's in his socks. Being in your socks is most definitely *not okay*. Then the nurse expresses confusion about the TAC. You are getting a TAC? Did you eat anything today? Why yes, after all, they brought him breakfast. *Oh.* Huh.

Three more nurses ask if Keith has eaten anything. He grows worried that perhaps his inadvertently eating breakfast will result in canceling the scan. He asks, and a nurse says that because he ate he'll likely throw up during the scan. Keith doesn't bother asking why they brought him breakfast if he wasn't supposed to eat it. His sights are set on Spello, rising out of the fog. He hounds the nurses, what about that scan? Finally, one types into a computer and tells Keith that there isn't space in the schedule for his scan. He can have it tomorrow. *Tomorrow?* No.

Keith puts his be-socked foot down. And reminds the staff that this appointment was made Sunday, he needs to have this scan *questa mattina*. A huff, and essentially a "we'll see." At which point Keith has visions of ripping out his IV port and bolting through the emergency doors and striding through the fields, all the way home. Belatedly, he remembers that the car is parked at the hospital. Driving is less dramatic, but probably more sensible. Pneumonia and all. Keith opts against the soundtracked, slow-mo escape, and instead settles for the steady glare of the annoyed American. Arms akimbo. Nurses keep passing. One informs him, "*Tu stai qui spesso.*" You stand here a lot. Yes, indeed.

Finally, they call him for the scan. Where he does not throw up. It's no worse "than being a human copy machine." He's dismissed, and told they will have the results tomorrow. *Tomorrow*? No.

The doctor had told him the results would be available immediately. Aggrieved sigh from technician. Okay, perhaps this afternoon. Keith is escorted back to his unit, where he catches sight of his doctor, and starts following him around. It's a busy day for the lung-compromised, so the doctor keeps gesturing, "Just one minute" while he is pulled by other doctors and nurses, engages in a shouting match for an hour with a family. Finally, Keith sees his other doctor and decides to harangue her instead. He is an equal opportunity haranguer.

The second doctor calls for the results of the scan and finds that it is inconclusive. But since he is clinically better, he can go home. As long as he adheres to the antibiotic protocol, gets serious rest, and comes back in ten days for a follow-up appointment. Which should be wonderful, but is actually vaguely unsatisfying. All this time, our sights have been set on the scan. *The scan*. It has taken on mythical proportions. With *the scan*, we would divine the state of the disease, the burgeoning health of Keith's lungs. It's *inconclusive*? But...he can still come home?

Maybe it's an issue of language. Or maybe the test doesn't show anything alarming, and that in concert with his clinical improvement is enough to earn him a get-out-of-hospital card. Keith does find out that all the blood tests for nasty bacteria came back negative. I suppose it's nice that something is ruled out. I just wish we knew what is ruled in. Keith asks if the blood tests suggested any problems with his other organs. The doctor says no, "*Ma, la polmonite non è sufficiente?*" But isn't pneumonia enough? Har har. The doctor also refers to the pneumonia as a "big pneumonia." Given the fact that his fever was never that high and he was fairly functional, we had assumed it was an average pneumonia. But no, it is a "big pneumonia." Now, why Keith couldn't get a run-of-the-mill pneumonia, I don't know. But he has always been a bit of an overachiever.

Despite his "big pneumonia," he's packing, getting his discharge paperwork, and will be home this afternoon. And maybe then I can write about how I had to iron Gabe's outfit this morning because his only clean clothes were damp and wrinkled beyond redemption. And then I can tell you about how I missed Siena's violin debut at Teatro Subasio today because I didn't know about it. And I can write about how grateful I've been for my children's adaptability—plans for pizza morph into plans for packaged *tortellini* when we find the *rosticceria* closed, and promises of read-aloud become read-to-yourself because it turns out reading still provokes my coughing to breathlessness. And then I can tell you about how I lost it with Siena when she refused to wake up Nicolas for school when I was making breakfast and trying to get everyone out the door so I could be ready for another day at the hospital. And then you'll understand what a mess I've been, and that I really suck at holding the edges together when the wind is blowing.

23 May (later)

Keith walks in looking shell-shocked. The persistent badgering has taken more out of him than he anticipated. He does arrive with good news, though. He met with another doctor and found out that the CT scan was, in fact, *not* inconclusive. And while it doesn't show the ponies and rainbows he'd been hoping for, it shows pneumonia. Not a "big pneumonia," nor a "strange pneumonia," nor the structural problems like clots or tumors that they feared after the initial x-ray. Just pneumonia. The follow-up imaging in ten days will give a better idea of his recovery, but his symptoms clearly indicate that he is improving. And he is home.

Periodically during the night, I find myself waking up to listen to Keith's breathing. It sounds a bit like an accordion, but for the most part it's the sleep of the highly contented. Now we can all draw a deeper breath, and exhale fully. And feel how lucky we are to be the five of us again, to have our loved one benefit from medical care, and to have been embraced by the community during our time of trial. Human kindness is overflowing.

26 May

There were times this year where I believed my daughter would surely shatter. But since *Carnevale*, I've watched as she's rebuilt herself. Her metamorphosis deserves a celebration, so when she asked me if she could have a birthday party, I agreed without hesitation. It's true that I wanted our Spello year to be without the trappings of our previous practices like birthday parties, but I am very clear that we need to honor Siena's friendship-building work. Just the arranging of the party forces her to confront the edges of her comfort zone. She calls each of the girls to get their addresses and then hand-delivers invitations she paints of local flowers.

As Siena and I walk to the *forno* to get bread for breakfast, she peers anxiously at the sky, hoping the rain holds off so she and her friends can go to the playground for her party. But it does rain. Torrents. Gushing. We meet her friends in the *piazza* and walk them up the hill to our house, the girls in fits of giggles huddled under their shared umbrellas. The party begins, as all parties should begin, with copious snacks. Puffs, chips, Haribo, popcorn, Siena's favorite sodas from Vinosofia (a gift from Brenda), and—the *pièce de résistance*—Oreos, a spectacular find. In addition to all this packaged goodness, I've made a platter of fried zucchini flowers. There seems to me something symbolic in this scene of chattering girls feasting on petals and blooms. After snacking, the girls move from one shared activity to another. Seamlessly. They do each other's hair, they paint each other's nails, they play with balloons, they draw, they ask Siena to play violin and burst into wild applause when she finishes, they are silly in a way that American tweens sometimes force themselves to grow out of too soon. I invite them to make their own pizzas, and they are drunk with their own pizza power. Throughout the afternoon, I'm struck with how sweet the girls are to each other. There is less of a "birthday girl" mentality, and more of a "shared community" mentality. Which is a gift for Siena, who hates being the center of attention.

Chiara assigns herself the role of the child Angelo. Whenever one of the girls talks to me, she stands by, to "translate" if I need it, speaking slowly and distinctly, and using more basic phraseology. She also writes birthday messages to Siena in two languages on our family white board ("Happy Birtheis"). And when it's time for cake, she secrets herself into the kitchen and asks if she can cover Siena's eyes when we bring out the cake. I thank her for this lovely idea, and she flushes with pleasure.

I bring the illuminated cake to the table, with Chiara's hands over Siena's eyes, the other girls grouped around excitedly. The girls sing in Italian, and then Chiara pulls her hands away with a flourish, and Siena's face glows with the light of eleven glorious candles. The girls then spontaneously burst into singing again, this time in English. My daughter eyes well with tears as she laughs in pleasure. This has been Siena's triumph. And she is radiant.

27 May

In Irvin Yalom's book *Love's Executioner,* he details his therapeutic process with ten different clients—exploring the dilemmas that grip his patients, touching on the truths underlying humanity. One chapter describes a young man who struggled with anxiety and self-worth. His transformative moment occurs during a seminar, when he realizes that everyone in the room is wearing polished shoes, while his are cheap, and battered besides. As his mind begins twisting around this uncomfortable fact, he has a revelation—"I am not my shoes." Yes. *I am not my shoes.* We so easily confuse what is core and what is extraneous. We respond to suspected criticism as if a lion is dragging off one of our young. When in actuality, there are very few things that demand that kind of defensiveness. I'm using the word "we" here tentatively. Because I'm really hoping it's not just me.

Decreasing my own defensiveness will probably be my life's work. It takes daily practice to accept opinions about me as just that—opinions. Not attacks on my character. I'm perpetually inspired when other people accept feedback with consideration, rather than indignation. In Spello, I'm perpetually inspired. Everyone is comfortable being advised, chided, wrong. Imperfect. When we went to lunch with Marcello in Collepino, I wanted to focus on the positives of the lunch, since it was Marcello's treat. But the men denigrated that lamb, because it doesn't occur to anyone that Marcello would feel ashamed that he'd provided a less than perfect meal. Marcello nodded easily along. Yes, unfortunate, old lamb. Smiles again. That lamb lunch? It's not him. Just his shoes.

And I've witnessed Paola and Doreen in conversation about Paola's ideas for her shop. Once Doreen told Paola directly when she thought an idea of Paola's wouldn't work. And Paola nodded thoughtfully. And when Doreen apologized for being blunt, Paola looked confused before telling her not to be sorry. She wants Doreen's input. It's not an attack. It's just her shoes.

And there is a *quinta* girl who is very, very tall. Taller than Keith. So tall that it took me awhile to stop remarking on it as an aside to Keith whenever I saw her. And even longer to stop remarking on it in my head. But she doesn't slouch or try to hide her height. She holds hands with the other girls as they walk to the bus after school, she carries her height like it's nothing startling or shaming. In fact, for *Carnevale*, she dressed as a genie—with a tall hat. She treats her height like someone might treat being left-handed in a class of north paws. She is not her shoes, or her shoe size.

Because this is not a culture of protecting everyone's fragile belief in their own perfection, we are getting lots of practice in separating our souls from our shoes. We get read the riot act by Patrizia for not calling her when we had to take Gabe to the hospital (we haven't told her yet about Keith's hospitalization, I'm a little scared). And every day I come home and tell Keith some piece of advice that someone has given me in regards to his health. Wear more clothes, don't go outside in this weather that is warm one minute and cool the next, eat turkey, don't eat pork. They don't couch it as, "you might want to consider...." They state it as, "you are doing it wrong."

Marcello stops by to talk to Keith. In his hand is the name and phone number of Keith's doctor in case we need to reach him. Marcello has made phone calls and compiled this information. 1) There are no complications from the pneumonia: *"Problemi no,"* 2) Keith must take his prescribed ten days of antibiotics, 3) The doctor is in the hospital on Tuesday, if Keith has questions or concerns. Then Marcello puts down the paper and speaks seriously. Keith really must dress more warmly. Everyone has agreed. It's dressing lightly that has led to the pneumonia. Keith tries to explain that he dresses the warmest of all of us. It is Siena who is continuously shocking the alley ladies with short sleeves in 70-degree weather. And it's Siena, not Keith, who *swam in Sicily*. Marcello just shakes his head and earnestly repeats, slowly, that Keith. Must. Bundle.

Being surrounded by this cavalier attitude toward being wrong or imperfect is loosening the shackles of my own restrictions. Lately I've been on a "we're leaving Umbria soon, I need to experiment with cooking all the foods I have a hard time finding in the States" kick. So at the *macelleria* I request a capon, and the butcher asks me if it's for broth, and I say no, it's to roast. And he and the customer behind me bellow with laughter. No, no, no, you silly American lady. Capons are only for broth. Okay, I then ask for a pheasant. More laughter. These only come frozen. The butcher says he can order me one, but he looks a little dubious about what I'd be doing with this specially ordered bird. I then point to an odd piece of meat and ask what it is. Chicken. Which I should probably know, even though it was the bottom half of the chicken, butterflied and prepared *"diavolo"* for the barbecue. The customer behind me instructs me to buy the *spiedini di agnello*, assuring me that they are delicious. I buy the skewers of lamb with thanks.

You see, I am not my bird, and I am not my shoes. But I am a woman making lamb *spiedini* and *agretti*—a green I had to ask the name of several times at the *fruttivendolo*, along with instructions for preparation—for dinner. And, right now, in this place that doesn't confound me with the mistakes I make, that is enough for me.

27 May

The adventurousness of my cooking has changed in the last ten months. Not just because I'm using pig skin as an ingredient and gutting calamari, but also in this way—I used to be recipe bound. A chronic list maker, ingredient checker, teaspoon level-er. Now, I've abandoned my assumption that I must have all information. I'll buy lamb skewers and *agretti* and tiny *carciofi* without clear ideas of how I'm going to prepare them. I've also learned to wing it when it comes to baking. For some time, I was stymied by Italian leaveners, but then I realized that what has butter and sugar can't be bad. So I gave up my requirements for clear directions and tossed myself into the floury fray. There is a distinct power in going off script. I whisk some eggs with sugar, add a mixture of flour and a package of leavener and a smidge of salt until the mixture is thick, then add in milk and maybe a little melted butter until the batter seems like cake batter. Sometimes I'll throw in some sliced apples. Sometimes I'll spice it up with orange zest. Sometimes I throw in a carton of yogurt. The cake is different, and devoured, every time.

Same with pizza. I'd hesitated to make pizza for so long, afraid of failing in the land of pizza perfection. Finally, I just decided to do it. No, my oven doesn't get hot enough. No, I don't have a pizza stone. No, I don't understand if *lievito di birra* is exactly like my yeast. But I just made it anyway. It wasn't fabulous, but it was pretty good. Maybe my food would be better if I knew exactly what to do. But in not knowing, I'm figuring it out.

Recipes engender unrealistic expectations. It's like a promise—follow the recipe exactly for a meal that resembles a glossy photograph. But it never does. So I'm chronically disappointed in my cooking. Whereas when I just dive in and try, there are no expectations. Good enough becomes wondrous, and the process is exhilarating. Having fun means I'm more likely to try again, and keep learning. Suddenly, hands and soul know what to do. It becomes instinctive. Easier. Forty minutes becomes plenty to whip up an apple cake, and Tuesdays become enough of an occasion for cake baking.

When I get scared of cooking without Mario Batali looking over my shoulder clucking at my lack of a ricer, I remember that women in Umbria have been making these foods forever, without gadgets or scales or measuring tools or written instructions. Sometimes the cooking is a flop. But even that makes success ultimately more possible, because it assists in learning to cook by feel. So I more instinctively adjust for variations in egg size and ambient humidity.

It's funny that not using a recipe is what's teaching me how to cook.

Festive Zucchini Flowers

zucchini flowers

1 cup flour

1 cup frizzante (sparkling) water

1 teaspoon salt

ricotta
(about 100 grams for 8 flowers)

lemon zest

mint leaves

frying oil

---

1. Combine flour, frizzante water, and salt.

2. Combine ricotta with a touch of salt, a bit of lemon zest and slivered mint leaves. Taste for seasonings.

3. Using a small spoon, fill the zucchini flowers with the ricotta mixture, then wrap petals up and around, twisting them at the top to close. Dip the flowers in the batter and let excess drip off before placing each flower in a pan of hot oil filled half-way. Turn occasionally. Remove to a paper-towel lined platter.

4. Alternatively, you can fill the flower with pieces of fresh mozzarella and tiny bit of anchovy.

JUNE

TANTI FIORI

1 June

The weather is the main topic of conversation in Spellani bars. Is it raining, will it rain, how hot will it get, where is the weather nice, who knows a catchy proverb that fits with our meteorological events? It's a particularly hot topic now, as the town gears up for the *Infiorata*. The festival is Spello's most beloved tradition, and her residents hold their collective breaths in hopes that nothing will go wrong. Everywhere, people are compulsively stepping outside to glare at the sky. There is a constant bemoaning of the diminished flower growth this year, the result of perpetual drizzle which has shackled sunlight. Any respite from the rain results in a flurry of neighbors potting, trimming, and cleaning. Along with the *Infiorata*, Spello participates in a national competition of balconies and patios and windows, and the judging begins right around the time of the *Infiorata*. It's flower hysteria in Spello.

2 June

Saturday morning of the *Infiorata* dawns drizzly, but it begins clearing by afternoon. Voices that were hushed and tense now take on a more characteristic lightness. Tents start popping up over the sites of the *quadrati*—the large, mural-like works, which are judged separately from the *tappeti*, the longer runs of flowers. According to the rules of the competition, the laying of flowers cannot begin until late at night. I watch teams feverishly vacuuming and drying the wet streets, creating masonry barriers to divert rain around the work, laying down the design templates or using chalk to draw a grid and transfer the image to the street square by square. Spello is burbling with conversation as adults and children sit on plastic chairs lining the streets, removing petals from flowers and placing them into shallow boxes.

As we stroll down Via Giulia, we are hailed by Riccardo. I'm surprised he remembers us from Barbara's cocktail party back in December. He pulls us into a cantina lined with boxes of petals, and then hands us a slip of paper emblazoned with Raphael's Madonna and Child. It's their *tappeto* design, he tells us with irrepressible pride. He hands each of our children a juice box and orders us to return at 9:30 PM to begin work. Keith and I consult with each other wordlessly. Yes, we will join Riccardo's *Infiorata* group. What this means we'll be doing, I don't know, but I find I'm impatient to find out. I'm willing to lay some masonry or copy chalk grids onto the street to be part of this.

The street buzz is so infectious, we have to force ourselves indoors for dinner. Over our new taste sensation—homemade pizza with dabs of ricotta and *salsa tartufata*, we process the alteration in our expectations. We had pictured observing the activity, now we'll be part of it. Another *passeggiata* takes us past Paola's shop, which is still open. Paola tells me that all the shops will be open until past midnight. The bars will be open until 2:00 AM. To accommodate the masses, there are tables and chairs set up in the area usually given over to the school. We sit and try to eat our cups of gelato, but we're too excited. Nicolas, it should be said, finds a way to finish our leftovers. He's hearty that way.

Once done, we amble to the cantina to join what I can now call *our Infiorata* group—*Pochi, ma Buoni*. The Few, but Good. We're introduced to a welcoming collection of Spellani who are energized for the night ahead. The *maestro*—the one in charge of directing the night's work—is Sauro, the baker. I wonder if this means there are baked goods in my future.

Our first step is to remove the tiny pods from the inner cores of daisies, while making conversation with other workers and fielding questions about how Gabe speaks effortless Italian. Once finished, Nicolas leaves to visit Mario, who is working on a design in the *piazza* for the middle school, while the rest of us stand in the street and watch as Sauro and Riccardo patch potholes and then slather wallpaper paste onto the asphalt to lay down the paper printed with a Rafael design. The rules stipulate that the template must not be colored, so groups indicate the colors to be laid in each section by number, color name, or flower name. With

Pochi, Ma Buoni, there are no color indications on the design, just a hand-held mock up of the image. Sauro determines which flowers to lay based on the abundance of each type of flower. The petals themselves are not allowed to be glued to the surface. They can be sprayed with water to keep them fresh, which keeps the petals safe from errant breezes, but they cannot be adhered in any way.

Some groups use store-bought flowers, evidenced by the plastic wrapped bunches of bright carnations. But *Pochi, Ma Buoni* only uses flowers gathered by group members, from gardens or in the wild. Some petals are dried to intensify their color, some are cut into pieces or ground up, others are processed at the last minute so they stay fresh and vibrant. Every group waits for the sun to set before chopping fennel. The licorice scent of the green fronds filling the streets and alleys will forever remind me of the *Infiorata*.

The group provides a design for children to work on as they please, and Gabe and Siena join the *bambini*, until work begins on the main design. Completely contrary to our low expectations of what we'd be allowed to do as novice *infioratori*, our family is given an entire segment of the design to complete together. I'm not sure we're ready for this level of responsibility. But I take comfort in Sauro's consistent supervision. He's constantly walking the length of the template, running upstairs to look down on the progress, and advising adjustments. The five of us sit down to work, laying flowers as dictated by the baker. I'm not surprised at Siena's engagement—handicrafts and flowers are her sustenance—but Gabe's focused concentration and Nicolas' investment in spending hours putting flowers between lines of a template both amaze me.

Nicolas' friends walk by at 11:30 and invite him on a *passeggiata* to see the progress of the other groups. He brushes off his knees and leaps to join them, which means he misses the dinner that is served at midnight, *penne* with wild asparagus and sausage. Luckily, he had all that gelato. As we eat, Riccardo shows me a photo of himself with a massive armload of the freshly collected asparagus. Nicolas rejoins us shortly after we return to work, and is present for our next break of hand-cut, homemade prosciutto, *salumi*, homemade wine, and pastries.

When we run out of the petals we're using to fill in a section, Siena dashes into the cantina to ask for more. Riccardo is omnipresent, taking Gabe for walks when his knees hurt from kneeling, or pressing another piece of Nutella cake into our free hands. Barbara, newly arrived from Virginia, is a flurry of motion herself—leading the children to her house for bathroom breaks, assisting in putting out the boxes of flowers. And we all talk and laugh and sip the *espresso* handed to us with a smile and a wink, as we work alongside our neighbors late into the cool night. Standing to relieve our knees, we watch the *maestri* bring the human figures in Rafael's painting to life. With their cups of seeds and pulverized petals like an artist's palette, in their meditative zone, delicately shading and layering. The figures look just like the painting, which I didn't expect to be possible with plant matter.

Petals all laid, we are handed a box of newly chopped fennel for the border. It's pliable, almost like clay and holds the flowers in place. After the large pink petals, which squirmed and shifted so much that Sauro awarded us *dieci e lode,* ten and praise, the easily matting fennel is a relief. It also pulls the whole design together. We stand back and breathe it in—the scents of fennel and jasmine-like broom mingled with aromas of *espresso,* the laughter, the flurry of activity getting more food and drinks to *infioratori,* the inky night patterned with worklights, and the art coming into fruition at our feet. I yawn, and hoist Gabe up so his nodding head can rest on my shoulder. It's 2:00, and we are released to go home. As we walk through the darkened alley, I send up a prayer that the weather holds.

3 June

Slumber doesn't come easily. Still jittery from the *espresso* thrust into my hand at 1:00 AM, my snippets of sleep are clouded with dreams of dropping flower petals. We wrestle ourselves out of bed and back onto the street. *Infioratori* are still feverishly working on the *quadrati,* desperate to finish before the judging that begins soon, and the procession that begins later in the morning. Most are nearing completion, and I'm enthralled at the intricate realism of the faces, the creativity of the designs, the boldness of the patterns, and the texture variations created by the petals and whole flowers. The *quadrato* of Noah's Ark captivates me with its swirling, elaborate design. We pass images of Saint Francis alongside the new pope, a fanciful rendering of Spello by the middle schoolers, and a modern day Madonna and Child, with long stretches of *tappeti* between them. The *borgo* boasts the largest and most complicated designs, with large petals placed as bird feathers and calla lilies used as butterfly bodies.

Once we have toured all the streets full of *quadrati* and *tappeti*, we return to Via Giulia to rejoin *Pochi, Ma Buoni*. As we approach, one of the team members stops in the street and holds our eye contact. Then he deliberately makes two gestures in succession—the slow thumb down the cheek for *bella*, beautiful, and then the moving of an okay symbol across the body as if pulling a string for *ottimo*, excellent. And it is. We can't stop looking at it. Riccardo invites us upstairs to view the complete work from above, and we are speechless. Back down the steps, I ask Riccardo when they had finished, and he replies, a half hour ago. I didn't count on how long all those fine details would take. Sauro spots us through the crowd and chuckles at our incredulous expressions. He moves toward us and tells us about the rain that had sent Barbara running home for tarps that volunteers had stretched over the workers. We'd sometimes felt light drops as we'd worked, but we'd loudly denied their existence or proclaimed that the moisture would hold down the petals. Tourists filing by had paused over our work and asked *"E, se piove?"* And, if it rains? I always answered, *"Non lo so,"* I don't know. Though Barbara told me she'd asked the same question many *Infiorati* ago, and was told, "It's okay if it washes away. God saw it."

We breakfast on baked goods the women order us to take, while we walk the perimeter of the design, pausing continually by "our section." As we wait for the procession to begin, we spy a careless tourist step into the fennel border. Nicolas flies to the *tappeto* to repair the damage, Siena running to fetch fennel from within the recesses of the cantina. Riccardo, though, is sanguine, joking with the tourist that her *multa* would be €500. His laughter adds to the carnival atmosphere, further heightened as friends pass to admire the work. Finally, we hear music floating up the hill, from the procession, which begins at Santa Maria Maggiore. Musicians and church members, some holding aloft gold flags, and then the priest, the first allowed to walk on the carpets of flowers. Goosebumps rise on my arms as I watch his feet scatter the petals our group had worked all night to place. It is no longer perfect, but in the eyes of the observant, now it is sanctified. And the thought of holiness taking the form of disruption, rather than perfection, gives me shivers.

We leave after the procession to make lunch, though we should have stayed— Barbara later tells us they brought out homemade lasagna and *porchetta*. We nap and then saunter out for popsicles at Bonci. I notice that all the vendors light up when they see us—I think with so many strangers, they thrill to a familiar face.

Keith and Siena decide to go to the flower vendors set up in the park, and I take the boys home. Some of our neighbors, including Anna, are sitting on the steps of the alley, and as Gabe overhears they are talking about cats, he calls over the ledge of the *terrazza*, *"I nostri gatti sono grassi."* Our cats are fat. Too true. The group breaks into peals of laughter, and begs him to join them. When I peek out ten minutes later to see him casually sitting with the adults, they call me down for a *un vetro*, a glass. They pour me a bubbly red wine, and though I catch very little of the conversation, and contribute even less, I'm glad to be included in this informal neighborhood assembly. Gabe leans against me and whispers, "Mamma, I love this."

4 June

Last night, I listened to the melody of hail tip-tapping on the rooftops. Drifting into an easy sleep, I imagined water and ice wending a tangled river of petals down the cobblestone streets to the *borgo*. When I yawn my way downstairs, I find Gabe on the couch reading *Pimpa*. I pull him onto my lap, and he plays with my fingers and talks about yesterday. He muses that the *Infiorata* was the most exciting day of his life. I'm not surprised. The vividness of scents and sights, the race to the finish, the turning familiar streets into canvasses, the festival vibe. And the art. The *Infiorata* is emblematic of Spello's commitment to the pursuit of art. Not just for rarefied individuals, but for everyone. Even six-year-old expats.

Gabe murmurs that he's hungry, so I decide to walk to the *forno* for *cornetti* and boxes of apricot juice. I slip on my shoes, and moments later I step in the shop, inhaling the now familiar scent of almonds and flour. Sauro calls me from the baking room, and when he catches my attention, he holds his index finger aloft with a grin. It takes me a moment to understand, and then I cannot believe it. We won. *Pochi, Ma Buoni* won first place in the *tappeti* competition. He laughs in delight as my jaw drops, and we whoop and applaud each other, while customers look at us curiously, before selecting bread for another day in Spello.

5 June

The end of school is fast approaching. Last religion class for Siena, last Saturday morning that Keith and Nicolas breakfast at Bonci before *scuola media* while the rest of us sleep in, last abacus homework for Gabe, last handful of times I'll race around the house in the morning to scare up pizza tickets, last *avviso*, last few times we'll be walking them to school, last few times we'll be gathered with the other parents waiting for their release five hours later. It's last, last, last all the way home.

In Charlottesville, the last month of school is a blur of class plays, end of year projects that sometimes require costumes and almost always require poster board, weekend soccer tournaments and multi-day soccer tryouts, violin and piano performances for private instructors plus music performances for school, juggling class parties, which are often over-the-top extravaganzas of "fun," and much more that I have blanked out of my consciousness. I usually move through May shell shocked, in constant fear that I'm about to drop a ball.

In Spello, the culmination of the academic year has been so mellow that I'm sort of surprised to find ourselves here, at the end of the road. Which makes me realize that the key to a sane spring is simple—no showcasing, no displays, few expectations. Our only requirements have been to provide Gabe with two apples for his class's fruit salad, and tonight's end of the year music concert. It's much easier to show up without resentment when one doesn't feel perpetually battered from all sides. Even if you have to show up at 9:00 PM for a children's concert. Even if that late concert includes twenty minutes of the same speeches you hear at every town event, including the speech from *il sindaco*, the mayor, that invariably begins, "In these difficult times of crisis…"

It's easy to be charmed, to feel the bittersweetness of the passage of time, when there is emotional space available. We were here in December for the Christmas concert, and here we are again. But this time, we can send Nicolas and Siena unchaperoned to the church, while the rest of us take 20 minutes to make this five-minute walk because it's impossible to get anywhere quickly when there are friends and neighbors who touch our arm to say hello at every turn. This time, as we find our seats, we can smile and wave at fellow parents. This time, Gabe asks to go on a *passeggiata* with his friends through the church while we wait. This time, we have the satisfaction of watching Siena laugh and chatter with friends, while Nicolas does the same with his friends on the other side of the church. This time, we feel a part of it.

6 June

This is my last week of lessons with Angelo. The kids are finishing school, and our leave-taking to-do list is long. A year ago I was also contemplating my leave-taking to-do list, but on that list was getting our visas, microchipping the cats, and wrapping up seven years of house renovations. And now it's walking through wildflowers in Castellucio, visiting the Perugina chocolate factory, setting foot in Keith's ancestral home of Abruzzo, sipping wine in the Piedmont, and hiking in the Italian Alps. We won't do half of that; I'm remembering that there are no *must-sees*. The only must is seeing what you see.

As I'm preparing for my lesson, Angelo stops by to ask if I might be interested in a family *lezione aperta,* an outdoor lesson. It is too beautiful a day to study indoors. He suggests following the course of the Chiona river. We throw on our shoes. Over the next two hours we drive through the *prato*, the meadow-like plain below Spello, stopping at *guadi*, places to wade through the water, and *cascate*, waterfalls. Angelo pulls over in one driveway to show us a house that is abandoned, surrounded by an overgrown thicket of rose bushes. He suggests, eyebrows waggling, that one could get a good price for it. We don't even pretend not to understand, and I can't help but look at this broken-down farm, nestled against a hillside, and wonder, "Could we live here?" Standing at the edge of the creek that crosses the driveway, Angelo spins possibilities of coming back for long vacations or, better, for a permanent home. I look at Keith, who is staring at the house. My mind tingles with possibilities, but I push the thoughts away.

We end our *gita* by walking to Bar Bonci for popsicles and greet 1) Marcello and Giorgio standing outside the shop, 2) the chef at Drinking Wine talking with Massimiliano the painter, 3) the new butcher by the school who gives me a lump of pork fat when I buy chicken, 4) Letizia in her car, who calls Gabe *tesoro* and asks if he's more awake than the morning of the *Infiorata*, 6) Paola, 7) the staff at Bar Bonci who wave us into the garden with jubilant smiles. Siena turns to me and announces, "This would never happen in America." Her voice rings with regret, at the thought of leaving this life that is slow enough for stopping.

Siena is more alarmed by the end of her Italian scholastic career than I ever would have anticipated back in November. She tells us about a dream she had, where we are leaving Italy and she's sobbing as she enters the airplane and whispers "Goodbye, Italy." Nicolas feels the same. It's not that they want to stay forever, but that they can't imagine leaving.

It is Gabe who wants to stay forever. When Anna stops watering her flowers to ask if perhaps when we go back to Virginia, we can leave our children with her, Gabe shoots me a look. *"È possibile?"* Last week we overheard him telling her that he's worried about going to school in America because he's not used to speaking English in school. While both Nicolas and Siena are both being mistaken for Italians, it's Gabe who is so a part of this life that he dances in the church at the *saggio* with total confidence and swagger. He has lost his physical hesitancy in Italy, and now throws himself into any fray. Gabe tells anyone who will listen, *"Non voglio tornare in America."* I don't want to return to America. We try to tell him that there are wonderful things there, too. But his memory of a life before Italy is hazy. His friendships have taken on the hue of a story; he can't remember what granola is; he can't remember the English word for scissors.

This is his life. The only one that feels real to him. The one that is a jumble of alley ladies kissing him, and neighbors calling him over when they see our *terrazza* door open to swing in hammocks together, with people constantly wanting to feed him, with people yelling at him if he's not wearing a jacket, with celebrations of blossoms that go on all night, with friends at school who hug him and hold his hand to walk united, with shopkeepers that call him *tesoro*, with Angelo to give him a candy and chatter while they drive, with local cat dynamics to ponder, with pizza for snack at school, with a close-to-certain chance of enjoying gelato in the course of any sunny day, with trips and adventures around every corner, with ancient Rome at his fingertips, with old men who invite him to play cards and pretend disgust when he wins. Again.

As Keith and I sit in the garden of Bar Bonci and the children scamper, I realize something that has been eluding me. Gabe was an anxious kid back in America. You would never know it now. I'm overcome with gratitude for this place that has allowed my child to access a wellspring of confidence he didn't know he had. I sheltered him from difficulties all his life, which did nothing to assuage his anxiety. Only when he had to acclimate to a class of 24 Italian-speaking, physically demonstrative children did he develop trust in himself. I feel guilt for taking Gabe away from this existence that resonates so deeply within him. But the leaving is a surety—our tickets were purchased this morning. July 25, we head home.

7 June

There's a hum on Via Garibaldi. But then again, there is always a hum on Via Garibaldi. This is the main street of Spello, but there is more here than the bustle of commerce. There is a thread of connectivity. Each shop is a link, and together they form the tapestry that is the heartbeat of Spello. Every shop is run by its owner. Instead of having an indifferent teenager with an eyebrow ring pull your *espresso* in the morning, it's Letizia who owns Bar Bonci. Instead of walking into a restaurant and feeling like it is a puppet play and the strings are pulled from an office in the next city, you are seated by the owner. The art shop is run by the painter. Teresa who makes your *panino* at the *panini* shop also ordered the *prosciutto* and decorated the window. Because of this, every shop is its own little hub of motion. Every shop is a transverse thread on the loom, a weft to build upon.

Since the owners work in their shops, the shops function as homes. With visitors popping in to say hello, to connect for a few minutes before moving on. This creates a cord between the shops and the community. And those cords are woven together with the shop owners themselves criss-crossing the street to connect with each other. I've spotted the chef at Drinking Wine having an espresso at Bar Bonci in the morning. And the butcher engaged in conversation with the painter on the sunny side of the street. Or Marcello lodged with Il Tribbio playing cards at a table outside Bar Tullia's side door. The people are the warp, the longitudinal threads across the weft—together they form the fabric of Spello.

This warp-and-weft spirit of connectedness hums in Paola's, La Bottega degli Intrecci. The shop is filled with scarves, clothes, bags, and jewelry, and always a friend stopping in to say hello. Like many shopkeepers, Paola keeps a chair next to her work desk, so a visitor can chat while she weaves simple threads into macramé. Often, that chair is occupied by Siena. Learning to twist and knot those strands together helped my daughter feel accomplished at a time when she was fixated on her limitations. Now, each time Siena visits, she sits beside Paola and makes *una portapianta*, a plant holder. My eyes can't even keep track of her flying fingers, as she twists and loops and knots. And when she is done, the *portapianta* is hung on the shop's hook, ready for sale. She's contributing.

Her attachment to Paola's shop has allowed this stretch of Via Garibaldi between our apartment and La Bottega degli Intrecci to feel known. It was the first place she could skip down to and back from on her own. It widened her home field. As part of the shop, she grew secure in her Spello life. Now, she stands straighter, she answers questions from customers who ask her what it's like to live in Italy for a year. Just last night, we went to a party and she introduced herself with a poise and surety I've never seen in her. Weaving her afternoons into the world of Paola's shop has tied her into the fabric of the town, and allowed her to feel like she has something to offer. She is a loop in the weave.

9 June

Siena has decided that when she gets home, she'd like to help people who feel as alien as she did when she first started school. I ask Nicolas what he's taking from his school experience, and he answers, "I've learned that anything is possible with the right attitude." And mugs to show he's being intentionally corny.

Siena curls up against me, sad about the end of school. She won't miss the academics, which she claims were either boring or redundant, but she regrets the loss of her friends and the school community. We talk about how I'd realized during the *Infiorata* that there are two kinds of beauty in the world: The kind that is beautiful because it seemingly lasts forever, like the Alps and the Mediterranean Sea, and the kind that is beautiful because of its very transience—childhood, the *Infiorata*, a sabbatical year.

Nicolas isn't as saddened as Siena. It's strange that of our three, Nicolas had the easiest adjustment to school here. His teachers were far more concerned that his hood was securely around his face than they were about his learning Italian long division. And yet, he's the most ready to move on. Gabe deflates every time he thinks about it, but Nicolas? He's fine. I wonder if school was almost a hazing experience for my younger two—not dissimilar to fraternity boys who feel banded with their house by virtue of submitting to a night of embarrassed discomfort. Now Gabe and Siena are tied to Spello, like it's vital to their personhood.

Funny though, with our focus on ending, we've clearly lost sight of what's beginning. Summer. When the bells rings on this last day of school, I hear the children in the school courtyard shriek in unison. They blow whistles and sing, *"È... finita la scuola!"* School is done. Right. I completely forgot about that rush of utter joy that accompanies the last day of school. The children's enthusiasm helps stir that fragile sense of possibility and warmth that summer embodies.

10 June

Keith thinks that if I ask Angelo about the origins of the *Infiorata*, he'll likely trace it to ancient Rome. Which is, in fact, exactly what happens. Over gelato at Bar Tullia, Angelo tells me that back in the time of Caesar, citizens tossed flowers onto the street for victorious generals to march upon—a sign of respect, since those sacred feet shouldn't touch the earth. This tradition was adopted by early Christians for sacred processions, including that of Corpus Domini, which isn't actually intended for the priest. It's for what he's holding: A monstrance, a chamber for the Eucharist, which Catholics believe is the body of Christ.

The throwing of flowers for processions was fairly standard, but around 1915, a Spellana named Carolina decided to create a flower carpet in front of her home for the Corpus Domini procession. This first *tappeto* was created on Via Consolare from *finocchio*, fennel, and *ginestra*, broom. Spellani liked the idea, and the practice spread through the town. With simple designs, and easily found plants.

There are photos of the *Infiorata* during the Fascist period in Italy—a particularly disturbing one features a swastika made of petals. But during the second World War, the practice of laying the flower carpets fell out of habit. The war was debilitating for the Italian people, and it took many years to recover. After the war, a woman in our neighborhood, Lella, revived the practice—with two simple tapestries, both long and narrow, with pointed top and bottom ends, and both lined with *finocchio*. One was filled with *ginestra*, and in the center included a circle lined with *finocchio* and filled with rose petals. The other featured stripes of alternating flower petals. Spello's civic organization, the *Pro Loco* wanted to spur more flower carpets as a way to breathe life back into a spiritually hobbled Spello. To that end, they created a competition. This encouraged more and varied efforts, and over the years, the competition has become fierce—with rivalries between groups, teams with a roster of upwards of 100 people, and a striving to win the honor and cash prize that comes with a *prima classificato*. That first place winner also receives what's called a *Properzio*. Angelo explains that Properzio was a lauded Roman poet, and several towns in Umbria claim to be his birthplace. Spello is one of these, and thus their award for the best flower carpet is called a *Properzio* and is a statue of the poet. It is bequeathed just as excellence in film-making is awarded with an Oscar.

Our chance to meet a *Properzio* is Saturday, when *Pochi, ma Buoni* celebrates the culmination of the *Infiorata*. We receive news of the party the Spello way—on the street. Four different people have stopped to invite us. The cantina is packed when we arrive, with chairs spilling out to line the road. Sauro points out our award then dives into his pasta with meat sauce. We accept plates laden with pasta, and when we are patting our stomachs, we are handed *porchetta* sandwiches. Then a table of food is unveiled—portions of turkey, marinated tomatoes, grilled vegetables, roasted potatoes.

Full as I am, I'm pressured to accept *un pinguino*, literally "penguin"—Nutella cake, stuffed with cream and a layer of Nutella—as the group keeps shouting, *"Dai, dai!"* It is a constant refrain at the *Pochi, ma Buoni* cantina. "Come on! Come on!" They are seriously worried about people not eating enough. I put out the apple pies I made, and am suddenly nervous. I neglected to remember that our team captain is the town baker, feeling a little sheepish setting out my humble pies next to the other desserts, despite the chatter of "American apple pie!" Keith whispers that he saw Sauro take a tentative bite of pie, pause appreciatively before nodding and muttering, *"Buono!"* and then set himself to eating the pie with *gusto*. I will make Keith tell me this story over and over, forever.

While our children play soccer in the darkened streets, there is a standing ovation for Luciana, who cooked dinner for 45 people. Twice. Then an elderly man shuffles from person to person, pouring plastic tumblers full of his homemade after-dinner liquor. I accept a cup with two hands, and thank him. Lifting the cup to my face, it smells sweet. The first sip reveals a gently woody edge.

I wish we could bring the *Infiorata* home. Keith thinks it would be a fragile husk of our experience here. But I think if we approach it like Lella, and keep it simple, it could be wonderful. I love the metaphor of the *Infiorata*—scattering petals on the inroads to our heart. Honoring where we are, where we are going, and the path in between. That we can compose beauty anywhere, and thereby create a sanctified space.

Plus, it's a fantastic opportunity for a party.

12 June

Many towns use tents for their festival *taverne,* but in Foligno, they are located in beautiful buildings, spilling out into the surrounding alleyways. There is a *taverna* for almost every *rione,* and when they are not in use as restaurants, they stand empty. Perhaps they can be rented for community events, but they only function as restaurants during festivals, such as the *Festa di Primi* or the *Quintana.* Each *taverna* offers a different menu and a different vibe, but they all offer traditional food at very low prices in a festival atmosphere.

With the Quintana on the horizon, Brenda and Graziano invite us to join them for a *taverna* meal. Since Foligno is Graziano's hometown, our meal is punctuated with him rising to embrace yet another old friend, each sporting the colors of their *riona.* Brenda tells us about the Quintana, and we realize that our upcoming trip to France means that we'll miss the entire festival. I feel lucky that we were able to at least attend the trials. Right now is all about learning to be okay with missing out—the events we'll miss, the places we won't visit, the friends we will have to leave behind—and focusing on the gift of being right here. Where we are. Like a pop-up restaurant.

20 June

Normandy is burnished like copper, like calvados in a glass, like sedge wound around a ripened round of Livarot. Simple in appearance, but *sfumato* in resolution. It is no wonder Monet painted in Normandy. It's a region that appears completely accessible—every village pristine, every market a thrill, every half-timbered house a museum piece. But though five days gives us a real appreciation for what the region has to offer, we have little insight into the people. They hold back. After 11 months in Italy, the difference between the northern reserve and the southern exuberance is palpable. Coming from Umbria, where a stranger is a friend in training, it's a little disorienting.

Thanks to RyanAir, we are forced to leave 14 hours earlier than we'd planned. Necessitating getting up at 2:00 AM (after tucking in late thanks to an impromptu invitation to Paola and Angelo to come over for pizza) to drive to Rome for our outbound flight, and eliminating the day I'd set aside to chart a rough itinerary. We arrive in Paris blind. After three days wandering the City of Lights seeking out nothing more than whatever is around the corner, we arrive in Normandy without preprinted maps or a list of sights. Instead, we visit the tourist office in Lisieux for a brochure on local attractions. Each suggested stop is nothing but a blurb, which means that we see everyplace for the first time. Media has given us access to sites in advance of our visits, and in a guidebook-driven culture where travel is a series of checklists, seeing something for the first time is not really seeing it for the first time. But no media can capture the bustle of a market, the smell of a bakery, the taste of fresh butter on a still warm baguette. The living. That is better than the seeing.

Living is almost all we do in Normandy. Because the Pays d'Auge region is far from D-Day sites, it's hardly touristed. And so the markets are authentic, with local people haggling and selecting radishes, mussels, inexpensive raw milk Pont l'Eveque, and more duck than we thought possible—duck salami, duck rillette, duck cassoulet. Our best meals are at our picnic table in the garden outside our rented cottage. With views to green hills or greener hills, irises and birch trees all around, and the burble of a nearby creek. There's a richness that we sink into. And yet we can't wait to get home. To Spello.

22 June

I wonder if "special" is an American concept. An American concept that defeats us, or at least constrains joy and connection. Everything must be special— holidays, birthdays, celebrations, school plays, ballet recitals, graduations, travel itineraries, class parties. We strive for a perfection that is unattainable. We hold back from challenging anyone else's striving for perfection, while squirming to establish our own. I speak from experience. It's something about me that I have wrestled with, but its deep roots have never been as clear as they are now, when I am surrounded by people who operate from a whole different ethos.

Here, it is not about being special or perfect (several Italians have opined to me that to Americans, perfect means, "better than everyone else"). I first noticed this when my children would come home with stories of their new classmates celebrating their artwork. Now, some of those classmates have lesser artistic skill than my children, and some have far more. But they all gathered to genuinely applaud anything my children drew. Initially, I thought that this praise was intended to make my children comfortable in their new environment. But now I believe that because these children don't have a hunger to be special, they don't compare other people to themselves to evaluate their "specialness," and therefore are able to genuinely appreciate the efforts of others.

So when Siena draws a cat, they don't think, "I can draw a better one," and therefore dismiss her skills. Nor do they say, "I could never do that, what's wrong with me that I can't do that; *mamma mia, is there anything about me that is special?*" This is a reaction I have witnessed over and over in the States, both in my work with children and adults, and also in observing a classroom of children deflate a little in the presence of their peer's talent.

Because here is the lie we Americans tell our children—"everyone has something about them that makes them special." It's just not true—not everyone has a talent, a skill that defines them. They are beloved, and they have beautiful spirits that move us in fabulous ways, that make them dear companions and cherished loved ones. But they don't all have talents that a little digging will uncover. And the constant searching for specialness and perfection is too much pressure. Every time we look at our experience in the light of someone else's, it uproots a little of our own soil.

I was raised in this American culture of specialness, and I can notice in myself a knee-jerk "what about me?" response when someone I know reaches a pinnacle of achievement. I feel suddenly, and embarrassingly, "less than." It takes actual work to note the reaction, forgive it (still working on that), and then remind myself of this message that Italy is teaching me.

We don't have to be special.

There is no need. It serves no purpose. It helps nobody. The striving to be special galvanizes the dark and twisty bits inside my chest. It is much nicer to step out of my ego, and swim with the wave, instead of against it. To feel a sense of shared joy at the accomplishments of someone in my community. To sense the unity among us, as opposed to the divisions of "you" and "me." And it's this "community" versus "self" approach that is responsible for why my children are experiencing a different social dynamic this year—with no bullies, queen bees, or king pins. If everyone has value, and the talents and skills that set one apart are irrelevant to that value, then there is an answering openness and acceptance. With no one trying to be special, it's so much easier to love each other. To hold hands and laugh.

To celebrate anything that sparkles.

26 June

Though it's true that because of the saturating effects of media, travel experiences often fall flat, this is not true for nature. You can know about what a natural wonder looks like. You can have it in your mind from different angles. But it doesn't detract from the experience of actually being there. With the light shifting, the wind bringing the smell of sun-warmed grasses, the swallows dipping and swooping, the 360-degree-surround-sound quality. Nothing can really prepare you for that. And that's what I realize at the Piano Grande, on the border of Umbria and Le Marche.

The Piano Grande is a windswept prairie set high in the Apennine Mountains. In late spring, it becomes iridescent with flowers. Lentils bloom a vibrant purple, poppies dip and sway their brilliant red crowns, and wildflowers put forth a glorious profusion. We've heard that June is ideal for experiencing a Technicolor Piano Grande. So we pack up, and head off. Nothing really works out as we expect.

First of all, we accidentally head in the wrong direction, so have to double back to Spoleto, and thus add an hour to an already long drive. This rarely creates camaraderie in a tight Fiat Punto. The delay also forces us to abandon our plans to lunch in Castellucio, the village that is perched over the Piano Grande, holding court as it were. We'll arrive late enough that restaurants may be closed. So we lunch in Visso. at a restaurant that does not offer the trout I've been craving since we drove alongside the glittering Nera river, renowned for fabulous fish. (Nicolas was so smitten with the crispy-skinned grilled trout that I ordered when we visited the Cascate delle Marmore, the stunning waterfall that drops into the Nera, that he asked for one for dessert.) The restaurant's only distinguishing feature is that it serves one of the few bad meals we've had in Italy. Undercooked pasta should be cause for shutting an Umbrian restaurant down.

We perk up walking through Visso. There is a walkway right outside the restaurant that runs alongside the town's canal. The sun warms us as the water patters and warbles. We stroll to the end of the town, then turn back to walk through the festival vendors. When we enter the curved *piazza*, I breathe a sigh of reverence. The buildings are a mesmerizing combination of sunset colors, and an array of brilliantly green mountains tower above. I take out my camera, and realize the battery light is flashing red. Danger! Danger!

Oh….*no*. I am about to enter one of the most divinely gorgeous places in Umbria, and my camera battery is low? I quickly switch it off and admonish my children to do nothing charming as I'm unable to capture it on film. They are only too happy to oblige and spend the next ten minutes bickering and neglecting our oft-forgotten "hands to yourself" rule. Keith emerges from re-caffeinating at the bar, and holds aloft his prize—chocolate-covered hazelnuts. This quickly distracts my children from their various grievances. Nicely done, Keith.

We leave Visso behind, contentedly munching on our treats and remarking on the shifting scenery. Until we crest the mountain range, and the Piano Grande spreads out below us. And then, there is only a hushed, "*Woooooooooow….*" The green fields undulate serenely before swooping into grass-draped hills at once gentle and stark. The landscape stretching below us is so spectacular that it takes a minute to realize—no blooms. Or, some blooms, but not the fields of color that we've seen. We must have mistimed the trip. Still, it is *insanely beautiful*, and it's hard to feel disappointed that an *insanely beautiful* place is not awash with colors. It is, however, easy to feel disappointed that an *insanely beautiful* place is experienced without a full camera battery. I take a few photos before the battery gives up. I can't believe I wasted any camera power on all the stupid things I took photos of, thinking my battery would last forever.

I'd like to say that putting down my camera makes me more fully present.

Engaged with my surroundings in a way I can't be when I put a lens between me and the world. That I learn a profound lesson about being in the moment, rather than recording the moment. But I'd be lying. Maybe I'm not evolved enough, but I feel that I see better with a camera. In framing a shot, I notice details, contrasts, lighting. It helps me savor my experience. I miss it.

My children ask if they can "just run" and when we say yes, they sprint into the distance, while Keith and I recline on a boulder, in deference to his weakened lungs. We watch, silently, as our children chase each other into the hillside. There are no trees, no people, no cars, to impede our view of sea green rises of earth, studded with the moving specks of our children. And we breathe in the freedom and joy of this stunning landscape. Castellucio perches above, achingly isolated, and the sky surrounds us.

Maybe we'll go back. With a picnic lunch, a firmer grasp on directions, and a full camera battery, and a surer sense of the flower schedule. Or maybe we'll let it linger deliciously in our memory. Just as it is.

27 June

The last half hour before Anna Maria, Stefano, and their boys arrive for our American breakfast, Gabe is lodged in front of the clock. Waiting. Our friends arrive, streaming light as they so often do. They film the making of pancakes, inhale deeply at the bacon Keith found at the Coop, and admire the browning potatoes. And how fun to sip smoothies, eat the "mini-*amburgers*" (what Lorenzo dubs the sausage patties I make from Italian sausage meat mixed with a touch of maple syrup and dried sage), and drizzle maple syrup while we talk about the Italian insistence that drinking wine is only proper when eating a meal. Our guests ask about our trip to Sicily, and then entreat us to join them next year for a vacation in Sardenia. Which, they add, we could combine with a trip to Spello. This sounds like heaven.

When they leave, Anna Maria asks if I can send her the recipe for pancakes. And we make another walking date and also plan for a dinner out, just us adults. Hugs, earnest cheek-pressing kisses, and goodbyes. We spend the rest of the day feeling blessed at our great fortune to have them as part of our Spello lives.

28 June

To our consummate delight, our dear friends from Charlottesville are here this week. The Henter family has been deeply wound with ours since before Keith and I were married. Ioline and Chuck both figured prominently in our wedding, and Ioline and I were pregnant with Nicolas and Luke at the same time. We like to think that our belly-to-belly conversations while they were *in utero* explains some of the boys' friendship. When Luke made an elite soccer team, Nicolas threw himself out of the window of our just-parked car in order to hug Luke with the appropriate fierceness. When Nicolas told Luke he was moving to Italy for a year, Luke asked him question after thoughtful question, and though he expressed sadness at his best friend's departure, he also shared excitement for the adventure ahead. Even James and Siena, despite the difference in their genders and the year-and-a-half gap in their ages, have been close since they were small—sharing a room each year on our beach trip, giggling late into the night.

So you can imagine the reunion—shrieks (this may well just have been me) and hugs and misty eyes (also me). Keith collected our friends from the airport, so he stands back and observes the scene with Angelo, whose journey home has been stalled by our filling the street with glee. When I look over, I see Angelo is standing easily beside Keith, beaming. At my eye contact, he deliberately makes the Italian gesture for "this is heavy with feeling." The waving-hand-at-hip-level gesture is soon replicated by the owner of Ristorante Drinking Wine where our families reunite over carefully crafted *antipasti* platters.

The next four days are a blur of spontaneous hugging, conversations light and deep, and enjoying the pleasures of Italy together. We dine at La Cantina, where we share the wonders of a perfect *scottadito* with a glass of intriguing Lacrima di Morro d'Alba. We walk along the aqueduct, after which we lounge with Aperol spritzes and a plate of Spellani salami on our *terrazza*. We take the train to Foligno where we visit the Sicilian pastry shop. We pick up *panini* at the *macelleria*, and lunch in the park. We eat spectacular shaved truffles on *bruschetta* at Vinosofia, alongside a stunning gin and tonic with cucumber and rosemary for the men, who consider themselves brothers in gin. We train to Perugia and share the "fun" of Italian train strikes and the sudden requirement of rethinking transportation. We laugh until tears catch in our eyes. We watch our children hug each other in sheer relief to be together again. We do the same. Siena says, "Having our friends here is like a piece of home. And it makes our house here feel like a home, not just a house. It's strange...and wonderful."

29 June

Spello is *pazza*, crazy, for flowers. Every nook and cranny is festooned, even the doorways secreted in blind alleys that tourists never venture. Spellani flower to please themselves. All day, as tourists pass, we hear them exclaiming, *"Tanti fiori!"* So many flowers.

Last week, after a dinner of trout and *bruschette* at Barbara and Mario's house, Keith and I walk to Piazza Vallegloria to watch the award ceremony for Spello's annual competition of balconies, steps, and windows. We arrive an hour late, pretty much when the award portion of the evening is beginning. It's taken us a year, but we've learned how to time our attendance. First, for Italian tardiness, and second, for the speeches. We do have to stand through the tail end of the speakers, but since there are photos of the bedecked doors and windows and alleys being projected onto the church wall, and the night is warm with sweet breezes, we don't mind.

Our neighborhood emerges victorious in the competition, with the stairs in the alley below us taking second place in the stairs and doors category, and the alley that leads to Anna's garden taking first in the alley category. There has been much neighborly support for each other's contributions, so the second place and first place winners cheer and celebrate together.

At the moment, there is more intensity around flowers. Every year, 12 European countries compete in the *Entente Florale Europa*, a competition designed to encourage a better way of life—greener and more vital—for those who live in urban areas. As such, there are several levels of judging. One is the beauty of the town, in particular focusing on the botanical richness. But the judges also observe the town itself. How it protects its heritage, how it encourages green living. In essence, how it preserves the old way of life while still looking to the future.

Each country selects a village and a town/city to compete in this European competition. Italy nominated Spello in its town/city category. And so a multinational jury has descended on our hill town. Gabe and Siena are selected by their school to take part in an English language presentation. Gabe greets the jury, introduces the middle school band which plays, "Waltz of the Flowers." He then leads the jury from station to station within the school. At each station, a student stands in front of a visual aid created by the children, and explains how the school incorporates learning about the environment, the seasons, and community. The last station is Siena's, who recites a quote from Saint Francis, *"He who works with his hands is a laborer. He who works with his hands and his head is a craftsman. He who works with his hands and his head and his heart is an artist."*

At the culmination of the performance, Gabe is the first of my two to emerge. He's glowing in his necklace made from gigantic orange paper flowers. Our neighbor, Anna, pulls Gabe against her, and asks me if they might be able to borrow Gabe, as the jury is visiting her garden. Gabe and I readily agree. From my stalking position on the *loggia*, I can't entirely tell what is happening, other than a line of people are ushered into the garden, Anna and others speak, with a translator for the jury. Gabe speaks as well, but I can't hear his words. And then Anna directs Gabe to dip his hands into what looked like a basin of petals. When he comes home, he informs us that this was in honor of Saint Giovanni's feast day, when Umbrians place flowers and petals in water and allow them to sit overnight to receive a blessing from the Madonna and Saint John in the form of morning dew. The next morning, family members clean their hands, face, or body with the fragrant water, in a sort of mystical ablution.

I sense that Spello doesn't expect to win the competition. Even so, it has given me a fuller appreciation for the amount of work that goes into making Spello, well—Spello. As I'm unlocking my front door, I notice a tourist taking photographs of our award-winning alleyway. He remarks, as people do, that *"Spello è piena di fiori."* Spello is full of flowers. I laugh and agree, while thinking that he probably doesn't know the half of it. Then he lowers his camera, smiles at me, and says, *"Complimenti."*

And I thank him. Feeling a little sheepish, because I have nothing to do with the bountiful flowers that grace the alleys and line the steps and window boxes. That is, unless you count the dead mint crinkling on our *terrazza*. And yet, I feel proud. I've been part of the motion and part of the celebration.

This is my city of flowers, now.

And I'm hopelessly in love.

Aperol Spritz

Aperol

prosecco

ice

orange slices for garnish

———————————————— ⋆ ⦿ ⋆ ————————————————

Clink several ice cubes into a large wine glass. Pour in *prosecco*,
then add a splash of Aperol, in proportions roughly 3:1. Add a half
of a thin slice of orange for flair, and stir. Serve with a warm smile.
Your old friend or new friend will now be your best friend.

JULY

CAPERS AND CLOUDS

1 July

When I pictured *Il Mercato delle Gaite*, Bevagna's festival of the medieval marketplace, I envisioned Ye Olde shoe cobbling and blacksmithing. So the demonstrations of bookbinding, animal husbandry, and chain-mail making are all surprises. Watching these arts in action is fascinating enough, but adding in the realization that Spello boasted the same bustle of linen-clad activity 500 years ago make the demonstrations more relevant. Then there is the pleasure of watching Gabe. He's a processor, routinely asking questions like, "How come nobody ever talks about Joseph and how sad he must have been when Jesus was crucified?" and when we answer him as best we can, his eyes open wide, his mouth gapes, and he stares off into the middle distance. While we smother our laughter and make the "Gabe's wheels are turning" gesture to each other.

All of his wheels are turning in Bevagna. Particularly at the stand showcasing paper and ink. He observes long past the attention span of his siblings, using all his Italian to ask about the writing, if the paper is made by hand, and how did they make ink. He asks, *"Quando io faccio inchiostro, io uso legno bruciato; perché le persone medievali non hanno usato questo?"* When I make ink, I use burnt wood; why did the medieval people not use that? And he listens with rapt attention when he's told that charcoal and water don't mix into a solution, so that when the ink dries, it turns to powder, but when the peel of the nut is boiled with water, it creates a pure solution that stays intact on drying. The demonstrator hands Gabe the nut in question, and peels a little of the skin away to show how quickly it darkens. *Processing, processing, processing.* The ink and paper man patiently answers each question and waits for the next one. Finally, the ink maker asks, *"Perché lui parla italiano così bene?"* How does he speak Italian so well? I love when things are other than what they seem.

At the pottery stand, a man kicks the shelf-like wheel to make the table turn, rotating round balls of clay into elegant pitchers and bowls. To the side is a pottery painter from Deruta. He hunches over a plate sitting on a spinner, rests his paintbrush on the plate, and then turns the plate to make a perfect circle—much as the potter puts one finger against the outside of the pot while it's turning to make a symmetrical indentation. Gabe wants to understand this process, and we talk about planting with intention, and allowing the figure to be changed simply by the cyclical press around a fingertip. I'm left to ponder while Gabe asks more questions.

Evening falls, and I enter Scottadito with a thrill of anticipation. This was the scene of my first *agnello scottadito,* and those chops are calling me. As we wait for our meal, a man sitting with his family at the other end of the table gestures to Gabe and Siena with their Italian Asterix and comments that it's nice to see children reading. We nod in acknowledgment, and point out that it's just a comic book. He asks if we speak Italian, and when we give a measured affirmative, he and his wife tell us about their recent trip to Tuscany where they observed more than one American family at dinner, locked into hand-held games. In the course of our conversation, we discover that the wife is from Foligno, but the family currently lives in Switzerland. We discuss our various travels, and they cheer that we'd been able to visit Sicily, and mourn that we'd missed Sardinia. All this time, their baby daughter is grabbing Siena's arm with her starfish hands and grinning up at her toothlessly. Siena's sweetness with the baby, and the baby's enchantment with Siena prompts the dad to ask if perhaps we'd like to have a family of four children and my heart leaps until I realize he's probably kidding.

We opt to get gelato elsewhere rather than dessert at the restaurant, which I regret when our neighbors are served *panna cotta* in dear little glass pots, with an accompanying shot glass of *espresso* thick with coffee foam. Our neighbor asks if we like Italian food while I'm fighting Gabe for the right to gnaw on my own lamb bones, and we burst out laughing. Do we like Italian food? Oh, *yes.* And just as much as the food itself, I love the parade. I love the *salumi* platters, unique to each region and restaurant, the plate of comforting pasta, the meat with caramelized edges, the bright salad to close, the little something sweet, the *espresso,* the *bella grappa.* We rarely indulge in the whole process unless it's an occasion, but even just a piece of the parade creates a bit of the gathered feeling the *antipasti* to *grappa* version engenders. When Alison and Andrew were here, we luxuriated in the Italian cavalcade of courses at La Cantina, and while we sipped the *grappa* the chef sent us after we closed our bill, we talked about how language can define the way we see the world. Alison looked out over the arcaded room, warmed with animated conversation, and told me about the Dutch word, *gezellig*, which most literally translates to cozy, but has elements of being relaxed, protected, a sensation akin to the feeling of being cuddled. I looked across the table at my new friends, and listened to the sound of Italian falling around my ears like soft rain, and watched how the candlelight flickered against the side of the wine bottle, and felt the satiated contentment of a lingering meal. Yes, a long Italian dinner is *gezellig*.

And I feel that again, now, as we lean toward the family at the other end of the table, laughing together over nothing really, just the pleasure of making a connection in the course of a meal. We say goodbye, reluctantly. But music pulls us into the *piazza* where we find jesters juggling flaming batons with concentrated ease.

Our time in Umbria has given me a new appreciation for backstory. Certainly knowing history has added a measure of brightness. But also just knowing the people we pass in the street have a backstory—ideas, dreams, griefs, and regrets. So much history, so much flavor, and all of us chronically cheated of knowing even the half of it. Which is frustrating, but the eternal mystery of what we don't know is also rather exquisite.

2 July

Dreaming has gotten a bad rap.

In this age of being in the present, and savoring gratitude for life's abundant gifts, the inclination for dreaming has been lost. Now, I'm as eager to ground in the present as the next quasi-practitioner of mindfulness, but I also like to use that position on the tallest hump in the timeline to look down at where I've been, and especially up to where I want to be. There's a power there—the shaping of a future from what was once just the fog of possibility.

This year of living abroad has been a dream of mine for over half my life. And for years, I resigned myself to what seemed the plain truth—it was never going to happen. At least not until our children were out of school. But the possibility continued to prickle, and here we are. At the end of that road. The dream was created, lived, narrated, and now...it's almost over.

When I was dreaming of this year, it would bother me to be told it wasn't possible or I couldn't do it or it would be bad for my practice/Keith's business/the kids' schooling. Perhaps that doubt spurred my own. Now, I find myself uninterested in the doubts of others. I know if something is important to me, I have the power to work toward it, and other people's opinions of the justness of my vision or my ability to make it happen are irrelevant. Circumstances may be beyond my control, but I know there lies a wellspring of determination, conviction, and tenacity within me. I believe in it. And so nowadays, I don't shy away from announcing my dreams.

And I strive to be a dream protector. Because when I hear about other people's dreams, at whatever level of intention, I feel honored and inspired. Partly because these dreams are usually exciting—hardly anyone writes me about a dream of becoming a storm drain cleaner. But partly because I have always been attracted to choice points—those moments when people stop and reflect, and realize that there is something different they want in their life. Louis Pasteur said, "Chance favors the prepared mind." I love to imagine that my support of other's dreams helps them create a fertile groundwork for making magic happen.

Since society doesn't support dreaming, I believe we must consciously nurture the dreamers. And we must nurture the dreamer in ourselves. I know it can be challenging to give ourselves permission to dive deep and consider—what do we want? Where are we right now? What do we need to feel like we are living at our potential and making the most of the lives we are blessed with? And what is stopping us? Shame that what we want may be different from what others expect? Fear of admitting what we want, and then failing to get it? Hesitation that the goal may require the overcoming of obstacles, and more work than we think we have the energy for? But here is the trick—once you allow yourself to imagine, really imagine, what you want, the energy follows. And those challenges that feel insurmountable? *Piano, piano.* One step at time. Rome wasn't built in a day.

There will be moments of self-doubt. That is part of the process. There were moments where I regretted this tendency to dream. Where the situation was so painful, I cursed this need of mine to endeavor to forge new pathways, live in the unexpected, challenge our existence. Because sometimes, it's just so hard. I suspect all dreamers have this experience, when reality knocks up against the dewy idealism of our imagination. Tough spots, those. Spots where the naysayers—around us and in the darkness of our souls—smirk in triumph. When my baby was spanked or my daughter refused to step into school because she was so afraid of her teacher's sarcastic belittling, all I wanted to do was grip each of them by the hand and jump on the earliest plane home. So, yes. It's hard. But worth it?

I look at myself—how I can speak without apology, now.

I look at my husband—who can breathe with ease, now.

I look at my eldest son—who has discovered his love of challenge, now.

I look at my daughter—who has revealed her own power, now.

I look at my baby—who has gained a surety I never thought possible, now.

Is it worth it?

Oh. Oh, *absolutely.*

3 July

It feels like a million years ago, rather than one, that I struggled through the bureaucracy to bring our cats to Italy. Rabies shots more than 20 days before we left, microchipping at the same time, flea noted on Juno during the rabies visit, necessitating large scale flea warfare, follow-up appointment within ten days of leaving for final flea check and clearance, documents sent to the FDA in Richmond for stamping, wrong form and black ink used by vet which is tantamount to murdered penguin in canned dog food in the FDA's book, requiring that all forms be immediately revamped and resent to the FDA.

It was on me to figure all of this out, along with the last well-child checks and dentist appointments, getting Keith's international driver's license, getting forms notarized, packing, selling our car, wrapping up my practice—the list is endless and gives me hives. Since all of the cat and child details fell to me on our outbound flight, I inform Keith that he's in charge of the cats' return. I'll go where I'm told, but I cannot steer that ship again, particularly in Italian. Keith's bureaucratic Italian is quite good. He's even managed to navigate his Italian citizenship application through the murky waters of the various offices that were sure it wasn't their responsibility. So—Tag! He's it.

Keith rolls his eyes a touch and turns so I don't notice his aggrieved sigh.

But I see it, and just smile and smile. Not me! You can't make me! Have I mentioned that bureaucracy, Italian or otherwise, awakens the obnoxious playground tyrant within me? You missed me, you missed me, now you've gotta kiss me!

This is all to say that it is Keith who discovers that the cats need another rabies shot, and may need a EU pet passport to get from Rome airport to Frankfurt airport, and makes the appointment at the vet. I do what I'm told, and carry Juno in a carrier to the vet. I'm surprised that there's no front desk or vet assistant. Just Dr. Ricci. We walk directly into his large examining room where he examines both cats, administers rabies shots, and easily clips Juno's scary claw that I was afraid would have to be pulled under anesthesia because it was thick and curled into her foot pad.

We ask about the timing of the rabies shot, and Dr. Ricci assures us that he'll redo the paperwork if needed. And we don't have to bring the cats to the follow-up visit. He can see them quite clearly at the moment. They are fine. I'm struck by how casual and breezy the process is. Cheap, too. The visit costs us the equivalent of $90. The same visit in the U.S. was well above $200. And our Italian vet gave us a pet picture frame as a souvenir.

So we'll bring back our paperwork to sign within ten days of our departure. Though not too close to ten days, in case our flight is canceled and we have to rebook for later, as the paperwork must be signed within ten days of them stepping on the plane. Keith will take the paperwork to an office in Foligno to complete the work for pet passports. Then our cats will be cleared for take-off.

Ready or not, here we come.

4 July

Over lunch at Barbara's house, we fall in love with her capers. She tells us that she collects them right here in Spello. How can we have missed capers growing around us? Barbara smiles, hands us plastic bags, and asks us to follow her. She walks in the direction of Marcello's garden, and our heads swivel, looking for the capers growing—out of the ground? On trees? I have never given the horticulture of capers a moment's thought. Barbara stops and points above our heads. I look up and find a profusion of plants, besprinkled with shiny capers and whimsical purple flowers, bursting out of the stone wall. They look like background scenery in a Disney tropical fairy tale. We collect hundreds of little caper berries, our hands growing slightly sticky, while we breathe in the day's caper-scented grace. Barbara instructs us to soak the capers in salt water for two days, and then place them in a sterilized jar and cover them with boiling vinegar. Our plastic bags growing fuller of plump green berries, Barbara asks Siena if she'd like to learn to paint clouds. Siena, who has admired Barbara's artwork, is humbled by the offer, and accepts.

A man opens his gate, and shuffles to stand with us as we gather. He launches into stories of delivering mail for 30 years throughout the hillsides. His wife joins us, and we talk about the slowness of Italian life compared to American life, and he and his wife say there must be good things about life in America, and I agree, but add that there are some hard things. And we all nod, this is how life is. *Bellezza e bruttezza*. Beauty and ugliness. It's everywhere. The couple's son arrives and offers to fetch a ladder to pick the higher plants. We decline and hold up our bags already filled with plenty of capers—we found some plants low enough for even Gabe to help. The son asks us to wait, and then he darts into the house, returning with a jar of home-brined capers which he insists we take. I hold the jar up to the sky, to allow the light to filter through the liquid suspended with merry balls of brininess. The son suggests we use the capers to make a *salsa verde* by grinding garlic, a big handful of parsley, two lines of anchovy paste, and two teaspoons of capers. When it forms a cream, add in olive oil to create a sauce. The family claims it is excellent with boiled meat.

Keith and the boys return home with our bags, while Siena and I walk to the *negozio* to fetch eggs to make pasta. We greet Letizia, who is trying to reach the chocolate chips. Because the area behind the bar at Bonci is raised, and she has such a considerable presence, it always startles me how small she is. I hand her the chocolate chips, and she tells me about the ricotta cake she's making for tomorrow, her day off. As she recites the ingredients, Cristian who is ringing up her purchases reminds her that he'll be getting the good ricotta on Tuesday.

Letizia walks out, I imagine dreaming of her ricotta cake and a leisurely morning *cappuccino*. Siena and I agree that we don't know anyone in the world as happy as Letizia. But as we cross the *piazza*, we are hailed by Sicilian Angelo, who cuts a caper of excitement when he sees us. He kisses both of our cheeks, eyes crinkling with joy. As we continue to walk to our house, I shake my head in wonderment. Spello is thick with happy people.

7 July

When I collect Siena from her first painting lesson, I hear Barbara telling her that a cardinal rule when painting clouds is to allow watercolors to be watercolors. I wish I'd heard this when I was busy trying to make my watercolor girl be something different. Siena skips home clasping her paintings to her chest, wafting the clean scent of triumph.

In the afternoon, Letizia asks us what we'll miss when we return home. I answer, "Spello," just as Keith sighs, "People." Over dinner, he elaborates that while he'll certainly miss specific people, what he'll really miss is a culture that values interaction. I think about how people here live modestly, in houses that have been in families for generations. They drive beat-up cars. They work jobs that provide for basic necessities—gardener, *barista*, baker, without feeling the need to do more, have more, or be *more*. Instead of striving for more, they relax into what they have. Time.

Time to write poetry. Time to play cards with friends. Time to knit in the alley. Time to play in the town orchestra. Time to exchange recipes while grocery shopping or in the street. Time to harvest what the earth so generously provides.

Time to stop and see the clouds.

8 July

Remember that when you leave this earth, you can take with you nothing that you have received—only what you have given.

—Saint Francis of Assisi

For 11 months we've lived less than ten kilometers away from the birthplace of Saint Francis, and yet we've never quite gotten there. It must be said, we visited Assisi nine years ago as part of a trip to Umbria. We left, shrugging our shoulders, muttering that it was a Catholic theme park. Scrubbed and picturesque streets, a looming castle of a basilica, monks bustling about, and shop after shop of souvenirs. You wouldn't think that one saint could inspire so many novelties, and so many of them made in China, but St. Francis was not your everyday saint.

Colleen learns that we still haven't been to Assisi, and is shocked at the heresy. She inveigles us to visit the Assisi she loves, to see where St. Francis actually prayed and to peek into the life of Umbria's beloved saint. We agree, and meet her at *Eremo delle Carceri*. It was here that Francis came to contemplate, preach to the birds, and sit in silence. Before we step into *Eremo*, Colleen holds us spellbound as she spins the story of Umbria's favorite saint.

Francis was born in the late 1100's, the son of a prosperous silk merchant. He was the consummate party boy—singing, drinking, wearing fancy clothes, heedless of anything but his own pleasure. He joined the Assisi army in the city's perpetual war with mightier Perugia and was taken prisoner. For a year he lived in a dungeon while the city of Perugia waited for Francis' father to save enough money to pay the ransom.

The experience left Francis a changed man. He battled chronic illness, suffering from fevers and bouts of weakness. He turned to prayer at the abandoned chapel of San Damiano for solace. It was during one of these times of prayer that he experienced his first vision. He saw the Byzantine cross lean toward him and say, *"Francis, go, repair my house, which as you see, is falling completely to ruin."* Looking around the disintegrating church of San Damiano, which was such a shambles it had been left to the lepers, Francis interpreted God's message literally. He began a mission to repair the chapel with his own hands.

His father insisted that Francis settle into a normal life, but neither punishing him nor beating him created compliance. Francis became increasingly defiant, finally throwing his clothes at his father's feet and declaring that he'd live under the rule of a different father. Before striding away naked. It's hard to storm off in your birthday suit, but I bet Francis pulled it off.

From that moment, he embraced a life of poverty, simplicity, and reflection. He lived and reflected in the hills around Assisi. His flour-sack garb eventually morphed into the shape of the tao cross that became his symbol. And though he'd lost his old party pals, he picked up followers, who were intrigued by his commitment to living a simple life, focused on connecting with God in all forms—through prayer, through preaching to God's creatures, through service to others.

One of these followers was Chiara. She was 14 years old when she was promised to a man 60 years her senior. She begged Francis for permission to follow in his footsteps. It wasn't common practice to accept women into a monastic order, but the thing about Francis? Whenever he was in doubt, he chose love. He set her up in the rebuilt San Damiano. The church became a convent for followers of Francis, and Chiara became a sought-after advisor to religious figures. Francis confided in her his wish to recede from the world, to focus on prayer in nature. And she insisted to him that he must keep one foot in the world of man, to spread his message. By this time, they understood that God's instruction wasn't literal, but rather that Francis was needed to repair the Catholic Church, which had become a wealth-building machine.

Having a frame, a richer understanding, of the time, people, and history makes our entrance into *Eremo* all the deeper. We step into the chapel built around Francis' slumbering spot, and down the stairs, through tiny doorways, to the stone on which Francis slept. The stone looks worn and soft, and I gaze at it, wondering about those nights Francis lay here, alone. From here, we exit the building to the woods that so moved Francis. We walk below the trees rustling faintly in the caressing breeze, noting the small wildflowers, until we arrive at the tao shaped cross that marks where Francis preached to the birds.

Colleen was right—*Eremo* is such a different Assisi experience than our visit to the opulent basilica years ago. These woods *breathe* Saint Francis. In the smell of green leaves, the delicious breeze, the pink Subasio stones jockeying for position with the roots of trees. It is sheer, mystical magic. Even the small chapel exudes the kind of quiet grace—with its rough crosses alongside smooth stone and fading frescos—that is unmatched by gilded cathedral ceilings.

As we leave, readying ourselves to say goodbye to our "Umbrian grandparents," we pass a guest book for leaving messages. Colleen and I watch as Siena practically floats to the book and stands considering, pen in hand, before writing, "*La luce d'amore brilla dentro tutti.*" The light of love shines in everyone. Gabe, not to be a outdone, writes, "*Il pace da more fare la buona.*" I think he means that to read, "The peace of love creates the good," but with his phonetic spelling actually reads, "The light from blackberries creates the good." As we exit the building, I imagine that all those times Gabe has asked to pray in church, his head and soul have been full of sparkly blackberries.

Lord, make me an instrument of thy peace. Where there is hatred, let me sow love, Where there is injury, pardon; Where there is doubt, faith; Where there is despair, hope; Where there is darkness, light; And where there is sadness, joy.

—Saint Francis of Assisi

9 July

Evviva! Yippee!

My friend Emily is visiting with her daughters. And all I can say is, "Hooray!" Seeing her face aglow when she jumps out of the taxi to fiercely hug me triggers a sense of flying. And I keep feeling it, every time I look over, and there she still is, beaming like life is an amazing amalgam of beauty and clarity. Emily lives with both hands on the ropes, fully engaged, and having her and her girls here is incredible. Eliza and Anne Marie have been Siena's friends since they were infants. Siena has spent so much time in their house that we joke that she is secretly drawing up adoption papers. When the three girls are together, they quickly create worlds, and dive in, headfirst, in unison.

My own joy is intensified in watching my daughter sink into the bliss of her friends' arms. Literally in their arms, as they've invented a ballroom dance to accompany the songs that Siena composed this year. Any pause in our *passeggiata* leads to girls dancing in the street as they sing *"Moontown,"* until they collapse in gleeful giggles or an adult calls, *"Macchina!"* to warn them of a coming car. Beyond the fun of non-stop slumber parties and running back and forth from our house to Emily's apartment and the bakery and the *negozio*, Siena has the joy of appreciating her voice. She helps her friends decipher menus, explains the patterns of Spellani life, and orders for them in restaurants.

Our days involve nothing more energy intensive than the park followed by gin and tonics at Vinosofia. Letizia has memorized everyone's drink orders, and as the sun begins to warm the stones in Bar Bonci's garden, and we sip our *cappuccinos* while gazing out over the olive tree adorned hillsides, I languidly turn to Emily and ask what she'd like to do today. She smiles and answers, "Pretty much this." Done.

10 July

Last week Keith and I had dinner with Anna Maria and Stefano at Osteria del Buchetto. We'd been charmed by the owner, the food, and the serenity of the view clear to Assisi twinkling in the distance. When Keith and I mull over where we should dine with Emily and the girls, del Buchetto is an easy choice.

We are warmly welcomed by the owner, Massimo, and shown to our seats. The terrace at del Buchetto is beautifully situated, with the convent of San Severino behind, the countryside ahead, an ancient Roman arch to one side, the swoop of Spello to the other. As an added bonus, our table occupies the whole right half of the *terrazza*, so it feels sheltered and private.

We begin with an *antipasti* platter of cured meats, *frittata*, *bruschette*, and other nameless savory treats. Everyone samples various offerings to exclamations of delight. Eliza, who has been anticipating her "meal of pig," orders a mixed grill of pork. I enjoy watching her tuck into her meal even more than I enjoy my own perfectly prepared *strongozzi*. Eliza announces, "I wish that when I got something to eat in America, the air above my plate would shimmer, and then I'd get the Umbrian version." I agree. Except, perhaps, for bread.

Dinner is characterized by a conversational flow. Usually the kids are at one end of the table, the adults are at the other, and we have at least two conversations happening. This time, the entire meal is one conversation. There is much laughter, storytelling, and appreciating. The sun slips behind the hills in a blaze of pink, and the cooling air settles around our shoulders. Massimo treats us to after-dinner drinks, which adds a gracious punctuation. He banters with us that Nicolas should get a taste of the liquor, and when we consent, he brings a glass with Nicolas' taste. A taste that is about as full as our own.

11 July

While I'm walking with Emily to the *negozio*, we run into Paola. She expresses admiration for the fact that Emily is a yoga teacher, and adds that she'd love a lesson from her. When Emily vaguely agrees that that would be fun, Paola asks,

"When?" Italians have no shame. I think it starts from the school years when students' grades are read aloud to the class with commentary, and everyone's flaws are turned into their nicknames. So Italians don't fear looking silly or hearing "no." Paola assumes that if Emily doesn't want to, she'll refuse, no problem. Where in the U.S., we'd hesitate to ask the question, out of fear of rejection or being perceived as pushy. It's freeing to live in a society where this shame of being wrong is as foreign as peanut butter. Questions are opportunities for connection, rather than platforms for having our inadequacies exposed.

So this morning, Paola and I stand on the terrace of Emily's apartment at 7:30, when the air is still cool. On three sides we are surrounded by the chiseled pink of Spello's medieval walls. On the other, the plains stretch toward the terraced hills, where the mists are just lifting. I sink back on my yoga mat, a new friend beside me, an old friend's voice creating a soothing counterpoint to the swallows calling as they sweep across the sky. There is an opening of space to sink into the moment. The utter exquisiteness of the moment. Everything clicks into place. I reverberate with a sudden surety of my connection to the divine spirit in others, in myself, in the world. I'm rooted in the earth, with my arms spread in warrior pose over my head to accept the grace of the sky.

12 July

This year is the 40th anniversary of Umbria Jazz. The Perugia-based music festival has boasted jazz greats such as Chick Corea and Sarah Vaughan, as well as artists not known for jazz—like Sting, the grand finale artist last year. The location of the festival used to vary; in fact, in 1997 Eric Clapton played at Villa Fidelia here in Spello. But now, the action is centered exclusively in Perugia, with music in the street all day, and bigger shows at the large stages at either end of the *corso* at night, as well as musical greats at the arena. Those big arena shows are ticketed, but all the other music is free.

With our love of free, and our aversion to crowds, we opt to visit Umbria Jazz on a weekday. As soon as we enter Corso Vannucci—the highest avenue of the city, anchored by the Rocca Paolina at one end and the cathedral at the other—we stumble upon our first music of the day. We cluster on the steps leading down to the where a trio is playing...and then quickly hop back up. Even the children are wincing. This is awful. Each musician is terrible, and they all seem to be playing different songs in different keys. We escape as quickly as possible. This does not bode well.

Continuing to the end of the *corso*, we find an Australian singer named Sarah McKenzie accompanying herself on piano. She is brilliant. Keith and Nicolas go in search of Umbrian hot dogs topped with onions frizzled in *pancetta* fat, while the children dance and Emily and I talk about what makes this music better than what we just left. Emily mentions the bass and drums that ground the sound, but then cedes that mostly it's just that Sarah McKenzie is actually good. After the performance, we loop through the park, and stop at the Chino tent to avail ourselves of free bottles of Nicolas' favorite drink. It is not universally beloved—Emily desperately searches for a way to rid her mouth of the offensive taste. I guess cola with the added sharpness of bitter, woodsy menthol is not for everyone.

Nicolas' pockets heaving with Chino cast-offs, we enter the Rocca Paolina. I tell our friends the history of this enthralling space—how in the 1500s, Perugia thumbed its nose at a papal edict controlling the trading of salt. Thus inciting the Salt Wars, which ended with the pope building a fortress, the Rocca Paolina, over the home belonging to the Baglioni, who were the kingpins of defiance against papal authority. The palace and the surrounding streets became the pope's basement, a place to store broken communion wafer irons and crates of wine, I suppose. Now the Rocca Paolina is the terminus for the network of escalators that lead up to the city's center, meaning that passersby hurry past old alleyways, a bakery, and lofted ballrooms, before taking the final escalator that brings them to the sunlit Corso Vannucci. History lesson done, the children scamper through the ancient stone rooms, posing in niches like statues and tracing the lines of streets, shops, and palace rooms. Over dinner at del Buchetto last week, Stefano told us that Perugia's Hotel Brufani Palace has a pool that shares a wall with the Rocca Paolina. The bottom of the pool is glass, and under the pool, one can see Etruscan remains. Wandering the Rocca Paolina leaves me with a feeling that wherever I go, I'm walking over expired castles and unremembered histories.

After romping through the Rocca Paolina, we step back into modern day Perugia. We stand for some time listening to Acoustic Spirit Duo—two guys who look like they are from San Diego, with sandals and turned back baseball caps and a come-as-you-are vibe. Gabe is more interested in the flower sticks on display across the *corso*. The salesman patiently teaches Gabe how to use the sticks, which thrills Gabe, who has been interested in all things tossed and twirled since we were entertained by jesters at Bevagna's medieval festival. He calls out how much fun it is to learn to toss the sticks while listening to music.

In the distance, I hear the familiar strains of one of my favorite pieces of music—"La Valse d'Amelie." Emily and I waltz down the *corso* toward the accordion player and decide that when we get home, we'll make a French dinner with French cheese and we'll watch *Amelie*. It's comforting to realize that going home is more than just the end of our year in Italy—it also means diving back into a life that's rich with love. I feel cherished by people here, but I do feel more known by people who have been in my life for years. It's Emily who tells me that when I speak Italian, my voice goes up, both in octave and in loudness. The way I sound when I'm particularly enthusiastic. And she sends my family into peals of laughter when she performs a pitch-perfect impression of me when I've been sick with a headache or illness and am on the upswing—in that burgeoning relief from the pain, I grow so overcome with gratitude that I'll cry over my mug that I am undeserving of such a wonder as a cup of coffee. Nicolas turns to me and says, "Emily does a dead-on impression of you." Old friends are the bass and drums. Grounding.

It's getting late, and Keith starts muttering about a *sacco di gente*, tons of people, so we take the train back to Spello. As we are sighing at the relief of putting our feet up, Emily suggest a "spa in a glass," Vinosofia's gin and tonic, on the walk home. She knows me so well.

13 July

The day begins like any day in Spello: A little cool, but with the promise of heat on the horizon. Swallows play their eternal game of "you can't catch me. " Clicking Legos form a quiet melody. A quick jaunt to Bar Bonci, where we are met with warm smiles and good coffee. On our walk back, Keith decides to make his weekly pilgrimage into the *comune* to inquire about the status of his Italian citizenship. He calls it his ritual "pester appointment." He's grown used to people groaning when they see him. It's the only way to keep his citizenship application on course. He submitted that application months ago, after a continual progression of head-banging trying to gather birth and death certificates that he eventually discovered he didn't need, getting all the documents translated by an official translator and certified by the courts in Perugia, creating an official-looking "application," and arguing with the *comune* that they really are legally required to process his application, even though they'd rather he go elsewhere.

I expect he'll come home from the pester appointment as he usually does—frustrated that there is one more hurdle, but excited that he's one step closer. So I continue home and start putting together lunch. It's just Friday.

Until, as it turns out, it's not just Friday...it's the Friday that Keith becomes an Italian citizen. Our home erupts in joy and applause! Wow! He did it! His name is now logged in the giant book of Spello as a resident of Spello and a citizen of Italy. Wow. I think I need to say it again. Wow. And now in Italian. *Uaou, uaou, uaou.*

Because this is Italy, nothing is ever as simple as one would anticipate. Once Keith achieved citizenship, the children's births were supposed to be recorded alongside his, allowing them the same dual citizenship status (United States law allows one to keep birthright citizenship along with American citizenship). *But.* My married versus maiden name is throwing a baboon-sized monkey wrench into the business, so there'll have to be some repair work before Italy believes I am who I say I am, and therefore, my children really are Keith's. More hoops, but how worth it to never again be denied a visa to live in Europe.

And how lucky that this happens now, rather than after we leave—because the joy on our friends faces as they shout, *"Un italiano in più!"* one more Italian, at Barbara's caper party feels like the ultimate celebration. Keith is their countryman now. They beam and dance, while the accordion music plays on.

We celebrate as Italy intended—with wine. First, at Vinosofia where we savor a bubbly Umbrian red. Then we head to La Cantina. Over our meal, we reminisce about the funny and heart-wrenching moments over the course of our year and toast the opening of horizons. We're still storytelling as we walk up the hill, though we pause so Gabe can dart into Bar Bonci when he hears Letizia call, *"Dov'è il piccoletto mio?"* Where's my little one. He stands before her, and stretches his hand high to the gathering stars and resounds, *"Eccomi!"* Here I am!

We near our home and Siena gasps and points above the pink tile rooftops. A blood moon hangs low in the sky. It sails through the heavens—oblivious and eternal.

15 July

I keep turning corners and have to blink back tears. Soon, this will all be a memory. The air in front of me is shifting, and the days and weeks ahead are a blur of fragmented half feelings and thoughts. Yes, I'm looking forward to hugging my friends again. Yes, I'm looking forward to having Chinese food delivered to my house. Yes, I'm looking forward to effortlessly supplying my family with dry socks. But then Spello will no longer be part of my present. It will be part of my past. I won't make any new memories here. I won't feel the blinding joy that is the simple rhythm of our life. Angelo, Bar Bonci, stone alleys frilled with vibrant flowers, simple days punctuated by drama among neighborhood cats—it will all be behind me. The life we've made here will just be—*over*.

Our plan has always been one year. It's all that we budgeted for. But now, Keith's eyes shimmer at the prospect of leaving. He sits me down and asks, "Can't we just stay?" My breath catches. It's not an entirely unexpected question—Keith resonates with our life here even more than I do. He shares the Italian tendency to throw oneself headlong into conversations and experiences, while I still have to sometimes talk myself out of holding back. So every trip to Bar Bonci, every streetside conversation with Marcello, every trip to the grocery store, underscores the Keith he is most comfortable being. At home, he works alone and can go a week without seeing anyone outside our family. Here, not even pneumonia can separate him from the community. I can practically see the Italian flag whipping behind his head as he leans toward me, waiting for my answer. Can we?

I want to. I do. Leaving feels impossible. The thought of Spello receding into our memories rather than a vibrant part of every day makes my heart plunge and shatter. I agree to talk about it. We break down the financial considerations. The only way we could make this work would either be to sell our house in Charlottesville or find another tenant whose rent would cover our mortgage and rent here. Both options seem daunting. Besides, though Keith has been bringing in some income, this trip was only possible because we'd saved for years. That fund is dry. It would take some serious creativity to figure out how to stretch his income, or find a way for me to supplement it. Is it worth it?

After all, there are other considerations, most notably education. I've spoken to people from all over Italy who tell me the system is broken. High schools are laborious and boring, and learning is rote. While I'm sure many American schools are the same, we've been historically lucky to have our children in classes that value inquiry, discovery, and creativity. When I ask Siena why she raises her hand only in Italian class, she says that English feels like cheating, the math and science teacher routinely jeers at students, and the other classes are entirely lecture, no dialogue, no engagement. Just never ending repetition—it's stultifying. Nicolas says, "Italian students learn how to put the pegs in the pegboard, but don't learn how to invent the pegboard." I remember Siena's art teacher who, after a year of having the kids draw circles and color them, told them that they could draw whatever they chose. To wild applause. The teacher added, yes, you can draw a flower with oval petals or a flower with heart-shaped petals.

When Gabe talks with pleasure that he escaped being spanked again, he adds that the teachers, other than Alessia, still yell a lot. I ask why they yell at him, and he tells me that he'll finish his work, and then get up and wander the classroom, and the teacher will yell that he's not doing his work. He'll respond that he's already finished, she'll check, and then the yelling will stop and he'll keep wandering. According to Gabe, this happens every day. All three of them report that the repetition and the sagging pace wear on them. Keith and I agree that if we stayed, our children's education would be a constant area of concern.

Of my three children, only Nicolas would have reservations about staying for reasons other than education. He misses aspects of American culture—pulled pork BBQ, sour gummy candy, alternative music (the air waves here are filled with American pop, unlike what we heard in Spain and France). But mostly he misses sarcasm. The kids here repeat the same physical jokes over and over, to riotous applause. Midway through the year, one of his friends said that he had never seen Nicolas laugh. It is not hard to make my kid laugh. One well-placed pun will make him double over with mirth. At first I wondered if there are shades to humor that he can't understand because of language—I know he's functionally fluent, but maybe it would be another year to understand humor? But I've heard from many others that Italian culture is too earnest to support sarcasm. It's a trade-off that doesn't bother me. But I can see Nicolas wanting a good belly laugh.

I've spent so much time learning to laugh at myself that Italian's humor stylings have escaped my notice. I do wish Italians would value forming a decent line.

Perhaps that line is a metaphor for my concerns for Italy's future. Because I feel sometimes like Italy is stuck. So self-congratulatory about her past triumphs in art and civilization that she doesn't look forward. Being behind much of the world can be rewarding. There is a focus on community and connection and authentic expression that is refreshing. Italian diners engage with their food and each other, rather than their smartphones. People and food are two things I am rather fond of, so perhaps self-servingly, are what I think of as keys to a grounded life. But there is a darker side to this reluctance to keep up with the rest of the world. In some ways, Italy is falling behind. There is an over-reliance on American notions of music and film, the dizzying bureaucracy is made preposterous by the refusal to embrace the internet, recycling is an afterthought, and Italian children are getting heavier and heavier, perhaps as they adopt American ideals of passive entertainment and packaged sweets. It makes me sad for this country, though it's not enough to make me want to leave. It gives me pause, but I would be happy to pause in a place with advantages that far outweigh these concerns.

When it comes down to it, it doesn't feel right to stay just because we can't imagine leaving. It feels right to go home, and consider in an intentional way if we want to return, for a month or a year or forever. To consider from a distance, not when we are wallowing in the grief of saying goodbye, how we'd want to handle our finances and our children's education. I'm glad Keith and I thought about it, and even more glad that we reached this point together.

No place is perfect, and one thing isn't necessarily "better" than another. I wonder if the trick is to see without judgment or ranking. There are beautiful things about Spello—some are apparent to the casual observer, some come into fruition with slower savoring. But part of the beauty of life here is that I've approached it with my arms open. With no expectations. And so I accept the whole package—from the fabulous butcher who reassembles a pig so we can see where different parts come from, up through a inefficient bureaucracy.

I hope I can do the same at home. I don't want to be blind to a place's drawbacks, because I want to honor what's important to us. But neither do I want to ignore the gifts of my life. Perhaps by being aware, without resentment or valuation, I can bring some of what I love about my life here home. Maybe I can make my Charlottesville life embody some of the lessons of simplicity and engagement that Spello has been so kind as to teach me.

16 July

We've been invited to dinner at Mario's, our first meal with virtual strangers who exclusively speak Italian. We arrive with wine, which is graciously accepted and put on the table, but then ignored. Mario points out the beer his parents purchased because he'd told them that he thought Keith would want beer. I wonder which American sitcom he's been watching.

Keith and I admire the outdoor wood-burning oven. As Mario's dad adds olive branches to adjust the temperature, he touts the ease of summertime cooking. They can make everything from pizza to *dolci* without heating the kitchen. We drift between watching him slip the pizzas in the oven to helping Mario's mom make *gnocco fritto*. She rolls pizza dough out like one rolls gnocchi, but instead of cutting the cords into pieces, she leaves them the length of her hand. She then fries them, drains them on paper towels, and wraps the end of the *gnocchi* with a slice of *prosciutto*. This is a revelation. The combination of the sweet doughiness with salty meatiness makes me wonder if *gnocco fritto* is like the love child of a doughnut and a bacon-wrapped date. I kind of want a whole meal of these.

But there is something else on the table that demands attention. *Coratella*. Sounds lovely, doesn't it? *Cor-a-tella.* Like a delicacy bedecked with flower petals and moistened with dew collected from ferns. Mario's father gleefully describes the *coratella*, and I think I hear the word for lungs. When he walks out to check the pizza, I turn to Keith and say, "Lungs?" Keith answers, "No, no, just liver." I'm not a fan of liver, unless it is whirled into pâté, but I can eat it. Mario's father returns and looks at my reassured countenance with some measure of confusion. I tell him that I had thought I heard him say, "Lungs." Ha ha! How silly! Only, he nods emphatically, yes! There are lungs! Lungs and liver and heart! Spurring me to act like this is even better than I'd imagined.

Once seated, Siena whispers to ask what kind of meat this is, and I say, "I don't know, just try it." She recoils faintly. I nibble a bit, and I can see how it could be good, the sauce is rich and layered. But I don't like that iron-y liver taste and I can't escape the alarming visual that I'm eating pneumonia. I try to eat more—after all, I'm sitting beside Mario's mother, who is sweetness itself, but I can't manage. Meanwhile, Keith and Nicolas are using their *torta al testo,* Umbrian flatbread, to sop up every last morsel. It is no surprise that Keith likes it—he thinks snails are akin to lifesavers—but Nicolas? I ask him, *sotto voce*, "You like it?" and he slowly shakes his head so no one notices. Pin a medal on that boy. He accomplishes what I cannot. Eating what one finds instinctively revolting, and doing it in a way that Mario laughingly points out places Nicolas misses a bite to ensure that his friend catches every last of the morsel of the dish he seems to adore. And Nicolas gives a *Properzio*-worthy performance, exuberantly scooping up those pieces of *coratella* that he'd skirted to the side in the hopes of avoiding. While I wish I could disappear.

Pizza scattered with rose petals follows, and I praise it far more than I usually would, to make up for the fact that when I relinquished my plate of *coratella*, it looked untouched. Despite my studious attempts to hide a bit under the *torta al testo*. Sigh. What a horrible guest I am. I feel so obtrusively American, with my American queasiness at the sight of meat not shrink-wrapped on a Styrofoam platter.

Dessert is cake filled with Nutella and rolled into a log. The Nutella provides a toothsome bite against the softly fragrant vanilla cake. Again, I almost prostrate myself in praise. Nicolas is right, Mario's mom is a wonderful cook. I remember Nicolas once told me that Mario remarked to him with some astonishment, "Your mom is a great cook." And Nicolas told him, "Well, so is yours." And Mario answered, "Yes, but my mom is Italian."

Mario's parents are the kind of people I think a more fluent language connection would turn into fast friends, which makes me regret that my grasp of Italian seems to be slipping away already. Maybe it's because I've been speaking so much English—having our friends here, I've gotten out of my habit of mentally translating my thoughts and conjugating verbs. Whatever it is, I watch myself making all sorts of dumb mistakes and I'm having an inordinately hard time constructing sentences. And I'm reverting to my Spanish ways, as Nicolas so helpfully points out.

To my frustration, my understanding is at 50%. Which is responsible for my next *faux pas*. When Gabe is moaning about not wanting to go home, they start talking about how difficult their younger son was. I laugh, thinking we are swapping parenting war stories. Keith surreptitiously nudges me with his foot, and then I realize that Mario's parents are wearing serious expressions. My mind scrambles, and I realize that they are actually saying that their youngest had a host of medical conditions that made his babyhood difficult. I switch gears quickly, express sympathy, ask questions. And hope that the darkness of the evening hides my flush of shame.

I feel like hitting myself on the forehead, but it's particularly amusing because of something that happened earlier today. I was engaging in my new favorite pastime—window communication. I lean out of my window like some old Italian *nonna*, gazing out to let my mind wander or talk to neighbors in their windows and on the street. So I was leaning out of my window and observed an alley lady, Maria, talking to an American about her cat Achilles. Spellani like to say that Achilles *"è sempre in giro"* He's always on the move. So twice a day, Maria calls him in to eat, walking up and down the street. This time, she was explaining to the young American woman about how Achilles and a neighbor cat like to play together. And the American, who had no idea what Maria was saying, responded with knowing sadness, "Oooooh, *oooooh...*" like Maria was telling her about the long line at the post office. She then added, "I understand!" When she so didn't. I giggled from my perch above. Remembering when we first arrived, alley ladies would talk to us and we would have no idea what they were saying so we tried to take our conversational cues from context—and then later worried that perhaps we were laughing gaily when they were actually telling us about their hemorrhoids. And now I was watching the same scene play out, but with full information about how neither of these people understood each other. I snickered in a self-congratulatory way. Hubris, oh, how I have missed thee.

Because here I am now, laughing in the face of these gentle people talking about their son's life-threatening allergies. I suppose one year in—even with a social network, advances in culinary skills, and traveling to other parts of this marvelous Boot—a peach is still a fish.

17 July

Il Tribbio is hosting a *porchetta* dinner in Marcello's garden. We arrive to find signs on the garden walls that read, "The Happening Garden." Happening? We gesture to the poster and ask Angelo what it means. He furrows his brow and says, "Happening. *Come, incontro.*" Oh! Meeting! He must mean "the garden where people meet." It lends the whole affair a retro-70's vibe. *The Happening Garden.*

Tribbio members and a few expats fill the seating, but the featured guest is the *porchetta*. *Porchetta* is a roll of whole, boned, roast pig, which is sliced so that each serving includes a bit of skin and fat, and light and darker meat. It's a staple of central Italy, found at outdoor markets, butcher shops, and *panini* counters. The quality of *porchetta* varies—sometimes the taste is meager and the skin is flabby, but sometimes it tastes like Thanksgiving. The *porchetta* at the Happening Garden is an excellent specimen. Crispy and tender and succulent, with an herb-infused layer of fat that melts like gravy. It is prepared the Umbrian way, with copious amounts of fennel.

We load our plates with slices of *porchetta* from the roll centered on the table, and Marcello glides like a waiter at a cocktail party, holding a plate of *lesso di porchetta*. He explains that *lesso* are the bits of pig removed before the animal is prepared. The pork pieces are cooked underneath the roasting *porchetta*, and thus are basted in pork juices. A system that works well for potatoes under rotisserie chickens in Paris, but I'm not so sure about pig scraps. Particularly when Marcello describes the bits. Let's see…there is a nose, two ears, four feet, and other parts that I can neither identify by sight nor by Italian description. I reluctantly admit I am too American for the *lesso*. Marcello nods, and says he suspected so, since I didn't like the *lumache*. I guess the street cred I acquired in my great *cotiche* experiment has flown the pigpen. That moment of derring-do has been outshone by my lack of love for snails. Keith, with his plate full of *lesso*, is lauded by Angelo and Marcello as a real Italian. Keith nods and laughs and takes a huge bite of pig ear.

When he pronounces the ear *delizioso*, I scoff. But then I wonder why I'll happily toss down fried pig skin—my father hailing from the Arizona-Mexico border means I grew up eating more *chicharrones* than potato chips—but not pig ears basted in pork juices. Well, maybe it makes a modicum of sense, based on texture alone. That which has the mouthfeel of Cheetos seems more palatable than that which looks like it has the mouthfeel of, well…rubbery ears. But I feel a leading to try it. I poise a bit of ear near my mouth, and my stomach lurches. I lower my fork. Angelo brings me a cup and says if I don't like it, I can spit it right into the cup, and nobody will mind. Angelo counts up to five and back down, signaling me to pop the forkful in my mouth at zero.

I do. And it's actually okay. Certainly better than snails. It doesn't feel rubbery. More like two layers of aspic around a noodle. And the flavor resembles pork consommé, light and delicate. I stop short of trying the foot—Keith describes it as fatty, meat-flavored jelly, hardly the pitch to prod me to overcome my delicate stomach.

Over plates of pork, I push myself to talk to people. We swap stories of *zanzare* and *porchetta*, nothing earth shattering, but it's enough to reassure me that I can string a sentence together. Gabe has no such concerns. Marcello asks him to check on the extinguished sprinkler unit, and when Gabe approaches it, Marcello turns on the faucet, leading to squeals and baleful glares. But then Marcello conspires with Gabe to play the trick on "unsuspecting" guests. Gabe rubs his hands together. One by one, Gabe lures guests onto the lawn and then, chortling, he springs the water. The Happening Garden is full of great sports, who pretend to flee or climb on the lamppost or pick Gabe up in a feigned attempt at retribution.

After the party, we stroll to Brenda and Graziano's for drinks. Sipping cocktails made with elderflower liquor, we stand on the *terrazza* to enjoy the breezes. It's closing in on dusk, and the golden air swims with light. Brenda points out the "tractor show" happening in the valley—she watches the tractor mow stripes in the hay like other people watch TV. Evening rolls in, and Graziano grills peach halves, which Brenda fills with squares of chocolate that turn oozy at the peach's warmth. The children scamper to the garden, and Graziano comments on how quickly Gabe has learned not just Italian, but the Spellani accent. He muses that perhaps this is because he learned Italian by sound, rather than visualizing letters or grammar. We talk about language, and Graziano says that our two eldest have also surprised him with how far they've come. Brenda adds how much they've enjoyed watching Siena come out of her shell. Nicolas comes to the *terrazza* for a drink of water and hears this last comment. He adds with pride that if Siena could stretch herself to speak a little more, she would be the best of all of us, as her ear is so good and her memory is incredible. I hadn't thought he'd noticed his sister's improvement at all.

We linger in the cooling night air, and Brenda and Graziano tell us that if we want to come back, they'll help us in any way. They speak with such warmth and friendship that Nicolas admonishes me not to cry. But it's too late. We have sown seeds in Spello, and are walking one more time among the fruits of that planting. Spello is our Happening Garden. How gratifying to stroll through the flowers at twilight, letting our hands brush the top of the blossoms, pausing to pluck a glorious bloom, lift to it our faces—and inhale deeply.

18 July

Two weeks ago, I received an email from Spello's *vice-sindaco*, the vice-mayor. He had stumbled across my blog while looking for news items about Spello's nomination in the *Entente Florale Europa* and wanted to schedule a meeting to talk about our experience in Spello. I was honored. But since then I've grown a little nervous. Am I being called into the principal's office? I have written, after all, of my children's less than stellar educational experiences. Am I in trouble?

When Keith and I climb the steps of the Palazzo Comunale, I am filled with apprehension. We pass the carved tablets hanging on the walls, including the revered notice from Emperor Constantine granting Spello the right to hold gladiator fights. We enter a room filled with frescoes and a large wooden table where the *vice-sindaco* is waiting. He begins by asking us about our impressions of Spello, citing his interest in our unique view—more connected than a tourist, yet separate enough to see things with fresh eyes.

The vice-mayor says some very lovely things about my blog (I didn't know that my writing is rich with *pathos*—I hope that is a compliment), and we talk about our year. In describing how we chose Spello, Keith and I explain that we had looked at other towns that felt, well, dead. But when we stepped into Spello's *piazza*, we were struck by its vibrancy. The *vice-sindaco* nods, and says that this is intentional. He goes on to tell us that 1,500 people live in the historical center of Spello, and 7,500 in the outskirts. So there has been a long-standing movement to get services and schools to move into the *borgo*—particularly after the devastating earthquake of 1997, when much of the town's infrastructure was being reconsidered and rebuilt. This movement, however, has been resisted by the administration of the town. And so the local police, the state *carabinieri*, the post office, the schools, and the pharmacy all remain in the historical center. This, to the great displeasure of many of those who have to find ways to park and walk to those services. I remember the twice-daily parade of kids walking to school, popping into one of the bars for a *cornetto* or a piece of pizza and putting it on their parent's tab. What would Spello be like if the school was in the *borgo*? If the town's physical center was not its emotional center?

We also mention that one of the highlights of living in Spello is the creative energy. The town is full of music, theater, art shops, poetry readings. He smiles, and says that this is because there are 52 different associations in Spello. Since they all sponsor at least one event each year, there is always something happening. The downside is that there is competition for space, time, energy and importance.

When we talk about the festivals—from the small ones like the feast day of San Martino to the big ones like the *Infiorata*—he asks if this is unusual where we are from. Keith and I look at each other, and Keith says that there are many festivals in our home town, but they all feel the same. The vegetarian festival and the chocolate festival and the festival of cultures all include the same vendors, the same organizations handing out leaflets. Here, each festival is so particular, with its own feeling, its own food-ways, its own history. So much variety in such a small place.

The meeting ends with the vice-mayor reiterating that reading my blog is like reading *letteratura*, literature, and he hopes that I will one day publish it. We close with expressions of mutual happiness to have met, and also regret that this meeting has taken place a week before our departure. But on further reflection, I like the timing. It was like an exit interview—to process our experience, and feel like the town of Spello is supportive of my chronicling the blessing it has been to live within her storied, pink walls.

19 July

We step onto American soil. Granted, we are surrounded by the hustle and honking of Rome, but since we are on the grounds of the American Embassy, we have to wrap our minds around the fact that we are technically in the United States of America. Complete with *People* magazine in the waiting room, CNN continually sludging through the happenings in the land of stars and stripes forever, and American-accented English barking on the intercom. Our appointment to have the United States notarize the fact that I'm me, even though my maiden name and my married name differ, is at 2:45. Our name is called at 2:45. I look up, startled.

We approach the window and explain the situation. Unfortunately, to Keith's eye roll, I can't talk normally. It happens whenever I speak English with a stranger nowadays. My English comes out too deliberate, with a quasi-Italian accent. The woman must be used to this. And my request. She smiles easily and hands me a bill to pay at the cashier, telling me that I'll be called when the form is complete. We pay, then start to sit down to wait, but we're called to window 5 before I can catch up on celebrity gossip. I walk to the window, sure there is a problem. But no, another woman stamps our paper and we are done. Fifteen minutes after we arrived, I have my notarized paper. It's very disorienting. Shouldn't there have been more waiting? More dithering? An argument or two? Moreover, the embassy bathroom toilet, which we avail ourselves of before leaving, boasts a toilet seat. And plentiful toilet paper. What a country.

Out on the street, we head toward the Vatican—I'm dreaming of seeing Michelangelo's Pietá, and the children want to be able to visit three countries in one day. A woman steps out of a restaurant and hails us with a trilling, "*Buongiorno!*" Lately I've been thinking about the fact that soon I won't be surrounded by this exuberant language. I'll miss hearing it. I'll miss speaking it. I'll miss it being my daily soundtrack.

The line into San Pietro is so long it looks like a mistake. The heat is oppressive, so we decide to just take an earlier train home. Besides, after a day of wandering the sweltering city, my thighs are chaffed beyond redemption. We head toward the train station, and by the time we are on the platform, my walk has turned into a waddle. Ladies, I think you hear me.

We board the train, and I exhale loudly, sinking into the seat. My face is flushed, my hair is standing on end, and my sweatiness is undeniable. It's fair to say that I am a hot mess. And not the good kind. As our train nears Spello, we agree on dinner at L'Orlando Furioso. With my proviso that everyone must walk to the restaurant with a wide straddle, so it looks like I'm imitating everyone, when I'm really trying to hold myself upright. We make quite a scene waddling down the street, Gabe in the lead, like a cartoon cowboy, fresh off a horse.

Our waitress ushers us to our usual table with a grin of welcome. Sitting down, we realize in unison that this will be our last meal here. We look around at each other and blink quietly. Keith breaks the silence, "I'm having actual *physical* reactions to the thought of leaving." Nicolas and Siena immediately respond that they know exactly what he means. I do, too. I say, "Whenever I think of leaving, my stomach becomes leaden, and my brain goes spacey." We all nod. It's akin to a mix of dread and anxiety.

We relish every bite of our pizza. When our waitress comes to check on us, we banter with her, and soak in the vibe of this restaurant that's become a staple of our Spello life. Hobbling out, we are filled with gratitude and regret. Next year navigating bureaucracy won't involve strolling through ancient civilizations, culminating in pizza that smells of home.

20 July

In Spello, days that begin with "Have you seen the cat?" are invariably unpleasant. Particularly when we're six days from our departure and have reservations to visit the Perugina chocolate factory.

I'm drinking my coffee when Nicolas asks the dreaded question; Freja didn't come when he poured her food. A troubling sign as our cat has not missed many meals. Since Juno's escape, we are vigilant about not leaving cats outside. The only exit from the house is our *loggia* door, open to catch errant breezes. But Freja never leaves Nicolas' side during the night, and besides it would take more motivation than I can imagine Freja summoning to leap from the ledge of the *loggia* down to the rooftops. But our perusal of the house turns up nothing, so the search begins.

The one comfort, we quickly agree, is that our more developed language skills make the experience easier than when Juno escaped. As I later tell Patrizia when we run into her at the *macelleria*, the first time around all we could really say was, "*Gatto....no. No gatto.*" When I tried to vary it up by saying we lost our cat, I ended up saying "We took our cat"—*abbiamo perso* is "we lost", *abbiamo preso* is "we took." To befuddled looks. Ten months later, we are able to outline the whole story, in much clearer detail. Our children can search on their own, thus widening the circle. The card-playing men outside Bar Tullia assure me that she will come home, and I respond, "*Spero, ma partiremo a giovedì.*" I hope so, but we leave on Thursday. Giorgio grandly offers to keep her if she's found after we go.

I call her from the window that overlooks the rooftops, then turn away, but Keith shushes us. He listens, stock still. Then we all hear it. Freja. Meowing.

We look toward our neighbor, Cristian's, *terrazza*, in time to see her jump onto the ledge, meowing in earnest, while we cheer. She's agitated, and looks like she's preparing to try to leap across the alley to our rooftop, rather than just running in a U-shape along the rooftops, back to our window. She is exactly that dumb. Giorgio, on his way home, looks up to see us calling her, and offers to fetch her. We wave him up, and he lopes easily up the steps. I will always remember Giorgio, standing tall in his ex-soccer star finery, black hair slicked back, stark against the *sfumato* Umbrian hills. Unfortunately, Freja doesn't find Giorgio nearly as captivating as I do, and she bolts as he approaches, through a doll-sized window into the attic between our window and Cristian's *terrazza*. Giorgio shrugs off our thanks for trying, apologizes for his lack of success, and continues home.

Keith decides to tackle the rooftops himself, and brings tools to jimmy the skylight of the attic room. Freja doesn't find this charming either, and scrambles through a hole in the wall into another room. A room with no entrance. The only way Keith can be sure she's in that space, and hasn't absconded into another room, is by thrusting the camera through the hole in the wall and videoing until he spots her. And then all he can do is wait. A storm thunders overhead, keeping Freja hunkered in her attic hideaway.

The children knock on doors, asking our neighbors how to access that attic. But no one knows. It seems to be an attic to nobody's house. I sit on the windowsill ledge, in case she darts through the little window before Keith can catch her. The waiting is unpleasant, as waiting generally is. Particularly when one can't turn one's head or move one's gaze from a small, dark window. But the fear is low. We know where she is. I allow my shoulders to relax as I listen to the rain fall on the terracotta roof tiles. Distant showers swoop across the valley with lightening crackling across the sky like God's signature. It's not too bad. As a general rule, I am too apt to distract. Being forced to sit and be *in* Umbria, to really feel this moment, is actually a weird kind of wonderful.

When the rain stops, Freja returns to the room where Keith is waiting. He perks, quietly. He had blocked the window to the rooftops, and now he quickly blocks the entrance to the inaccessible room. Then, he turns his attention to catching our cat. Freja, dumb as she is, is wise to him. She presses herself into the space where the rooftop meets the wall. He tries waiting for her, calling her, talking to her, singing to her. She purrs lightly, but doesn't move. He tries putting tuna on a stick to lure her out. She ignores it, even when he knocked her nose with the tuna stick. He tries luring her out with the toys we made for her out of earbuds and rubber bands. *Niente*. And now Nicolas needs new earbuds.

Keith continues to wait. In the broiling, dusty stone attic that smells of dead animal. He puts his hand through some unidentified and desiccated creature, and tries to avoid putting his feet in the copious animal feces. Eventually Keith uses the stick to prod Freja out of her tight spot. She darts in a circle around the attic, like a horse in the *Quintana*, expressing as she runs. Our only experience with cats' predilection for expressing a foul, musky liquid was during the move to Italy, when Juno expressed so much it was leaking out of her carrier. Good times.

Freja settles back in her safe, unreachable corner. Keith prods her again and herds her into an accessible spot, all the while speaking soothingly. She is not soothed. She is panicked and soon deranged. Expressing, hissing, pooping, bellowing. All at once. And then she bolts. From my perched position, I see her claw her way out of the window that Keith had attempted to block. She must have sucked in her in all-too-significant gut to fit through that small space. But fit she does, and then flees back onto Cristian's *terrazza*. Keith follows and sees her dash into what looks to be a laundry room. He closes the door, sealing her in.

Nicolas runs to the *negozio* to tell Cristian that our cat is trapped in his house. Cristian hops on his scooter, Nicolas hard on his wheels. They enter the house, with instructions that only Nicolas should approach Freja. She no longer recognizes Keith, she is delirious (we go with the simple *pazza*—crazy—to describe her state to Cristian). Nicolas opens the door of the laundry room and Freja is immediately docile. Panics briefly at the sight of the cat carrier, but once she is in, and Nicolas touches her nose through the mesh, she begins purring.

And so we bring our smelly, relieved cat home.

Not as good as a trip to the chocolate factory. But at least she's in her accustomed place, curled like a burr against Nicolas. Wondering where her favorite earbuds are. But not really able to keep that thought in her vacant brain, what with all the important purring work she needs to catch up on.

22 July

Our cupboard is bare. When I reach past the broken shards of dried linguine and the heavy dusting of cornmeal and the scattered grains of *farro*, the pickings are slim. Just half a bag of lentils from Colfiorito, a handful of dried mushrooms, one potato, and a sheaf of cookies largely ignored by my family on account of their blandness but really quite tasty with Nutella. Bare. And I'm not motivated to shop, considering I can count the number of days we have remaining on one hand, and two of those days we have dinner plans. I've been putting together the oddest assortment of foods to avoid going shopping. I am reminded of our pre-launch days, when out of desperation, I considered ice cream sandwiches a balanced breakfast. Yesterday, my family winced when I served stale bread with the last of the tuna and past-its-prime *prosciutto*. This adds to the anticipation of having lunch with our friends in Bettona.

I do pick up ingredients to make banana bread, knowing how much our friends enjoy American treats. Along with a pot of miniature roses, to thank them for the generosity of their friendship this year. I also arrive armed with pad and paper to have Conci walk me through her recipes. I recently made *ragù*, remembering her instructions, and while it was good, it wasn't the same. I clearly cannot trust my memory.

The lunch provides more fodder for note-taking: Pasta with cream and peas and both *prosciutto cotto* and *crudo*, succulent Italian fried chicken (Conci tells me the secret is bathing the chicken pieces in lemon water before cooking), meatballs in savory sauce, *frittata*, couscous, tomato salad with green olives and shaved onion. And of course, their homemade wine. One of the secrets to Conci's fabulous cooking is something that I learn constantly, but never stop forgetting; perhaps this time I'll remember. The secret is—*more is not more*. I always think, "If one piece of *pancetta* in my sauce is good, two must be better." Until my sauce is thick with ingredients, and my pasta is swimming in sauce, and the subtlety is lost. Pasta itself is a beautiful thing. The sauce should be made with a light hand, so the pasta can shine.

Our conversation this time is easier than ever. At one point, Roberta asks Nicolas if he's learned to cook, and he responds he can only "cook" bread with Nutella, which he manages quite well. Roberta says he'll have a much better time with the ladies if he tells them that he makes pasta. So he should go ahead and tell them he cooks Italian food, and then contact her for help if anyone calls his bluff.

So much laughter. Relaxing with our adoptive family over cups of *caffè corretto* flavored with a dash of Varnelli anise liquor, I ease into a sweet contentment, tasting the nuanced corners of bliss. It's suddenly evident to me that our friendship developed over their lunch table. What would have happened if, when they first invited us for lunch, we refused out of politeness? This whole relationship would never have existed.

The heat is growing by the time we say goodbye, so when we get home, I call Patrizia to see if we can come swimming. She answers, *"Come no?"* Which literally means, "Why not?" but with Italian emphasis, it really translates to, "Obviously!" With a tone of such welcome, it feels like she's been waiting for us.

And oh, that cool water is gladness itself. As the sun slips behind Spello, I join the adults while the kids, wrapped in towels, delve into iced tea and almonds. It occurs to me that sunsets mean I should be thinking about dinner. I announce that we need to go so I can feed our children. Patrizia, on the heels of asking me what Umbrian dishes I've learned to cook, wants to know what I'll be making. Oh. Good question. I think of those lentils. Is there a package of smoked salmon in our fridge or am I making that up? While I'm mulling, Patrizia invites us to stay for dinner. I thank her, but decline. She wants to know, *"Perché?"* Why? Well, there are five of us. She rolls her eyes. She knows how many of us there are. Then I decline again. *"Ma, perché?"* Well, the kids need to eat immediately, and I know they don't eat until late. She insists, but it's ready now!

I accept, as graciously as I can. While the children and Filippo play on the lawn, I help Patrizia—slicing fresh figs to serve with *prosciutto* and dicing tomatoes to sprinkle with oregano and Spellani oil. Patrizia pulls an Umbrian rice salad, with tuna, slices of hot dog, diced ham and Emmentaler cheese, out of the fridge. And then she produces a platter of *vitello al tonnato*—cold slices of veal covered with a creamy and tangy tuna-mayonnaise sauce. A lovely hot weather dinner, especially eaten on their poolside *terrazza*.

As we banter, we slowly realize that Siena is speaking effortless Italian. And once she starts, she doesn't stop. Nicolas stares at me and mouths, "She speaks!" Siena smiles and says that we aren't with her at school and when she's with her friends. Yes, I know—I was aware this was happening, I just hadn't witnessed it for myself. Her Italian accent is praised as virtually accent-less, and her smile is radiant.

Patrizia scoops gelato into bowls, and we remember our first time at their house, when Gabe broke an ice cream bowl and burst into tears. Now they only have seven bowls, so Gabe is handed a plastic one. He doesn't notice. Gelato inhaled, the children race to play soccer with Filippo while Keith and I sip *limoncello* with our hosts. We reminisce about the year, and they tell us the kids can keep the fuzzy blankets they've grown so attached to. And they hope we return to Spello. I nod and blink back tears. It occurs to me that maybe the truest sustenance comes from letting ourselves be fed, rather than trying to feed ourselves all the time.

As an added bonus to our grand day out, the fact that we were fed by two Italian families forced me to communicate in Italian all day. So not only do I go to sleep high on Italian food, and embraced in Italian love—I dream in Italian. For the first time.

23 July

I don't tell the butcher that it's my last visit. I think I want to pretend that I'll be back in a few days for *salumi* and chicken wrapped in *pancetta*. This *macelleria* has been a fixture of our year, and I'm not entirely sure how to say goodbye. Instead, I attempt to fix into my memory the volubility of the shop, and the butcher's warm smile as he hands me the white paper package of lamb *spiedini*. At the *fruttivendolo,* I stop to take in how the dim shop smells of sun-warmed tomato leaves and plump apricots. My sack strangely light, I step onto the *navetta.* I choose a spot behind the driver, and leave a poppy on Luciano's customary seat, whispering a goodbye.

I prepare our meal deliberately, breathing in the stone-warmed breeze coming in from the open *terrazza* door. I notice how the sunlight glances off the waxed wooden table, and wonder if I've properly stopped to appreciate the sight during this year. As I stretch the pasta dough along the board, I listen to the rhythm of the rolling pin, followed by the clack of the knife cutting the pasta into neat ribbons. The water I squeeze from the dried and soaked *porcini* mushrooms smells of earth.

The food heaped onto platters, I call the family to gather for dinner. We're quiet as we slide the tender pieces of lamb from the *spiedini* onto our plates, alongside string beans doused with the last of our Spello oil and crisp, balsamic-laced salad. But it's the pasta that we pass with hushed reverence. My hands have been trained by Conci, and the *tagliatelle* is golden and beautiful. It's tossed with a mushroom cream sauce, inspired by the meager contents of our pantry, but the taste speaks of fullness rather than void. In our slurping and praising of the rich and fragrant pasta, the silence is broken. We speak with incredulity that this meal, which now seems relatively ordinary, will be hard to come by in just a few days.

25 July

Readying our goodbye recalls for me the beginning. All these memories of our first week here are rising up, demanding attention, just when I am bidding my beloved Spello *adieu*—the first time the kids saw the city gate rising in front of our car, our first trip to the *negozio,* our first visit to Vinosofia, our first gelato at Tullia, our first coffee in Bonci's garden. I feel like the memories are pressing me from all sides, and walking down the street, my mind is crowded with images from the past.

I wish leave-taking wasn't so energy intensive. There is so much to pack, so many errands to cross off our list, so much to prepare. Working down an agenda is antithetical to our lives here the last 11 months and 25 days. Where is that slowness? Where is that sense that a full day is one where I go out for coffee twice? Where is that tranquility that draws me to the open window, to lean out and observe life, feeling comfortable with the quietness of my thoughts?

Somebody hand me my spritz.

And then there are the goodbyes. We say goodbye to Letizia, since Bar Bonci is closed tomorrow, our last day here. She brings us our drinks and pastries, and seems oddly restrained. When I ask if I can take her picture, she bites her lip, and then starts to cry. She tells us, laughing—because Letizia can't stop laughing even when she's crying—that she considers us Spellani, and it's hard to see us go. I never would have thought that we would grow so attached to the woman who pours our coffee. I hadn't considered what exchanging conversation with the same person every day for a year, through hard spots and celebratory spots, who stops her car to talk to us, who winks at our daughter when she's taken to Bonci for a school trip and secretly serves her extra gelato, who calls out to our children when they pass her shop in their transition to another building during school hours—how much that would influence our attachment. We hug Letizia and weep together.

It's strange. Sometimes I can be completely in a goodbye. Feeling it, even embracing that pain as a mark of entwined affection, the glory of which trumps the tear of separation. And sometimes I feel myself pulling back. Leaving is hard, sometimes I just want it done and over. I want to stop straddling where I am and where I am going. Since I'm not staying here, it's easier on my heart to just put myself forward a few days. I think the kids are the same. In one conversation they'll swing between talking about how painful it is to say goodbye to friends or how they can't remember what life is like back home, and then all of a sudden, they are talking about what candy they want to find on Friday. Quite the heel turn. Even Gabe is looking forward to aspects of American life that I thought he'd forgotten. He, too, is waltzing between frames.

We have our celebratory meal out with Brenda and Graziano at a steakhouse outside Cannara. La Hazienda is beautifully situated in agricultural fields, with views out to Assisi and Spello. The night is clear and almost cool. And the meal is excellent—a perfect steak, with a board of seasonings to select, such as smoked salt or Persian salt or a jot of rich balsamic or mustard sauce or peppery olive oil. But I notice in myself a tendency toward emotionally wandering off. I have to periodically twirl myself back to the present. I'm not thinking about home, but I feel myself detaching. Which, yes, does make it easier. But I need to stay with the rhythm of the moment, even when it would be much nicer to glide into the sidelines of my emotions.

Staying with painful moments is, well, painful. I understand my desire to loose hands, but I know it's best for me to stay with the dance until the house lights rise.

26 July

Our Spello home is empty. Walls once polka-dotted with art and postcards are bare. Boxes are packed and ready for shipping. Garishly colored luggage is full to bursting with reminders of our year in Italy. The house is quiet—my family is still sleeping off the late night. The Umbrian breeze floats sweetly by as I sit on the *terrazza* with my cup of coffee, listening to the three-wheeled *ape* rattling down the street and the alley lady calling her cat in for breakfast. Both of my cats are wandering around confused. We're all a little confused. It's hard to take it all in. We're on a precipice of our own devising. It should make more sense than it does.

I've realized that the blessing is that we have a home in Italy now. We can travel here, and it can feel like a vacation and like we're home at the same time. But as wonderful as that is, there is no way to deny that our life here is over. And I am, we all are, processing that in waves.

There's so much I want to hold onto. Oddly, one of the things I am most loath to let go of is me. Who I am is different now, and I don't know how to bring home this Spello version of myself. It is Spello-me that grasps the beauty of standing in the window and watching the world go by. Who hears music in the swooping swallows. Who finds the earth in a glass of wine. Who can smell the approach of rain behind Subasio. Who sips an Aperol spritz and marvels at the shadows in the eaves as the sun reluctantly slips behind the ancient walls. Who notices that the smell of stone in the ubiquitous winter fog is deep and restorative. Who stands in a bar and listens to the harmonies of language surround and engulf my soul. Who appreciates that a single clove thrust into an onion can heighten a simmering *ragú*. Who understands how to use water to paint clouds. I don't know what will happen to my Spello self once we arrive on American soil.

This Spello version of myself understands that things don't have to be perfect. I don't have to be perfect. I simply need to connect. I have forged relationships with people here, not because they dovetailed with my personality or values or history, not because the fit was "perfect," but because love was the only option that felt right. And I have felt loved, not because of what I give or what image I project, but just for being who I am. What I've learned from Spellani schoolchildren holds fast in my center: Making the heart encompass what is oddly shaped increases the depth and capacity of love. Realizing this has reconciled me to loving even my own odd shape—my imperfections, my vulnerability. These oddities serve to both make me human and connect me with the divine.

The old me spent a lifetime pretending to be average, the Spello-me had to struggle with being a peach out of water. In doing so, I have learned what it's like to flit on the borders. A year of kissing strangers on the cheek and now I don't so much feel my common humanity as I hear it thrumming deep within me. Making a home on foreign soil has made me realize—we are all one. I want to reach across to hold hands, to look into the eyes of the marginalized and the mainstream, and hold that space in the circle together. Because we *are* together.

We are all one.

It's important to me that as a family we cultivate the lessons of our year abroad. That we maintain our Italian, that we remember how to remove a squid's ink sac, that my hands can divine when a pasta dough is ready to roll. But what I really want to keep alive in my soul is love. Love for myself and where I am in my process, love for you and where you are in yours. Love for my children's learning through growing. Love for the soil on which I stand. Love for people I've never met but am nonetheless tied to.

In our vulnerability that makes us human, we love.

In our weakness that gives us heart, we love.

In our imperfection that allows us to knit our souls to each other, we love.

Insomma, I rise. I plant my feet and share my message. Because I think I know what lies at the beautiful center—that space within us that cradles our deepest, undefended selves. It's no secret; I'm not sure why it took me so long to figure it out.

This whole year illuminates one indelible truth.

Pasta is good.

Love is better.

27 July

I wrote this post. I wrote it already. It feels like I've been writing it forever, in my mind. And then I sit down. It's time to write it. Really write it; you know, like with words one can see again later. Typed. And I do. I write it.

And it is horrible.

My mind refuses to stay composed and focused. Instead, it darts like a fish too close to the shore. I get the words out, but it's listless. Limping. Empty. Hardly how I want my last post to feel. Why can't I write about this last day? Why can't I write about the feeling of my heart dropping into my knees when Assunta tells us that she won't accept payment for our afternoon gelatos and spritzes? And how that feeling of being overwhelmed by a gripping wave of gratitude will be the theme of the day?

I want to tell you about all of it.

About the farewell party at Marcello's shop. How Marcello tells Gabe that Giorgio is going to frame the replica of Luigi Silvi's work that Gabe made for them and hang it alongside the art. Gabe, so puffed with pride—his own work, hanging in a gallery. His proudest artistic moment since his drawing of the pope was turned into a poster by Angelo and hung outside the shop. Now the old men call him *"maestro."* I wish you could see him as he sits on a white plastic chair next to Marcello and swings his crossed feet, and talks. About what? I don't even know. I'm not sure it matters.

I want to be able to describe the feeling of being crowded into the gallery, surrounded by neighbors. And how taken aback we are to be presented with gifts. My hands shake as I accept a tablecloth lovingly embroidered by Maura. My eyes swim with tears as we are given an engraving of Rome from 1700 from Giorgio and his wife, Laura. The amazement in our hearts as Angelo and Marcello hand us a framed tile with the seal of Spello, and with it they declare that the tile inducts us as citizens of this town that has become our home. We read the dedication that Angelo has typed and affixed to the back, and then everyone signs it while we mingle with glasses of *prosecco*. And then the relief as I look at Giorgio, and he tells me, despite his assurance the day before that this party would not be for crying, *"Ora va bene piangere."* Now it's okay to cry. And I do. But so does he.

I wish I could write this in a way that I can explain the depth of my gratitude that we found these people. Laura, who tells me that she will miss leaning out of her window to talk with whoever happens to be on our *terrazza*. Giorgio, who has taken to tossing candy high across the alley onto our *terrazza* to the delight of our children, and hugs me goodbye with American ferocity. Marcello, whose face loses its mirthful grin, replaced by an expression of stillness and grief.

Then, we hold hands and walk away. Down the hill, to Vinosofia, for more goodbyes that I also can't write with any clarity. And I want to. I want to be able to describe how Brenda carefully planned treats for us all—from excellent local cheese, to beautiful *mortadella*, to aged balsamic vinegar for Nicolas—all elegantly arranged and served with perfectly paired wines. And how it twists my heart to see my friend so intent on easing this moment, yet I catch her eye, with a tear that matches my own. A last *"Cin!"* merry with joy to be together this last time, which fades with anticipation of the moment we must leave.

And we do leave. And it's exactly as hard as you'd expect. I wish I could share with you the images that flood my mind, of all those merry meals with these friends that valued us for exactly who we are, who guided us to memories we never would have had otherwise, who somehow feel like family.

I want to be able to tell you how the goodbyes felt like waves crashing at this point—powerful and endless. With no time to catch a breath. Because then we meet Patrizia at the house, and she looks at our house cleared of cheerful clutter, and asks, *"Perchè non apri la confezione bagaglio, ti aiuto, dai!"* Why don't you unpack your bags, I'll help, come on. Once again, we feel the blind luck that placed us in her family's hands a year ago.

Yet another goodbye, and then we walk to Paola's house. On the walk, Stefano calls Keith to say goodbye. I already said goodbye to Anna Maria, who gave us each lace bookmarks with our initials and a card thanking us. Their earnest farewells are bewildering. I can't imagine what they got from this friendship, but I know what we did—a connection in the school, a set of people who always looked genuinely thrilled to see us, a beautiful friend for Gabe, and a family willing to help and assist us anytime. How can I convey the intensity of their goodbyes, and how it pulls from us an incredulity that we are walking way from all of this. How can I capture the tug of that longing? And of that love?

And still there is more. Dinner at Il Trombone with Paola and Angelo is spectacular. It was the first place we ate as a family in Spello, but we haven't eaten there in months. We can't get over how perfectly chewy and yeasty the pizza dough is, the perfect sauce, the wonderful toppings. I can talk about the pizza forever, no problem. If you want a description of the food, I'm your girl. But writing about how the valley glows with one last resonance of light before darkness begins gathering in the distant valleys and then over the farmland—that, I can't seem to manage. Nor can I describe the awareness that settles like moonlight around our shoulders—the joy of speaking in Italian around pizza with friends, laughing about anything and nothing, is nearing its end.

And then we can't put it off anymore. We leave, and say goodbye to Paola, with assurances that we will see her soon, as she will visit us, and we will be back. And yet, we know it's not the same. I wish I could adequately paint the picture for you, of Siena who begins to shrink at this leave-taking—she's had a relationship with Paola outside of ours as a family. The goodbyes are hitting her hard. This child of mine who spent months craving Charlottesville, now looks up at me with starlight in her eyes, and wonders aloud why we have to go.

And we continue to walk with Angelo through the darkened streets.

Past In Urbe, where our friends stayed when they visited, past the parking lot that housed the *taverna* for the olive oil festival, past Teatro Subasio where we watched shows and school performances, past Il Cacciatore where we enjoyed a dinner among communists and an Easter benediction, past Anna Maria and

Stefano's home in a former monastery, past the double doors that once housed workers in folding chairs filling boxes with petals for the *Infiorata*, past steps down to the church where I did my poetry reading, past the alley where a cat that looks just like Juno lives, past the *forno* that glowed warmly when I would enter in the morning to buy bread from the scantily clad bakers, past the alley ladies.

The alley ladies, sitting there, now. Enjoying the last warm breezes and the companionship for just a little longer before turning into their respective homes. Ready even at this moment to pull unsuspecting little boys in for a hug. And to warmly shout out affectionate greetings and wishes.

The alley ladies.

They sit on their chairs, sharing stories of marketing and foraging and cats and town drama. They sit there as we turn the corner to say goodbye to Angelo, my heart filled with emotions I'm helpless to describe—a combination of gratitude and grief that defines the edges and fills the contours of today. Angelo holds it together until he says goodbye to Nicolas, and then they both have to duck their heads and wave goodbye. The alley ladies sit while we enter our house and close the door with an audible click. They sit there while I hold my weeping daughter. They sit while I stand on the *loggia* and weep myself. They sit while Keith goes outside to say goodbye to the darkened hills and glittering lights of Umbria.

And in the morning, after we are gone, they assemble again. The stone arches rise high above them, framing the Umbrian blue of the sky. The cool, pink walls invite them to sit, to gather, against their surety. Their green chairs wait to enclose this congregation.

And now...I'm here. An ocean away.

But I know them. And I know their patterns, and I know that *pausa* is over in Spello, and so I know in my heart...

The alley ladies are sitting there even now. Even still.

Bare Cupboard Tagliatelle

tagliatelle, preferably fresh

butter

2 garlic cloves, minced

a handful of dried porcini mushrooms,
soaked in about a cup of water

fresh thyme,
preferably Apennine thyme
from a nearby *terrazza*

white wine, just a splash

a cup of heavy cream

---

1. Remove porcini from the water, and chop roughly. Reserve the water! It's flavor gold.

2. While the water heats to boiling to cook the pasta, heat butter in a pan. Add garlic, and cook for a few seconds. Don't let it brown. Add the porcini mushrooms, and cook until the mushrooms are fragrant and cooked through. Deglaze with a splash of wine, scraping up any browned bits from the bottom of the pan. Now add the mushroom-soaking liquid, making sure to pour carefully so that the dirt remains at the bottom of the pouring vessel.

3. Add fresh thyme leaves, and a bit of salt and pepper. Boil the mixture until the mushroom-soaking water is a rich, dark brown and almost has a syrup consistency. Stop the cooking at this point, and wait for the pasta to complete it's cooking. Drain the pasta.

4. Fire up the mushroom pan, and when it starts bubbling, add in the cream. Stir until thoroughly combined, taste to correct seasoning.

5. Place pasta in a bowl, cover with the porcini sauce, and serve with a bowl of grated parmesan.

6. Inhale the scent of home.

——— * ❋ * ———

Thank you, beautiful reader, for staying with us to the end of this journey. I'd be so grateful if you would take a moment to head back to the Amazon listing for this book and leave a review, to help new readers discover *Il Bel Centro*. Without reviews, independently-published authors are, for all intents and purposes, invisible.

Now that we're friends, please stay in touch! Sign up for *Contorni* (a little something extra on the side) and I'll send you periodic updates (about one every few months) on the family, Spello, culinary discoveries, and future books, as well as information on promotions and contests. You know me enough to know that I'll never share your information with anyone.

Visit *www.ilbelcentro.com*, like *Il Bel Centro* on Facebook, or send me a message to *michelle@ilbelcentro.com*. Mail from readers makes me happy.

I hope we can sit down over a cappuccino one day.

Until then, keep dreaming.

—*Michelle*

——— * ❋ * ———

42912855R00292

Made in the USA
Lexington, KY
10 July 2015